Michael Langhammer

Automated Coevolution of Source Code and Software Architecture Models

The Karlsruhe Series on Software Design and Quality
Volume 23

Chair Software Design and Quality
Faculty of Computer Science
Karlsruhe Institute of Technology

and

Software Engineering Division
Research Center for Information Technology (FZI), Karlsruhe

Editor: Prof. Dr. Ralf Reussner

Automated Coevolution of Source Code and Software Architecture Models

by
Michael Langhammer

KIT Scientific Publishing

Dissertation, Karlsruher Institut für Technologie
KIT-Fakultät für Informatik

Tag der mündlichen Prüfung: 10. Februar 2017
Erster Gutachter: Prof. Dr. Ralf H. Reussner
Zweiter Gutachter: Prof. Dr. Colin Atkinson (Universität Mannheim)

Impressum

KIT Scientific Publishing

Karlsruher Institut für Technologie (KIT)
KIT Scientific Publishing
Straße am Forum 2
D-76131 Karlsruhe

KIT Scientific Publishing is a registered trademark
of Karlsruhe Institute of Technology.
Reprint using the book cover is not allowed.

www.ksp.kit.edu

Print on Demand 2019 – Gedruckt auf FSC-zertifiziertem Papier

ISSN 1867-0067
ISBN 978-3-7315-0783-3
DOI: 10.5445/KSP/1000081447

Abstract

To develop complex software systems, source code and other artefacts, such as architectural models and behaviour descriptions, are used. Keeping these software architecture-based models consistent with the systems' source code during software development and software evolution helps software architects.

Having up-to-date architecture models eases the development and evolution tasks since questions such as *how* and *where* to add new features in the software systems can be answered more easily. Furthermore, it is possible to predict the performance of a software system with architecture models that include behavioural specifications, such as the Palladio approach.

Architecture drift and architecture erosion are, however, two well-known problems that can arise during architecture-based software development and software evolution. These problems arise when software architecture models are not kept consistent with the source code, e.g. when code is evolved without updating the architecture accordingly. Eventually, this leads to out-dated and thus useless architecture models.

Most existing solutions to avoid these problems either focus on keeping UML class diagrams and source code consistent during software evolution, or embed architectural information into the source code to avoid the need of consistency preservation.

In this thesis, we introduce a novel approach to keep high-level component-based architecture models consistent with source code during software development and software evolution. In particular, the approach can be used to keep instances of the Palladio Component Model (PCM) consistent with Java source code. To do so, the architectural elements are created, changed, or deleted as soon as their corresponding source code elements have been changed and vice versa. We also present a change-driven consistency preservation process that preserves consistency based on user-defined change-driven consistency preservation rules between the architectural model and source code. We introduce four different sets of consistency preservation rules between architectural models and source code, which are realised in our prototypical implementation. Within the consistency preservation process, we introduce a user disambiguation concept, which can be used if the consistency preservation cannot be achieved automatically. In this case, users need to clarify how consistency can be achieved. As the presented approach is a change-driven approach, we need to retrieve each change performed in the involved architectural editors and the source code editors. To enable users to reuse existing editors, which with they are familiar, we implemented monitors for the Eclipse Java source code editor and PCM architectural model editors. The presented approach enables, furthermore, users to keep source code consistent with behavioural architectural models as well. Therefore, we have implemented an approach that incrementally reverse-engineers the PCM *Service Effect Specifications* based on changes performed to source code methods. The *Service Effect Specifications* are used to describe the behaviour of components.

For reusing existing source code and existing architectural models within the presented approach, we present different integration strategies. For architectural models, we present an approach that simulates the creation of architectural models. During the creation, we monitor the emerging changes and use them as base for the creation of the corresponding source code. For source code, we propose an approach that uses reverse engineering tools to create an architectural model, which can be integrated to the consistency preservation approach presented in this thesis. Arbitrary code, however, is seldom build according to the defined consistency preservation rules. To deal with this fact, we present an approach that is able to deal with integrated source code for which the actual consistency preservation rules cannot be used. The approach is able to keep even those elements consistent using specific consistency preservation rules for integrated source code elements.

We have evaluated the presented approach in different case studies. We showed that it is possible to integrate existing architectural models by simulating their creation. Within the performed case study, we were able to integrate between 98 % and 100 % of the supported elements for the different consistency preservation rules. Next, we evaluated the integration of existing source code and showed that it is possible to keep changes to source code consistent with the architecture and vice versa. Therefore, we integrated four open source projects into the presented coevolution approach. We showed that changes performed to source code are kept consistent with the architectural model, by integrating an old version from the Version Control System (VCS) and replayed changes to a newer version using a change replay tool. During this evaluation, we also showed that the presented approach is able to keep changes performed to method bodies consistent with the behavioural model. We also conducted a performance evaluation to measure the overhead of the presented change-driven approach during the software evolution. We showed that the presented approach is in most cases able to keep the architectural model consistent with changes performed to the source code within one to five seconds. Finally, we evaluated that the coevolved architectural models can be used for performance prediction. Therefore, we first parameterised the models with resource demands. After the parameterisation step, we execute the performance prediction using the performance prediction capabilities of the PCM. To analyse the accuracy of the performance prediction, we compared the predicted value with actual measured values. In our case study, we observed a prediction error for the response time of approximately 10 %, so that the coevolved models can be used to estimate the performance of the real software system.

Zusammenfassung

Zur Entwicklung komplexer Softwaresysteme, werden neben dem Quelltext zusätzliche Artefakte, wie beispielsweise Architekturmodelle, verwendet. Wenn die verwendeten Architekturmodelle während der Entwicklung und Evolution eines Softwaresystems konsistent mit dem Quelltext sind, können Softwarearchitekten und Softwareentwickler bei der Entwicklung der Systeme besser unterstützt werden.

Architekturmodelle, die auf dem aktuellem Stand sind, vereinfachen Entwicklungs-und Evolutionssaufgaben, da einfacher beantwortet werden kann *wie* und *wo* neue Funktionen implementiert werden sollen. Außerdem ist es möglich, modellbasierte Analysen mit Hilfe der Softwarearchitekturmodelle vorzunehmen. Beispielsweise können mit dem Palladio Komponentenmodell (PCM) Performanzvorhersagen durchgeführt werden, wenn ein Architekturmodell des Softwaresystems vorhanden ist und dieses Verhaltensspezifikationen beinhaltet.

Wenn Architekturmodelle bei der Softwareentwicklung und Softwareevolution verwendet werden, können die beiden bekannten Probleme Architekturdrift und Architekturverletzung auftreten. Diese Probleme treten für gewöhnlich auf, wenn bei voranschreitender Entwicklung des Quelltextes die Architektur nicht konsistent zu diesem gehalten wird. Dies führt zu veralteten und schlussendlich nutzlosen Architekturmodellen.

Viele existierende Ansätze, zur Vermeidung dieser Probleme, zielen darauf ab, Quelltext und UML-Klassendiagramme konsistent zu halten, oder sie zielen darauf ab, Architekturinformationen in den Quelltext einzubetten. In letzterem Fall wird die Notwendigkeit, die Architektur konsistent mit dem Quelltext zu halten, umgangen, da die Architektur integraler Bestandteil des Quelltextes ist.

In der vorliegenden Dissertation beschreiben wir einen neuen Ansatz, um komponentenbasierte Architekturmodelle, welche sich auf einer hohen Abstraktionsebene befinden, konsistent mit dem Quelltext zu halten. Wir beschreiben, wie Instanzen des PCMs konsistent mit Java-Quelltext gehalten werden können. Um Konsistenz zu erreichen, werden Architekturelemente erzeugt, gelöscht oder geändert, sobald ihre entsprechende Quelltextelemente geändert wurden, und umgekehrt. Für die Umsetzung der Konsistenzerhaltung stellen wir einen änderungsgetriebenen Ansatz vor. Dieser verwendet benutzerdefinierte, änderungsgetriebene Abbildungsregeln, um die Konsistenz zwischen den beteiligten Modellen sicherzustellen. In dieser Dissertation stellen wir vier konkrete Mengen von Abbildungsregeln zwischen Architekturmodellen und Quelltext vor. Diese haben wir in einer prototypischen Implementierung des Ansatzes umgesetzt. Wir stellen außerdem einen Mechanismus vor, der mit den Benutzern des Konsistenzerhaltungsansatzes interagiert, wenn die Konsistenz nicht automatisch erhalten werden kann, sondern die Benutzer zuerst ihre Intention, die sie mit einer bestimmten Änderung verfolgen, dem Ansatz mitteilen müssen. In diesem Fall müssen die Benutzer das genaue Vorgehen für die Konsistenzerhaltung spezifizieren. Da der vorgestellte Ansatz änderungsgetrieben funktioniert, ist es notwendig, dass wir alle Änderungen in den beteiligten Architektur- und Quelltexteditoren aufzeichnen können. Um es Benutzern zu erlauben, vorhandene Editoren, mit denen sie sich auskennen, wiederverwenden zu können, haben wir Beobachter für diese Editoren implementiert. Diese Beobachter zeichnen alle Änderungen an einem Modell auf und informieren unseren Ansatz über jede durchgeführte Änderung. Der in dieser Dissertation vorgestellte Ansatz erlaubt es auch, verhaltensbeschreibende Architekturmodelle konsistent mit dem Quelltext zu halten. Um dies zu erreichen, haben wir einen Ansatz implementiert, der es ermöglicht, *Service Effect Specifications* des PCMs inkrementell aus Methoden zu erstellen, nachdem diese geändert wurden. Die *Service Effect Specifications* werden innerhalb des PCMs genutzt, um das Verhalten einer Komponente zu spezifizieren.

Um bereits bestehende Architekturmodelle und bestehenden Quelltext innerhalb unseres Ansatzes verwenden zu können, stellen wir je eine Integrationsstrategie für die Architektur und den Quelltext vor. Um bestehende Architekturmodelle zu integrieren, simulieren wir deren Erstellung. Während dieses Erstellvorgangs zeichnen wir die Änderungen auf, die nötig sind, um das Architekturmodell zu erstellen. Diese Änderungen werden als

Eingabe für den Konsistenzerhaltungsprozess verwendet, um daraus den entsprechenden Quelltext zu erzeugen. Um vorhandenen Quelltext einzubinden, stellen wir einen Ansatz vor, der auf Architekturrekonstruktionsverfahren basiert, d.h., zuerst wird die Architektur eines bestehenden Softwaresystems rekonstruiert. Die erstellte Architektur wird anschließend zusammen mit dem bestehenden Quelltext in unseren Coevolutionsansatz integriert. Oftmals ist bestehender Quelltext jedoch nicht so aufgebaut, wie es die Abbildungsregeln vorschreiben. Innerhalb der Integrationsstrategie für Quelltext stellen wir deshalb einen Ansatz vor, der in der Lage ist, solche Quelltexte dennoch zu integrieren. Dieser Ansatz ermöglicht es, nicht nur diese Art von Quelltext zu integrieren, sondern diesen auch mit speziell definierten Abbildungsregeln automatisch konsistent zu halten.

Wir haben unseren Ansatz in verschiedenen Fallstudien evaluiert. Dabei haben wir zunächst gezeigt, dass es möglich ist vorhandene Architekturmodelle zu integrieren, indem ihr Aufbau simuliert wird. In der durchgeführten Fallstudie ist es mit unserem Ansatz und den vorgestellten Abbildungsregeln möglich, zwischen 98 % und 100 % der unterstützten Elemente zu integrieren. Als nächstes haben wir gezeigt, dass unser Ansatz in der Lage ist, existierenden Quelltext zu integrieren und Änderungen am integrierten Quelltext konsistent mit der Architektur zu halten. Für diese Fallstudie haben wir zunächst den Quelltext von vier quelloffenen Projekten in den Ansatz integriert. Als nächstes haben wir gezeigt, dass es möglich ist, Änderungen am Quelltext konsistent mit der Architektur zu halten. Dazu haben wir eine alte Version des Quelltextes integriert und Änderungen die zwischen einer alten und neueren Version durchgeführt wurden, aus einem Versionskontrollsystem extrahiert und erneut auf den Quelltext angewendet. Im Rahmen dieser Evaluation haben wir auch gezeigt, dass es möglich ist Änderungen, die innerhalb von Methoden durchgeführt werden, mit einem Verhaltensmodell konsistent zu halten. Wir haben außerdem eine Evaluation der Leistungsfähigkeit unseres Ansatzes durchgeführt und gezeigt, dass unser Ansatz in den meisten Fällen in der Lage ist, die Architektur in einer Zeit zwischen einer und fünf Sekunden konsistent zu halten, nachdem eine Änderung am Quelltext durchgeführt wurde. Als letztes haben wir gezeigt, dass es möglich ist, coevolvierte Modelle für die Performanzvorhersage zu verwenden. Dazu haben wir zuerst die Modelle in einem Parametrisierungsschritt mit den nötigen Ressourcenverbräuchen angereichert. Als nächstes konnten wir die Performanzvorhersage durchführen. In unserer Fallstudie zeigte sich, dass der Vorhersagefehler für die Antwortzeit eines Systems bei ca. 10 % liegt, und damit die coevolvierten Modelle für die Abschätzung der Performanz eines realen Systems verwendet werden können.

Contents

List of Figures

List of Tables

List of Listings

1. Introduction

This introduction first motivates the advantages of an approach for coevolving source code and architectural models and highlights the advantages of having up-to-date architectural models (Section 1.1). In Section 1.2, we describe the goals and questions of this thesis. Afterwards, we shortly describe the approach and the contributions of this thesis (Section 1.3). Finally, the introduction chapter gives an overview of the structure of the remainder of this thesis (Section 1.5).

1.1. Motivation

For the development and evolution of a software system, software architects and software developers usually use multiple artefacts. An important artefact is, of course, the source code of the software system itself. Another important artefact that is often used, is the architectural representation of the source code [KOS06], which usually allows users to get an high-level view on the source code.

Such architectural models can be useful in the planning phase of software development and software evolution. Software architects can, for instance, specify which components in the architectural models need to be adapted or created in order to realise a requirement in the software system. Moreover, architectural models can be used to analyse Non-Functional Properties (NFP) of a software system. The Palladio Component Model (PCM) [Reu+16], for instance, can be used for model-based performance predictions. The prediction is possible even before the implementation of the software system has been started. To do so, software architects need to specify the expected behaviour of software components. Architectural models can also be used for forward engineering, i.e. the architectural models can be used in order to create source code. This source code can either be executed directly without any changes or it can be source code stubs, which need to be completed by software developers in order to obtain an executable software system. Architectural models can also be used for the documentation of the software system.

If architectural models are used in the processes of software development and software evolution, the well-known problems of architecture drift and architecture erosion can occur. Perry and Wolf [PW92] described both problems initially. They defined architecture erosion as violation of the architecture, while they defined architecture drift as insensitivity about the architecture. These problems occur if changes to source code are not kept consistent with the architectural model or if changes in the architectural model are implemented incorrectly in the source code. Having these problems leads to architecture models that are out-dated and thus become useless. Such outdated architectural models are neither a good source for planning and conducting software evolution nor can they be used for precise analysis of NFP.

Hence, having up-to-date architectural model is a necessary perquisite to profit from the benefits architectural models provide. Creating up-to-date architectural models can be done using reverse engineering approaches. Therefore, the research area of reverse engineering provides tools that are able to reverse-engineer architectural models. Most reverse engineering approaches use the source code as input [DP09]. Changes performed to an already existing model, however, are often lost if the architecture model is regenerated from source code. Approaches combining forward and reverse engineering enable the round-trip engineering between source code and architectural model. These approaches can be used to keep architectural models and source code consistent during the development and evolution of a software system. Most existing approaches focus, however, on preserving consistency between object-oriented source code and UML class diagrams.

In this thesis, we present an approach that is able to keep component-based architectural models consistent with the source code. The used architectural models can be used during the actual evolution of a software system by supporting users to keep changes performed to source code consistent with the architecture and vice versa. Moreover, the architectural models can be used for analysis of NFP in a subsequent step.

The initial need of keeping the architecture models and source code consistent arises because both models can be seen as views on the same software system and thus contain redundant information. Even though architectural models are an abstraction from the underlying source code, the information contained in the architecture model, such as components and interfaces, often have a representation in the source code. The complexity of defining the overlap between architectural model elements and source code elements depends on the used architecture model. It is easy, for instance, to define the overlap and the mapping between UML class diagrams and object-oriented source code, as most elements from UML class diagrams have a direct representation in object-oriented source code. It is, however, not a trivial task to define the mapping between component-based software system and object-oriented source code, because the mapping between source code and components can vary depending on the used project and the underlying source code technology. The mapping can even be specific for a certain set of architectural elements. The approach that we present in this thesis is able to support user-defined consistency preservation rules between architectural models and source code.

1.2. Goals and Questions

As we shortly mentioned above, we introduce a coevolution approach for source code and architectural models, which can be used to avoid architecture erosion and ease the detection of architecture drift. Hence, we formulate the main goal of this thesis as follows:

> *Develop a coevolution approach that is able to keep changes performed to source code consistent with architectural models and vice versa.*

To achieve the main goal, we need to achieve the following subgoals:

1. *Define a consistency preservation process for architectural models and source code.*

2. *Define exemplary consistency preservation rules between architectural models and source code, which can be extended and reused.*
3. *Show that the coevolved architectural models can be used for performance prediction in a subsequent step.*

After we have achieved the above-mentioned subgoals, the coevolution approach can be used to develop new software systems. Potential users of the coevolution approach usually have existing source code and existing architectural models already. In order to allow users to reuse already existing artefacts, the approach needs to be able to integrate existing architecture models and existing source code. Hence, we formulate the fourth subgoal as follows:

4. *Integrate existing source and existing architectural model into the coevolution approach.*

From the four defined goals, we can derive the following high-level research questions:

1. *Which steps are necessary to achieve change-driven consistency for architectural models and source code?*

   To enable the coevolution of source code and architectural models in a change-driven way, we need to define a change-driven consistency preservation process. The challenge arising from this question should be solved in a generic way, in order to solve the challenge for both the presented coevolution approach and the view-centric engineering Vitruvius approach.

2. *How can component-based architecture models be mapped to source code?*

   An important challenge for the coevolution of component-based architecture models and source code, is to define bidirectional change-driven consistency preservation rules. For the realisation of the approach, we use the component-based software architecture model PCM and Java as object-oriented source code language. As we mentioned above, the mapping between source code and the component-based architectural model depends on the used project and the used source code technology.

3. *What steps are necessary to enable performance prediction for coevolved models?*

   As we stated in the motivation, models can be used for the analysis of a software system's NFP. An important challenge when using the PCM is to show that the coevolved models can be used for the performance prediction.

4. *How can the approach within this thesis be tailored in order to support existing source code and existing architectural models?*

   As we want to use the coevolution approach for existing source code and existing architecture models, we need to define how existing artefacts can be integrated into the coevolution approach. Therefore, we need to define a process how users can reuse existing source code and existing architectural models.

1.3. Approach and Contributions of this Thesis

In this section, we give a brief overview of the approach and the contribution of this thesis. Both are aligned to the goals presented in the section before. Moreover, we show how we have evaluated the contributions of this thesis.

In this thesis, we present our Coevolution approach, which is a novel approach for coevolving architectural models and source code during the development and evolution of a software system. In particular, the approach can be used to keep instances of the PCM consistent with Java source code. Therefore, *PCM* elements are created, changed, or deleted as soon as their corresponding source code elements have been changed and vice versa. To store the correspondences between architectural model elements and source code elements, we use a correspondence model. Consistency is preserved based on user-defined change-driven consistency preservation rules between the architectural model and source code. Within this thesis, we present four different consistency preservation rules between architectural models and source code, which are implemented in our prototypical implementation. The presented consistency preservation rules are reusable and extendable. We use the concept of user change disambiguation, which can be used if the consistency preservation cannot be achieved automatically. In this case users need to clarify how the consistency can be achieved. As our Coevolution approach is a change-driven approach, we need to retrieve each change performed in the involved architectural editors and the source code editors. To allow users to reuse existing editors, which they are familiar with, we implemented monitors for the Eclipse Java source code editors and PCM architectural model editors. We also present a UML class diagram editor [KLK16], which can be used to edit the source code using a projective UML class diagram view. Our Coevolution approach allows, furthermore, users to keep source code consistent with behavioural architectural models as well. Therefore, we propose an approach that incrementally reverse-engineers the PCM *Service Effect Specifications* based on changes performed to source code methods. The *Service Effect Specifications* are used within PCM to describe the behaviour of components.

To be able to deal with existing source code and existing architectural models, we present different integration strategies. For architectural models, we present an approach that simulates the creation of architectural models. During the creation, we monitor the emerging changes and use them as base for the creation of the corresponding source code. For source code, we propose an approach that uses reverse engineering tools to create an architectural model and a correspondence model, which we can use within our Coevolution approach. Arbitrary code, however, is seldom build according to the defined consistency preservation rules. To deal with this fact, we present an approach that is able to deal with integrated source code for which the actual consistency preservation rules cannot be used. The approach is able to keep even those elements consistent using specific consistency preservation rules for integrated source code elements.

1.3.1. Contributions

In the following, we present a brief overview of the contributions of this thesis. The contributions are aligned with the research questions.

1.3.1.1. Consistency Preservation Process

In this thesis, we present a change-driven consistency preservation process. To be able to use the change-driven process, we need to react to changes performed by users or tools. To retrieve all performed changes, we decided to monitor the used editors. To realise the consistency preservation between architectural models and source code, we contribute a source code monitor as well as an architectural monitor. Both are able to monitor existing editors, i.e. they allow the reuse of existing editors within the consistency preservation process. The architectural monitor is implemented in a generic way and can be used for arbitrary Eclipse Modeling Framework (EMF) models, i.e. it can be used to monitor arbitrary EMF models.

We also contribute the process used to achieve consistency. This process is triggered by the monitors. In particular, the monitors notify the process about a specific change, which has been performed on a model element. After the notifications, the consistency preservation process executes the following steps to achieve consistency: First, we initialize the process by retrieving the consistency preservation rules that need to be executed. Therefore, we check which models are affected by the performed change. Secondly, executable commands are created based on the changed element and the actual performed change operation, using the active consistency preservation rules. The commands that we use in our implementation are generic commands of the EMF framework. In the third step, these commands are executed, which leads to updated models. Even though we introduce and instantiate the process specific for architectural models and source code in this thesis, the presented process is generic for arbitrary models. In particular, it is embedded within the Vitruvius framework and thus can be used to keep arbitrary pairs of EMF models consistent.

The idea for the code monitor has been presented in the publication [LK14]. The initial idea of how to keep models consistent is part of the publication [KBL13].

1.3.1.2. Coevolution Approach for Software Architecture Models and Source Code

We define our Coevolution approach and explain how users can use it to keep architectural models and source code consistent. As we reuse some concepts from the view-based engineering approach Vitruvius, we classify our Coevolution approach with respect to Vitruvius. Moreover, we define the Virtual Single Underlying Model (VSUM) of our Coevolution approach, which contains the architectural models and the source code models.

For the consistency preservation rules, we present the following three different dimensions: i) a technology-specific dimension, ii) a project-specific dimension, and iii) an element-specific dimension. This thesis contributes the following four different consistency preservation rules between architectural models and source code: First, we present the package mapping consistency preservation rules can be used to keep instances of the architectural model PCM consistent with Java source code that is based on Plain Old Java Objects (POJOs). Next, we present two technology-specific consistency preservation rules. The first one can be used to keep instances of the PCM consistent with Java source code based on Enterprise Java Beans (EJBs). The second technology-specific consistency preservation rules, can be used to keep instances of the PCM consistent with Java source code that is created using a dependency injection framework. We also present consistency preservation rules between instances of the PCM and artefacts used for the Eclipse plugin development. The defined consistency preservation rules specify how architectural models need to be changed if a change in the source code occurred and vice versa.

To allow users to detect architectural violation, this thesis contributes an approach for the coevolution of behavioural models and source code during software evolution. Therefore, we have developed a novel approach that creates behavioural models from a source code method as soon as the method has been changed and warns users if the change introduces an architectural violation.

The coevolution of software architecture models and source code is part of the following publications: [Lan13], [LK15], [Kra+15a] and the associated tech report [Kra+15b]. Within these publications, we introduced how we can keep architectural models consistent with source code. We also introduced the package mapping consistency preservation rules.

1.3.1.3. Including Existing Architectural Models and Existing Source Code

As it is important to deal with existing architectural models and existing source code, we contribute an approach that is able to integrate these existing artefacts. Therefore, we present the two integration strategies Reconstructive Integration Strategy (RIS) and Linking Integration Strategy (LIS).

A Reconstructive Integration Strategy simulates the creation of a model. During the simulated creation, we monitor the performed changes using the implemented change monitors. These changes can be used as input for the consistency preservation process, which then creates respectively updates the corresponding model elements. The concept of a RIS is generic for models and can thus be used within the Vitruvius framework as well. We implemented RIS generic for arbitrary models and applied it to the PCM in order to include existing architecture models.

A Linking Integration Strategy, in general, first uses an existing Model-to-Model (M2M) transformation or Model-to-Text (M2T) generation from the existing model to the model that needs to be integrated in order to create the corresponding instance. The M2M transformation respectively M2T generation is required to create a kind of trace model, which contains the mapping between the model elements from the existing to the created model. As a LIS requires a generation step from the existing model to the model that needs to be integrated, the first step towards implementing a LIS for existing source code, is to use reverse engineering tools to create an architectural model from existing source code. To do so, we present the two reverse engineering approaches *Extract* and *EJBmoX*. *Extract* is able to reverse-engineer Java source code implemented with POJOs using different extraction algorithms of the underlying reverse engineering tool Architecture Recovery, Change, and Decay Evaluator (ARCADE). *Extract* is able to reverse-engineer Java source code based on EJB source code. Both approaches are necessary for the integration of an existing source code base. The second step to implement a LIS is to use the output models of the reverse engineering approach to create a correspondence model, which can be used within our Coevolution approach. For the integration of existing source code, we defined four different integration levels. If the existing consistency preservation rules can be used for the coevolution of the integrated source code elements and their corresponding architectural model elements, the elements are considered as elements integrated with Integration Level 1. If the existing consistency preservation rules cannot be used, the elements are considered as elements integrated with Integration Level 2 by default. If elements, considered as elements integrated with Integration Level 2, are changed, users are notified that the consistency needs to be preserved manually. If integration specific consistency preservation rules are defined for specific changes performed on elements in Integration Level 2, the elements are considered as integrated with Integration Level 3. By using specific consistency preservation rules for integrated elements, we are able to support automatic consistency preservation for integrated elements. Elements considered as integrated using Integration Level 4, are elements for which element-specific consistency preservation rules need to be defined in order to support automatic consistency preservation. Within our prototypical implementation, we support the first three integration levels.

The idea and implementation how we can include existing artefacts into our Coevolution approach has been published in [Leo+15]. The reverse engineering approach *Extract* has been published in [Lan+16].

1.3.2. Evaluation

This section provides a quick overview of the conducted evaluation. A detailed description of the evaluation can be found in Chapter 6. We conducted evaluation aligned to the goals presented in Section 1.2. In particular, we conducted the following evaluations:

1. *Evaluation of the reverse engineering approaches*

   We evaluated the developed reverse engineering approaches *Extract* and *EJBmoX*. We showed that both are able to reverse-engineer a component-based software system from the underlying source code. For *Extract*, we reverse-engineered 14 different open-source systems with a size of up to 644.000 Source Lines of Code (SLoC). For *EJBmoX*, we reverse-engineered two relatively small open source case study systems with a size of approximately 5000 SLoC. For *EJBmoX*, we furthermore compared a manually created architecture model of a software system with the reverse-engineered model.

2. *Evaluation of the consistency preservation rules and the integration of existing architectural models*

   We evaluated the developed consistency preservation rules by integrating seven existing architectural models for the developed consistency preservation rules. We showed that it is possible to create the corresponding source code for a given architectural model.

We are able to integrate 98% up to 100% of the supported elements per consistency preservation rule set. Regarding all architectural elements, the number differs between 30% for the Eclipse plugin consistency preservation rules, and 100% for package mapping consistency preservation rules.

3. *Evaluation of the existing source code and consistency preservation of changes*

   We successfully integrated four open source projects into our Coevolution approach with a size of up to 112.000 SLoC. For the four projects, we showed that our Coevolution approach is able to keep changes performed to the source code consistent with the architecture. As changes, we use changes extracted from a Version Control System (VCS) and applied them to source code. We evaluated Integration Level 2 and Integration Level 3 with this evaluation. We showed that the presented approach is able to react to more than 70% of the overall recorded change respectively to more than 90% of the changes if we take out the changes, to which we currently not reacting to on purpose. For the case study, over 99% of changes affected integrated code, i.e. they need to be kept consistent manually (Integration Level 2) or by executing consistency preservation rules specific for the integrated code (Integration Level 3). Hence, using Integration Level 3 and the defined specific reactions, our Coevolution approach is able to process more than 90% of the changes it reacted to using a specific consistency preservation rules. We were also able to show that changes performed on method bodies can be kept consistent with behavioural architecture model and that changes performed on the architectural model can be kept consistent with the source code.

4. *Performance evaluation of the consistency preservation*

   We conducted a performance evaluation of our Coevolution approach by measuring the time it consumes to keep changes performed on source code consistent with the corresponding architectural elements. Even though we observed one exception, we were able to show that it usually takes between one and five seconds to update the architecture model. We were also able to show that the time needed to process a change is dominated by the time the used Java parser needs to parse the changed compilation unit. Even though we observed some exceptions, the duration of the parsing step usually increases with the size of the compilation unit. We conclude that the time is acceptable but by optimizing or replacing the used Java parser, we could reduce the time needed to process a change.

5. *Model-based performance prediction*

   We conducted a model-based performance prediction with a coevolved model, to show that coevolved models can be used for NFP analysis. Therefore, we used mRUBiS[1] as case study system. We first used *EJBmoX* to reverse-engineer an architectural model. Secondly, we performed an evolution scenario for mRUBiS. During the evolution, we kept the architectural model and the source code consistent using our Coevolution approach. To use the extracted model and the coevolved model for performance prediction, however, users need to enrich the model in an upfront step. This step involves setting up the software system and instrumenting the software system in order to measure its performance. Afterwards, we use a load driver to create a specific workload for a provided service. During the execution of the load driver, we gather measuring data for the performance behaviour of the software system. This data can be used to parametrise the architectural models of the software system. After enriching the models, we perform the performance simulation and compare the predicted value with the actual measured values. The prediction error for the response time is approximately 10%, which is a usable result to estimate the performance of the real software system.

1.4. Existing Approaches

There are multiple existing approaches developed in academia and industry related to at least one of the contributions presented in this thesis. None of the existing approaches, however, combines the coevolution of source

[1] https://www.hpi.uni-potsdam.de/giese/public/mdelab/mdelab-projects/case-studies/mrubis/

code and high-level architectural models and its behavioural models in a change-driven way.

We grouped existing approaches in the following three main groups:

1.4.1. Approaches that keep architectural models and source code consistent during software development and software evolution

Approaches supporting the consistency preservation between architectural models and source code can be subdivided in four groups:

Coevolution approaches for source code and high-level architectural models

IBM Rational Rhapsody[2] is a popular tool that aims to keep architectural models consistent with source code. It is able to keep UML package diagrams (including classes) consistent with the source code. KobrA [Atk+01] keeps UML diagrams consistent during the development of a software system using a Single Underlying Model (SUM). None of the approaches, however, allows to keep component-based architectural models and source code consistent.

Approaches supporting change-driven extraction or coevolution of behavioural models

Existing approaches to extract behavioural models, such as ArchLint [Maf+13] and Just-in-Time Tool for Architectural Consistency (JITTAC) [Buc+13] can be used to detect architectural violations in the source code based on extracted behavioural models. Approaches such as mbeddr [Voe+13] and From UML to Java and back again (Fujaba)[Nic+00] enable the coevolution between source code and UML behavioural models, such as activity diagrams and statecharts. They, however, do not focus on the coevolution between source code and behavioural models based on a high-level architectural model.

2 `http://www-03.ibm.com/software/products/en/ratirhapfami`

Approaches supporting round-trip engineering between UML class diagrams and source code

Many existing approaches, such as UML Lab[3] and Borland Together[Bor05], focus on the consistency preservation respectively round-trip engineering between source code and UML class diagrams. These approaches, however, do not use high-level architecture models as we do within our Coevolution approach.

Approaches embedding architectural information into source code

Another popular field of research is to embed architectural constructs, such as components, interfaces, and roles, into source code. This is usually done by either extending the source code language with architectural constructs [Voe+13][ACN02] or by using existing language features to describe architectural constructs [MM03] [Kon+13]. These approaches, however, do not have an explicit architectural model as the architectural information is embedded into the source code directly.

1.4.2. Architecture reverse engineering approaches

Reverse engineering approaches usually aim to create a high-level architectural model from source code. A popular survey on reverse engineering approaches has been carried out by Ducasse and Pollet [DP09]. They state that some architecture reverse engineering approaches are developed in order to use the reverse-engineered architectural model for coevolution between source code and architecture[TH99][HMY06][Wuy01]. The existing approaches, however, do not present different integration levels for the existing source code and most of them also do not focus on change-driven consistency preservation.

[3] `http://www.uml-lab.com/`

1.4.3. View-based software development approaches

Related view-based software development approaches, such as Orthographic Software Modelling (OSM) [ASB10], using a single underlying model in order to describe all artefacts used for the software development. Mens et al. [Men+06] introduce an approach for keeping high-level architectural views consistent with the source code. The existing approaches, however, do not address the consistency preservation between source code and component-based architectural model including behavioural models.

1.5. Structure of the Thesis

The remainder of this thesis is structured as follows.

In Chapter 2, we introduce the necessary foundations for the thesis. In particular, we present foundations of Model-Driven Software Development (MDSD) and view-based software development. Furthermore, we present used approaches, tools, and standards. We especially introduce Vitruvius, Palladio, and Source Code Model eXtractor (SoMoX).

In Chapter 3, we first explain the terminology used in this thesis. Afterwards, we describe the change metamodel and the correspondence metamodel. Moreover, we explain how existing editors can be monitored. Finally, we explain the consistency preservation process used in Vitruvius and in our Coevolution approach.

In Chapter 4, we present the approach of this thesis. To do so, we introduce how coevolution for source code and architectural models can be realised using our Coevolution approach. We also introduce three dimensions for the consistency preservation rules and four different consistency preservation rules between architectural models and source code. Furthermore, we present consistency automation levels and the user disambiguation our Coevolution approach uses to involve users in the consistency preservation process. We introduce how our Coevolution approach can be used to keep behavioural models consistent with source code during the evolution of a software system. In the last part of this chapter, we present different roles of users have if our Coevolution approach is used.

In Chapter 5, we introduce how we can integrate existing architectural models and existing source code into our Coevolution approach. We first present two generic integration strategies for models. We secondly, instantiate the approaches to show how to i) integrate architectural models using the first approach, and ii) integrate existing source code using the second approach. We also introduce different integration levels for the source code.

In Chapter 6, we present the evaluation of our Coevolution approach. We present different case studies to evaluate the contributions of this thesis. We present an evaluation of the reverse engineering approaches, the consistency preservation rules, the integration levels, and the coevolution of source code and architecture. We also show how the coevolved models can be used for performance prediction.

In Chapter 7, we present related work to the approach, we presented in this thesis. Therefore it explains related research approaches as well as existing industrial tools enabling the coevolution of source code and architectural models.

Finally, Chapter 8 concludes the thesis by summarizing the thesis. Based on the open questions, we give an outlook on future work.

2. Foundations

In this section, we present the necessary foundations for this thesis. We first present foundations for Model-Driven Development (MDD) (see Section 2.1). Next, we present the foundations for view-based software development (see Section 2.2.2). In Section 2.3, we give an overview of the Palladio Component Model (PCM). Section 2.4 introduces the foundations of Source Code Model eXtractor (SoMoX). In Section 2.5, we present the tools and standards, we used in this thesis. As last part of this chapter, we present the evaluation concepts (see Section 2.6), we used in this thesis to evaluate the contributions of the thesis.

2.1. Model-Driven Software Development

Model-Driven Software Development puts models in the center of the software development process. Hence, within Model-Driven Software Development (MDSD) models are not used for documentation only, but play a central role [VS06]. They are treated as first class elements in the development process, i.e. they are as important as the source code of a software system. An important purpose of the models in MDSD is that they can be used as input for code generators in order to create source code from the model. This code can be either executed directly or refined by developers in order to retrieve a running software system.

Within MDSD, one important concept is the creation and use of Domain Specific Languages (DSLs). DSLs are generated in order to allow the modelling of a domain specific concern. For instance, the PCM is a DSL for the creation of architectural models. To create and use a DSL, users can create, for instance, a domain specific metamodel and further tooling, such as graphical editors.

In MDSD, multiple models are often used to create a software system. These models can be tailored specific for the users who use them. Therefore, the models can have different levels of abstraction. The used models are conform to a defined metamodel, which itself is a model.

A well-known example for MDSD is the Unified Modeling Language [Obj15], which can be used to create models of a software systems. Therefore, UML allows the creation of different diagrams, such as class diagrams, to support software architects and software developers during the development and evolution of a software system.

Models used within MDSD usually have the properties defined by Stachowiak [Sta73]. Stachowiak defines the following three properties for models: [1]:

- representation, which means that models need to represent their originals,
- reduction, which means that a model needs to be reduced to the attributes of the originals that contain the necessary information for the creator or user of the model,
- pragmatism, which means that models need to be created for a certain purpose.

2.1.1. Meta Object Facility

The Meta Object Facility (MOF) standard has been defined by the OMG [Obj16]. MOF provides, amongst others, a metadata management framework to enable the development of model driven systems. It introduces, furthermore, a four-layered architecture. The four metalevels are the metalevels M3 to M0 and defined as follows:

- M3 is the metametamodel layer,
- M2 is the metamodel layer,
- M1 is the model layer, and
- M0 reflects the reality.

[1] Stachowiak originally presented the properties in German as follows: Abbildungsregeln (representation), Verkürzungsmerkmal (reduction), Pragmatisches Merkmal (pragmatism). To translate them into English, we use translation provided by Burger [Bur14]

The elements from a lower level need to be conform to elements of the higher level. MOF metamodels are described in an UML class diagram like syntax. The MOF metametamodel is self-describing, i.e. the metametamodel can be described using a MOF metamodel. To exemplify the four levels, we consider a software system modeled with the UML class diagram. In this case the MOF is metametamodel, UML is the metamodel, the UML class diagram is the model, and the implemented software system is the realisation of the model.

Essential MOF (EMOF) [Obj16] is a subset of the MOF standard. It is a simple framework allowing to map MOF models to implementations, for instance, the XML Metadata Interchange (XMI) format. Ecore, which is used in the Eclipse Modeling Framework (EMF) framework, is an implementation of EMOF. The metamodels and models, we use in the remainder of this thesis are Ecore-based.

2.1.2. Eclipse Modeling Framework and Ecore

The Eclipse Modeling Framework[2] [Ste+08] is a framework that allows model-driven development within the Eclipse Integrated Development Environment (IDE). Therefore, it offers the following notable features:

- creating metamodels,
- source code generation from metamodels,
- generation and creation of editors that allow creating and editing of instances of metamodels.

A variety of tools using th EMF framework have been created in order to ease the development of software systems. Model transformation languages, for instance, can be used to transform instances of models into instances of other models. Notable examples of Model-to-Model (M2M) languages are Query View Transformation Operational (QVTO) [Obj09] and Atlas Transformation language (ATL) [JK06] can be used. While QVTO can be used for unidirectional transformations, ATL can be used for bidirectional transformations as well. Tools, such as Xtext [EV06] and EMFtext [Hei+09a], allow the creation of textual DSLs. Both provide the automatic creation of textual editors based on the defined DSL.

[2] `https://www.eclipse.org/modeling/emf/`

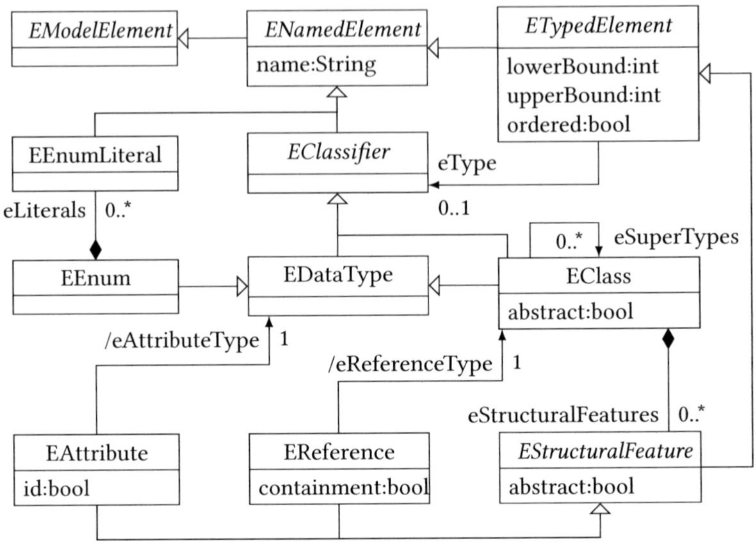

Figure 2.1.: Classes of the Ecore metametamodel. The figure has been published already in Kramer [Kra17].

Within the Eclipse Modeling Framework, Ecore is the metametamodel that can be used to create metamodels. As mentioned above, Ecore itself is an implementation of the EMOF standard. Figure 2.1 shows the classes of the Ecore metametamodel. Metamodels created with Ecore need to conform to this metametamodel. To create a metamodel using Ecore, the main task of users is to model classes with attributes and references amongst each other. The metamodels can be defined using a class diagram, which has very similar syntax as class diagrams within UML class diagrams.

In the work carried out within this thesis, we present a change-driven approach for model consistency. One step to implement such a change-driven approach is to retrieve all changes from Ecore-based models. The first step towards retrieving the changes is to identify possible changes. Therefore, Kramer [Kra17] has identified possible changes in Ecore-based models. Figure 2.2 depicts the feature model Kramer [Kra17] created for possible changes in Ecore-based models. In particular, the feature model shows the different

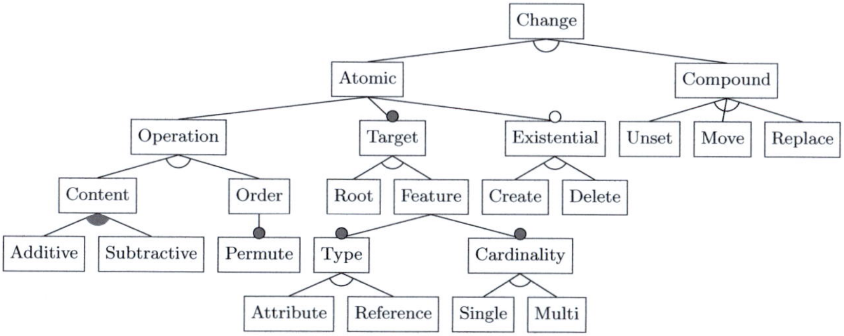

constraints:

1. Permute ⇒ Multi
2. (Multi ∧ Content) ⇒ (Additive ⊕ Subtractive)
3. Single ⇒ (Additive ∧ Subtractive)
4. Existential ⇒ (Root ⊕ Reference)
5. Create ⇒ (Additive ⊕ Root)
6. Delete ⇒ (Subtractive ⊕ Root)
7. Root ⇒ (Additive ⊕ Subtractive)

Figure 2.2.: Feature model for all possible changes in Ecore models [Kra17]

operations that can be performed by users. From the feature model, we were able to create a change metamodel, which we integrated into the VITRUVIUS framework. The actual used classes of the change metamodel and the concepts used in the VITRUVIUS framework are explained in Chapter 3.

2.2. View-based Software Development

View-based software development has the paradigm that multiple views are used to develop and implement a software system. Hence, views play a central role in the development process. The views itself are instances of view types, which are the metamodel of the views. The used views can be tailored, for instance, to the user using them. The UML [Obj15], for instance, uses different viewpoints for the different user roles involved in the development of a software system. For instance, software architects use a special view onto the software architecture while software deployers use a special view for the deployment.

The ISO 42010 [ISO11] standard defines architectural view types and architectural views. As Burger [Bur14] pointed out, the definition used in the ISO does not precisely define viewpoints. As Burger [Bur14] mentioned, Goldschmidt et al. [GBU10; GBB12] provide the following more precise definition for view types:

Definition 1. *A* view type *defines the set of metaclasses whose instances a view can display. It comprises a definition of a concrete syntax plus a mapping to the abstract metamodel syntax. The actual* view *is an instance of a view type showing an actual set of objects and their relations using a certain representation. A* viewpoint *defines a concern.*

Within the ISO 42010 [ISO11] standard synthetic and projective view-based are differentiated. In synthetic approaches users can construct views using model correspondence approaches. In projective approaches an underlying repository is used to create all views. The views are generated dynamically using a creation mechanism view.

One major challenge in view-based software engineering is to keep the used views consistent in order to avoid inconsistency. In synthetic approaches the views need to be kept consistent among once another and the correspondences need to be maintained during the development. In projective approaches a major challenge is to define the underlying repository and the generation mechanism for the views. In Figure 2.3, peer-to-peer approaches, which can be used by synthetic approaches, are compared to hub-and-spoke approaches, which can be used by projective approaches. The necessary number of transformations to keep views consistent increases in a linear matter in projectional approaches, while it increases in a quadratic matter in peer-to-peer approaches.

2.2.1. Orthographic Software Modelling

The Orthographic Software Modelling (OSM) approach, introduced by Atkinson et al. [ASB10], is a view-based engineering approach. The main concept of OSM is the use of a Single Underlying Model (SUM), which is used to store all information about the system under development in one single model. The SUM needs to be redundancy-free, i.e. no duplicated information is allowed within the SUM. Using such a SUM avoids the need of consistency

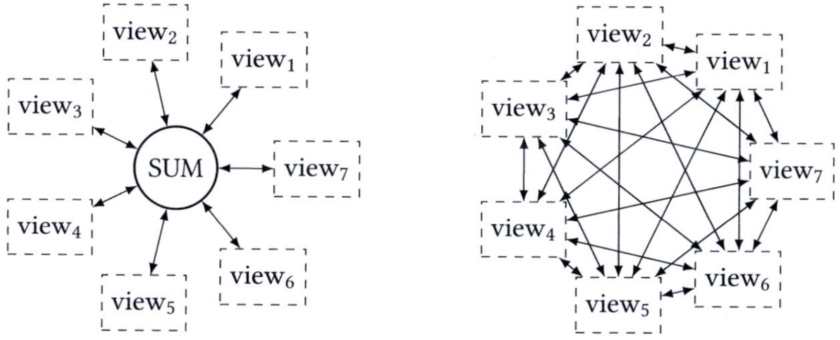

Figure 2.3.: Hub-and-Spoke approach vs. Peer-to-Peer approach [Bur14]

preservation between the models involved in the development. It is, however, hard to define such a redundancy free metamodel. Furthermore, using such a SUM hinders the reuse of existing tools if they are not tailored specific for the SUM. Accessing the SUM is possible via views solely. The views are instances of view types and can be generated dynamically from the SUM using transformations. As soon as the views have been edited by users, the information is stored in the SUM. Hence, keeping the views consistent between one another is not necessary, because they are kept consistent using the SUM.

2.2.2. VITRUVIUS

The VITRUVIUS approach is a view-based engineering approach, which Burger [Bur14] and we [KBL13] introduced. VITRUVIUS can be used to keep instances of different metamodels consistent during the development of a system. Therefore, it uses a Virtual Single Underlying Model (VSUM), which contains all information that is necessary to describe the system. The access to the models contained in the VSUM is solely possible via views. The idea of storing all information in one underlying model is inspired by the SUM used in OSM. However, within the VSUM of VITRUVIUS existing metamodels can be reused. Hence, existing tools working with instances of the metamodels can also be reused using VITRUVIUS. The overlap between the model instances of the used metamodels is kept consistent using consistency preservation rules between the models. Hence, Vitruvius can be considered as a hybrid approach combining projective and synthetic elements. Within the VSUM, a synthetic approach is used that keeps the overlap between the models consistent. From an external view the VSUM, however, can be seen as projective because the views itself need to be kept consistent with the VSUM only.

The used views for manipulating the models are instances of view types. The views-types are either projectional view types or combining view types [Bur14]. Projectional view types are view types, which show information from one metamodel only. Hence, they can be used to show and manipulate instances of one metamodel within the VSUM. Using projectional view types also allows us to integrate and reuse already existing view types for a metamodel within Vitruvius. Combining view types are able to combine information from more than one metamodel and present them to users. They can be created using ModelJoin (see [Bur+14] and [Bur13]). ModelJoin allows the creation of a metamodel for a view type using a DSL that can be used to query information from different metamodels and combine them in one metamodel. The syntax of the ModelJoin query language is inspired by the well-known Structured Query Language (SQL), which can be used to query information from databases. Burger and Schneider [BS16] showed how it is possible to create combining view types for Vitruvius that can be edited. Using this approach, changes conducted to the combining view types are kept consistent with the models in the VSUM. Combining view types can even be flexible view types, which are created during the development process on demand. An overview of Vitruvius is shown in Figure 2.4.

Within this thesis, we use the Vitruvius framework as base for our implementation. In Chapter 3, we present the contributions of this thesis to the Vitruvius framework. In the initial Vitruvius vision, Burger [Bur14] and we [KBL13] envisioned the application of Vitruvius to the Component-based Software Engineering (CBSE) domain. The approach presented in this thesis can be seen as first step towards the realisation of this vision. The differences of the approach presented in this thesis and the Vitruvius vision is presented in Section 4.2. Therefore, we first present the vision how Vitruvius can be applied to the CBSE domain and secondly, classify the approach developed within this thesis into the Vitruvius vision.

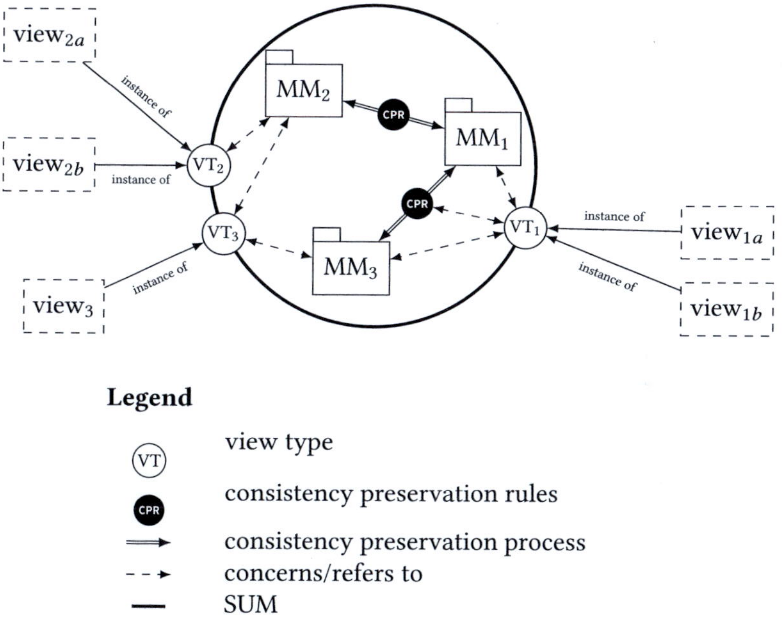

Figure 2.4.: Overview of the VITRUVIUS VSUM and the views that allow The overlap need to be defined within the consistency preservation rules (arrows with CPR), which are defined either in a GPL or in DSLs tailored to specify the overlap between model instances. The views can be used to manipulate instances within the VSUM. The figure has been published already in [Bur13]. We, however, changed it slightly in order to match the terms used in this thesis.

2.3. Palladio Component Model

The PCM (see Becker et al. [BKR09], Reussner et al. [Reu+16]) can be used to create a component-based software architecture model. Hence, it can be seen as an Architecture Description Language (ADL).

Based on the created architecture models the PCM allows users to perform model based analyses. These analyses include, for instance, performance prediction and reliability analysis [Bro+12]. To allow this analysis, Palladio proposes the use of five different models, which created by different users (see Becker [Bec08]). Figure 2.5 shows the models and the transformations respectively interpretations provided by the Palladio bench. The Palladio bench is the implementation of the Palladio approach. In Reussner et al. [Reu+16] a component for Palladio is defined as follows:

Definition 2. *Software Component A* software component *is a contractually specified building block for software, which can be composed, deployed, and adapted without understanding its internals.*

Hence, within Palladio a similar component definition is used as the one introduced by Szyperski et al. [SGM02], who define a component as a unit of composition block with specified interfaces, which can be deployed independently.

Component developers are responsible for creating the software architecture in terms of components, interfaces, signatures, data types, provided roles, and required roles. Roles in the *Repository* describe the relation between components and interfaces. Component developers are, furthermore, responsible for creating the behaviour of components by specifying one *Service Effect Specifications* (*SEFF*) for each provided signature of a component. Software architects are responsible for assembling the software system in the *System* model. The assembling is done based on the components in the *Repository*. Software architects need to connect the instantiated components using connectors and specify provided roles and required roles of the software system. System deployers are responsible for creating the *ResourceEnvironment* model and the *Allocation* model. Within the *ResourceEnvironment* model, they need to specify the servers, their CPUs, HDDs, and network connection between them. In the *Allocation* model, they need to specify which assembly from the *System* is deployed on which resource. Domain experts are responsible for modelling the behaviour of users in the *UsageModel*. Therefore, they specify the interaction of users with the system, for instance, they specify which provided services of a *System* are called in which order. They also specify the characteristic of the relevant input parameters, and the arrival rate of new users at the system. The QoS analyst uses the Palladio bench and analyses the properties of the software system.

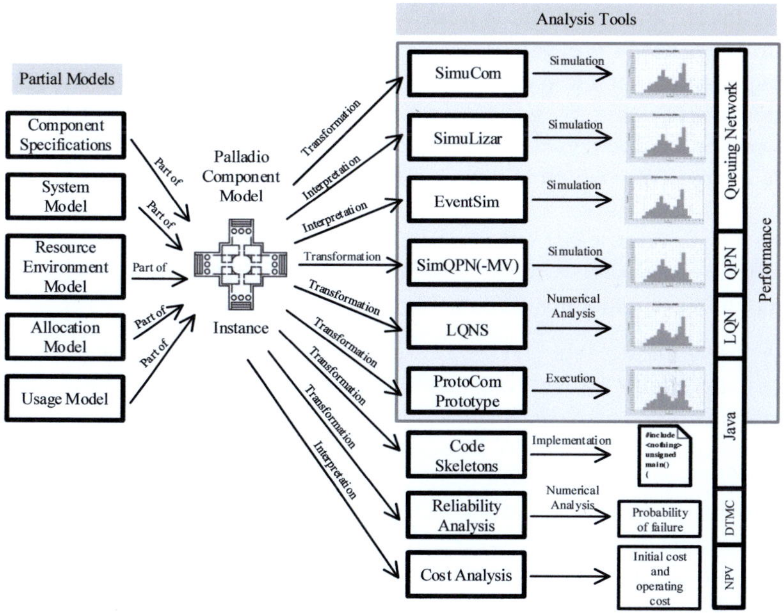

Figure 2.5.: Overview of the partial PCM models [Mer+16]. The Palladio bench provides the transformations respectively interpretations for the different analysis models and tools.

In this thesis, we focus mainly on the PCM *Repository* including the *SEFFs* and the PCM *System*. Based on Becker [Bec08] and Reussner et al. [Reu+11], we explain the structure of both below.

2.3.1. PCM *Repository* with *SEFFs*

As we mentioned above, component developers are supposed to implement the architecture of a software system using the *Repository* model. Figure 2.6 shows the metaclasses and example instances of them. In the following, we explain the elements from the PCM *Repository* that are relevant for this thesis. The *Repository* itself is the root object of the *Repository*, which contains all other elements. A *BasicComponent* is a single component, which is implemented by developers. It is not intended to be split up in more components. Using object-oriented languages a *BasicComponent* is usually implemented using classes. A *BasicComponent* contains the *SEFF*, which are describing the behaviour of the provided signatures. A *CompositeComponent* is a component, which is composed of other components. Therefore, it connects the internal components using connectors. It does not define own behavioural elements in terms of *SEFFs*. The internal structure of a *CompositeComponent* is similar to the structure of a *System*, which we explain in the following section.

OperationInterfaces are first level entities in the PCM, i.e. they are not bound to a component. Instead they can be provided or required by components. *OperationInterfaces* have *OperationSignatures*, which are defining the service that need to be implemented by a component that provides the *OperationInterfaces*. Hence, a component using implementations of the interface can be assured that the services are fulfilled as expected. *OperationSignatures* contain *Parameters* and *ReturnTypes*. Even though *Parameters* can be specified as *in*, *out*, or *inOut parameters* in the PCM, we only use *in Parameters* in this theis. The PCM introduces data types, which are used for the *Parameters* and the *ReturnTypes* of a *OperationSignature*. Within the PCM the following three different kinds of data types can be used:

- *PrimitiveDataTypes*, which are predefined primitive types, such as `integer`, `double`, and `string`
- *CollectionDataTypes*, which represent a collection of another data type. The inner type of the collection is stored in the reference *InnerType*.
- *CompositeDataTypes*, which represent a combination of other data types. The data types, which are composed by the *CompositeDataType*, are stored in a list of *InnerDeclaration*.

CompositeDataType and *CollectionDataType* are user-defined types.

To connect components and interfaces the PCM introduces so called Roles. This roles are separated in to required and provided roles. The roles are contained in a *BasicComponent*. A *OperationRequiredRole* indicates that the *BasicComponent* requires the specified *OperationInterface*, while a *OperationProvidedRole* indicates that the *BasicComponent* provides the specified

OperationInterface. Relevant for this thesis are the *OperationProvidedRole* and the *OperationRequiredRole*, which are able to connect *BasicComponents* with *OperationInterfaces*. As we only use *OperationProvidedRole* and the *OperationRequiredRole* in this thesis, we refer to them as *PrvovidedRoles* respectively *RequiredRole* to ease the reading of the thesis. Even though we also use *OperationInterfaces* only in this thesis, we refer to them as *OperationInterfaces*. This makes it easier to distinguish between architectural interfaces and code interfaces. Code interfaces are simply addressed as *interfaces* or *Java interfaces*.

Service Effect Specifications (SEFFs), which are introduced by Koziolek [Koz08], are used to describe the behaviour of a software system. They specify, similar to a UML activity diagram, the control flow performed by a *BasicComponent* in order to fulfill one of its provides services. The PCM metamodel foresees the usage of different *SEFF* classes. Up until now, however, only the class *Resource Demanding SEFF (RDSEFF)* is specified as subclass of *SEFF*. In the remainder of the thesis, we refer to *RDSEFFs* as *SEFFs* in order to increase the readability. The main elements of *SEFFs*, we are using in this thesis, are explained in the following. The main elements of a *SEFF* are the *ExternalCallActions*. They indicate the call of a component-external service within the *SEFF*. A *LoopAction* indicates that the control flow within the *LoopAction* is executed multiple times. A *BranchAction* specifies branches within the control flow. From the specified branches only one is executed based on either a probability or a input parameter. *InternalActions* abstract from internal behaviour of a component. An *InternalAction*, for instance, can abstract away from a complex internal algorithm. The component developers specify the resource demanding behaviour of the *SEFF* actions. Therefore, they indicate, for instance, the loop count of a *LoopAction*, the probability for a *BranchAction*, and the CPU and HDD demand of an *InternalAction*. *ResourceDemandingInternalBehaviour* define behaviour, which can only be used within a specific component. The behaviour, which can be described within a *ResourceDemandingInternalBehaviour*, is the same as in a *SEFF*. *ResourceDemandingInternalBehaviours* can be compared to private methods in classes of object-oriented languages. *InternalCallActions* can be used to call *ResourceDemandingInternalBehaviours* from within a *SEFF* or another *ResourceDemandingInternalBehaviour*.

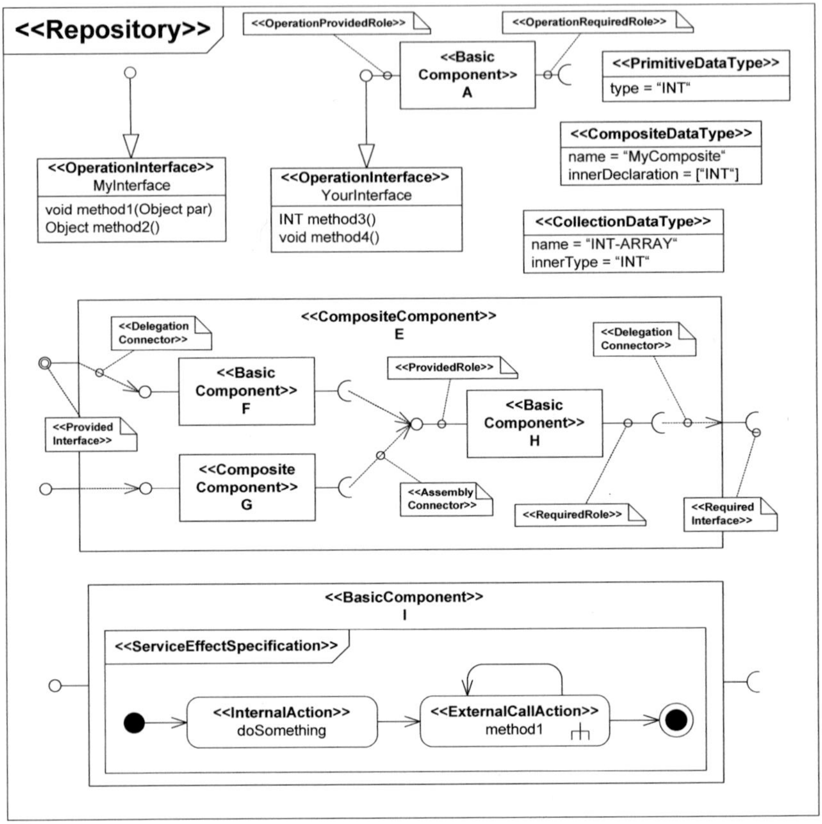

Figure 2.6.: Metaclasses in the PCM *Repository*[Reu+11], which are used within this thesis. The upper part depicts *BasicComponents* and *OperationInterfaces* and the relations between them. The middle part shows the internal structure of a *CompositeComponent*. The lower part shows a simple *SEFF* contained in a *BasicComponent*.

2.3.2. PCM *System*

The second important model for this thesis is the *System*. Figure 2.7 gives an overview of the elements within a *System*. Within a *System* components from on or more *Repositories* are composed to one *System*. The important elements

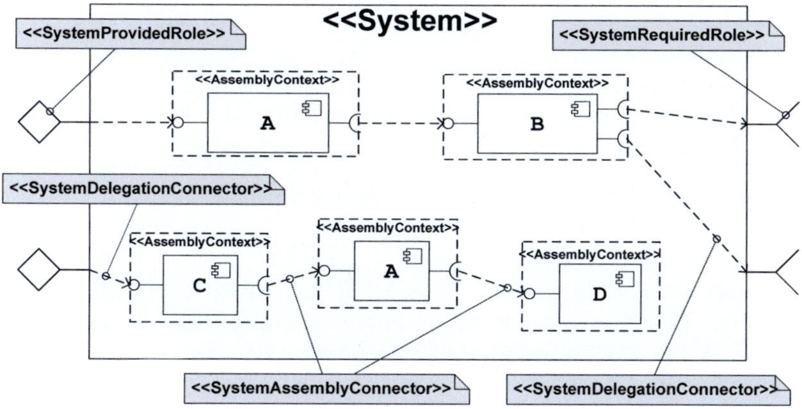

Figure 2.7.: Metaclasses in the PCM *System*

of a *System* are explained in the following. An *AssemblyContext* assembles a component from a *Repository*, i.e. it creates an instance of a component in a *System*. The *SystemProvidedRoles* indicates the provided interfaces of a *System*, while the *SystemRequiredRoles* indicates the required interfaces of a *System*. Technically, a *SystemProvidedRoles* is a *ProvidedRole*, while a *SystemRequiredRoles* is a *RequiredRole*. The provided and required interfaces of the *AssemblyContexts* are connected using *DelegationConnectors*. To connect *SystemProvidedRoles* with *AssemblyContexts ProvidedDelegationConnectors* are used. To connect *AssemblyContexts* with *SystemRequiredRoles RequiredDelegationConnectors* are used. The internal structure of a *SubSystem* and a *CompositeComponents* is the same as the internal structure of *System*.

2.4. Source Code Model eXtractor

SoMoX, which has been introduced by Krogmann [Kro12], is a reverse engineering approach, which is able to reverse-engineer Java code into PCM instances. In particular, SoMoX is able to create a PCM *Repository* from source code and a PCM *System* derived from the *Repository*. It also creates a default *ResourceEnviroment* model and a default *Allocation*. The created

Repository contains components, interfaces, roles, and *SEFFs*. Krogmann [Kro12] points out that SoMoX performs best if the analysed project follows a component-based architecture. Together with Beagle [KKR10], SoMoX is able to reverse-engineer a component-based architecture, which can be used for performance prediction.

In this section, we present only the necessary details about SoMoX, which readers need to know in order to understand the parts of the thesis, where we refer to SoMoX. Therefore, we first give an overview of the SoMoX approach. Next, we explain the SoMoX *SEFF* reconstruction in detail. The detailed explanation is necessary, because within this thesis, we explain an incremental version of the *SEFF* reconstruction.

2.4.1. Overview

To reverse-engineer the statical architecture of a software system, SoMoX uses the following four steps:

1. parsing the source code into a model representation,
2. reverse engineering components and interface using metrics,
3. extracting data types and signature using metrics, and
4. reverse engineering of the *SEFFs*.

For the first step, SoMoX currently uses either Model Discovery (MoDisco) [Bru+10] or Java Model Parser and Printer (JaMoPP) [Hei+09a]. Both tools allow us to parse the source code into an EMF model representation. Within this thesis, we use JaMoPP for the parsing. Based on this model, the other steps within the SoMoX reverse engineering phase are executed.

As second step, SoMoX reverse-engineers the statical architecture of the source code. Therefore, it uses different metrics. Details about the used basic metrics can be found in Krogmann [Kro12]. The weighting of the different metrics need to be defined by users of SoMoX. If the users are familiar with the software system, the they are usually able to define the metrics. The metrics need to be weighted between 0 (low impact factor) and 100 (high impact factor), to determine the impact factor of the metric during the anlayses. An example for the metric is the package metric, which specifies the impact of the package hierarchy on the architecture. If it has a high impact factor classes within the same package are more likely to be in the same component. Another example, for a metric, is the interface violation metric, which investigates whether classes communicate to each other via interfaces or directly. The value of the interface violation metric specifies, whether classes with direct communication between each other are more likely to be part of the same component or not. After applying the metrics to the source code SoMoX tries to iteratively combine classes to components and *BasicComponents* to *CompositeComponents*. After the reverse engineering of components and interfaces SoMoX reverse-engineers the necessary *OperationSignatures* and *DataTypes* for the interfaces.

The last step towards the reconstruction of a software architecture is to reverse-engineer the statical behaviour, in terms of *SEFFs*, of the source code by analysing the source code methods. As we extend the *SEFF* reconstruction in this thesis, we explain the SoMoX*SEFF* reconstruction in detail within the next section.

2.4.2. SoMoX *SEFF* Reconstruction

The main goal of the SoMoX *SEFF* reconstruction is to reverse-engineer the behaviour of the source code into *SEFFs*. To do so, the *SEFF* reconstruction approach analyses the source code methods, which have been identified by SoMoX as provided methods of a detected *BasicComponent*. The *SEFF* reconstruction also abstracts from the source code, i,e., non-architectural-relevant control flow elements are not represented in the resulting *SEFF*.

Prerequisites for the analyses are that it needs the parsed source code model of the software system, the reverse-engineered statical architecture, and an instance of the Source Code Decorator Model. The source code model is available, because it is created during the first step of the SoMoX reverse engineering process. The statical architecture model is the result of the second SoMoX reverse engineering process. The Source Code Decorator Model (SCDM) contains the information, which source code element is reverse-engineered into which architectural element. It is created during the reverse engineering of the statical architecture models, i.e. it is created in the steps two and three of the above-mentioned reverse engineering steps. It contains the information which classes are composed to one component.

For *OperationInterfaces*, it contains the information which class respectively code interface are the corresponding elements. For each *OperationSignature* it contains the corresponding Java method, i.e. the Java method that lead to the creation of the *OperationSignature*. For complex *DataTypes* it contains the class that corresponds to the *DataType*. The *SCDM* is created during the second step of the SoMoX reconstruction process. Hence, for each reconstructed architectural element an entry in the *SCDM* is either created or the existing entry is updated.

The actual *SEFF* reconstruction step for a given method is separated in two phases: In the first phase all method calls within a method are visited and classified as either

- *component-external* method calls (respectively *external* method calls), which are calls to classes or interfaces that are contained in another component,
- *library* calls, which are calls to third party library used by the software, for instance, calls to classes in `java.lang` are considered as *library* calls, or
- *component-internal* method calls (respectively *internal* method calls), which are calls to methods within the same component. Theses calls are visited recursively by the *SEFF* reconstruction in order to get a classification of all method calls called directly or indirectly by the parent method.

To classify the method calls the *SEFF* reconstruction first retrieves the classifier of the called method. Next, it checks whether the SCDM has an entry for the classifier of the called method. If this is not the case, the call is considered as a *library* call. If the SCDM has a corresponding entry it checks whether the classifier of the method performing the call (the source method) is contained within the same component as the called method (target method). If this is the case the call is an *internal* call. If the classifier of the source method is contained within a different component as the classifier of the target method, the investigated method call is a *component-external* call. The parent statements, such as `branches` and `loops`, of component-external method call statements and the component-internal method call statements are marked, i.e. it is possible to decide for parent statements whether they contain an architectural relevant method call.

After recursively classifying all method calls, the *SEFF* reconstruction performs its second step, which is the creation of the actual *SEFF*. The main supported elements from the *SEFF* metamodel, are i) *ExternalCallActions*, which are created for *component-external* method calls, ii) *BranchActions*, which are created for `if` and `switch` statements, iii) *LoopActions*, which are created for loops in the source code, and iv) *InternalActions*, which are created for source code sections, which are not relevant for external behaviour of the component. To create the *SEFF*, a control flow analyses is conducted and all statements are visited again. The *SEFF* is created based on the *component-external* method calls, i.e. `loop` statements, `if` statements, and `switch` statements are made explicit in the architectural model only if they contain an external method call. If they do not contain a *component-external* method call, they are combined within an *InternalAction*. By combining the calls, which are not relevant for the component-external behaviour, the *SEFF* reaches a higher abstraction level from the source code. The *SEFF* reconstruction is also able to abstract from component-internal method calls by inlining them in the *SEFF* by default. If a component-internal method contains a component-external method call and is called at least twice from within its component, however, the *SEFF* reconstruction is able to make the call explicit in both *SEFFs*. This avoids the reconstruction of the same source code methods for multiple *SEFFs*. Instead the *SEFF* reconstruction creates a *ResourceDemandingInternalBehaviour* for the component-internal method. In the *SEFF* itself an *InternalCallActions* calling the created *ResourceDemandingInternalBehaviour* is created. After executing all steps, the *SEFF* for a provided service has been created. As Krogmann [Kro12] points out the *SEFF* reconstruction does not use any heuristics but follows a strict order to create a *SEFF*. An example for the reconstruction of a *SEFF* from a given method is given in Section 4.5. Within this thesis, we propose an approach to incremental reconstruct a *SEFF* as soon as a method body of a source code method corresponding to a *SEFF* or a *ResourceDemandingInternalBehaviour* has been changed by developers.

2.5. Used Tools and Standards

In this section, we explain tools and standards we used within the thesis.

2.5.1. Java Model Parser and Printer

JaMoPP [Hei+09b] [Hei+10] provides a parser and printer for the Java language. The parser parses Java into an EMF model representation, while the printer prints Java code from the JaMoPP EMF model. The EMF metamodel of JaMoPP is a metamodel of the Java language. In particular, it is a metamodel of Java 1.5. Hence JaMoPP supports source code created with syntax features, such as generics, which were introduced in version 1.5 and older versions. Source code, which uses syntax features of newer Java versions, however, can neither be parsed nor printed using JaMoPP. JaMoPP allows us to use treat Java source code as any other EMF model and use model driven technologies, such as model transformations, for Java source code. JaMoPP is created with EMFtext [Hei+09a]. EMFtext is an approach, which allows the creation of textual syntax for a given metamodel. It automatically creates text editors for the specified metamodels.

2.5.2. Eclipse Plugin Development

Eclipse plugin development using the Eclipse Rich Client Platform (RCP) [Vog13], is a foundation for this thesis in two different ways. First, the implemented approach as well as the VITRUVIUS framework, are implemented as Eclipse plugins, i.e. they can be used within the Eclipse IDE. Secondly, we use artefacts of Eclipse plugins for the consistency preservation between Eclipse plugins and the PCM *Repository* (see Section 4.6.3). In this section, we mainly focus on the artefacts and their EMF model representation, which are used for the consistency preservation rules. As we explain the artefacts, we partly also explain how they can be used for the Eclipse plugin development.

```
Manifest-Version: 1.0
Bundle-ManifestVersion: 2
Bundle-Name: Example BundleName
Bundle-SymbolicName: my.organisation.example.bundle
Bundle-Version: 1.0.0
Export-Package: example.package
Require-Bundle: org.eclipse.emf.ecore,
 com.google.guava,
 org.apache.log4j
```

Listing 1: An example for an Eclipse Manifest file

```
<?xml version="1.0" encoding="UTF-8"?>
<plugin>
  <extension-point id="example.id" name="ExampleExtensionPoint" schema="schema/
       examle.id.exsd"/>
  <extension
        point="example.id.provides">
    <provides
        provider="example.id.provides.ProviderClass">
    </provides>
  </extension>
</plugin>
```

Listing 2: An example for an Eclipse plugin XML file

2.5.2.1. Overview of Eclipse Plugin Development Artefacts

One Eclipse plugin is represented as one Eclipse project in the IDE. The main artefacts for the plugin development are the *Manifest.mf* file, the *plugin.xml* file, and the *feature.xml* file.

The manifest file refers to plugin project as a bundle. It contains necessary information about the plugin respectively the bundle. It contains, for instance, the name, the exported packages, the imported bundles, and the imported packages. Listing 1 shows an example of a manifest file.

The relevant information in a plugin.xml file for this thesis, are the information about the extension point a plugin provides and the extension points a plugin implements. An example of a plugin.xml is given in Listing 2.

```
<?xml version="1.0" encoding="UTF-8"?>
<feature
    id="example.feature"
    label="Example Feature"
    version="1.0.0"
    provider-name="My Organisation">

  <plugin id="example.plugin1"/>
  <plugin id="example.plugin2"/>

  <includes id="example.my.other.feature"/>
</feature>
```

Listing 3: An example for an Eclipse feature XML file

To combine different Eclipse plugins, Eclipse allows users to combine existing plugins to features. One feature is defined in one project. The main artefact within a feature is a *feature.xml*, which contains the information about the included plugins. As features can contain each other, the *feature.xml* can also include other features. Listing 3 shows an example of an Eclipse feature XML file.

2.5.2.2. Model Representation of Eclipse Plugin Development Artefacts

As we use Eclipse plugins in one of the consistency preservation rules and the EMF for the realisation, we need to be able to access the artefacts using techniques of MDSD. Hence, we need to have EMF metamodels of the Manifest file, the Plugin.xml, and the Feature.xml. Metamodels for the Manifest file and for XML files are part of the EMFtext concrete syntax zoo[3]. From EMFtext, we get a parser and a printer for the textual syntax as well as textual editors for them. Hence, we can use them to treat the content of the files as models, which means that the models contain the same information as the files.

The EMFtext XML model is generic for all XML files, while the EMFtext Manifest syntax and metamodel are already tailored specific for Eclipse manifest files. Hence, we need to implement helper classes to ease the use

[3] http://emftext.org/index.php/EMFText_Concrete_Syntax_Zoo

```
public final class WebGUIImpl implements IWebGUI {

    private final IMediaStore iMediaStore;

    @Inject
    public WebGUIImpl(IMediaStore iMediaStore){
        this.iMediaStore = iMediaStore;
    }
}
```

Listing 4: An example for dependency injection using the `@Inject` annotation

of the EMFtext XML implementation with Eclipse plugins XML and Eclipse feature XML files.

2.5.3. Dependency Injection Frameworks for Java

In this section, we present dependency injection frameworks for Java. Similar to EJBs and the Eclipse plugin mechanism, we present consistency preservation rules between architectural model and a dependency injection framework within this thesis (see Section 4.6.1.2). Dependency injection frameworks for Java are standardized in JSR330[4]. They are based on the dependency injection pattern proposed by Fowler[5]. The dependency injection pattern itself allows to inject a dependency of a class either via the constructor, via a setter, or via interface injection. The dependency injection pattern allows an inversion of control, because the dependencies are injected into classes and the classes do not need to care about the creation of the actual instances. We focus on constructor injection using dependency injection frameworks for Java. Using constructor injection means that dependencies from classes to interfaces are injected via the constructor. An example of the constructor injection can be seen in Listing 4. Within this listing, an instance of `IMediaStore` is injected to the instance of `IWebGUI` using constructor injection. To compose the classes, users need to specify which class is actually used for which interface. This can be done specific for the used dependency injection framework. Within this thesis, we use Google

[4] `https://jcp.org/en/jsr/detail?id=330`

[5] `http://martinfowler.com/articles/injection.html`

```
public class MediaStoreModule extends AbstractModule {
  @Override
  protected void configure() {
    bind(IMediaStore.class).to(MediaStoreImpl.class);
  }
}
```

Listing 5: An example of a Google Guice module

Guice[6] [Van08] as dependency injection framework. We use it to show that it is possible to keep architectural models and source code, which is based on Google Guice, consistent during the development and evolution of a software system. Google Guice offers the possibility to compose the classes within the source code. An example is shown in Listing 5. It shows the class `MediaStoreModule`, which extends the Google Guice class `AbstractModule`. Within Google Guice each module class needs to configure respectively compose the classes in its `configure` method. Therefore, a Google Guice module class either needs to extend class `AbstractModule` or implement the interface `Module`. Within the example listing, the class `MediaStoreModule` extends the class `AbstractModule` and uses its `configure` method to bind the `IMediaStore` interface to the `MeidaStoreImpl` class.

2.5.4. Enterprise Java Beans

In this section, we explain the necessary foundations for Enterprise Java Bean (EJB) based on the EJB standard [Sak09]. In this thesis, we only use EJB version 3.1 and above. EJB introduces component-based classes and interfaces into Java. To mark a class as EJB component-class Java annotations are used within EJB version 3.1. Component-classes are either annotated with `@Stateless`, `@Stateful`, or `@MessageDriven`. A component-class annotated with `@Stateless` is not allowed to hold a state, while a component-class annotated with `@Stateful` is allowed to store information and reuse them during another call. A component-class annotated with `@MessageDriven` is

[6] `https://github.com/google/guice`

used for message driven communication. Usually the Java Message Service (JMS)[7] is used for the message driven communication.

Similar to EJB classes, EJB relevant interfaces, which are called EJB business interfaces, are also marked with annotations. For interfaces it can be distinguished between local and remote interfaces. Remote interfaces are annotated with `@Remote`. Remote interfaces support the access through remote servers. Local interfaces are annotated with `@Local` and support local access only.

An EJB component-class realizes an EJB business interface, if it implements the interface through a standard Java `implements` relation. If a class only implements one interface, it is automatically exposed as EJB business interfaces, even if the interface is not annotated with `@Remote` or `@Local`. To use an implementation of an EJB business interface within a component, a field with the type of the interface needs to be created and annotated with either `@EJB` or `@Inject`. The EJB runtime environment than uses dependency injection to inject an instance of the component-class implementing the interface. Another possibility to use an implementation of an EJB business interface, is to create a field with the type of an EJB business interface and lookup the EJB implementation of the business interface within the code manually. In this case the field does not need to be annotated with `@EJB`.

Within EJB 3.1, it is also possible for an EJB component-class not to implement any EJB interfaces but to be exposed as EJB component anyhow. This can be useful if a class should be used local only, but be managed through EJB.

For the deployment of EJB components a deployment descriptor can be used, which usually is an XML file.

2.5.5. Replaying Changes from a Version Control System

During the evaluation of the approach, we need to replay changes from a Version Control System (VCS) in order to evaluate the main contributions of this thesis. Therefore, all changes from an old version in the VCS to a newer version in the VCS are replayed within the IDE to simulate the development

[7] `https://java.net/projects/jms-spec/pages/Home/`

process. The changes need to be replayed on a fine-grained level for each file, which have been affected between two versions of a software system. Such fine-grained changes are, for instance, changing the signature of a method, adding or removing an import, or changing a statement. The differences between two versions within a VCS, however, typically span a set of such fine-grained changes. For the realisation of these requirements, Petersen [Pet16] implemented a tool, which is able to replay changes from a VCS.

The change replay tool performs the following three steps to enable the replay of fine-grained changes between two versions of a VCS:

1. extracting VCS changes from a VCS,
2. apply Abstract Syntax Tree (AST) differencing calculation, and
3. replay the extracted changes in the IDE.

The first step is to extract all changes between two versions, as they are stored in the VCS. After this extraction, we have coarse-grained changes based on the commits. Such changes, however, usually span many of fine-grained changes, and can not be used for the change replaying directly.

To get fine-grained changes, the change replay tools compares the coarse-grained changes based on the AST representation of both. This is the second step of the change replay tool. Petersen [Pet16] compared different AST based diffing tools and decided to reuse GumTree [Fal+14] within the change replay tool. GumTree is by default only able to compare changes based on AST. The results are highlighted and presented to users in an editor. Hence, users are able to easily see differences between two versions. Petersen, however, extended GumTree so that it is also possible to store the necessary additional information for the change replay.

As last step, the extracted fine-grained changes are applied subsequently in the IDE. Therefore, the change replay tool resets the entire content of a file based on the Eclipse Java Development Tools (JDT) AST.

The change replay tool is currently not able to preserve the layout information during the change replay. This, however, turned out not to be an issue for our evaluation, because we are only interested in the non-layout information, i.e. we are interested in actual code changes.

2.6. Evaluation foundations

This section presents the foundations, which we used to structure the evaluation of our contributions. We first explain the Goal Question Metric (GQM) concept introduced by Basili et al. [BCR94]. As second foundation for the evaluation, we present the three validation levels introduced by Böhme and Reussner [BR05].

2.6.1. Goal Question Metric

The concept of having a GQM plan for the evaluation has been introduced by Basili et al. [BCR94]. To apply the GQM approach for evaluation in software engineering, first it is necessary to define evaluation goals. According to Basili et al. [BCR94], goals are defined on a conceptual level and should be defined for an object of measurement. Measurement objects are categorized in i) products, which are artefacts produced during the life cycle of a system, e.g. the design of a product and its implementation, ii) processes, which are activities associated with time, e.g. designing and testing, and iii) resources, which are items used in the process, for instance, hardware or software. Next, questions need to be defined that can be used to define whether the goals have been reached. These questions are defined on the operational level and should characterize the object of measurement. Finally, metrics, which can be used to answer the questions, need to be defined. To answer the question using the defined metrics, the metrics should be quantifiable, i.e. metrics are defined on the quantitative level. They are either objective, if they depend on the measured object only, or subjective if they depend on the measured object and the viewpoint from where the measurements are taken [BCR94]. Figure 2.8 gives an overview about the hierarchical structure of a GQM plan.

2.6.2. Validation Levels of Böhme and Reussner

Böhme and Reussner [BR05] introduced three different levels for the evaluation of prediction models. As Klatt [Kla14] points out the levels can be applied for the validation of software analysis approaches in general.

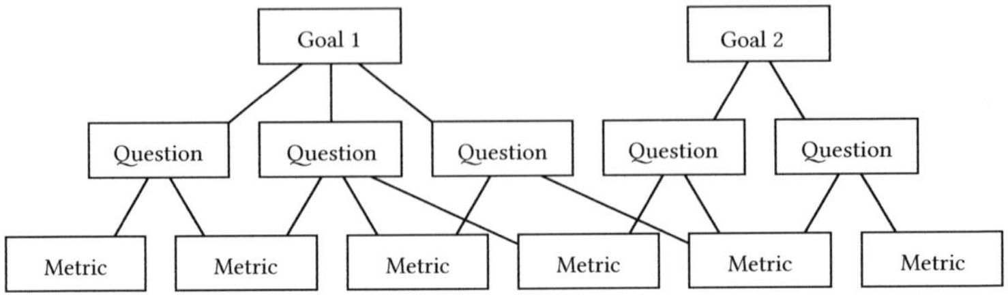

Figure 2.8.: Hierarchical structure of a GQM plan [BCR94]

Hence, we can apply the levels to structure the evaluation of our Coevolution approach as well. Böhme and Reussner [BR05] did not explicit introduce a *Level 0* validation level. Even though they state that a *Level 0* validation would be the level for implementation validity, i.e, a functional implementation is necessary to evaluate an approach. As Klatt [Kla14] points out, the validation *Level 0* is validated implicitly by performing validations for the other validation levels if a prototype is required for all other validation levels.

The first level (*Level I*) is called metric validation by Böhme and Reussner [BR05]. For performance prediction approaches, this level can be used to show that the predicted performance of a software system equals the measured performance. Klatt [Kla14] calls this level the result validation and points out that this level can be used to compare the result of an approach with the reality.

The second level (*Level II*) is a called applicability validation. For approaches that use performance prediction this means that it needs to be validated whether the input data of an approach can be acquired reliable and whether the results can be interpreted meaningfully. As for the SPLevo approach, which has been introduced by Klatt [Kla14], this means for our Coevolution approach, that we need to show that our Coevolution approach can be applied to real world project. To perform a Level II validation, Böhme and Reussner [BR05] recommend to perform a case study.

The third level (*Level III*) is called benefit validation. A benefit validation evaluates the benefit of an approach compared to competing approaches using an empirical validation. A possible example of a *Level III* validation using our Coevolution approach would be to develop a software system with our Coevolution approach and a competing approach, such as IBM Rational Rhapsody Developer. As Böhme and Reussner [BR05] state, setting up such a validation study requires high effort, because different developer teams need to develop the same software system using different approaches. Since the proposed study involves developers, a possible threat to validity is that the results can depend on the performance of the developers. Hence, the study needs to be repeated in order to rule out this threat to validity. This fact requires additional effort to perform a *Level III* validation. Within the scope of this thesis no *Level III* validation has been performed.

3. A Change-driven Consistency Process for Models

To achieve architecture and code consistency, our Coevolution approach uses the change-driven framework of VITRUVIUS. The VITRUVIUS framework itself is based on the VITRUVIUS vision, which Burger [Bur14] and we [KBL13] have introduced. The VITRUVIUS framework is implemented using Eclipse plugins, i.e, it can be used within the Eclipse IDE. Within this chapter, we present the contributions of this thesis to the change-driven framework VITRUVIUS. We will present our Coevolution approach in Chapter 4. In particular, this chapter presents the following contributions to the VITRUVIUS framework:

- change monitoring for the existing source code editor and Eclipse Modeling Framework (EMF) editors,
- the definition of consistency preservation rules using a General Purpose Language (GPL), and
- the process how change-driven consistency can be achieved.

The VITRUVIUS framework can be used to keep arbitrary models consistent during the evolution of the models. Even though the focus of this thesis is to keep architectural models and source code consistent, the contributions in this section can be generalized for other models as well. Especially, the monitoring for EMF models and the consistency preservation process are generalizable for arbitrary models. The focus of this section and the thesis and the current VITRUVIUS framework is to support the consistency preservation between two metamodels. Easing the consistency preservation for more than two metamodels and solving arising conceptual challenges, such as propagating the changes caused by another change propagation, is part of future work.

The remainder of this section is structured as follows. First, we introduce the scientific challenges for this chapter in Section 3.1. In Section 3.2, we present the terminology, which we use throughout this thesis. Next, we present the change metamodel and the correspondence metamodel from the VITRUVIUS framework. In Section 3.5, we present how we can monitor existing source code editors and existing architectural editors. Next, we explain how consistency preservation rules can be created using either a GPL or a Domain Specific Language (DSL) (see Section 3.6). We explain the used consistency preservation process of the VITRUVIUS framework in Section 3.7.

3.1. Scientific Challenges

In this chapter, we address the following scientific challenges:

- *What steps are necessary to monitor the existing editors, such as the architectural editor and the code editor, which we use in our Coevolution approach?*

  For the change-driven approach VITRUVIUS, we need to monitor the views that are used within the VITRUVIUS approach. For our Coevolution approach between source code and architectural models, this means that we need to monitor the existing architectural views and the existing code view. Both monitors need to create an output model that can be used by the VITRUVIUS framework.

- *Which steps are necessary within a change-driven approach to achieve consistency between different models?*

  Since VITRUVIUS is a change-driven approach, it needs to be notified as soon as users or tools change a model. After this change, VITRUVIUS needs to keep the corresponding models respectively the corresponding model elements consistent with this change. Therefore, we need to define a process specifying the consistency preservation process after a change.

3.2. Terminology

In this section, we introduce the central terminology, which is used throughout this thesis.

We first explain the concept of *change-driven* in the model-driven environment. The consistency preservation process we describe in this section and that we use in the remainder of the thesis to keep architectural models and source code consistent, is a change-driven process. Hence, we define the term change-driven as follows:

Definition 3 (Change-driven consistency). *Change-driven consistency means that changes play a central role in the consistency preservation process. The consistency preservation process itself is triggered based on changes performed to models, which are involved in the process [Kra17]. A change contains the information about the performed change type and the changed element.*

Bergmann et al. [Ber+12] and Ráth et al. [RVV09] investigated change-driven model transformations and defined them as transformations using changes as input, i.e. consume changes, or produce changes as output. They point out that an important fact for change-driven model transformations is to incrementally update models instead of regenerating them every time. The changes that we use, are generated by specific monitors, which monitors editors, i.e. we monitor existing editors to notifiy about changes performed by users. These changes are used as input for our consistency preservation process. The output of our consistency preservation process, however, are not changes but models, which have been updated incrementally based on the changes. The consistency preservation process is change-driven but not *edit-based*, because the changes do not necessarily need to result from editing operations. The process itself could also be used in an environment where the changes are created by an approach that computes the difference between two versions of a model. Approaches, such as EMFCompare [BP08] or the model differencing approach proposed by Burger and Toshovski [BT14], can be used to compare models and create the necessary changes for the change-driven process.

Next, we define the term *correspondence*:

Definition 4 (Correspondence). *A correspondence specifies as a set of elements that correspond to each other. The corresponding sets of elements describe the overlap of different models.*

To identify corresponding elements, we use the *Vitruvius correspondence model*, which we explain in Section 3.3. The correspondence between elements are created and updated during consistency preservation operations.[1]

Next, we define the term of a *consistency preservation operation*. Therefore, we use a similar definition as Kramer [Kra17] uses for *consistency preservation*.

Definition 5 (Consistency preservation operation). *A consistency preservation operation defines the actual operation, which is executed to preserve consistency between models.*

As we are in a change-driven environment, this consistency preservation operations are executed based on changes performed to the models. Based on the consistency preservation operation, we can define *consistency preservation rules*.

Definition 6 (Consistency preservation rules). *Consistency preservation rules are rules defining how a pair of metamodels can be kept consistent. They consist of a set of consistency preservation operations.*

In general, the consistency preservation rules can be implemented in a GPL or a transformation language, such as Query View Transformation Operational (QVTO)[Obj09], or in specific DSLs tailored to change-driven consistency preservation process. Within this thesis, we define consistency preservation rules between architectural models and source code. They can be defined in either in the GPL Xtend or in the a DSL tailored to our consistency preservation process.

[1] Even though the elements corresponding to each other are usually instances of different metamodels, it is possible that the corresponding elements are instances of the same metamodel.

3.3. Change Metamodel

Within this section, we describe the change metamodel from VITRUVIUS. The change metamodel is based on the feature diagram for possible changes in EMF models, which has been introduced by [Kra17] and which we explained shortly in Figure 2.1.2. From this, Kramer [Kra17] has derived a change metamodel. The complete metamodel is available within the VITRUVIUS framework[2].

The supported non-abstract classes, i.e. the classes, which can actually be instantiated, are shown in Figure 3.1. The change metamodel and especially its non-abstract classes are central artefacts within our change consistency preservation process. The monitors for the different models create instances of the change metamodel respectively instances of the non-abstract classes. The change consistency process itself reacts to these changes and creates commands based on the changes in order to achieve consistency between different model instances. The changes are separated into atomic changes and compound changes. Compound changes representing changes composed of other changes, while atomic changes representing a single change. New compound changes can be added by composing existing atomic or compound changes. For the monitoring of Java code, for instance, we added the change `MethodBodyChange`, which is a compound change describing the change of a method body. In Figure 3.1 the changes `ExplicitUnsetEFeature`, `MoveEObject`, and `ReplaceInEList` are examples of compound changes.

3.4. Correspondence Metamodel

In this section, we present the VITRUVIUS correspondence metamodel. The VITRUVIUS correspondence metamodel is used to describe the corresponding elements for two metamodels. In VITRUVIUS, we use one instance of the VITRUVIUS correspondence metamodel for each pair of metamodels within the Virtual Single Underlying Model (VSUM). Consider Figure 2.4, which we presented in the foundations (see Section 2.2.2): The VITRUVIUS correspondences model instances between the elements are part of the consistency preservation (CP). For the approach of keeping source code consistent with an

[2] `http://vitruv.tools`

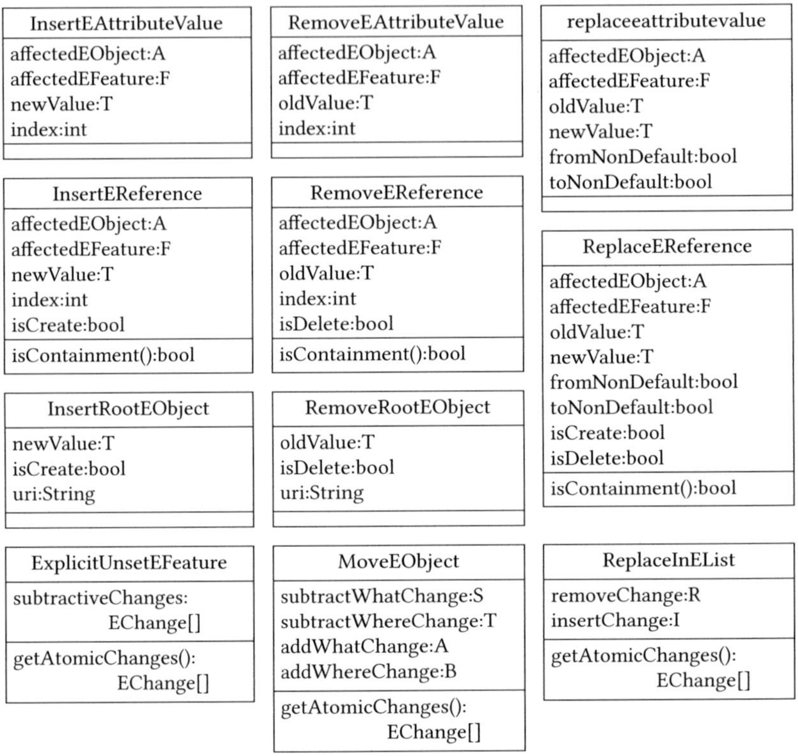

Figure 3.1.: Non-abstract, i.e, final classes of the change metamodel for Vitruvius ([Kra17]). Kramer [Kra17] presents a feature diagram for changes in EMOF and Ecore based metamodels and derived the change metamodel for Vitruvius from it. In the figure, we omitted the permute changes, because they are not supported yet. We have also simplified the name of the classes and omitted the type parameters.

architecture model, we use one Vitruvius correspondence model containing the information how the source code elements correspond to architectural elements.

The Vitruvius correspondence metamodel itself is generic and can be used for arbitrary metamodels. The metamodel, which is depicted in Figure 3.2, consists of only two classes: The `Correspondences` class is the root element

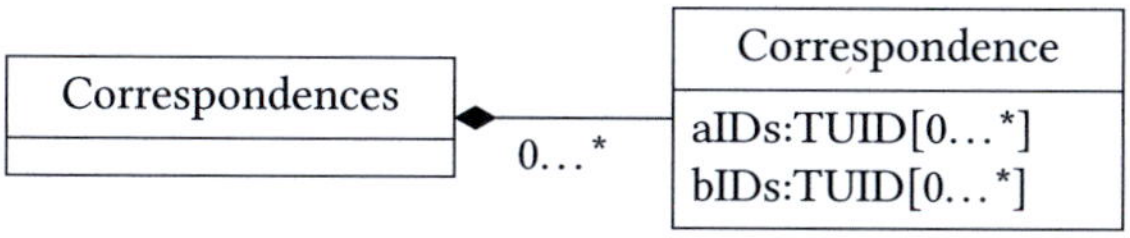

Figure 3.2.: The correspondence metamodel we used in the consistency preservation process. All actual `Correspondence` instances are contained in the root class `Correspondences`.

of the metamodel contains a list of `Correspondence`. The `Correspondence` contains two lists of identifier references. One list contains identifiers to reference models in one metamodel, while the other list contains identifiers to reference models in another metamodel. Hence, one `Correspondence` represents the actual correspondence between a set of objects from one metamodel to a set of objects from another metamodel. One reference in the reference list can be used to identify one element in one model instance. To reliable identify an element the reference in the `Correspondence` needs to be unique, i.e. only one concrete element needs to be identified for a given ID. Therefore, we currently use our Temporarily Unique Identifier (TUID) mechanism, which basically is a string that uniquely identifies an element. Therefore, it contains the path to the file containing the element and an identifier, which is able to identify an element within this file. The ID is only temporarily as it can change for a specific element as soon as, for instance, the file name changes or the element is moved to another file. We need to be able to calculate a TUID for each element, which potentially can be used in a `Correspondence` list. A TUID of an element can also be used to retrieve the actual element.

Consider the following examples on how to calculate a TUID for metaclasses of the Palladio Component Model (PCM) metamodel and for metaclasses of Java Model Parser and Printer (JaMoPP) metamodel. To identify an element in the PCM, we can use the path to the file and Universally Unique Identifier (UUID) of the element. This approach only works for metamodel classes containing an `id` field, i.e. it only works for metaclasses extending directly or indirectly from `Identifier`. For metaclasses not extending `Identifier`, such as the metaclass `Parameter`, however, need to be identifiable as well. For instances of these metaclasses, we use the `enityName` attribute of the instance and the TUID of the parent element. Hence, the TUID is build hierarchically. All classes directly or indirectly extending class `NamedElement` contain the `enityName` attribute. Using this mechanism, we are able to calculate a TUID and resolve objects for a given TUID for all metaclasses in the PCM.

For the elements in JaMoPP, it is more complex to calculate a TUID, because the JaMoPP metaclasses do not contain an `id` element. It is also not possible to extend the JaMoPP metamodel with an `Identifier` class, because JaMoPP stores the elements as Java source code. Within the Java language itself no `id` is foreseen for the elements. Hence, we need to identify the elements using their Java Fully Qualified Name (FQN). To identify a method, for instance, we use the name of the method, the return type of the method, the parameter types of the method, the class name of the class containing the method and the name of the package and its parent packages recursively, i.e. as the PCM TUIDs the JaMoPP TUIDs are build hierarchically as well. Using this mechanism allows us to uniquely identify a method, because Java methods in one class need to be unique in terms of their parameter types. Even though the TUID calculation mechanism for the PCM can be generalized for metamodels having a similar `Identifier` class as the PCM, the TUID mechanism, in general, is specific for each metamodel.

One part of future work is to check, whether the TUID mechanism can be replaced or eased by the standard Ecore mechanism for identifying objects in an instance of a metamodel.

3.5. Change Monitoring

As we mentioned above, we use a change-driven approach to keep models consistent. To do so, we react to changes performed in involved editors, i.e. we use a change-driven approach that uses edit-based changes to ensure consistency. To realise such an approach, we need to get notifications about each change users performed in one of the editors involved in the consistency preservation process. As one goal of the presented work is to allow users to use familiar editors, we need to develop mechanisms to get notified about changes in each editor. It is furthermore unfeasible to create new editors for every model involved in the consistency preservation process. These statements are true for the work presented in this thesis and the Vitruvius approach as well.

For the work presented in this thesis, we need to get notified about changes in source code and in the architectural model. Therefore, we developed an approach to monitor existing architectural model editors as well as monitoring in an existing Java source code editor. Both approaches are explained in the following sections. Hence, the following sections address the first scientific challenge defined for this chapter.

3.5.1. Monitoring Changes in Architectural Models

In order to keep changes that users apply to architectural models consistent with the source code, we need to monitor the changes in architectural models. The architectural models used within the presented work are either edited or manipulated by users using the standard EMF Ecore editors or graphical editors. The graphical editors are currently either created with Graphical Modelling Framework (GMF) or Eclipse Sirius. Allowing the reuse of all existing editors is one goal of our consistency preservation process. This is especially important for the graphical editors, as they allow convenient editing and manipulating of architectural elements.

All graphical editors as well as the standard EMF Ecore editors manipulate the underlying EMF models. To avoid the effort of monitoring each existing editor separately, we have decided to monitor changes on the underlying EMF models. As the architectural models that we use are standard EMF models, the monitor presented in this section can be generalized for arbitrary EMF models, i.e. the presented monitor can be used for arbitrary EMF models.

For the realisation of the monitoring, we use the built-in EMF mechanism of listening to changes in models. The built-in mechanism notifies registered listeners about each change in an EMF model. To ensure that we get notified about all changes performed to any EMF model, we start listening to changes as soon as users opening an editor that is capable of manipulating the architectural models. The information about the performed changes that we retrieve from the EMF change notification mechanism, are represented as a set of `ChangeDescriptions`. The EMF `ChangeDescriptions` contain the information about the changes that has been occurred in EMF-based models.

This model, however, can not used directly, because we need the changes in specific form for our consistency preservation mechanism. Therefore, we transform the EMF `ChangeDescription` to instances of the above-presented change metamodel. After we have created instances of our change metamodel, we submit the changes to our consistency preservation mechanism. The change consistency mechanism uses the information within the change to preserve consistency between model elements. The implementation of the EMF monitor is available as part of the VITRUVIUS framework.

Using the approach of monitoring the underlying EMF model has the advantage that changes are monitored regardless of the used editor. If it is important, however, to keep information consistent, which are solely available in the graphical editors, such as the layout information, the graphical editors have to be monitored separately. This is the case, for instance, if the position of two elements from different metamodels need to be kept consistent in the graphical editors. To this date however, the requirement of keeping layout information consistent among instances of different metamodels, did neither occur in the work presented in this thesis nor in any other case study of VITRUVIUS.

3.5.2. Monitoring Source Code Changes

This section explains, how we monitor changes performed to Java source code during the software development and evolution. To perform source code changes software developers usually use the source code editor of an IDE. Further possibilities to edit the source code, such as reafactorings or quick fixes, however, exist as well and need to be considered for the change monitoring. In this section, we explain the monitoring for the source code editor and additional artefacts, as well as our implementation of the change monitoring.

Messinger [Mes14] developed the Java code monitor within his master's thesis. We presented the Java code monitor in [Kra+15a] and the associated technical report [Kra+15b]. This section is based on the mentioned publications.

3.5.2.1. Monitoring the Source Code Editor

For the source code editor itself, it would be possible to reuse the EMF editor implemented for the monitoring of architectural elements. To reuse this monitor, however, would require users to use model-based editors for Java code, such as the standard EMF editor or the JaMoPP editor for Java, to manipulate the source code. One goal of our work, however, is to allow users to use familiar tools. This is especially important for existing source code editors provided by modern IDEs, because this editors provide powerful editing support, and they are widely used and accepted. To allow the reuse of this editors, we need to monitor the source code editor of the used IDE. As we use the Eclipse IDE, the description of the source code monitoring process is closely aligned to the behaviour of the Eclipse IDE. The concepts, however, can be applied to other IDEs, with similar behaviour as the Eclipse IDE as well. To monitor the changes, the IDE needs to provide a mechanism, which is able to notify interested listeners about a change performed by developers. After the actual notification from the IDE, we need to classify the changes. This is necessary, as the change reporting of the IDE is based on basic operations, such as adding and removing characters in the editor. For the classification Messinger [Mes14], created a change catalogue for changes on object-oriented source code. Messinger [Mes14] evaluated, whether existing change metamodels can be used within the Java code monitor. Therefore, he focused on the existing change catalogues, proposed by Herrmannsdoerfer et al. [HVW11], Fowler et al. [Fow+99], and Dig and Johnson [DJ06]. The change catalogue of Herrmannsdoerfer et al. [HVW11], is mainly designed for coevolution of models and metamodels, i.e. adapting model instances to changes of the metamodel. The change catalogue of Fowler et al. [Fow+99], and Dig and Johnson [DJ06] list changes on object-oriented source code. Fowler et al. [Fow+99] presents refactorings to object-oriented source code and present necessary changes in object-oriented source code representing such a refactoring. As refactorings usually preserve the semantic of source code, the changes in the change catalog presented by Fowler et al. [Fow+99] are only a subset of all possible source code changes. Dig and Johnson [DJ06] discuss API evolution in object-oriented source code and list changes, which can be performed to object-oriented source code. None of the existing change catalogues, however, fits our needs. Hence, Messinger [Mes14] created a special change catalogue for the change monitor. The change catalogue classifies changes into the following three categories and sub-categories.

- Primitive changes, which are primitive changes performed by developers. They are subdivided in three categories:
  - create and delete changes of root elements, such as classes or packages.
  - structural changes, such as adding or removing methods, fields, parameters etc., and
  - modification changes, such as renaming method, changing modifiers.
- Composite changes, which are composed changes leading to semantically changes. They are subdivided in two categories:
  - 1st order composite changes, which consist of composed primitive changes, such as moving classes or moving interfaces, and
  - 2nd order composite changes, which consist of composed composite changes, such as extracting methods or inlining methods.
- Type hierarchy specific changes, which are specific for changes affecting the type hierarchy in object-oriented languages. They are subdivided in three categories:
  - type changes, for instance, specializing or generalize the return type of a method,
  - move changes, for instance, pull-up or push-down a method, and
  - composite move changes, for instance, extracting a super-class or inlining a super-class

The complete change catalogue can be seen in the Appendix (see Section A.1).

One technical limitation of Eclipse Java Development Tools (JDT) Abstract Syntax Tree (AST) change notification is that no exact changes are reported for statement changes within method bodies. The Eclipse IDE only reports the information about a fine-grained change. Seifermann [Sei14] provides an extension for the Java source code monitor. The extension allows us to classify, amongst others, such fine-grained changes in order to figure out whether the change affected a method body. Even though we do not get notified about the actual statement, which has been changed, the information about the changed method turned out to be sufficient for our use cases.

3.5.2.2. Monitoring additional Code Manipulation Editors

As mentioned above, it is not sufficient to only monitor changes performed in the source code editor, as developers usually have other possibilities to manipulate and edit the source code. For instance, modern IDEs usually have a built in refactoring support. For many changes, such as renaming, developers often use refactorings in order to speed up the development process and avoid manual renaming. Even though these changes affect the source code and could be monitored implicitly using the monitor for the code editor, we decided to monitor this kind of changes by observing the IDE. Even though we can try to figure out whether a specific list of changes represents a refactoring or not, we argue that it is simpler to monitor the IDE, because we can be sure that we observed the correct change. To give an example for a refactoring, we consider the refactoring pull-up, which pushes a method from a subclass to one of its super classes. If the changes necessary to perform a *pull-up* refactoring are only monitored via the source code, we would get the notification that a method has been removed from one class and a method has been inserted into another class. To monitor this refactoring through the source code monitor solely, we would need to match the removed method in one class with the added method in another class.

Another possibility for developers to edit source code is to use quick fixes offered by the IDE. A quick fix can, for instance, used to correct a statement, which is syntactically incorrect. Similar to the refactorings, these changes can be monitored using the monitor for the IDE itself. It can be beneficial, however, to know if developers used a quick fix to perform a change.

During the monitoring of refactorings and quick fixes, we need to ensure that the monitor for the source code editor does not report the changes as well, i.e. the source code editor itself needs to be deactivated during the execution of refactorings and quick fixes or we need to develop a mechanism to detect and remove duplicated changes.

Besides the advantage of getting changes performed through refactorings or quick fixes directly, the monitoring of these additional mechanisms helps us to clarify the intent of the developers automatically. Knowing the intent of developers upfront can be beneficial during consistency preservation process itself. If a method has been renamed by developers, for instance, they might be asked by the consistency preservation process whether the corresponding architectural model elements should be renamed accordingly or whether the change in the source code should be rolled back in order to avoid renaming of architectural elements. If a method has been renamed using a quick fix to avoid a compiler error, for instance, it is clear that developers needed to perform the change in order to fix that error. In such a case the example intent clarification described above, can be avoided.

3.5.2.3. Implementation of the Change Monitoring in Source Code

Messinger [Mes14] implemented the change monitoring as Eclipse plugin for the Eclipse IDE. Hence, as the other artefacts we implemented in this thesis, the monitor can be used within Eclipse IDE. To monitor the source code editor of the Eclipse IDE, we use the Eclipse JDT, which provides the possibility to notify listeners during the reconciling of changes. Hence, listeners are notified as soon as the Eclipse JDT AST parser incrementally parses the performed change. The monitor also monitors performed refactoring within the Eclipse IDE. For instance, it is able to monitor rename refactorings performed using the refactoring capabilities of Eclipse. The implementation is in principle also able to monitor quick fixes performed by developers. It turned out, however, that for the kind of changes we are interested in, we do not need to monitor quick fixes, because the Java code monitor is sufficient to get all changes. The consistency preservation rules, we present in this thesis, do not have benefits from an intent clarification through quick fixes. In future work, however, the quick fix monitoring functionality can be used if the monitoring of quick fixes turns out to be helpful. One current technical limitation for the monitoring of refactorings and quick fixes is that the Eclipse IDE does notify listeners only about performed refactorings and quick fixes for a certain class of refactorings and quick fixes. Hence, we are not able to get notified about all performed refactorings and quick fixes at the moment.

3.5.2.4. Transforming the Monitored Changes into Instance of the Change Metamodel

After we have monitored the source code changes as described above and classified them according to the change catalogue, we need to transform them into a representation of the above-mentioned change metamodel. This task is considered as the second main task of the source code monitor. The changes that we get from the IDE and the classification is done based on the AST representation of the used IDE. In case of Eclipse, this is performed using the Eclipse JDT AST. Even though the Eclipse JDT AST itself is a model, it cannot be used within the change metamodel and by our consistency preservation mechanism directly, as it is not an Ecore based model. For the change metamodel and the consistency preservation process itself, however, we need to have an EMF model representation of the performed change. To bridge the gap between the models and the change representation, we transform the observed changes into an Ecore based model representation. We decided to use JaMoPP to parse Java source code into an Ecore based model representation. We use JaMoPP instead of other existing approaches, such as Model Discovery (MoDisco) [Bru+10], because JaMoPP also allows printing the parsed model into as Java source code. The latter is necessary, as the main goal of the work presented in this thesis, is to create and use bidirectional consistency preservation rules between architectural model and source code. After parsing the changed compilation unit using JaMoPP, we match the changed elements with the elements within the JaMoPP elements. As next step, we are able to create the change instances of the above-described change metamodel. As last step of the monitoring, the Java code monitor triggers our consistency preservation process with the change. This consistency preservation process itself is explained in the next section. By using this approach, we do not need to parse the whole source code of the project but we need to parse the actual changed compilation unit using JaMoPP.

More technical details how we create the instances of the change metamodel can be found in the master's thesis of Messinger [Mes14]. In future work, however, propose the use of the Eclipse JDT AST instead of JaMoPP if it is extended in a way that it makes it possible to use the Eclipse Java AST model as an Ecore based model.

3.6. Defining Consistency Preservation Rules

To keep changes in models consistent using VITRUVIUS and our Coevolution approach, consistency preservation rules between pairs of metamodels need to be defined. The consistency preservation rules need to define consistency preservation operations for each change. Therefore, they specify which elements of one metamodel in the metamodel pair needs to be changed after a specific change in the other metamodel of the metamodel pair has been performed.

If more than two metamodels need to be kept consistent, consistency preservation rules for each pair of metamodels are necessary. In this thesis, however, we mainly focus on the consistency between one pair of metamodels. Arising challenges during the consistency preservation of more than one metamodel pair is part of our future work.

The consistency preservation rules, can be defined either in a GPL or in a Domain Specific Language. For the VITRUVIUS framework, [Kra17] provides a language family to specify the consistency preservation rules in specific DSLs.

In the following, we outline our implementation to keep a pair of metamodels consistent using a GPL. We also give a small overview of the Mapping Invariant Response (MIR) languages, which are a family of DSLs and tailored to keep arbitrary models consistent using the VITRUVIUS framework. In this section, we focus on the realisation of how to keep pairs of metamodels consistent. The actual used consistency preservation rules for architectural models and source code and the different kinds of consistency preservation rules we identified, are explained in Section 4.3.

3.6.1. Defining Consistency Preservation Rules using a GPL

By using a GPL to define the consistency preservation rules, the occurred change needs to be analysed in order to preserve consistency between model instances. As we described above, the Vitruvius framework is notified about changes as soon as a change has been performed. The information in the change can be used by the GPL implementation to preserve consistency. As the change information is an instance of the change metamodel, it contains the information about the performed change and the changed element. The GPL implementation can use the information to decide, which corresponding elements need to be updated accordingly.

During the execution of consistency preservation operations the instances of the `Correspondence` between elements need to be created and updated. An update, for instance, is necessary if an TUID affecting attribute of an affected element has been changed. For JaMoPP, for instance, the `name` attribute of a method affects the TUID of the method as well as the TUID for the methods parameters. Hence, if a method name has been changed the TUID needs to be updated for the method and its parameters.

Within our initial implementation, we used the GPL Xtend[3] to implement consistency preservation rules. The implemented mechanism can be seen as internal DSL embedded into Xtend. To execute the correct updating method, we first need to call the correct consistency preservation operation based on the instance of the change and the changed element. Therefore, we first use the dispatch functionality offered by Xtend to determine the type of the change by dispatching the incoming change over all possible non-abstract changes. To determine the affected object and call the correct consistency preservation operations, we use a map that stores the consistency preservation operations for all possible elements between two metamodels. All transformations need to implement the generic class `EObjectMappingTransformation`. This allows us to store them in a map and execute the correct transformation based on the class of the actual changed element. Listing 6 shows an excerpt of the dispatching for the change types and the use of the map to call the actual implemented transformation.

[3] `http://www.eclipse.org/xtend`

The method `executeTransformationForChange` can be called from outside the class with the occurred change. It first dispatches the change in order to determine the performed change. As second step, it updates the TUID of the affected object if necessary. The first dispatch method is called if the change is unknown to the `TransformationExecuter`. It logs an error and returns `null`, i.e. the corresponding models are not updated. The other two example dispatch methods, we show in the listing, are called if a new root object has been inserted respectively if a root object has been removed. In these cases the `create` method respectively `delete` method for the object are called. Within this transformation the corresponding model can be updated accordingly. After this, we call the transformation `createdAsRoot` respectively `deleteRootEObject` to indicate that the performed change affected a root object, which allows the transformation to react accordingly, for instance, by deleting all corresponding child objects of the deleted root object. The map `mappingTransformations` needs to be initialized during the creation of the `TransformationExecuter`.

Listing 7 shows the transformation that is executed after an *OperationSignature* in the PCM model has been renamed and needs to be kept consistent with the source code. Therefore, we first need to retrieve the corresponding interface method. As second step, we calculate the old TUID. As next step, we can update the name and then update the TUID of the method. Hence, to keep the source code consistent, we update the name of the corresponding source code interface method. As last step, we also update the name of the methods implementing the code interface.

Using the described approach allows us to keep consistency for all non-compound changes. For compound changes, such as method body changes or replace in list changes, we need to either flatten the contained non-compound changes and react to the atomic changes contained in the compound changes or we need to implement a special treatment for these changes.

3.6.2. Defining Consistency Preservation Rules using the MIR Languages

Instead of using a GPL to define the consistency preservation rules, they can also be defined by using a DSL or a family of DSLs. One instance of

```
def public TransformationResult executeTransformationForChange(EChange change) {
  //dispatch the incoming change
  val TransformationResult transformationResult = executeTransformation(change)
  updateTUIDOfAffectedEObjectInEChange(change)
  return transformationResult
}

def private dispatch TransformationResult executeTransformation(EChange change) {
  //log an error if the concrete change is unknown
  logger.error("No␣executeTransformation␣method␣found␣for␣change␣" + change)
  return null
}

def private dispatch executeTransformation(InsertRootEObject<?> insertRoot) {
  val clazz = insertRoot.newValue.class
  // for insert root changes: call the create transformation for the created
       object
  val EObject[] created = mappingTransformations.get(clazz).createEObject(
       insertRoot.newValue)
  // call the created as root object for the created object
  mappingTransformations.get(clazz).createRootEObject(insertRoot.newValue,
       createdObjects)
}

def private dispatch executeTransformation(RemoveRootEObject<?> removeRoot) {
  // for remove root changes: call the remove transformation for the removed
       object
  val clazz = removeRoot.oldValue.class
  val EObject[] removed = mappingTransformations.get(clazz).removeEObject(
       removeRoot.oldValue)
  // call the delete root method for the removed object
  mappingTransformations.get(clazz).deleteRootEObject(removeRoot.oldValue,
       removedEObjects)
}
```

Listing 6: Excerpt of the dispatch functionality in Xtend used for the dispatching of incoming changes to distinguish the type of change.

a possible DSL are the MIR languages, which are tailored especially for the Vitruvius framework. Kramer [Kra17], presents the MIR languages and introduces a formal background. Klare [Kla16] introduces the reaction

```
override updateSingleValuedEAttribute(EObject affectedEObject, EAttribute
    affectedAttribute, Object oldValue, Object newValue) {
  val transformationResult = new TransformationResult

  // retrieve the single interface method corresponding to the
      OperationSignature
  val interfaceMethod = correspondenceModel.getCorrespondingEObjectsByType(
      affectedEObject, InterfaceMethod).claimOne
  val oldTUID = correspondenceModel.calculateTUIDFromEObject(interfaceMethod)
  interfaceMethod.name = newValue.toString

  //update the changed TUID of the method manually
  correspondenceModel.updateTUID(oldTUID, interfaceMethod)
  updateImplementingMethods(affectedEObject, newValue)
  return transformationResult
}
```

Listing 7: Executed Xtend transformation after an *OperationSignature* has been renamed

language, Werle [Wer16] introduces the mapping language, and [FKL16] the invariant language. All languages are created using Xtext[4].

The reaction language allows the definition of solution-oriented imperative reactions to achieve consistency. Similar to the defined solution in the GPL it is possible to react to specific changes performed to specific model elements. Hence, by using the reaction language, all non-composite changes can be handled. The invariant language is a problem-oriented language, which allows consistency checking using parameterised invariants. The mapping language offers the possibility to declarative define bidirectional consistency preservation operations. A common example, where the mapping language can be used is the name attribute of different metaclasses, which should kept consistent.

The MIR languages hide the complexity of updating the used ID manually, i.e. in the current implementation they update the TUID of changed elements automatically. One current disadvantage of the MIR languages is the lack of handling composite changes within the languages. For instance, changes on method body changes cannot be handled directly. The language framework,

[4] http://www.eclipse.org/Xtext/

```
reaction RenameOperationSignature {
   after value replaced for pcm::OperationSignature[entityName]
   call renameMethodForOperationSignature(change.affectedEObject)
}

routine renameMethodForOperationSignature(pcm::OperationSignature
      operationSignature) {
   match {
      val interfaceMethod = retrieve java::InterfaceMethod corresponding to
            operationSignature
   }
   action {
      update interfaceMethod {
         interfaceMethod.name = operationSignature.entityName;
      }
      call {
         updateImplementingMethods(change.affectedEObject, change.newValue)
      }
   }
}
```

Listing 8: Executed reaction after an *OperationSignature* has been renamed

however, supports the identification of such changes and provides specific handling routine adhering to a common interface. The reaction to this kind of changes need to be defined within an GPL, such as Java or Xtend. An example for this kind of changes is a change performed to method bodies in the Java source code.

Listing 8 shows an example transformation that is executed after an *OperationSignature* in the PCM model has been renamed and needs to be kept consistent with the source code. The reaction is the same as in the GPL implementation: the corresponding Java interface method and the implementing class methods are also renamed. As we can see the executed reaction is executed after the name of an *OperationSignature* has been replaced. The retrieving of objects from the correspondence model is executed within the `match` block. The update of the interface method is done in the `update` block. Within the `call` block arbitrary Xtend code can be executed. In our case, we execute the same method as in the GPL implementation in order to keep the implementing class methods consistent with the architectural change.

3.7. Consistency Preservation Process

Within this section, we describe consistency preservation process used in the VITRUVIUS framework and therefore in our Coevolution approach as well. Hence, we address the second scientific challenge defined for this chapter. The consistency preservation process consists of three main steps:

- the trigger of the change consistency preservation process and the initializing of the process,
- the creation of executable commands, which uses the information from the change in combination with predefined consistency preservation rules to define the necessary action to keep models consistent, and
- the execution of this commands and the saving of the changed models.

A visualisation of the three steps is shown in Algorithm 1. For the commands, we use the transactional command framework of EMF. Within our consistency preservation process the creating of commands and the executing of commands is separated. Using this approach, allows us to create a generic mechanism for executing the changes and saving the changed models. Hence, developers of the consistency preservation rules do not need to take care of the actual creation and executing of commands. Furthermore, the used approach should eases the evolution and maintenance of the used framework. For instance, a part of future work is to allow the rollback of user changes and the resulting changes executed by the consistency preservation process. This rollback functionality can be realised generic for VITRUVIUS considering the separated command execution part only. The three steps, which are currently used, are explained in the next sections.

3.7.1. Change Triggering and Initializing Change Consistency Preservation Process

The first steps within the change consistency preservation process are the change triggering and the initializing of the consistency preservation process.

Algorithm 1 An overview of the Change Consistency Preservation Process, which can be used to keep models consistent.

```
Require: Changes ← Set<Change>,
    source2Metamodel ← Map<FileEnding, Metamodel>)
    consistencyRulesMap
    ← Map<Metamodel, Set<consistencyOperation>
    commandExecuter ← CommandExecuter
    ▷ Initializing the consistency preservation process
validateChanges(changes)
metamodel ← source2Metamodel.get(change.source.fileEnding)
consistencyRuleSet ← consistencyRulesMap.get(metamodel)
for all change ∈ Changes do
    for all consistencyRules ∈ consistencyRuleSet do
    ▷ Creating the commands using the active consistency preservation rules
        commands ← consistencyRules.createCommands
    ▷ Execute the commands using a generic command executer
        commandExecuter.execute(commands)
```

The triggering process itself equals the last step of the monitors, we already described in this chapter, because the monitors trigger notify the consistency preservation process after a change respectively a set of has been performed and the consistency needs to be preserved. Form the perspective of the change consistency preservation process, however, this is the first step. In Algorithm 1 an existing set of changes is a requirement for the consistency preservation process.

For the set of retrieved changes, we first check whether the changes are valid. We currently only check whether the changed elements have the same metamodel. Hence, it is currently not possible to change elements from different metamodels simultaneously. This limitation can be overcome in future work. The limitation is not affecting the work presented in this thesis, as we currently only use changes performed to one metamodel. For the work presented in this thesis, however, it has no affect, because we only change elements adhering to the same metamodel at a time. As next step in initializing phase, we first collect the necessary information to execute the consistency preservation process. We first collect the information which consistency preservation rules need to be executed, i.e. we need to identify the To do so, we first retrieve the metamodel of the changed element. The

Vitruvius framework allows us to retrieve a set of target metamodels, for which consistency preservation rules are defined, from a given source metamodel. Hence, we have the information about the consistency preservation rules between the metamodels.

After we retrieved this information, we can start the consistency preservation process by executing the consistency preservation rules individually for each change (see line 4 in Algorithm 1).

3.7.2. Command Creation

The command creation, step is executed for each change individually. Within the command creation process, we retrieve the commands needed to be executed in order to preserve the consistency between the changed models and affected models. As we mentioned in Section 3.6 above, the consistency preservation rules itself can be defined either using a GPL or the MIR languages. As we separate the command creation process from the actual consistency preservation definition, users defining the consistency preservation rules do need to deal with the actual creation of commands. The output of this step is a set of commands, which can be executed in the next step.

3.7.3. Command Executing

Within the command-executing step, the actual consistency preservation step is performed. As the command creation step, this step is executed for each step individually (see line 7 of Algorithm 1). Within this step, we iterate over all created commands and execute them. During the execution of the commands the defined consistency preservation rules are executed and the affected models are actually changed. The saving of models involved in the current consistency preservation process is the last part of the command-executing step.

4. A Method for keeping Architecture Consistent with Source Code

In this chapter, we introduce our Coevolution approach and present how it can be used to keep component-based architectural models consistent with source code during software evolution.

As we have mentioned in Chapter 1, the well-known problems architecture drift and architecture erosion [PW92] can occur if the architectural model and the source code are evolved independently from one another, e.g. if the source code is evolved without updating the architecture model accordingly. Up-to-date models, however, can ease software evolution because, for instance, software architects can decide more easily how to integrate a new requirement into the software system. Depending on the used architectural model language, model-based analyses, such as predicting the performance, are possible. If architecture models are not kept up-to-date, they become out-dated and eventually useless. If the architectural models and source code can be kept consistent automatically or semi-automatically, the manual effort is omitted or reduced.

To achieve the goal of having up-to-date architectural models and reduce the effort of keeping them consistent with source code manually, we introduce our Coevolution approach. ,Since our Coevolution approach uses bidirectional consistency preservation, it is furthermore possible to keep the source code consistent with changes to the architecture model. The creation of a new component in the architectural model, for instance, leads to the creation of a new package and a new class in the source code model.

To avoid architecture drift, our Coevolution approach uses change-driven consistency preservation, which means that we keep the models consistent as soon as one of the models has been changed by users. Our Coevolution approach is able to keep static architecture models in terms of components, interfaces, and signatures as well as behavioural models consistent with the source code. Code elements that are kept consistent with static architecture model elements only are considered as *static code elements* within this thesis. Static code elements are usually packages, class declarations, interfaces declarations, interface methods, method declarations, and fields in classes. Code elements that are kept consistent with behavioural models are considered as *behavioural code elements*. These code elements are usually statements within method bodies of a class method.

To keep the changes performed on behavioural source code elements consistent with the behavioural models, we analyse the behaviour of the changed method in the source code and incrementally recreate the corresponding architectural behaviour models. Since our Coevolution approach works in a change-driven way and keeps the behaviour of source code also consistent with behavioural architecture models, it is able to detect method calls that introduce architecture erosion. These method calls are method calls that introduce, for instance, a call from a class in component *A* to a non-public service from component *B*. Such calls are possible from within the source code, but not allowed, as they would introduce architecture erosion. Using our Coevolution approach, users are supported by avoiding this kind of architecture erosion during the software evolution.

To map architectural models to code and code to architectural models, our Coevolution approach requires the availability of bidirectional consistency preservation rules between the architecture model and source code. Since the mappings between architectural models and source code are not the identical for all projects and used technologies, we provide a mechanism to create and refine existing consistency preservation rules and embed them into our consistency preservation process.

Within this section, we explain our Coevolution approach applied to Palladio Component Model (PCM) as architectural model and Java as source code. The concepts, we propose can, however, be applied to other component-based architecture models, such as UML component-diagrams, and other object oriented languages as well.

We introduced the basic idea of our Coevolution approach in [Lan13]. We presented the first realisation for source code and architectural elements in

[Kra+15a; Kra+15b]. We (Kramer, Burger and Langhammer [KBL13]) as well as Burger [Bur14] performed preliminary work and presented Vitruvius, which is an approach to keep the overlap between models consistent (see Section 2.2.2). From a Vitruvius perspective our Coevolution approach can be seen as an application of Vitruvius to the Component-based Software Engineering (CBSE) domain.

The remainder of this Chapter is structured as follows: In Section 4.1, we explain the scientific challenges for this chapter. In Section 4.2, we give an overview of our Coevolution approach and explain the main concepts. After the explanation our Coevolution approach, we we classify our Coevolution approach into the Vitruvius vision (see Section 4.2.5). As next step, we introduce bidirectional consistency preservation rules between source code and architecture and give an example for the consistency preservation rules. In Section 4.4, we present the different kinds of automation levels and user change disambiguation within our Coevolution approach. Section 4.5 introduces, how consistency between behavioural models and their implementing source code can be achieved. In Section 4.6, we introduce technology-specific bidirectional consistency preservation rules between source code and architecture as well as mappings to code related artefacts. Section 4.7 introduces different roles if, our Coevolution approach is used in the software development process.

4.1. Scientific Challenges

In this chapter, we address the following scientific challenges:

How can the architectural models and the source code of a software system kept consistent during the evolution of a software system? To enable change-driven coevolution of source code and architectural models in a change-driven way, our Coevolution approach needs to fulfill the following requirements: First, we need to define bidirectional consistency preservation rules between architectural models and source code. Secondly, we need to find a way to reuse existing editors within in our change-driven approach, because we want users to be able to use existing editors.

How can the abstraction gap between architectural models and source code be closed using consistency preservation rules? Architectural models often abstract from implementation details. One architectural component, for instance, can be realised by several classes in the source code. To bridge the abstraction gap between architectural models and source code, we need to define consistency preservation rules, which can be used to keep architectural models and source code consistent. The consistency preservation rules need to be define a mapping between source code elements and architectural model elements. The consistency preservation rules heavily depend on the project environment and the used code frameworks and techniques. For instance, the consistency preservation rules need to take into account if the project is developed using Enterprise Java Beans (EJBs), because EJB already defines components and interfaces on source code level.

Which steps are necessary to also enable coevolution of source code and a behaviour model? Architectural models often contain high-level information about the behaviour of the software system. These models cannot be translated into source code directly because they do not contain the necessary implementation details. They can, however, be reverse-engineered from source code. To include behaviour models into our Coevolution approach, we have to solve two challenges: The first challenge is that the behavioural models of the architectural models needs to be updated incrementally when developers change code. The second challenge is that it is necessary to figure out which code needs to be adapted, if architects change the behavioural model.

What are the different roles in a software development process when our Coevolution approach is used? A challenge is to define how the different users that have different roles, such as developer and architects, are involved in the software development processed when using our Coevolution approach. Since the consistency preservation rules between architectural models and code can be technology-specific or even project-specific a role needs to be defined that is responsible for creating the consistency preservation rules between architecture and code.

4.2. Coevolution of Architectural Models and Code

Within this section, we introduce the concepts of our Coevolution approach and outline how it can be used to keep architectural models and source code consistent. Furthermore, we explain models and the editors for architectural models and source code that we use in our Coevolution approach. Even though we explain our Coevolution approach on the example of the PCM as architectural modelling language respectively Architecture Description Language (ADL) and Java as object-oriented language, the concepts can be applied to other architectural modelling languages, such as UML component diagrams, and to other programming languages, such as C# or C++, as well. As mentioned above, we presented the idea for our Coevolution approach in [Lan13] and instantiated it for [Kra+15a].

To preserve consistency between different models our Coevolution approach uses the two main concepts: model-driven engineering, and change-driven engineering. Furthermore, our Coevolution approach reuses concepts from Vitruvius, which we presented in [KBL13] and which was refined by Burger [Bur14]. In this section, we only explain these concepts from the Vitruvius approach that we reuse and how we reuse them, while we classify our Coevolution approach into the Vitruvius vision in the next section.

The first concept we use is the concept of model-driven engineering, which means that the development process is model centric, and models are the main artefacts within our Coevolution approach. In fact, we consider all involved artefacts as models. Hence, the architecture and especially the source code are also considered as models within our Coevolution approach. Even though from a technical perspective, Java source code is not an Eclipse Modeling Framework (EMF) model, approaches such as Java Model Parser and Printer (JaMoPP) [Hei+10], allow us to parse models in such a way that they can be treated as EMF models. Treating the source code as a model allows us to apply model-driven techniques, e.g. model to model transformations, to the source code and use the source code together with model-based artefacts.

Change-driven means, that our Coevolution approach reacts on changes that users perform in either the architectural model or the source code. Hence, the consistency preservation steps that are necessary are executed after changes in either of the involved models. This also means that the editors that we use in our Coevolution approach need to report changes users perform. As we mentioned in Chapter 3, it is necessary to define bidirectional consistency preservation rules in order to react to these changes. To keep architectural models and source code consistent, we need to define consistency preservation rules between the architectural metamodel and the source code metamodel. In particular, we need to define bidirectional consistency preservation rules between the PCM metamodel and the Java metamodel. This bidirectional consistency preservation rules can be defined and implemented either in the general purpose language XTend, which we explained in 3 or in the Mapping Invariant Response (MIR) languages introduced by Kramer [Kra14; Kra15; Kra17], Klare [Kla16], Werle [Wer16], and Fiss [FKL16]. Regardless of whether the internal language or the MIR is used to implement the bidirectional consistency preservation rules, the consistency preservation rules need to specify specific change preservation operations for each change respectively for a specific set of changes performed by users.

We use the following concepts, which were originally introduced for the Vitruvius approach: the Virtual Single Underlying Model (VSUM) (see Section 2.2.2), the correspondence metamodel (see 3.4), the change metamodel (see 3.3), and the user change disambiguation. We use the VSUM to store the model instances of the architectural models, the source code represented as models, and the correspondence model. We are using instances of the correspondence metamodel to keep track of the corresponding elements. Since we use the same correspondence metamodel as the Vitruvius approach we refer to our correspondence metamodel as Vitruvius correspondence metamodel and to instances of the model as Vitruvius correspondence models. The change metamodel allows us to define changes from different editors in the common model instance, which can be used as input parameter for the consistency preservation process. This has the advantage that we can use the same consistency preservation mechanism for changes that are performed in different editors respectively views. We furthermore use the concept of user change disambiguation, which is used if changes users perform cannot be kept consistent automatically without additional information. In this case, our Coevolution approach needs to ask the users in order to clarify their intent, which can take place either before or from within the consistency preservation operations. We proposed a mechanism how user change disambiguation can be realised for changes in code in [LK14] by asking the users to clarify the intent of a change. More details about the different kinds of user change disambiguation are explained in Section 4.4. Like the Vitruvius approach, we currently make the assumption that only one model is changed at a given time. As a part of future work, it should be investigated how concurrent editing on different models by multiple users can be enabled.

Figure 4.1 gives an overview of our Coevolution approach. In particular, it explains the different steps that are necessary to keep the models consistent. As the step zero (0), users edit either the PCM *Repository*, the PCM *System*, or the Java source code, which automatically changes the underlying models (either the architectural model or the source code). This step is neither changed by nor influenced by our Coevolution approach. The first step, in which our Coevolution approach is involved, is step (1). In step (1), the monitors observe changes on the models and trigger the Vitruvius framework in step (2). Within the trigger step, the monitors also pass the performed changes to the Vitruvius framework. Based on these changes, the Vitruvius framework executes the consistency preservation transformations (3). These transformations can use the information from the changes as well as the information stored in the correspondence model (4) to update the models (5). If a change is performed to behavioural code, the change is kept consistent using a similar mechanism as depicted in Figure 4.1. However, in step (5), we execute a incremental *SEFF* reconstruction step instead of a transformation. We will explain more details about the incremental *SEFF* reconstruction in Section 4.5. To simplify Figure 4.1, the concept of user change disambiguation is not shown. A user interacting step, for instance, is possible from within the consistency preservation operations (step (5)).

4.2.1. The VSUM of our Coevolution Approach and the Definition of Consistency Preservation Rules

As mentioned above, the metamodel level of our VSUM our Coevolution approach consists of the architectural metamodel, the source code metamodel, and the correspondence metamodel. In particular, we use the PCM as a metamodel for the architecture, JaMoPP as metamodel of Java, and the Vitruvius correspondence metamodel. The consistency preservation rules are also part of the VSUM and need to be defined upfront, i.e. during the design time of the VSUM. On the instance level, our VSUM contains

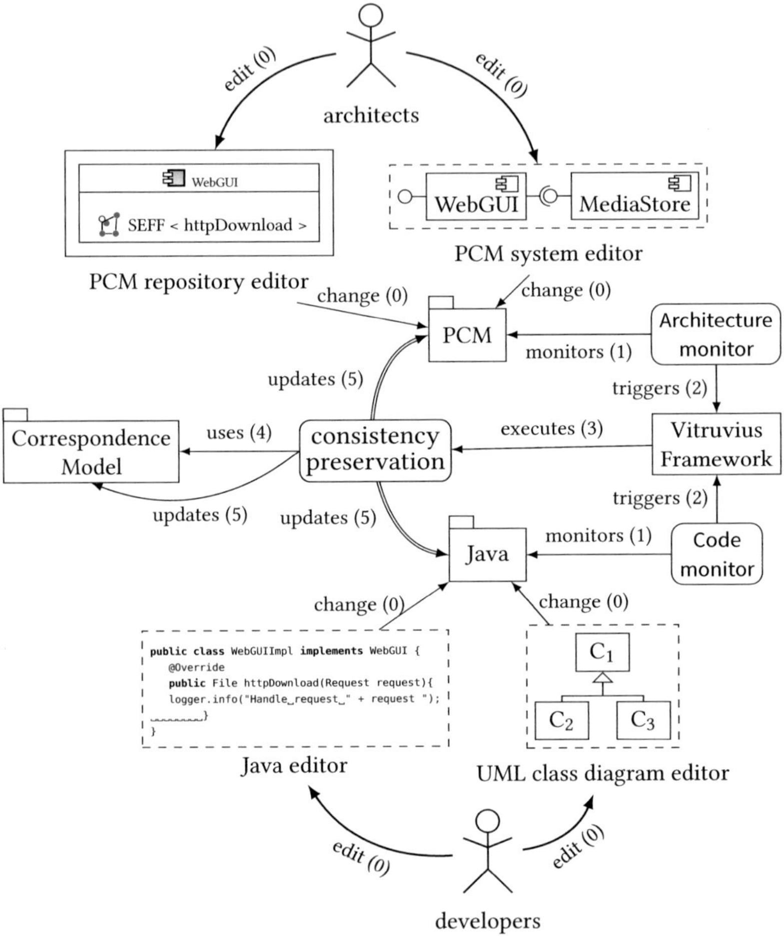

Figure 4.1.: The steps our Coevolution approach executes to keep architectural models consistent with the source code. Step zero (0) is performed by users of the architectural model editors or the source code editor. This step is not influenced or changed by our Coevolution approach. In reaction to step zero, however, our Coevolution approach performs the steps (1) through (5) in order to keep architectural models and the source code consistent.

instances of these metamodels, which are JaMoPP instances for the Java source code, PCM instances for the PCM metamodel, and instances of the Vitruvius correspondence metamodel. Figure 4.1 shows that the consistency preservation rules can access both models within the VSUM as well as the Vitruvius correspondence model instances to keep the models consistent after a change.

4.2.2. Monitored Source Code Editor

As editor for the JaMoPP metamodel, we use the standard Eclipse Java code editor. Even though JaMoPP offers a textual editor for the Java model as well, we have decided to use the standard Eclipse Java editor for the following reasons: First, the standard Eclipse code editor is more powerful than the JaMoPP editor. For instance, it offers state of the art code completion and powerful refactoring operations. Secondly, users of our Coevolution approach can stick with the editor they are used to and can still use the tools the IDE offers (e.g. refactoring, quick fixes etc.).

Since our goal is to use the standard Eclipse Java editor, we need to obtain all changes that a developer performed within editor. As we explained in 3.5.2, we created an approach to monitor the code editor in order to retrieve changes and convert them into compatible changes, i.e. changes are converted to changes in the Vitruvius change metamodel. For changes performed to classes, interfaces, methods, fields, or annotations, we get exact information about the change, e.g. we get the information that the class `WebGUIImpl` has been renamed to `NewWebGUIImpl`. For changes in method bodies, however, we get the information that the method body of a method has been changed, e.g. we get the information that the method body of the method `donwnload` in the class `WebGUIImpl` has been changed. Even though we implemented the monitor for the Eclipse Java editor, the concept can be adapted to other IDEs under the condition that the IDE offers a method to add a listener to the code editor that reports changes based on the Abstract Syntax Tree (AST) changes and enabling plug-ins during runtime of the IDE.

Figure 4.2 shows how our Coevolution approach keeps models consistent from the perspective of the code editor with our plugged in extension. The first task is that the change (1) a developer performed to the source code is

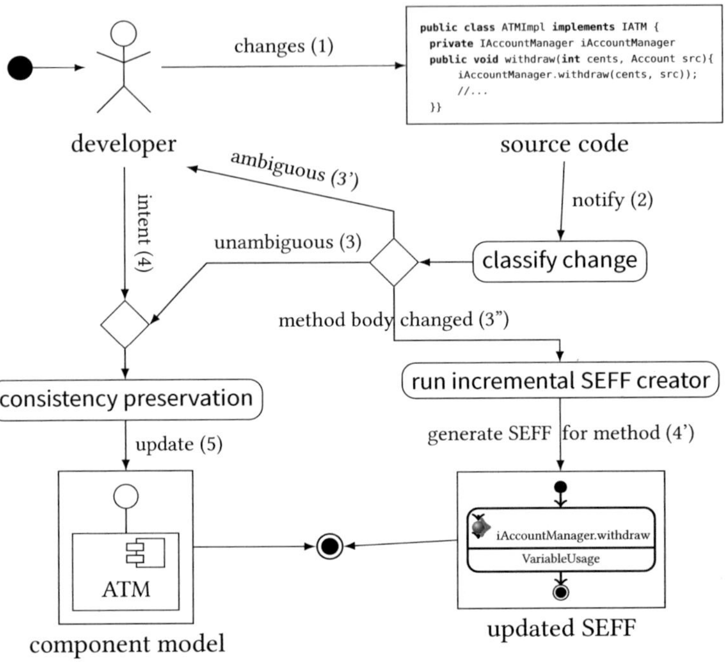

Figure 4.2.: The process how our Coevolution approach keeps source code changes consistent with the architectural model (see [LK14])

detected (2). After that the change is classified (3) either as unambiguous (3), ambiguous (3'), or as method body change (3"). If it is an unambiguous change the consistency preservatican can be triggered directly and the architecture can updated (5). If the change is classified as an ambiguous change, this means that our Coevolution approach is not able to keep the change consistent without additional information from the developer. Hence, they need to clarify their intent (4), in order to allow consistency preservation to keep the change consistent with the architecture (5). If the change is classified as method body change, we can run our change-driven incremental *SEFF* creation that keeps the behavioural model corresponding to the method body consistent (4'). Detailed information how the change-driven incremental *SEFF* creation works can be found in Section 4.5.

4.2.3. Monitored Architectural Editor

As architectural editors, we use the standard PCM editors. Since our Coevolution approach focuses on the PCM repository, the PCM system and the behavioural model *SEFF*, we use these three editors onto the PCM metamodel as editors, which we already explained in 2.3. To include this editors within our Coevolution approach, we need them to report the atomic changes. To do so, we can use the generic EMF model monitor, which we implemented for the VITRUVIUS approach and explained in 3.5.1. The generic EMF model monitor is able to monitor changes on the PCM models and reports the performed changes as instances of the VITRUVIUS change model. The process of the consistency preservation from the editors point of view is similar to the process, we explained for the code monitor (see Figure 4.2). The main difference is that an architectural model is changed instead of the source code and the source code is update instead of the architectural model.

4.2.4. UML Class Diagram Editor for Java Code

In [KLK16], we presented Projective UML class diagram editor for Java. Hence, this section is based on the mentioned publication. Even though many editors exist that keep source code and UML class diagrams consistent, we decided to create a model-based UML class diagram editor as a projective view on the source code. In Chapter 7, we introduce aproaches for keeping source code consistent with UML class diagrams, which are related to our Coevolution approach as well as to Projective UML class diagram editor for Java (ProjUMLed4J). Most related tools, such as UML Lab[1], use an explicit UML model and use an explicit consistency preservation consistency mechanism to keep source code and UML models consistent. A popular tool, which also only uses the source code as source for information is Together from Borland [Bor05]. The so called LiveSource mechanism allows to keep source code consistent with the UML class diagram during the evolution of a software system. Information, such as the multiplicity of annotations, which is part of the UML diagram editor only, is stored in source code comments. The layout information is stored in a separate folder within the project.

[1] `http://www.uml-lab.com/`

```
public MyClass {
   @Association(targetLowerMultiplicity=0,targetUpperMultiplicity=-1)
   private MyString[] myStringList; }
```

Listing 9: Example for an Association annotation

ProjUMLed4J dynamically generates a UML class diagram view from the underlying Java source code when opened. It is created with Eclipse Sirius [VMP14]. As underlying model, we use JaMoPP [Hei+10]. It allows users to use an UML class diagram view of the source code and furthermore, it allows them to create, update, and delete operations for classes, interfaces, methods, fields, parameters and return types. Associations based between classes are shown in the editor and can be specified using the editor. An association between two classes is created if one class has a field with the type of the other class and if both classes are shown in the view. If the latter is not the case, the field in the source code is displayed as field in the UML class diagram editor. The associations between the classes are added to the source code using annotations added to the field. We decided to use annotations instead of, for instance, comments, because annotations are checked by the Java compiler. The association annotations specify the multiplicity of the association and whether the association is an aggregation association or a composition association. The annotations can be added manually during the evolution of the software system. To omit the manual effort, they are also automatically created by ProjUMLed4J in a preprocessing step during the creation of the UML class diagram editor view. The automatic creation of annotations is able to detect the multiplicity of the annotations as follows: We assume an infinite upper bound if the type of the field is a collection type, for instance, `ArrayList`, or if the field is an array. If this is not the case, we assume an upper bound of 1. If the upper bound is 1, i.e. the field is neither an array nor is the type of the field a collection type, we are also able to figure out the lower bound. This can be done by checking whether the field is final or not. If the field is final, we assume a lower bound of 1, otherwise we assume a lower bound of 0. Automatically detect precise multiplicities, such as limited ranges, is both hard to assure in source code and hard to extract from source code. Listing 9 shows an example of an `Association` annotation.

During the generation of the UML diagram, ProjUMLed4J generates `@Association` for the attribute `myStringList` if MyString is in the same package as MyClass. The multiplicity values are represented by annotation attributes and are set to 1 by default. As `myStringList` references an arbitrary number of `MyString` objects, however, we are able to set the target multiplicity to `-1`. This value represents `0..*` in the UML class diagram editor, i.e. an arbitrary objects of `MyStrings` can be contained in the field `myStringList` number.

To use the editor within our Coevolution approach, it is necessary to monitor the performed changes. As the editor changes the underlying source code automatically, we can use Java source code monitor to monitor the changes. Hence, we currently do not monitor the editor itself, but the underlying model. If information solely available in the class diagram editor shall be kept consistent with another mode, we need to add explicit monitoring for ProjUMLed4J. Currently, the only information not available in the source code is the layout information. The layout information is stored by Eclipse Sirius in a separate file.

Currently, the UML class diagram editor is tailored in order to support the package mapping consistency rules, i.e. it is able to present the classes contained in a package. Hence, when using the package mapping consistency preservation rules, the class diagram editor can be used to show the classes within one component. The UML class diagram editor, however, can be extended easily in order to support an arbitrary set of classes.

Figure 4.3 shows an example of our running example and its corresponding UML class diagram. The lower left part shows an evolution scenario: A new interface method (1) is added through in the source code. After this new method has been added the affected element in the UML class diagram editor is updated automatically (2).

4.2.5. Classification of our Coevolution Approach into the View-based Engineering Approach Vitruvius

As we explained in 2.2.2 the Vitruvius approach is a change-driven view-based engineering approach, which can be used to keep model instances of different metamodels consistent during the development process. To this end, Vitruvius uses a VSUM to store all involved models. The access to

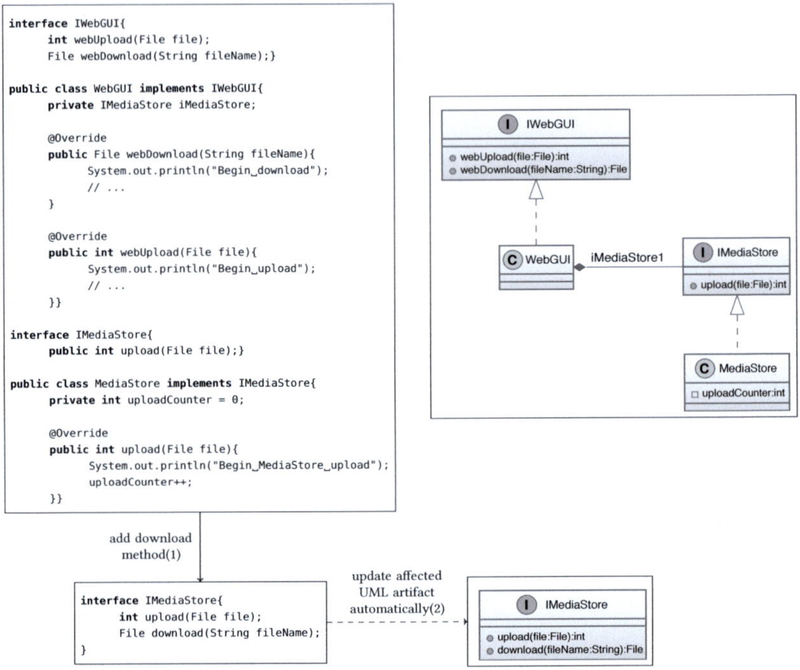

Figure 4.3.: The UML Class Diagram Editor applied to our running example [KLK16]. The left upper part shows the source code of the MediaStore. The right upper part shows the corresponding UML class diagram.

the models within the VSUM is solely possible via views, which monitors all changes. In this section, we classify our Coevolution approach into the Vitruvius approach and point out the contributions of this thesis to the application of Vitruvius to the CBSE domain.

In the initial idea of Vitruvius, Burger [Bur14] and we [KBL13] introduced the Vitruvius vision. Within this vision, we focus on the consistency preservation of arbitrary models and use as example the CBSE domain, which can be seen in Figure 4.4. As initial models to explain the vision, we used PCM, UML, Java source code and the Sensor Model, which stores the simulation results, from the PCM. As views, we use the existing standard views for the models included as view types, and flexible view types and flexible views (see Section 2.2.2) to combine information from more than one underlying models and the correspondence model if necessary. For the definition of the consistency preservation rules, we proposed the use of the MIR languages and a correspondence model. The correspondence model allows us to store the information about corresponding model elements. In order to ease the understandability of Figure 4.4, the correspondence model is not made explicit, but comprised in the arrows between the models. To conclude the vision: We [KBL13] as well as Burger [Bur14] focused on the introduction of the Vitruvius idea and its general application to heterogeneous metamodels. Burger [Bur14], furthermore, focuses on the creation of flexible views. In both publications, however, the main focus are neither the concrete consistency preservation rules nor the coevolution of behaviour models and code. Hence, the novel contributions for the application of Vitruvius to the CBSE domain within this chapter are the definition of:

- reusable and extendable consistency preservation rules from PCM to Java source code,
- a projective UML class diagram editor/view for source code,
- a Coevolution approach behavioural source code elements and a behaviour model, and
- the specification of different user change disambiguation levels.

Furthermore, we extend the existing Vitruvius development roles by defining roles for software architects, component developers and architectural consistency methodologists.

In the following, we list the concepts that our Coevolution approach and the Vitruvius approach have in common. This concepts are the

- change-driven change propagation, which means that changes users perform are monitored, converted into a Vitruvius change model representation, and propagated immediately,
- use of a VSUM to store all involved models, and
- use of a correspondence model in order to keep track of corresponding model elements.

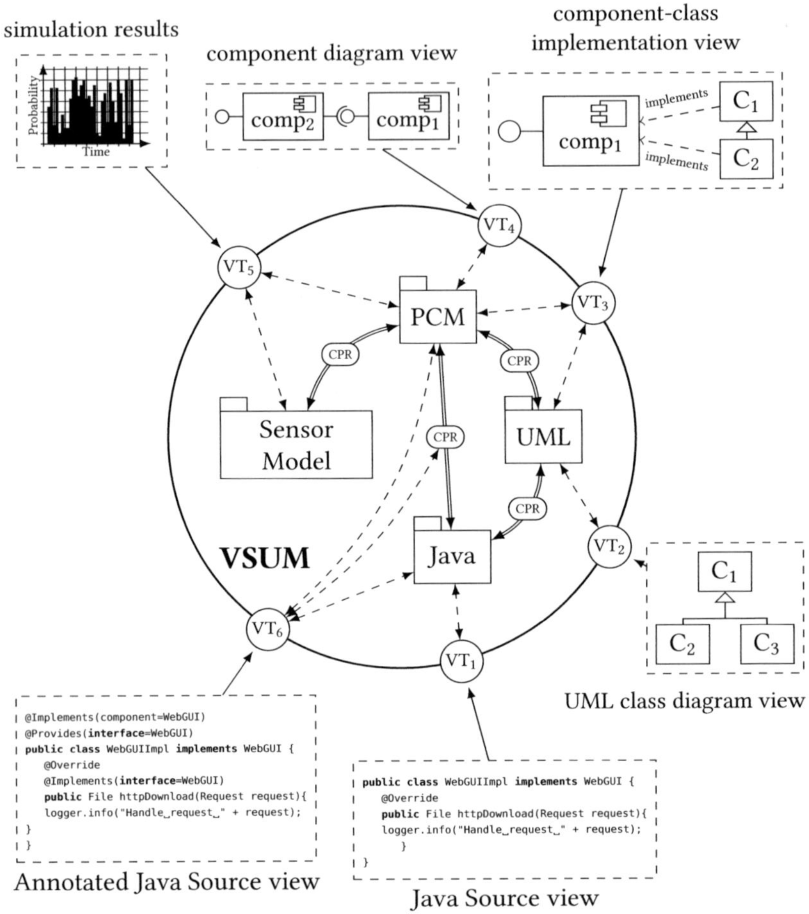

Figure 4.4.: The Vitruvius vision applied to the CBSE domain, as we [KBL13] and Burger [Bur14] proposed. As models we use the PCM, UML, the PCM Sensor Framework model, and a model of Java source code. The consistency preservation rules between the model instances are depicted as the arrows annotated with CPR. The view types are either combining view types (if they contain information from more than one metamodel) or projectional view types (if they contain information from one metamodel only).

Hence, our Coevolution approach can be seen as the first step towards the realisation of the VITRUVIUS vision for the CBSE domain. As metamodels, we use the Java metamodel provided by JaMoPP and PCM. As view types, we use the existing Java source code editors as views to the source code view type, the view type and existing views for the PCM, and a UML class diagram view on to the source code. Parts of future work are to include flexible view types within our Coevolution approach in order to allow users to use views such as the component-class implementation view as well as the annotated source code view, and include more metamodels, such as the UML metamodel and the Sensor metamodel into the VSUM.

4.3. Consistency Preservation Rules between Component-based Architecture and Source Code

In order to keep architectural models and source code consistent during software development and software evolution, we need to define bidirectional consistency preservation rules between architecture and code. These consistency preservation rules have to define how architectural elements are represented in code and vice versa. Hence, we address the second scientific challenge that we defined for this Chapter (see Section 4.1). To do so, the mappings specify the consistency preservation operation that has to be executed if users of our Coevolution approach add, change, or delete either code elements or architectural elements. A typical example for a consistency preservation operation is that an architectural element should be renamed automatically after its corresponding source code element has been renamed by developers. However, not all information in the source code relevant for the architectural model. Helper methods, for instance, which are used within a component to help the component to fulfill its provided services are not architectural relevant.

Hence, the consistency preservation rules describe the overlap between the source code and the architectural model. We define the overlap as information that is contained in both models, the architectural model and the source code model. Identifying the overlap and defining according consistency preservation rules to keep architectural models and source code consistent is the main task of the architectural consistency methodologists (see 4.7.1).

4.3.1. Dimensions of Consistency Preservation Rules

We identified the following three dimensions for the consistency preservation rules: i) a technology-specific dimension, ii) a project-specific dimension, and iii) an element-specific dimension. Technology-specific in this case means that the mapping between architecture and code depends on the used existing technology and how it describes architectural artefacts, such as components and interfaces, in source code. Defining technology-specific consistency preservation rules allows us a) to reuse the consistency preservation rules for projects that use the same technology, and b) to use our Coevolution approach together with already existing tools and frameworks. An example for an existing technology is EJB, which has a concept of component-like classes build in the framework already. If EJB is used in the current project to realise the architectural model in source code the consistency preservation rules should be created with respect to EJB concepts and should use the built-in concepts of the EJB framework. Another example of technology-specific mapping is the mapping between the architectural model and Plain Old Java Objects (POJOs). The standard Java source code does not have a built-in language feature to represent components or other architectural elements. Hence, architectural consistency methodologists needs to define how architectural elements and code elements correspond to one another based on the existing elements in the source code, such as classes, interfaces and packages.

The project-specific dimension means that even if the underlying technology is the same for different projects, the consistency preservation rules can vary depending on the project their are used in. For instance, in one project every source code interface should be represented as architectural interface, while in another project only those interfaces, which are contained in a specific package/folder, are considered as architectural relevant interfaces. Project-specific consistency preservation rules can be reused within all projects that have the same mapping between code and architecture as well as the same technology.

As last dimension, we have identified the element-specific dimension, which allows us to define consistency preservation rules for specific elements. The element-specific dimension itself is divided into two dimensions: a) an element-specific dimension for specific set of elements, and b) an element-specific dimension for a specific element.

The first element-specific consistency preservation rules are element-specific consistency preservation rules that are valid for a set of elements. They can be defined for elements that do not follow the general consistency preservation rules, which are defined for the current project and technology. Hence, the element-specific consistency preservation rules overrides the existing consistency preservation rules for a specific set of elements. During the evolution of a software system our Coevolution approach checks whether such an element-specific mapping rule exists for the element that has been changed before the application of the consistency preservation rules. If this is the case only the element-specific consistency preservation rules are executed. Within our Coevolution approach, we use element-specific consistency preservation rules for the integration of existing source code, which are not compliant to the current consistency preservation rules (see Section 5.4.4).

The second dimension are element-specific rules for a specific element. The difference to the first kind of element-specific consistency preservation rules is that these rules are valid only for a specific element, not for a set of elements. The consistency preservation rules specific for one element override the set of element-specific consistency preservation rules, i.e. if an element has consistency preservation rules specific for that element these consistency preservation rules are executed. Within our Coevolution approach, we currently do not use this kind of element-specific consistency preservation rules. We outline, however, how they can be used for integrated elements.

Within this thesis, we present project and technology-specific consistency preservation rules between PCM and source code using the technology EJB and consistency preservation rules between PCM and POJOs. Furthermore, we present a project and technology-specific mapping between the PCM and a dependency injection framework, where the dependency injection framework is used to compose components. We also present technology-specific consistency preservation rules between the PCM and artefacts from the Eclipse Plugin Development, which are Open Services Gateway initiative (OSGi) based, to show that it is possible to support technology-specific consistency preservation rules, where the components and interfaces are partly defined in other artefacts than the source code itself. All consistency preservation rules, we present in this thesis, can be reused in other projects or can be used as base rules for project-specific extensions.

4.3.2. Package Mapping Consistency Preservation Rules as Example

This section presents an example for bidirectional consistency preservation rules between architectural models and source code. We use these consistency preservation rules in the remainder of this section to explain our Coevolution approach.

As architectural model for the consistency preservation rules, we use a PCM *Rrepository* and a PCM *System*. As source code, we use Java source code build with POJOs. POJO, in this case, means that no specific mechanism, such as EJB, is used to define components or interfaces. An overview for the mapping of a PCM repository can be found in Table 4.1, while an overview of the mapping to the PCM system can be found in Table 4.2. As the consistency preservation rules are based on the package hierarchy in Java, we call them package mapping consistency preservation rules.

4.3.2.1. Mapping the Repository Elements to Source Code

Using the package mapping consistency preservation rules, we map a *Repository* to three packages in the source code. This means if a new *Repository* has been created we create one package that corresponds to the repository. This package will contain all components. Furthermore, the package contains one contracts package for the interfaces and one datatype package for all data types. If users start with the source code and create a package first, we create the *Repository* as well as the both necessary packages inside the new package. Hence, we assume that the newly created package corresponds to the *Repository*.

PCM metamodel element	Source code language element
Repository	Three *packages*: main, contracts, data types
BasicComponent	Package within the main *package* and a public component realisation *class* within the package
OperationInterface	*Interface* in the contracts package
Signature&Parameters	*Methods&parameters*
CompositeDatatype	*Class* with getter and setter for inner types
CollectionDatatypes	*Class* that inherits from a Java collection type (e.g. `ArrayList`)
RequiredRole	*Field* typed with required interface in the component-class and *constructor parameter* for the field in the component-class
ProvidedRole	Main class of providing component *implements* the provided interface
SEFF	*Method* in the component realisation *class* that overrides the corresponding interface method

Table 4.1.: Example mapping between PCM repository metamodel elements and source code language elements

Each *OperationInterface* is mapped to one Java interface within the contracts package with the same name. *Signatures* and *Parameters* are mapped accordingly to the matching Java interface. In the case of interfaces the opposite mapping is straight forward: if a Java interface has been created in the contracts package a new *OperationInterface* is created automatically. The same is true for Java methods and their parameters. Java interfaces that are not created in the contracts package, are not considered as architectural relevant interfaces by default. Users of our Coevolution approach and the consistency preservation rules, however, can specify those Java interfaces as architecture relevant if they want to override the consistency preservation rules.

For each *CompositeDatatype* created in the architectural model, we create one class in the datatypes package. For the innertypes of a *CompositeDatatype*, we create a field for the innertype and one getter and one setter for the field.

For each *CollectionDatatype*, we also create a class in the datatypes packages. This class inherits from a Java Collection type (e.g. `ArrayList`). Users of our Coevolution approach need to specify which Java Collection type shall be used for the specific *DataType*. To do so, the consistency preservation operation, which is executed after a *CollectionDatatype* has been created, asks users after they added a *CollectionDatatype* in the architectural model which Java Collection type should be used. The reason why users need to disambiguate this change is that the PCM abstracts from the concrete used collection type and only specifies that a collection of elements shall be used. The type parameter for the created collection class equals the corresponding Java class for the *innertype* of the *CollectionDataType*. If no *innertype* has been added upon the creation of the *CollectionDataType*, we use `Object` as type parameter. As soon as users add the *innertype* to the *CollectionDataType*, we replace `Object` with the Java class that corresponds to the *DataType* of the *innertype*. To map *DataTypes* from source code to the architecture two possibilities exist: The first one is straight forward: If a class in the datatypes package has been created, we automatically create a corresponding PCM *DataType*. To determine whether a *CompositeDatatype* or a *CollectionDataType* should be used, we again, ask the users of our Coevolution approach. The second possibility to create an architectural *DataType* based on a change in the source code is more complex: We create a PCM *CompositeDatatype*, for classes that are used as parameter or return type in architecture relevant methods. Even though this does not match our mapping exactly, we create the data type in order to enable the coevolution. This, however, could cause the effect that a class can correspond to a component as well as to a data type. This approach is also realised within Source Code Model eXtractor (SoMoX), where a component class can be used as data type as well. Using our approach, we could avoid allowing the use of a component class as parameter or return type by forbidding the use of a component-realisation class or any class that is not in the datatype package as return type or parameter. If a developer would try to do so, a warning or error could be displayed and the action could be undone automatically. Implementing this approach allows us to detect this kind of architectural violation.

Each *BasicComponent* is mapped to a package inside the *Repository* package that has the same name as the *BasicComponent* and one component-realising class inside the component package that has the same name as the *BasicCom-*

ponent with the suffix *Impl*. This class serves as Facade or Proxy class for the component. Furthermore, this class is marked as final to forbid inheritance from this class. If we map from code to the architecture we create by default a *BasicComponent* automatically if the above-mentioned mapping becomes true. This means, if a developer creates a package within the repository package and a class within this package that has the same name as the package, we create a *BasicComponent* in the architectural model. Since this mapping is hard to match for developers we soften this mapping. For instance, a new *BasicComponent* can be created in the following cases:

- no class has been created within the package yet, and
- the class name does not match the package name.

To allow such a softening of the mapping, we use user change disambiguation (see Section 4.4), which allows us to let developers and architects decide whether they want to create a *BasicComponent* and which class should be the component-realising class for the *BasicComponent*.

A *RequiredRole* is mapped to a field in the realisation class of the *BasicComponent* and a constructor parameter within this class as well as an assignment statement in the constructor that assigns the value of the constructor parameter to the field. This means that we use the dependency injection pattern[2] with injection through the constructor. Hence, a component realisation class cannot be instantiated without an instance of each of its required interfaces. The mapping from the source code to the architectural model can be softened as follows: as soon as a field is added to the component-realisation class that has the type of an architectural relevant interface, a *RequiredRole* and the constructor parameter as well as the assignment in the constructor can be created.

A *ProvidedRole* means that an architectural component provides an architectural interface. To map this to the source code, we let the component-realising class implement the Java interface that corresponds to the provided interface. The mapping from code to architecture is straight forward: if developers add an implements relation between the component-realisation class and an interface that corresponds to an architectural interface, we create a provided role in the architecture model.

[2] `http://martinfowler.com/articles/injection.html`

PCM metamodel element	Source code language element
System	*package* and public class within the package
CompositeComponent & Subsystem	*Package* within the main Repository package and public class within the package
AssemblyContext	*field* in the class and *instantiation* of the mapping class
RequiredRole	*Member* typed with required interface and *constructor parameter* for member
ProvidedRole	class of the *System implements* the provided interface
ProvidedDelegationConnector	delegation call to the corresponding field within the overwritten method of the provided interface
RequiredDelegationConnector	*constructor parameter*, typed with the interface of the required delegation connector that is given to the constructor of the requiring components-realisation class
AssemblyConnector	assignment of the constructor parameter from the field that corresponds to the requiring AssemblyContext with the corresponding field that corresponds to the providing AassemblyContext

Table 4.2.: Example mapping between PCM system metamodel elements and source code language elements

A *SEFF* is mapped to a class method, which overrides a Java interface method that corresponds to the *SEFF*'s *OperationSignature*. The mapping from source code to architecture is straight forward: As soon as a method in the source code is created that overrides an interface method, which corresponds to an *OperationSignature*, a new *SEFF* is created in the *BasicComponent*, which corresponds to the method's class.

4.3.2.2. Mapping between Composed Entities from PCM and Source Code

To enable the use of PCM composed entities in our consistency preservation rules, we need to define bidirectional consistency preservation rules for them as well. The super class of composed entity in the PCM is the class *ComposedProvidingRequiringEntity*. Concrete CPREs are the PCM *Systems*, *CompositeComponents* and *SubSystems*. The difference between them is that the *System* is a first class entity in the PCM, while the *CompositeComponents* and the *SubSystems* are contained in the *Repository*. Hence, the difference in the mapping is as follows: *CompositeComponents* and *SubSystems* map to a own package within the *Repository*'s package. A *System*, however, maps to its own package that is not inside the *Repository* package. Similar to the mapping of a *BasicComponent* the package that is created for the *CPRE* has the same name as the *CPRE* and the realisation class within the package also has the same name with an appended `Impl`. To map these elements from source code to architecture we use the following approach: If a new package or class is created, which is not covered by the correspondences yet, we request users to disambiguate the change in order to figure out whether the created package respectively the created class should be mapped to a *CompositeComponent* a *Subsystem* or a *BasicComponent*. If users create a new package on the same hierarchical level as the package that corresponds to the *Repository*, we also request users to disambiguate the change in order to figure out whether a *System* should be created.

Even though the first mapping rule is different depending on the kind of the *ComposedProvidingRequiringEntity* (CPRE) the remainder of the bidirectional consistency preservation rules for CPREs is identical for the package mapping consistency preservation rules. Hence, for all CPREs an *AssemblyContext* is mapped to a field in the CPRE-realisation class. The field has the type of the component's realisation class from the encapsulated component of the *AssemblyContext* and the name of the *AssemblyContext*. Furthermore, we create an instance of the component's realisation class in the constructor and connect the *AssemblyConnectors* as well as the *DelegationConnectors* accordingly. To map an *AssemblyContext* from source code to the architecture, we use, again, a soften mapping rule: A new *AssemblyContext* is created each time developers create a field in the class that corresponds to a CPRE.

ProvidedRoles and *RequiredRoles* of CPREs are mapped the same way as they are mapped for *BasicComponents*.

A *ProvidedDelegationConnector* is a connector that connects one public accessible interface from the CPRE to the inner *AssemblyContexts*. To map this to source code we create a delegate call within the overwritten corresponding method of the CPRE's realisation class. The code created by the consistency preservation rules, delegates the call to the field that corresponds to the encapsulated component of the *AssemblyContext*.

A *RequiredDelegationConnector* is mapped to a constructor parameter. This parameter is typed with the Java interface type that corresponds to the required interface within the *RequiredDelegationConnector*. The mapping from code to architecture is straight forward in this case: If a constructor parameter, which corresponds to an architectural interface or to an architectural component, is added by developers, we create a new *RequiredDelegationConnector*. If the constructor parameter maps to a component-realisation class, we create *RequiredDelegationConnectors* for all *RequiredRoles* of the component.

An *AssemblyConnector* is a connection between two *AssemblyContexts* and connects the required interfaces with the provided interfaces. This means that we assign the constructor parameter of the field that corresponds to the requiring *AssemblyContext* with the field that corresponds to the providing *AssemblyContext*.

4.3.2.3. Discussion and Limitations of Architecture to POJOs Consistency Preservation Rules

The presented bidirectional consistency preservation rules are only one example, how instances of the architectural model PCM can be mapped to Java source code and vice versa. When using the presented consistency preservation rules it is not possible to map all valid PCM instances to source code. Hence, the consistency preservation rules introduce some constraints to the PCM instances. For instance, within the PCM it is possible for one *BasicComponents* to provide the same *OperationSignature* twice. This is not possible using the package mapping consistency preservation rules, we explained in the section above. In general, two approaches are possible to overcome the limitation of introducing new constraints. The first solution is to check the constraints that are introduced by the consistency preservation rules and resolve occurring conflicts before executing the consistency preservation operation. If a constraint violation is detected, an error can be generated and reported to the users. Hence, users need to resolve this manually, for instance, by removing one conflicting element. The resolution of some conflicts, however, can be done automatically as well. The second solution is to change the consistency preservation operations in order to remove the introduced constraints. Therefore, the consistency preservation operations can be extended, for instance, to use the same mapping from architectural model to source code as proposed by Becker [Bec08]. He proposes the use of explicit classes for *ProvidedRoles*, i.e. the roles are made explicit. This approach is implemented, for instance, for SimuCom and ProtoCom. The approach has the advantage that it is possible to map all valid PCM instances to source code. It, however, has the disadvantage that more source code needs to be generated. The additional generated code introduces some indirections to source code, which makes the source code harder to understand for developers. This is not an issue for SimuCom and ProtoCom, as they are used to generate code that a) is used for performance prediction, or b) is used to generate code stubs. This becomes an issue, however, when the source code should be used by developers to create actual software systems.

In the current shape of the consistency preservation rules, we use one package for the *Repository*, which contains all packages for all *Components* directly. If a project uses many *Components*, many sub-packages are created within the *Repository* package. Having many of sub-packages in the *Repository* package, could decrease the understandability of the source code. To overcome this issue, it is possible to create more container packages for the elements within the *Repository* package as follows: The *Repository* package could contain own sub-packages for *BasicComponents* and *CompositeComponents*.

Using the consistency preservation rules, it is not possible to deploy the created components and systems on different machines. To overcome this issue, one possibility is to use Remote Procedure Calls (RPC)[3] for calls from one component to another component. This means that all interfaces are realised

[3] `https://docs.oracle.com/javase/8/docs/platform/rmi/spec/rmiTOC.html`

as RPC interfaces. Thus, it would be possible to deploy the components on different machines.

Furthermore, using the package mapping consistency preservation rules, it is complicated to create CPREs from the source code, because developers need to comply to explained consistency preservation rules for CPRE within the source code. Hence, we recommended to create CPRE via the architectural model instead of creating them from within the source code directly.

4.3.2.4. Example using the Package Mapping Consistency Preservation Rules

In this section, we introduce a small example project that consists of an architectural model and source code, which are created using the above-mentioned package mapping consistency preservation rules. We introduced the simple example in our previous work [Lan13]. The example is a simplified version of the MediaStore example introduced by Koziolek et al. [KBH07] and recently described by Strittmatter and Kechaou [SK16], which enables users to download audio files from a server and upload audio files to a server.

In our simplified version, the *Repository* of the MediaStore consists of the two components *MediaStore* and *WebGUI* and the two interfaces *IMediaStore* and *IWebGUI* (see Figure 4.5). The component *MediaStore* provides the interface *IMediaStore*, while the *WebGUI* component provides *IWebGUI* and required *IMediaStore*. The *WebGUI* interface contains the two methods *httpUpload* and *httpDownload*. The *IMediaStore* interface contains the two methods *upload* and *download*. Hence, the *WebGUI* component has the *SEFFs httpUpload* and *httpDownload*, while the *MediaStore* component has the *SEFFs upload* and *download*.

Figure 4.6 shows the *System* of our simple example: each component is instantiated once within an *AssemblyContext*. Furthermore, the *System* provides the *IWebGUI* interface and delegates calls to the *AssemblyContext WebGUI*. Hence, users can communicate with the *WebGUI* component to access the media files that are stored within the *MediaStore* component.

Figure 4.7 shows the UML class diagram of the MediaStore example, which contains the classes as well as the packages our Coevolution approach creates using the package mapping consistency preservation rules. Figure 4.7

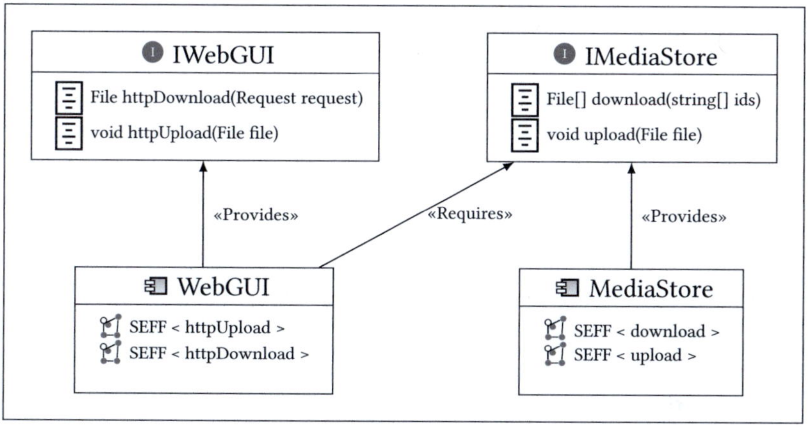

Figure 4.5.: The *Repository* of the MediaStore example that contains the components *MediaStore* and *WebGUI*

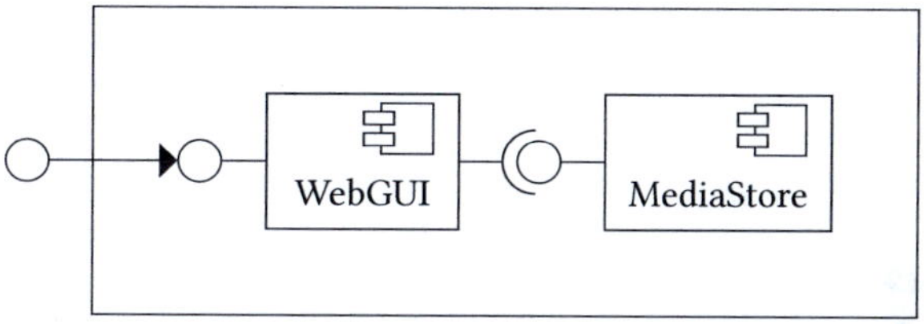

Figure 4.6.: The *System* of the MediaStore example. The *System* provides the interface `IWebGUI` through a *ProvidedDelegationRole.*

focuses on the packages created for components. Hence, we omit the default-packages for the *OperationInterfaces*, the *DataTypes*, and for the *Repository* itself.

To show how a *BasicComponent* with one provided *OperationInterface* and one required *OperationInterface* is realised in source code, consider Figure 4.8. The *OperationInterface* named *IWebGUI* and its *OperationSignatures* correspond to the `IWebGUI` interface and its methods. The *OperationInterface* named *IMediaStore* is mapped accordingly. The component-realising class is named `WebGUIImpl` and is contained in the package `webgui`. According to the package mapping consistency preservation rules it implements the `IWebGUI`

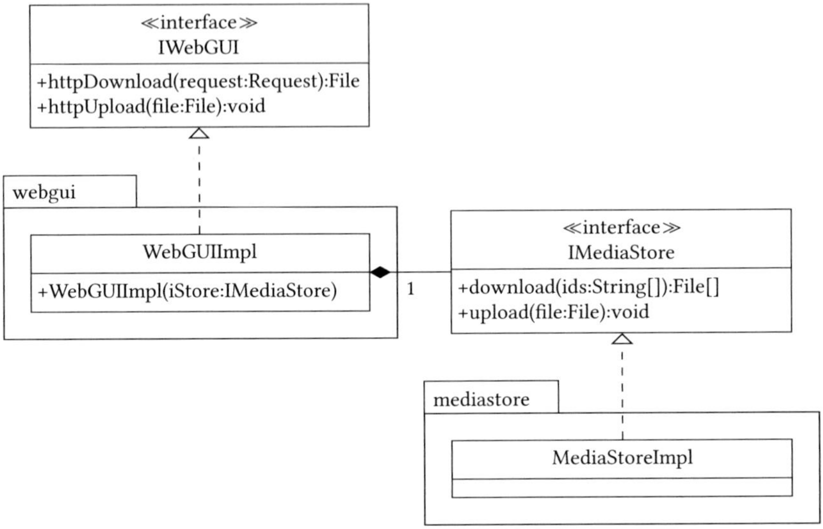

Figure 4.7.: The UML class diagram of the MediaStore example. To ease the diagram, we omitted the `contracts`, the `repository`, and the `datatypes` package.

interface and implements the methods `httpUpload` and `httpDownload`. Furthermore, it needs an instance of the *IMediaStore* as constructor parameter that is assigned to the field `mediaStoreImpl`.

Listing 10 shows how the System of our simple example is mapped to source code. According to the consistency preservation rules it has one private field for each of the System's AssemblyContexts, which are instantiated and connected in the System's constructor. Since the *System* provides the *IWebGUI* interface and delegates calls to the *AssemblyContext* that contains the *WebGUI* component, the *System*'s realising class implements the `IWebGUI` interface, overrides the methods from the `IWebGUI` interface, and delegates the calls to these methods to its field of the `WebGUIImpl` class.

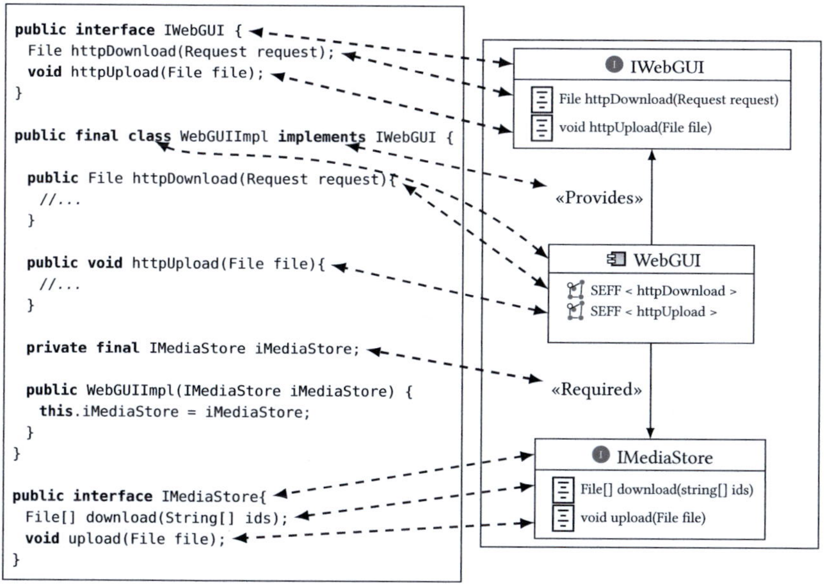

Figure 4.8.: The mapping between a *BasicComponent* and its provided and required *OperationInterfaces* to the corresponding source code elements using the package mapping consistency preservation rules

4.3.3. Outline on How to Verify and Validate our Consistency Preservation Rules

Even though we do not present a formal verification of the used consistency preservation rules in this thesis, we outline how the consistency preservation rules can be verified. Our consistency preservation rules could be verified using mechanisms, which can applied to the General Purpose Language (GPL) Java. Besides of the evaluation, we will show in Chapter 6, the consistency preservation rules can be validated using N-Version Programming (NVP). We explain these two techniques in the following.

We do not focus on the verification techniques for model transformations, because the consistency preservation rules are written in languages, which

```
package mediastoresystem;

public class MediaStoreSystemImpl implements IWebGUI{

	private final MediaStoreImpl mediaStoreImpl;
	private final WebGUIImpl webGUIImpl;

	public MediaStoreSystemImpl(){
		mediaStoreImpl = new MediaStoreImpl();
		webGUIImpl = new WebGUIImpl(mediaStoreImpl);
	}

	@Override
	public void httpUpload(File file){
		webGUIImpl.httpUpload(file);
	}

	@Override
	public File[] httpDownload(String[] ids){
		return webGUIImpl.httpDownload(ids);
	}
}
```

Listing 10: Mapping from the example PCM *System* to source code using the package mapping consistency preservation rules

translate to Java code and directly manipulate the models. Calegari and Szasz [CS13] provide a state-of-the-art overview of model verification techniques. They point out that many tools, used for the verification of model transformation are based on relational and graph-based transformations, because both can be translated into formal domains. Furthermore, they state that transformation languages, which are closely related to standard programming languages, introduce similar verification problems as standard programming languages (see Calegari and Szasz [CS13]). As a result, traditional code verification approaches can be applied to verify such transformation languages.

4.3.3.1. Using Standard Java mechanisms for the Verification

As we explained in Section 3.6, we use Xtend and Domain Specific Languages (DSLs) for the creation of the consistency preservation rules. As both of this languages are translated into Java source code, we can use standard mechanisms for Java to verify the correctness of the consistency preservation rules. Using the behavioural specification Java Modelling Language (JML) (see Leavens et al. [LBR99]), for instance, allows users to specify contracts for each method. The contracts can be used to verify the code against the contracts. This can be done, for instance, by using the verification framework KeY introduced by Beckert et al. [Bec+07]. It combines automatic and interactive proving.

To use such an approach for the verification of our consistency preservation rules, we would need to specify contracts for each consistency preservation method. For the consistency preservation rules implemented in the GPL Xtend, this can be done by adding the contracts to each Xtend method and by instructing the Xtend code generator to add this JML contracts to the generated Java method. For the MIR transformations this can be done either by adding the JML specification to the generated Java source code or by adding the JML specifications to the part of the source code, which is translated to Java methods. To ease this approach for the MIR languages, they could be extended in order to support users by adding the JML specifications. Therefore, a new language feature can be implemented, which allows users to add JML specifications within the MIR languages directly.

4.3.3.2. Using NVP for the Validation

One possibility to validate the correctness of the consistency preservation rules is to use NVP (see Chen and Avizienis [CA78]). NVP, in general, proposes the idea of implementing multiple versions of a software system using different teams and different languages. For the implementation, the teams get the same specification for the software system. The goal is to get fault-tolerant software systems by having redundant implementations performed by different teams in order to rule out programming errors. NVP is used, for instance, for aircraft control systems. During the runtime of the software systems, a voter collects the output of the different implementations.

If the output of the systems is not identical the voter assumes that the majority of systems computes the correct output and uses this output. Knight and Leveson [KL86] performed an experiment using 27 implementations of the same specification to investigate, whether the programs fail for different tests. They found out, however, that many implementations fail for the same tests. Hence, it turned out that different programming teams perform similar mistakes and that NVP should be used with care.

To validate the correctness of our consistency preservation rules using NVP, we would require different developers to implement the same consistency preservation rules. This could be done, for instance, with students in a practical course. For the package mapping consistency preservation rules, we already have two implementations for consistency preservation rules from PCM to Java. We performed the initial implementation using the GPL Xtend (see Section 3.6.1), while the other implementation has been performed by Klare [Kla16] in the reactions language. Both implementations can be used for change-driven consistency preservation for the direction from PCM to Java code. They both pass the tests we implemented for the package mapping consistency preservation rules from PCM to Java (see Klare [Kla16]). We do not consider our solution as NVP because Klare did know the Xtend implementation and was even able to partly reuse parts of the Xtend implementation. The implementations show, however, that we get the same result using the GPL and the reactions language for the implemented test cases.

4.4. Consistency Automation Levels and User Change Disambiguation within our Coevolution Approach

As we mentioned in the sections above, our Coevolution approach communicates with the users, if the consistency between architecture and code cannot be preserved fully automatically. The communication is usually triggered by the consistency preservation operations to either notify the user, e.g. about the creation of a new element in the architecture as reaction of a source code change, or to ask the users intention. To give an example for the user change disambiguation mechanism, consider our running example in Section 4.3.2. We introduced the mapping for *CollectionDatatypes* to source code, where we map each *CollectionDatatype* to its own class that inherits from a Java `Collection` class. On architectural level, however, only generic *CollectionDatatypes* are known. Hence, it is unclear which Java collection should be used as base class for the new Java class. One possibility is to determine the Java collection class, e.g. `ArrayList`, in the consistency preservation rules operation already. This has the disadvantage, that for all collections the same base class is used by default even though the class is not suitable for all specific requirements. To overcome this disadvantage, we proposed to ask the users in order to disambiguate a performed change and let them decide which Java collection class should be used after a new *CollectionDatatype* has been added. Hence, the approach in this case is semi-automatic, because we request users to disambiguate the change.

In this small example we illustrated that a fully automatic consistency preservation not intended for every change using our Coevolution approach. To ensure semi-automatic consistency within our Coevolution approach, we identified two kinds of possible user change disambiguation. The first one is an interactive user change disambiguation using dialogs, and the second one is a postponed user change disambiguation using a task list.

In this section, we first explain and classify the different levels of automation for consistency preservation, we used in our Coevolution approach. Afterwards, we explain the possible time and kind of user change disambiguation. In the last step of this section, we explain the different kinds of user change disambiguation our Coevolution approach uses to clarify the intent of a user change if necessary.

4.4.1. Levels of Automation used in our Coevolution Approach

The problem of not being able to keep changes in models consistent automatically with the other models in the VSUM is not specific to our Coevolution approach, but also applies to the Vitruvius approach in general. For Vitruvius in general Werle [Wer16] and Kramer [Kra17] identify six levels of automation for the consistency preservation, which are depicted in Figure 4.9. We adapted the terminology slightly in order to match the terms used in this thesis. Using our Coevolution approach only the following three automation

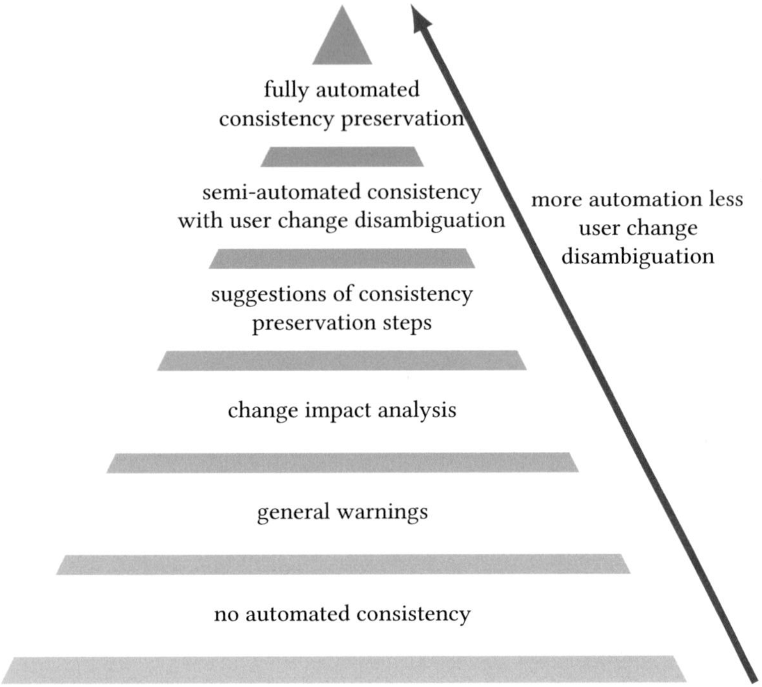

Figure 4.9.: Different levels of automation in Vitruvius for consistency preservation based on [Wer16] and [Kra17]. For our Coevolution approach only the top three levels are relevant.

approaches are relevant: fully automated consistency preservation, semi-automated consistency preservation with user change disambiguation, and automated suggestions for consistency preservation steps.

Fully automated consistency preservation means that after either a source code element or an architectural element has been changed the corresponding model elements are changed and kept consistent automatically. Using our package mapping consistency preservation rules the most changes fall into this category. Especially for the mappings from the statical architectural elements, e.g. components and interfaces to source code almost all changes can be kept consistent automatically.

Semi-automated consistency preservation means, that additional information is necessary to preserve the consistency after users performed a change to a model. Based on this additional information from users, the changes on the corresponding model elements can be executed automatically by our Coevolution approach. Hence, the additional information is usually required by the consistency preservation operation itself to get additional information from users in order to keep the models consistent. Using the package mapping consistency preservation rules, this approach is used mainly for the source code to architecture mapping. For instance, the approach is used if a new package is added. In this case, users need to clarify whether the new package should be mapped to a new component or a new system or if they want to decide later, whether the new package should be mapped at all. The approach is also used if users add a class into a package without a corresponding component or system yet. For the package mapping consistency preservation rules from architectural model to source code, the users only need to disambiguate a change if they created a new *CollectionDatatypes*.

Automated suggestions for consistency preservation means that the corresponding elements cannot be created automatically. In this case only suggestions can be provided automatically. These suggestions specify which elements need to be changed respectively adapted by the users to achieve consistency between the models. Using our Coevolution approach and the package mapping consistency preservation rules changes to the internal behaviour of a *SEFF* fall in this category. These changes fall in this category, because, it is in general not possible to determine automatically the code for the actions within a *SEFF*. For instance, an *InternalAction* in a *SEFF* could span multiple methods and call arbitrary third party libraries. Hence, if an action is added to a *SEFF*, we cannot change the code accordingly, but we can point to the method that needs to be adapted by developers. Further details to the mapping between the behaviour in terms of *SEFFs* and code are explained in Section 4.5.

If our Coevolution approach is used it depends on the implemented consistency preservation rules, whether models can be kept consistent automatically or whether users are request to disambiguate a change. Especially, the first two levels are depending on the used consistency preservation rules, because the implemented consistency preservation operations can decide hard coded which actions should be executed, instead of asking the user to disambiguate the change. Avoiding the kind of user change disambiguation, where the users need to provide additional information, has the advantage that users are not interrupted often during the development. It has, however, the disadvantage that the options for the end users are limited. These limitations can be acceptable for certain domains or projects where such decisions are clear and can be made during the design time of the VSUM. To give an example for a user change disambiguation that could be avoided, consider the example for *CollectionDatatypes*. In this case, we currently request users to disambiguate the change in order to get the information which Java collection type should be used for the corresponding class. In order to avoid users to disadvantage a change, we could change the mapping, for instance, in a way that the Java collection `ArrayList` is used for all *CollectionDatatypes*. To avoid user change disambiguation for changes in source code, we could specify, for instance, that for each new package in the source code, a new *BasicComponent* is created automatically. Hence, in both cases a user change disambiguation could be avoided, but the options for end users of our Coevolution approach would be limited.

4.4.2. Point in Time and Kind of User Change Disambiguation

In the section above, we introduced the automation levels used in our Coevolution approach. Three other challenges for the user change disambiguation in our Coevolution approach are to determine i) the point in time when a user change disambiguation should be executed, ii) the amount of information that is necessary, and iii) the kind of user change disambiguation, which determines how users are requested to disambiguate the change. These challenges are not independent from each other in our Coevolution approach, because the time and the amount of information necessary for a user change disambiguation usually determines also the kind of the user change disambiguation.

For our Coevolution approach, we identified two points in time when a user change disambiguation can take place: They either can take place directly after a user performed a change, or they can take place in a future point in time. Hence, the first one is an interactive user change disambiguation, for which we propose the use of dialogs. The second ones are future interactions that do not interrupt the users during the development, but the users need to take care of the consistency preservation in a later step. The requested information from a specific user change disambiguation can vary between a single information that needs to be provided by users, up to the request of changing many elements in the source code or architecture after one corresponding element has been changed.

As we mentioned above the kind of user change disambiguation depends on the point in time as well as on the requested information. For our Coevolution approach, we currently use dialogs and task lists as kinds of user change disambiguation. Dialogs are suitable if only one or few information from the same user that performed the change, which caused the immediate execution of the current consistency preservation operation. Task lists are suitable if at least one of the following conditions is true: i) many information are necessary to ensure consistency, ii) the user that performed the change is not responsible or able to ensure consistency, or iii) the user that performed the change should not be interrupted.

Similar to the automation level challenge the above-mentioned challenges for user change disambiguation are also challenges for the whole VITRUVIUS approach. Kramer [Kra17] also identifies that it is necessary to determine the time (*when*) and the kind (*how*) of user change disambiguation. For the time challenge he proposes three possibles points the time: before the transformation, during the transformation (when needed), and after the transformation. For the kind of user change disambiguation he proposes interactive as well as postponed user change disambiguation. While the interactive kind is suitable for immediate user change disambiguation, the postponed user change disambiguation is suitable if different users respectively different user roles are involved in the consistency preservation process. While our point in time and kind of user change disambiguation are specific for our Coevolution approach, the challenges and solutions Kramer proposed are more general and tackle bidirectional transformation challenges using different automation levels in general.

4.4.3. Interactive Interactions using Dialogs

As mentioned above, this interactive dialogs are used by our Coevolution approach if information are needed from the same user that performed the change in an interactive way to finish the execution of the current consistency preservation operation. On the automation levels, we presented above, the user dialogs can be classified on the second level (semi-automated consistency preservation).

For the dialogs itself, we propose two dimensions. The first dimension determines whether a modal or a non-modal respectively modless dialog should be used. Modal dialogs are used by our Coevolution approach if immediate user reaction is necessary to execute the current consistency preservation operation. Since modal dialogs are blocking dialogs, the advantage of modal dialogs for our Coevolution approach is that no other changes can occur until the dialog is answered and closed. The disadvantage of modal dialogs, however, is that they need immediate response from the users and block them until they disambiguated the change. Modless dialogs on the other hand are non-blocking dialogs. For our Coevolution approach this means that users can continue to work on the models even if the dialog is not answered and closed yet. Hence, modless dialogs should be used when possible in general. Within our Coevolution approach modless dialogs are used if an interactive interaction with the users is necessary, but the answer to the dialog is not necessary immediately. The challenge of modless dialogs for our Coevolution approach are that changes in one of the models can occur even if the dialog remains unanswered. Hence, they can be used for those information that are not critical for other model elements.

The second dimension is the kind of dialog that is used to display the user change disambiguation to the users. The kind of the used dialog depends on the information that is requested by the current consistency preservation operation. We currently use the following three dialog kinds: If the transformation can provide a choice between different options, we use a radio button dialog. It the transformation needs to have an information that needs to be user-defined, we use a free text input box. As last kind, we use yes/no dialogs if the consistency preservation operation needs the information, whether for a performed change a corresponding element should be created or changed as well.

In the following, we give some examples for dialogs using our Coevolution approach and the package mapping consistency preservation rules. Let us first consider the example of PCM *CollectionDatatypes* again. If a *CollectionDatatype* has been created in the PCM it is unclear for the consistency preservation operation which Java collection class should be used. Hence, additional information from the user is required. Since only one information is required and the possible selection can be defined upfront, we use a modal dialog box that uses radio buttons where users can choose from different Java collections types.

If a new package has been added, we use a modless dialog box with radio buttons to get the information from the user whether a new architectural element should be created as corresponding element for the new package. This new corresponding element can either be a *BasicComponent*, a *CompositeComponent*, or a *System*. Another option is to not create a corresponding architectural element respectively decide later whether a new architectural element should be created. If a new class has been added in a package that already has a corresponding component or a corresponding system, but no realisation class for the component or system yet, we use a yes/no dialog to ask the user whether the new class should be the realisation class for the corresponding architectural element or not.

4.4.4. Task list to enable late resolving of inconsistency

Another way to interact with the users, which we use within our Coevolution approach, is a task list, which contains future tasks for software developers and software architects. Using our Coevolution approach, the following additional domain specific information are stored in the task list to ease the task of the users: i) information which element has been changed respectively which element has been added or removed, and ii) a pointer to the corresponding element(s) that should be changed to keep the models consistent. The task list can be used for semi-automated consistency preservation as well as for the suggestion of consistency preservation steps. One advantage of the task list is that it can be used for consistency preservation tasks that require users to add many information to either one of the models, e.g. implementing a whole method or class. Another advantage is that it can be used if the current user is not the right user to keep the current change consistent with the other models.

Using the package mapping consistency preservation rules within our Coevolution approach, we use the task list for changes within a PCM *SEFF* as follows: After an action has been added to a *SEFF*, we add a task to the task list that points to the method, which corresponds to the *SEFF*. The created task contains the information which element in the architecture has been changed and provides information about the change that should be performed in the source code method. This is easy for control flow elements, such as *ExternalCallActions*, *Loops*, and *Branches*. For *InternalActions*, however, we only can point to the corresponding method and can add information between which control flow elements the new change has been introduced.

4.5. Coevolution of Source Code Behaviour and Architectural Elements

In this section, we present an approach that keeps behaviour models consistent with the source code during the software development and software evolution. Hence, this section addresses the third research challenge, which we defined in Section 4.1 for this chapter. Having an up-to-date behaviour model enables users of our Coevolution approach to get an abstract view about the behaviour of the software system. Furthermore, the behavioural model can be used to perform model-based analyses. Since we use the PCM as architecture model, we use the *SEFF* as behavioural model that should be kept consistent with the source code. Even though we focus on the *SEFF*, the concepts we propose can be applied to other behavioural models, such as the UML activity diagram, as well. Since we use the PCM and propose a possibility to keep the PCM *SEFFs* consistent with the source code, the models we use can be used in a later step to predict the performance of a software system using the performance prediction capabilities of the PCM (see 2.3).

In the sections above, we explained how we can keep the static architecture in terms of packages, classes, interfaces, fields and parts of constructors of a software system consistent with the source code. Hence, we consider that code as static source code. Code that needs to be kept consistent with behavioural models is the code within method bodies. Hence, we consider that code as behavioural source code.

To keep a behavioural model and behavioural source code consistent, we could use bidirectional consistency preservation rules between source code and models. This would be a similar approach to the consistency preservation between static architecture and static source code. It turned out, however, that this approach can only be used as unidirectional mapping from behavioural architecture models to source code. To keep code changes consistent with the architecture, we extended the *SEFF* reverse engineering approach from SoMoX [Kro12]. This approach is able to reconstruct a *SEFF* incrementally after users changed the source code using the code editor. The *SEFF* reconstruction depends on the used consistency preservation rules between architectural model and source code, i.e. the *SEFF* reconstruction needs to be defined specifically for the used consistency preservation rules.

In the remainder of this section, we first explain how changes on architectural behaviour models can be kept consistent with the source code (see Section 4.5.1). In the second part of the section (see Section 4.5.2), we explain how we can keep the behavioural architecture models consistent after the source code has been changed and explain how this approach can be used to detect architecture violation (see Section 4.5.2.4). To ease the understandability of this approach, we give an example for the incremental-change-driven reconstruction in Section 4.5.2.6. In Section 4.5.3, we explain how this two approaches can be combined to support coevolution.

4.5.1. Mapping from *SEFF* to Source Code

Keeping changes in a *SEFF* consistent with source code is challenging, because the *SEFF* is an abstraction from the source code and does not specify how the underlying source code is implemented. An *InternalAction*, for instance, can abstract a complicated algorithm that spans over several component-internal classes and is used by the component to fulfill its provided service. Hence, generating meaningful code if a *SEFF* element is added or changed is in general not possible for all *SEFF* elements. As mentioned above, however, we can define consistency preservation rules from behavioural models to source code. To this end, however, we are not generating code if a user changes the *SEFF* because the *SEFF* is an abstraction from the source code. We are, however, able to generate tasks for developers who are responsible for implementing the software system. This tasks are generated in the task list for developers and point to the method that corresponds to the *SEFF* in which the *Action* has been changed. After implementing the tasks developers need to mark them as done and remove them from the task list. The approach of using a task list to restore the consistency later, is similar to the approach described by Balzer [Bal91]. He describes an approach for resolving inconsistency. In his approach, tolerated inconsistencies are marked and its values leading to them are stored. The inconsistencies need to be resolved in a later step.

Even though we currently only generate tasks in the task list, it is possible to generate code stubs in the code for certain domains or *SEFF* elements. It is possible to create code for the control flow elements within the *SEFF*, such as *Loops* and *Branches* as well as for *ExternalCallActions*. This can be done using the information from the VITRUVIUS correspondence model. For instance, it is possible to generate stubs for a switch-case statement within the code after a *Branch* action has been added in a *SEFF*. Doing so can be useful in certain domains, such as the embedded systems domain. However, since the goal of our Coevolution approach is not to enable visual programming and we do not focus on the embedded systems domain, we have not further investigated the possibilities on how to generate stubs for the control flow elements within a *SEFF*.

4.5.2. Incremental *SEFF* Creation to Create up-to Date Behavioural Models

As mentioned above, to incrementally create the *SEFF* from the source code, we extend the *SEFF* reverse engineering approach from SoMoX [Kro12]. We explained the SoMoX *SEFF* reconstruction approach as proposed by Krogmann [Kro12] in detail in 2.4. For this section, it is relevant to know that the *SEFF* reconstruction performs a control flow analyses for each method that corresponds to a *SEFF* in order to create the actions within a *SEFF* from source code. To do so, the *SEFF* reconstruction approach uses a two-state process. Within the first step of the process all method calls within a method are classified. Herby, the calls are divided in component-internal calls, component-external calls, and library calls. Component-external calls are calls to a method of another component or to an interface method that corresponds to an *OperationSignature*. A library call is a call to a third party library or a language API a or a data type. Internal calls are those calls that are neither of the above, i.e they are calls to a method that is in a class within the same component. In the second step of the process, the actual control flow analyses is executed in order to build the *SEFF*. Based on the component-external calls the *SEFF* reconstruction approach creates the corresponding *SEFF* elements for loops, switch and if statements. The *SEFF* reconstruction process of SoMoX, however, only works if the whole source code of the software system has been parsed upfront. Furthermore, a Source Code Decorator Model (SCDM), which can be used to classify the method calls within a method, needs to be available. The first point is not an issue for the SoMoX *SEFF* analysis, because the whole source code of the software system under investigation is parsed before the SoMoX reconstruction process starts. The second point is also not an issue for the SoMoX *SEFF* analysis, because SoMoX creates a SCDM within the reconstruction steps that are executed before the actual *SEFF* reconstruction.

4.5.2.1. Goal and Challenges for the Change-Driven Incremental *SEFF* Creation

The main goal of the incremental *SEFF* reconstruction is to built a *SEFF* for only the part of the source code that has been changed. Hence, only the affected *SEFF*(s) should be recreated during an incremental *SEFF* reconstruction. This reconstruction needs to be done without the need of parsing the complete source code of a project. For instance, a possible unit that can be reconstructed incrementally is a *SEFF* for the method after the method body has been changed by a developer. As SoMoX creates the SCDM during the first phase of the reconstruction of a software system, we do not have a SCDM within our Coevolution approach. Hence, another goal is to enable the *SEFF* reconstruction without having a SCDM available. The SoMoX *SEFF* reconstruction uses the SCDM for the following tasks:

1. check which component belongs to which class, i.e. the SCDM is used to classify the method calls, and
2. find the called interface and the called port for a found component-external call.

From these tasks the SCDM is used for, we can identify the first three challenges that appear if we want to use the SoMoX *SEFF* reconstruction approach within our Coevolution approach: i) we need to circumvent the fact that we need to have the parsed source code of the whole project, ii) the classification of method calls need to work either without the SCDM or with an incrementally updated SCDM, and iii) the called interface and the ports also need to be identified either without the SCDM or with an incrementally updated SCDM. These challenges are not independent from each other, because the second and third steps not only need an up-to-date SCDM, but they also need the parsed source code of the whole project. Hence, if an approach solves the second and third challenge without parsing the source code of the whole project it would automatically solve the first challenge as well.

Another challenge, challenge iv), comes with the incremental reconstruction of component-internal methods after their code has been changed. Using the SoMoX *SEFF* reconstruction as introduced by Krogmann [Kro12] component-internal methods are either inlined in the *SEFF* or made explicit in *ResourceDemandingInternalBehaviours*. They are made explicit if the following two conditions are true: i) the method is called more than once within a component, and ii) the method contains at least one component-external method call. In the following, we refer to *SEFF* and *ResourceDemandingInternalBehaviours* as *ResourceDemandingBehaviour* if the statement we make is true for both of them. From the standard reconstruction of component-internal methods, we can derive the following two sub-challenges for the change-driven reconstruction of *ResourceDemandingBehaviour*: iv).1: adding or removing a method call, which destination is a component-internal method, to a method that corresponds to a *ResourceDemandingBehaviour*, and iv).2: changing a component-internal method in a way that affects the component external-behaviour of the component. Since in the standard SoMoX *SEFF* reconstruction approach component-internal methods are inlined within their parent *ResourceDemandingBehaviour* if their called only once respectively made explicit if they are called at least twice, we need to make this behaviour incremental. This sub-challenge, however, only occurs if a component-internal method contains at least one component-external call. Otherwise it would be inlined to an *InternalAction* in the affected *ResourceDemandingBehaviour*. The second sub-challenge, iv).2, occurs, for instance, if a component-internal method does not contain a component-external call yet, but the latest change has introduced a new component-external call. The exemplified change of introducing the first component-external call to a method, also affects *ResourceDemandingBehaviours* that correspond to other methods, because the component-internal method would have been ab-

```
public final class WebGUIImpl implements IWebGUI {

      private final IMediaStore iMediaStore;

      public File httpDownload(Request request){
        if(RequestHelper.isValid(request)){
              File file = this.doDownload(request);
              return file;
        }else{
              logger.warn("Request␣" + request + "is␣not␣valid");
              return null;}
      }

      private File doDownload(Request request){
        String[] id = RequestHelper.getId(request);
        if(id == null || id.length == 0)
              return null;
      }
}
```

Listing 11: An implementation of the download method

stracted to an *InternalAction* using the SoMoX *SEFF* reconstruction in those *SEFFs*. One consequence that follows from both of the two sub-challenges is that changes on one method in the code can potentially affect more than one *ResourceDemandingBehaviour* of one component. Like the other challenges, the fourth challenge does not occur in the standard SoMoX *SEFF* reconstruction, because the code is not analysed incrementally within SoMoX, i.e. the code under investigation does not change during the reconstruction.

Example for the Challenges Consider Listing 11 that represents an implemention of the `download` method of the `WebGUIImpl` class, which we introduced in Section 4.3.2.4: Let us assume, that SoMoX reconstructed the same static architecture as depicted in the running example (see Figure 4.5). Hence, the SCDM would contain the information that the components *WebGUI* contains the class *WebGUIImpl* and the component *MediaStore* contains the class *MediaStoreImpl*. Furthermore, the SCDM contains the information, that the *OperationInterface IWebGUI* as well as its signatures corresponds to the `IWebGUI` Java interface and its methods, and that the *OperationInterface IMediaStore* as well as its signatures corresponds to the `IMediaStore` Java interface

```
    private File doDownload(Request request){
      String[] id = RequestHelper.getId(request);
      if(id == null || id.length == 0)
           return null;
      return this.iMediaStore.download(id)[0];
    }
}
```

Listing 12: The `doDownload` method after a developer added a component-external method call

and its methods. As mentioned above, the SoMoX *SEFF* reconstruction mechanism uses the SCDM to identify whether a component-external method is used. Using the provided SCDM, the SoMoX *SEFF* reconstruction considers the method calls `doDownload` as component-internal call. We assume that the method calls `isValid`, `getId` and `log` are calls to third party libraries. Hence, these calls are considered as library calls. Since no component-external methods are used in the method `httpDownload` and in the methods that are called directly or indirectly the created *SEFF* contains only one *InternalAction*.

Evolution scenario Let us assume the evolution scenario in Listing 12, in which developers change the `doDownload` method and add a component-external method call as follows: The new call to the `download` method of the `IMediaStore` interface is a component-external call. As the SoMoX *SEFF* reconstruction does not work incrementally, all above-mentioned challenges occur after after such a change: i) if no information is available in which part of the source code the change occurred and if the model of all source code files from the project is necessary, the source code of the whole project needs to be parsed, ii) since our Coevolution approach does not have a SCDM available, we do not know whether a given method call is a component-external method call or a component-internal method call. iii) if the call is a component-external method call our Coevolution approach does not know how to represent the method call on the architecture model, because it is unclear which architectural interfaces and which architectural ports are used to realise the call, and iv) to update the *SEFF* accordingly the *SEFF* needs to be analysed for both: the method `doDownload` and all methods that call the `doDownload` method as well as the methods that call these methods. In our

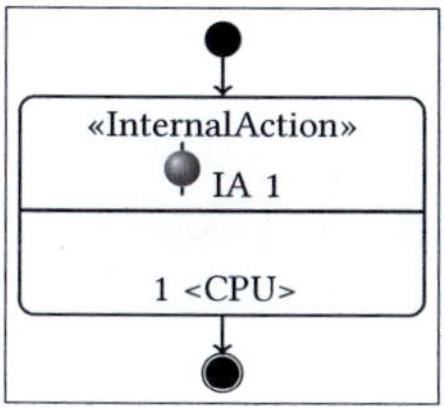

SEFF without component-external method call

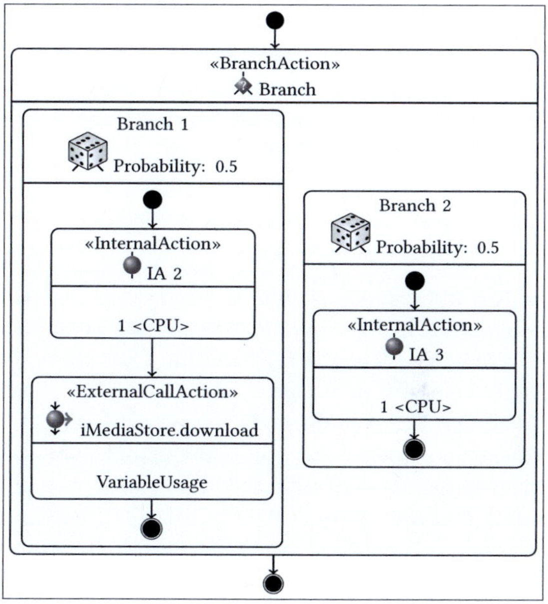

SEFF after a component-external method call has been added

Figure 4.10.: Comparison between the *SEFF* before a new method call has been added (left side) and the reconstructed *SEFF* after the new method call has been added (right side).

example, this means that we need to analyze the `httpDownload` method as well. Within the `httpDownload` the if-else statement needs to be made explicit into a *BranchAction*, because the if branch contains an external method call. Figure 4.10 shows the resulting *SEFF* before the change (left side) and after the change (right side). The figure illustrates that multiple *SEFF* changes can be necessary after one component-external method call has been added to a method.

4.5.2.2. Change-driven Incremental *SEFF* Reconstruction based on the SoMoX *SEFF* Reconstruction

In this section, we propose an approach that solves the above-mentioned challenges and is able to reconstruct a *SEFF* incrementally in an change-driven way. The approach neither needs a SCDM nor the parsed source code of the whole project. Hence, the first challenge is implicitly solved by solving the second and third challenge.

To solve the second challenge, we propose the following approach: Even though no SCDM is available, we can use the current consistency preservation rules as well as the information from the VITRUVIUS correspondence model to classify each method call. Since, the classification of method calls depends on the current consistency preservation rules our classification mechanism is specific for the used mapping. The specific part, however, only applies to the external calls and library calls since internal calls can be found generic, because component-internal calls are those calls which are neither a component-external call nor a library call. This means that we need to have a mapping-specific external call finder as well as a mapping-specific library call finder.

To solve the third challenge, we need to find an approach that is able to find the matching *OperationSignature* and the matching *ProvidedRole* for a component external method call. As for the second challenge, this can be done using the information from the current consistency preservation rules and the VITRUVIUS correspondence model. Hence, this information is mapping-specific as well, because the information how a *ProvideRole* and a source code method is mapped to a *OperationSignature* can vary between different consistency preservation rules.

Hence, we can state that to use an incremental version of the SoMoX *SEFF* creation approach within our Coevolution approach, one needs to implement the following functions specific for the used consistency preservation rules:

- a method call classification that classifies component-external calls and library calls, and
- a matcher that finds the corresponding *OperationSignature* and *RequiredRole* for a component-external call.

To solve the fourth challenge, we propose two different approaches: The first one, recreates the *SEFF* the same way as proposed by Krogmann [Kro12]. The second one, slightly changes the existing *SEFF* reconstruction approach: it makes all method calls that are considered as component-internal calls explicit within the *SEFF*. Both are presented in the following.

Change-driven *SEFF* Reconstruction by Inlining Component-internal Calls
The first approach to solve the fourth challenge including its sub-challenges, creates the same output as the SoMoX *SEFF* reconstruction process. Hence, methods that are considered as component-internal methods are treated the same way as in SoMoX. This means they are inlined within the *SEFF* by default. As mentioned above, Krogmann [Kro12] proposed an optimization of this approach by creating *ResourceDemandingInternalBehaviours* for all methods that are i) considered as component-internal method calls, and ii) called at least twice within the component. In the *SEFF* an *InternalCallAction* is created for the method calls to those component-internal methods. For the internal-method itself a *ResourceDemandingInternalBehaviour* is created. This approach has the advantage that it omits the redundancy of having the same source code method represented in more than one *SEFF*s. If this approach would not be used, a method that is called multiple times would be analysed multiple times and would be represented in multiple *SEFF*s.

To reconstruct *SEFFs* in an incremental, change-driven way and solve the fourth challenge using the approach presented by Krogmann, our Coevolution approach needs to be able to change not only the *ResourceDemanding-Behaviours* elements corresponding to the changed method, but it also needs to be able to reconstruct the actions within *ResourceDemandingBehaviours* for affected methods. Hence, the approach needs to able to change more than one *ResourceDemandingBehaviours* for one change. We first need to decide whether we need to change more than the *SEFF* elements that correspond to the current method. For sub-challenge iv).1 this is the case if either of the following cases is true: i) if a call is added that calls a component-internal method so that this component-internal method is called twice, or ii) if a call has been removed that calls a component-internal method so that the component-internal method is called only once. For sub-challenge iv).2 this is the case if either of the following cases is true: iii) the first component-external method call has been added to a component-internal method, or

iv) the last component-external call has been removed from a component-internal method. If either of these four cases is true, we secondly need to calculate the affected *ResourceDemandingBehaviours.* Since the VITRUVIUS correspondence model contains the correspondence information from a method to its *SEFF* respectively *ResourceDemandingInternalBehaviour,* we can figure out the affected *ResourceDemandingBehaviours* directly by using the VITRUVIUS correspondence model. Since we know all actions that are affected by the change, we also have the information which parts of the corresponding *ResourceDemandingBehaviours* are affected.

As last step, we need to update all affected *ResourceDemandingBehaviours* as shown in Algorithm 2 and described in the following: If the first case (i) is true, our approach creates a *ResourceDemandingInternalBehaviour* for the method that has been called and creates an *InternalCallAction* within the *ResourceDemandingBehaviour* that corresponds to the method that has been changed. Furthermore, it replaces the actions, which correspond to the called method with an *InternalCallAction* to the newly created *ResourceDemandingInternalBehaviour* in their current *ResourceDemandingInternalBehaviour.* Hence, actions that correspond to the method are made explicit in an *ResourceDemandingInternalBehaviour* and this *ResourceDemandingInternalBehaviour* is called in the existing *ResourceDemandingBehaviour,* where the actions were inlined. If the second case (ii) is true, our approach rolls back the steps done for case i). This means, that the corresponding *ResourceDemandingInternalBehaviour* for the method is removed and the actions of it are inlined in the *ResourceDemandingBehaviour,* that calls the *ResourceDemandingInternalBehaviour* using an *InternalCallAction.*

If the third case (iii) is true, we need to create an *ExternalCallAction* in the *ResourceDemandingBehaviour,* which corresponds to the changed method. Furthermore, we need to recreate the *ResourceDemandingBehaviour* of the method that calls the component-internal method and the methods calling this method until we reach a method that directly corresponds to a *SEFF* or a *ResourceDemandingInternalBehaviour.* The reason for that is that the call to the component-internal method can be executed, for instance, within a for-loop or an if statement, which has been abstracted to an *InternalAction* until the new component-external method call has been introduced. However, with the new component-external call action in the component-internal method, this control-flow elements become relevant for the behavioural model as well and need to be made explicit in the *ResourceDemandingBe-*

Algorithm 2 Change-driven *SEFF* reconstruction that inlines component-internal calls

```
Require: changedMethod ← source code method,
    vcm ← VITRUVIUS correspondence model
behaviour ← reconstructBehaviourForMethod(changedMethod)
internalMethodChanged ← ¬vcm.hasSeffFor(changedMethod)
if 2nd overall call to any internal method introduced then
    internalMethod ← getInternalMethodCalledTwice(changedMethod)
    rdib ← createResourceDemandingInternalBehaviourForMethod(internalMethod)
    affectedRBs ← vcm.getCorrespondingResourceBehaviours(internalMethod)
    for all affectedRB ∈ affectedRBs do
        internalCallAction ← newInternalCallActionCalling(rdib)
        affectedRB.replace(rdib.actions, internalCallAction)
else if removed second to last call from any internal method then
    internalMethod ← getInternalMethodCalledOnlyOnce(changedMethod)
    rdibForMethod ← vcm.getCorrespondingBehaviour(internalMethod)
    internalCallAction ← findInternalCallActionThatCalls(rdibForMethod)
    callingBehaviour ← internalCallAction.parentBehaviour
    callingBehaviour.replace(internalCallAction, rdibForMethod.actions)
    delete(rdibForMethod)
else if internalMethodChanged ∧ (first external call added ∨ last external call removed) then
    affectedMethods ← newEmptySet
    invokingMethod ← findInvokingMethod(changedMethod)
    corresponding ← vcm.correspondingBehaviour(calleeMethod)
    while corresponding = ∅ do
        affectedMethods.add(invokingMethod)
        invokingMethod ← findInvokingMethod(changedMethod)
        corresponding ← vcm.correspondingBehaviour(invokingMethod)
    for all affectedMethod ∈ affectedMethods do
        reconstructSEFFforMethod(affectedMethod)
```

haviour. If the fourth case (iv) is true, we need to abstract the method call into an *InternalAction.* As in the third case, we need to recreate the *ResourceDemandingBehaviour* for the current method as well as the *ResourceDemandingBehaviour* that calls the internal method. Again, this has to be done until a method is reached that either corresponds to a *SEFF* or a *ResourceDe-*

mandingInternalBehaviour directly. To figure out, whether a method directly corresponds to either of both or not, we can again use the Vitruvius correspondence model. For methods with a direct correspondence the matching *ResourceDemandingBehaviour* is stored, while for other methods only their actions are stored in the correspondence model.

This approach has the advantage that the abstraction level remains the same as in the original SoMoX *SEFF* reconstruction. However, it has the disadvantage that multiple *ResourceDemandingInternalBehaviours* need to be updated for specific changes, e.g. if the first component-external call has been added to a component-internal method.

Change-driven *SEFF* Reconstruction by making all Component-internal Calls explicit The second approach to solve challenge iv) and its sub-challenges is to change the existing *SEFF* reconstruction approach. Instead of inlining component-internal method calls within the current *ResourceDemanding-Behaviour*, we propose to make every component-internal method explicit within its own *ResourceDemandingInternalBehaviour*. Hence, we create a *ResourceDemandingInternalBehaviour* for each component-internal method if it is called the first time from a method that corresponds either to a *SEFF* or another *ResourceDemandingInternalBehaviour*. In the *ResourceDemandingBehaviour* that corresponds to the actual changed method, we create an *InternalCallAction*, which calls the *ResourceDemandingInternalBehaviour*. During the creation of the *InternalCallAction*, we do not know whether the called *ResourceDemandingInternalBehaviour* will contain a component-external method call in the future. Hence, the surrounding control flow elements of the component-internal method calls are need to made explicit as well, even if the called method does not contain a component-external method call yet. If, for instance, a component-internal method is called within a for-loop, we need to make this for loop explicit in the corresponding *ResourceDemandingBehaviour* as well. Sub-challenge iv).1 is solved since no inlining is done using this approach. Instead every component-internal method is made explicit in a *ResourceDemandingInternalBehaviour*, regardless whether it is called only once or whether it contains a component-external method call. Sub-challenge iv).2 is omitted, as *ResourceDemandingBehaviours* behaviours are made explicit as soon as they are called the first time, i.e. during the development time it cannot occur that more than one *ResourceDemandingBehaviour* is affected by one change. Hence, the challenge that multiple *ResourceDemandingBehaviours* are affected by one change is omitted, since only the *ResourceDemandingBehaviour* is affected that corresponds directly to the changed method.

This approach has the advantage that it usually does not need to deal with the reconstruction of multiple *ResourceDemandingBehaviours* after a single change in one method has been performed by a developer. The reconstruction of multiple *ResourceDemandingBehaviours* after a change needs to be executed only if a change has been performed that introduces the first method call to a method that has not been reconstructed to a *ResourceDemandingBehaviour* yet. In this case, the newly called method is reconstructed first and a *ResourceDemandingInternalBehaviour* for it is created. Furthermore, for component-internal methods and their corresponding actions in the behavioural model neither the inlining strategy into the parent *ResourceDemandingBehaviour* nor the strategy of making them explicit into an own *ResourceDemandingInternalBehaviour* has been done dynamically.

The approach, however, has the disadvantage that abstraction is lost, because every component-internal method that is used is made explicit regardless whether it contains a relevant component-external behaviour or whether it is called at least twice within the component. Hence, the created behavioural model potentially contains unnecessary information, which can make it hard for users of the architectural view to get a quick overview to the insights of a component's behaviour. To overcome this disadvantage, we propose a view that hides unnecessary *ResourceDemandingInternalBehaviours* dynamically by inlining them as follows: In the first step, all *ResourceDemandingInternalBehaviours* that are either only called once within all *ResourceDemandingInternalBehaviour* or only contain *InternalActions* can be inlined into the *ResourceDemandingBehaviour* where they are called. In the next step, control flow elements, such as loops and branches, that internally consists only of *InternalActions* can be composed to one *InternalAction.* In the last step, consecutive *InternalActions* can be merged to one *InternalAction.* This view can be created dynamically from the underlying model and can be shown to users of the behavioural model. This view has the disadvantage, that if users perform a change on the architectural behaviour model we cannot figure out the correct position in the source code where to add the new element respectively to which method a task in the task list should be added. However, we can add the task for the developers to the parent *SEFF.*

4.5.2.3. Mapping-Specific Call Classification and *RequiredRole* Finder for the Package Mapping Consistency Preservation Rules

In this section, we present a mapping-specific call classification and a mapping-specific matcher that finds the matching *RequiredRole* for a component-external call for the package mapping consistency preservation rules we introduced in Section 4.3.2. This, consistency preservation rules map each component to its own package and a class within this package that is the component realisation class.

Call Classification for the Package Mapping Consistency Preservation Rules
Within the package mapping consistency preservation rules, we can define component-external calls with each one of the following definitions:

1. calls, where the called method corresponds to an *OperationSignature*,
2. calls, where the called method corresponds to either an *OperationSignature* or a *SEFF*, or
3. calls, where the destination of the call is an interface method that corresponds to an *OperationSignature* or if the destination of the call is a class whose package or parent package corresponds to another component as the class of the current method.

The first approach has the advantage, that it follows exactly the mapping we defined in Section 4.3.2. Hence, the check whether a call is a component-external call can be done directly using the Vitruvius correspondence model, because the only check that is necessary is whether the destination method corresponds directly to an *OperationSignature*. The disadvantage of this approach, however, is that calls, whose destination is outside of the package but does not fulfill the mapping directly are not covered. Hence, this approach assumes that developers are aware of the consistency preservation rules and only introduce component-external calls by calling the required interfaces directly. Similar to the first approach the second approach assumes that the users are aware of the consistency preservation rules. It adds the possibility to call methods, which are not interface methods but correspond directly to a *SEFF* of another component.

This disadvantage can be overcome when the third approach is used. For the third approach, we define a component-external call as a call that calls a method that is contained within a package that corresponds to a another component as the package of the calling method. This approach, has the advantage that we can figure out if a call has been introduced that is not covered by the current architectural mapping yet. For instance, we can figure out if a developer adds a component-external call that is a call to a class method of another component, that does not correspond to a *OperationSignature* or a *SEFF* and can react accordingly. We will discuss possible reactions to this architecture violations in Section 4.5.2.4. To figure out whether a call is a component-external call, we need to implement a mechanism that returns the corresponding architectural component for a given method. To do so, we use the following approach: First we check, whether the class of the current method is the component realisation class for the current component. If this is not the case and the class does not have any correspondences, we check whether the package of the class corresponds to a component. Again, if this is not the case, we recursively check the parent packages until we find a correspondence to a component. After getting the component of the current method and the component of the called method, we can check whether the call is a component-external call by checking whether the components of the methods are identical or not.

Using the example package mapping consistency preservation rules, a library call is a call to a third party library or a call to the method within the Java language API or a call to method, whose class corresponds to a PCM data type, but not to a component. Hence, to figure out, whether a call is library call or not, we can check whether the class of the called method corresponds to a component. If this is the case the call is not a library call. As mentioned above, calls that are neither component-external calls nor library calls are component-internal calls. Hence, only calls to the methods that are contained in the same component are considered as component-internal calls.

***RequiredRole* Finder for the Package Mapping Consistency Preservation Rules**
Based on the above-specified external call finder, we also need to define a mapping-specific *RequiredRole* finder. In the following, we explain one possibility to do so. The used approach is depicted in Figure 4.11. We propose is an architecture-centric approach, i.e. we use architectural models and the

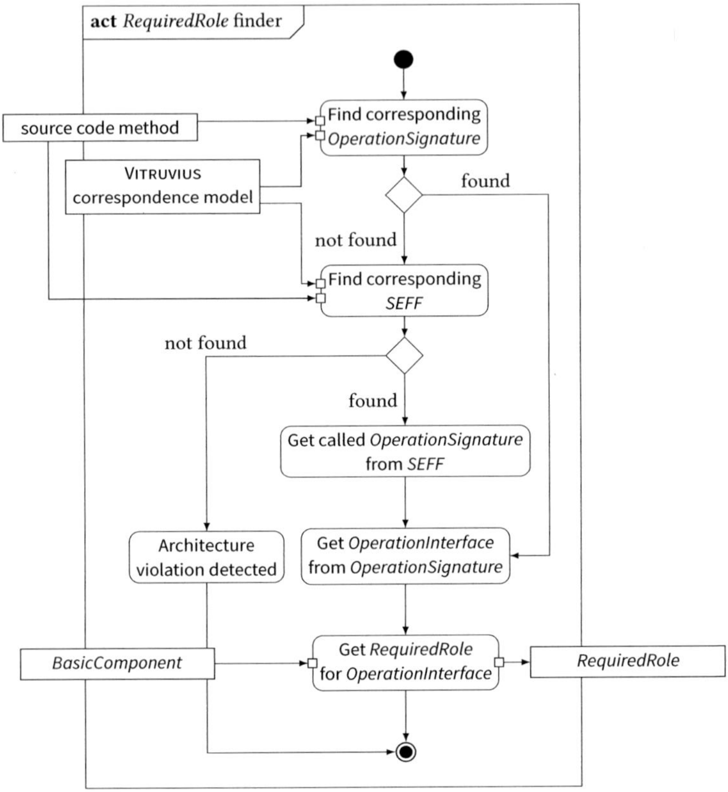

Figure 4.11.: Activity diagram that shows, how the *RequiredRole* finder for the package mapping consistency preservation rules is realised. The input for *RequiredRole* finder are the changed source code method, the VITRUVIUS correspondence model, and the current PCM *BasicComponent*. The output is the corresponding *RequiredRole*, which is used by the method call. We left out the object flow inside the activity diagram to simplify the diagram and improve its clarity.

existing correspondence model elements, in order to find the *RequiredRole*. The source code elements are only used as helper elements in order to find the corresponding architectural elements.

The first step, is to figure out which *OperationSignature* corresponds to the called method respectively which architectural *OperationInterface* has been used for the call. To do so, the approach checks whether the called method directly corresponds to an *OperationSignature*. If this is not the case, the approach checks whether the called method corresponds to a *SEFF*. If this is the case, we can get the *OperationSignature* that is called from the *SEFF*. If a called method neither corresponds to an *OperationSignature* nor to a *SEFF*, we consider the change as an architecture violation. How we can react to this kind of architecture violation is explained in the next section. If we detected an architecture violation, we end the lookup for a *RequiredRole*. If we found an *OperationSignature*, we can get its *OperationInterface*, i.e. we can retrieve the *OperationInterface* that has been used for the call. As next step, we need to figure out which concrete *RequiredRole* of the component has been used to perform the call. This can be done by iterating over all *RequiredRoles* of the source component and use the first *RequiredRole* that requires the interface. We can use this *RequiredRole* as the *RequiredRole*, which is used for the component-external call. This approach, however, has two disadvantages: To make sure that the used *ProvidedRole* can be determined automatically, it adds the limitation that each component is allowed to require each interface only once. To overcome this disadvantage, we could slightly change the iteration over all *RequiredRoles* of a component. Instead of taking the first matching *RequiredRole*, we can continue the iteration and collect all matching *RequiredRoles*. If more than one *RequiredRole* matches, we can ask the users to disambiguate which *RequiredRole* is actually used for the call. The concept of user change disambiguation and their different levels are described in Section 4.4. The second disadvantage is that this approach does not check, whether the performed method call actually uses the field that corresponds to the *RequiredRole* to execute the external call. A simplified approach that checks whether the field is used for the call can be implemented within the component-realisation class, because we can check whether the call uses the field directly.

4.5.2.4. Detecting Architecture Violation using the Change-driven Incremental *SEFF* Reconstruction

As outlined above, our change-driven incremental *SEFF* reconstruction, is able to react and hinder architecture violations that can occur from wrong component-external method calls. If a developers adds a method call to a different method our *SEFF* reconstruction approach classifies this method call. If it is a component-external method call our Coevolution approach finds the corresponding *OperaitonSignature* and the used *RequiredRole* on architectural level.

The first possible violation is that a corresponding *OperationSignature* is found for the called method, but no *RequiredRole* can be found. The violation in this case is that the current component does not require the called method respectively its interface yet. A simple solution is to just add a *RequiredRole* from the *OperationInterface* to the component performing the method call. However, this would probably violate the current consistency preservation rules since be a specific mapping could exist that specifies how *RequiredRoles* are mapped to the source code. Consider our package mapping consistency preservation rules: using these rules a *RequiredRole* is represented by a field in the component-realisation class. For these consistency preservation rules the violation can be solved by creating a new field in the component-realisation class and ensure that the performed call uses this field to execute the method call.

The second possible violation is that no *OperationSignature* can be found for the called method. Hence, the called method is not part of the offered services of the called component. This means, that the method, which has been called, should probably not be used from external components. To preserve consistency and avoid the architecture violation in this case, the following strategies are possible: One possibility is that we roll back the change of the developers and inform them that the method they just called should not be called from outside of the destination component itself. Another possibility is to add the called method to the provided interface of the called component automatically and inform users that their change let to the creation of a new *OperationSignature*. Another option is to ask the users whether the *OperationSignature* should be added for the new call or whether the change in the source code should be rolled back. Hence, a corresponding *OperationSignature* can be found after doing this and our approach can execute the same steps that are executed that are executed for the first architecture violation. Within the second step the users need to disambiguate the change,i.e. software developers and software architects need to clarify whether the method call should be allowed.

In our prototypical implementation, we inform the users which kind of architecture violation has been detected. We currently do not support an automatic solving of the architecture violations.

4.5.2.5. Implementation of the Change-driven Incremental *SEFF* Reconstruction

We implemented the change-driven incremental *SEFF* reconstruction for the package mapping consistency preservation rules within our Coevolution approach. For the implementation, we implemented respectively reused the following mechanisms: To react on changes that have been performed to a method body within the source code, we reused the implementation of Seifermann [Sei14] and Messinger [Mes14]. As next step, we refined the call classification strategy interface, which is used by the *SEFF* reconstruction of SoMoX, to detect component-external calls, library calls and internal calls. In particular, we extended the existing basic classification strategy in a way that it is possible to add mapping-specific classification strategies easily.

For the behavioural reconstruction itself, we implemented the approach that makes all component-internal method calls explicit. This has the advantage that we do not need to parse more than one source code file for each method body change. Furthermore, we only need to reconstruct the *ResourceDemandingBehaviour* for the changed method. The reason for this decision is that we want to avoid the need of parsing more than one source code files after each change. Hence, the output models we generate are different from the output models SoMoX generates. As mentioned above, this disadvantage can be overcome by creating a new view onto the reconstructed *SEFF*.

4.5.2.6. Example of Change-driven Incremental *SEFF* Reconstruction using the Package Mapping Consistency Preservation Rules

In this section, we present an example of the change-driven incremental *SEFF* reconstruction using the package mapping consistency preservation rules. For the *SEFF* reconstruction, we use the approach of making the calls to component-internal methods explicit within the *SEFFs* respectively the *ResourceDemandingInternalBehaviours*.

```
public File httpDownload(Request request){
  if(RequestHelper.isValid(request)){
  }else{
        logger.warn("Request␣" + request + "is␣not␣valid");
        return null;}
}
```

Listing 13: The `download` method after the first change

As example code, we use the code introduced in Section 4.5.2.6. For the explanation of the change-driven incremental *SEFF* reconstruction, we focus on the following steps: At first, we consider changes in the `httpDownload` method. Here we focus on the change that introduces the component-internal method call to `doDownload` method. As second step, we consider the same change, we used in Section 4.5.2.6. Hence, a new component-external call is added to the `doDownload` method.

Let us assume that neither the method `httpDownload` nor the method `doDownload` contain any code. As first implementation steps let us assume that a developer adds the if-else block and the logging statement to the `httpDownload` method. The resulting `httpDownload` method is depicted in Listing 13: After our Coevolution approach detects the changes it creates respectively updates the corresponding *SEFF*. Therefore, it classifies the newly introduced method calls using the Vitruvius correspondence model and the mapping-specific classification for the package mapping consistency preservation rules. Using this classification mechanism gives us the information that the calls `isValid` and `log` are considered as library calls, because the classes, of the method are neither corresponding to a different component directly nor they are contained in another component. Hence, our incremental *SEFF* reconstruction approach creates one *InternalAction* for the method calls within the corresponding *SEFF*. The left side of Figure 4.12 shows the corresponding *SEFF* after the first steps.

As next implementation step, we consider the addition of the call to the `doDownload` method within the `httpDownload` method. After this change the resulting `httpDownload` method contains the code in Listing 14: Again, after this change is detected the *SEFF* for the `httpDownload` method is analysed by our incremental *SEFF* reconstruction. Using the Vitruvius correspondence

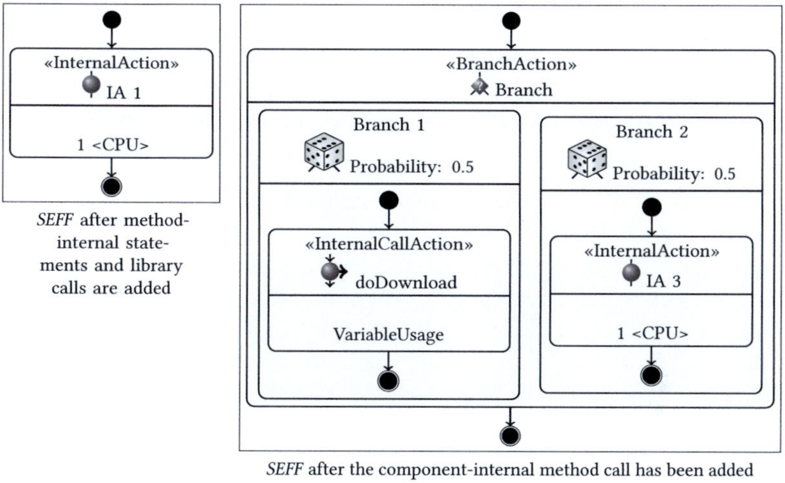

Figure 4.12.: The resulting *SEFF* of the incremental SEFF creation from the `download` method. On the left side the result after the first two changes is depicted. These changes introduce library calls or method internal statements only. The right side shows the result after the third change. This change introduces the component-internal method call to the `doDownload`.

```
public File httpDownload(Request request){
  if(RequestHelper.isValid(request)){
        File file = this.doDownload(request);
        return file;
  }else{
        logger.warn("Request␣" + request + "is␣not␣valid");
        return null;}
}
```

Listing 14: The download method after the call to the `doDownload` method has been inserted

model gives us the information that `doDownload` is considered as component-internal method call because the class of the target method `doDownload` is neither a component-external call nor a library call.

```
private File doDownload(Request request){
  String[] id = RequestHelper.getId(request);
}
```

Listing 15: The `doDownload` method after the first change

Since this is the first call to `doDownload` method, we create a corresponding *ResourceDemandingInternalBehaviour* for the `doDownload` method. The reconstructed *ResourceDemandingInternalBehaviour* for the `doDownload` method is empty because the method does not contain any statements yet. Since component-internal method calls are made explicit the corresponding *SEFF* contains an *InternalCallAction*, that calls the newly created *ResourceDemandingInternalBehaviour*. Since the method call is contained in an if-else branch, the *SEFF* reconstruction also makes this if-else branch explicit within a *BranchAction* in the corresponding *SEFF*. The resulting corresponding *SEFF* is depicted in Figure 4.12.

As next step, we consider the changes in the currently empty method `doDownload`. As first change in the method we assume that a developer adds the `getId` call to the method, which results in the following method: After our Coevolution approach has detected the change in the method it recreates the new behaviour for the *ResourceDemandingInternalBehaviour*. Therefore, it first uses the VITRUVIUS correspondence model to classify the method call, which is classified as library call since the class of the called method is neither contained in any component nor corresponds to an architectural interface. This means, that we can create a corresponding *InternalAction* for the method call. Hence, the resulting *ResourceDemandingInternalBehaviour* contains only an *InternalAction* (see left side of Figure 4.13).

As next change we assume, that the check whether the length of the array `id` is null or not, which changes the method to: Again, our Coevolution approach detects this change and updated corresponding *ResourceDemandingInternalBehaviour*. Since the change does neither introduce a new component-external method call nor a component-internal method call, our Coevolution approach merges the resulting *InternalAction* with the created *InternalAction* for the first change. Hence, the resulting *ResourceDemandingInternalBehaviour* is not changed and still looks as depicted on the left side of Figure 4.13.

```
private File doDownload(Request request){
  String[] id = RequestHelper.getId(request);
  if(id == null || id.length == 0)
       return null;
}
```

Listing 16: The doDownload method after the second change

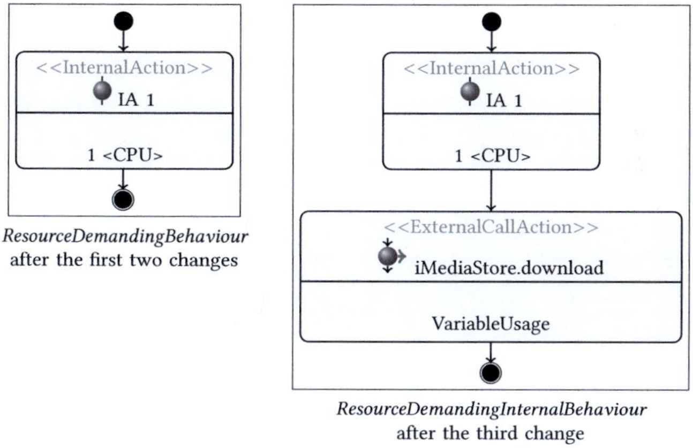

Figure 4.13.: The resulting *ResourceDemandingInternalBehaviour* of the incremental SEFF creation from the doDownload method. On the left side the result after the first two changes is depicted. On the right side the result after the third change, which inserts the call to the download method of the IMediaStore interface, is depicted.

As next change we assume, that the return statement that executes the call to the download method of the field iMediaStore is added by a developer. This change gives us the following method: After our Coevolution approach has detected this change, it runs the *SEFF* reconstruction for the doDownload method again and classifies, amongst the other method calls, the newly introduced method call. Therefore, it uses the Vitruvius correspondence model, which contains the information that the download method corresponds to the *OperationSignature download* in the *OperationInterface IMediaStore*. Hence, our Coevolution approach identifies the call to the download method as component-external method call and creates an *ExternalCallAction* in the

```
private File doDownload(Request request){
  String[] id = RequestHelper.getId(request);
  if(id == null || id.length == 0)
       return null;
  return this.iMediaStore.download(id)[0];
}
```

Listing 17: The `doDownload` method after the third change

ResourceDemandingInternalBehaviour that corresponds to the `doDownload` method. The resulting *ResourceDemandingInternalBehaviour*, which is depicted at the right side of Figure 4.13, now contains one *InternalAction* and one *ExternalCallAction*.

The difference between the resulting incrementally created *SEFF* and its called *ResourceDemandingInternalBehaviour* and the introduced *SEFF* in the example of the Figure 4.10 is that the change-driven incremental *SEFF* reconstruction creates a *ResourceDemandingInternalBehaviour* for the `doDownload` method and an *InternalCallAction* for the method call to the *doDownload* method instead of inlinig it in the *SEFF*.

4.5.3. Coevolution of Behavioural Architectural Models and Source Code

In the sections above, we described independently from each other how we can i) keep behaviour models consistent with the code by describing the mapping from the behaviour model to the source code, and ii) reconstruct behaviour models from code using a change-driven incremental *SEFF* reconstruction approach. To integrate the two approaches into a coevolution process, we propose two different approaches. The first one works as follows: After a change occurred in the architectural behaviour model, our Coevolution approach creates a task in the task list for developers and point to the method that needs to be changed. If developers changing this method in a later step, our Coevolution approach recreates the architectural behaviour of the method. Since, we recreate the corresponding *ResourceDemandingBehaviour*, we override changes that have been performed in the architecture and that are not implemented in the corresponding code yet. This has the advantage that the behavioural model represents the implemented code as soon as the source code has been changed. However, it has the disadvantages that developers can include component-external method calls without getting informed that these calls are not intended by the architecture. This approach is an code-centric approach, because the incremental *SEFF* creation overrides architectural changes to the *SEFF* with the actual reconstructed *SEFF* elements.

The second approach, we propose, is an improved approach that overcomes the disadvantage of the first approach for component-external method calls within a *ResourceDemandingBehaviour*. The reason that we focus on component-external method calls is that usually the implementation of component-internal behaviour falls into the scope of the component-developer. To check whether the component-external behaviour of a *ResourceDemandingBehaviour* has been changed we propose the following approach: Instead of recreating the corresponding *ResourceDemandingBehaviour*, a comparison between the existing *ResourceDemandingBehaviour* and the newly created *ResourceDemandingBehaviour* can be performed. If the result of the comparison is that the existing *ResourceDemandingBehaviour* is different than the recreated one regarding the component-external behaviour, we first check whether a task in the task lists for this method exists that requires to add or remove a component-external method call. If this is true and if the change meets that requirement, we can remove the task from the task list automatically and use the new *ResourceDemandingBehaviour* in the architectural model. If this is not the case, our Coevolution approach can warn developers and architects that an inconsistency has been found and they need to decide whether the code should be changed or the behavioural model should be replaced with the new *ResourceDemandingBehaviour*.

4.6. Consistency Preservation Rules between Architectural Models and Code

To use our Coevolution approach, bidirectional consistency preservation rules between the architectural elements and source code elements are necessary to enable coevolution of source code and architectural models. As example consistency preservation rules, we already introduced the package mapping consistency preservation rules in Section 4.3.2. In this section, we introduce source code technology-specific bidirectional consistency preservation rules between architectural models and source code. As example of source code specific technologies, we use EJB as well as a dependency injection framework. We, furthermore, introduce consistency preservation rules between two different architectural models and source code. In particular, we introduce bidirectional consistency preservation rules between architectural models and Eclipse plugin artefacts in terms of the manifest files and Eclipse plugin.xml files, which are related to OSGi bundles.

All consistency preservation rules, we introduced, are reusable and extendable. The latter means that they can be extended for other project-specific or technology-specific bidirectional consistency preservation rules. The defined consistency preservation rules address the second scientific challenges of this chapter, as they can be used to close the abstraction gap between architectural models and source code.

4.6.1. Source Code Technology Specific Consistecncy Preservation Rules

To develop a software system, specific technologies or frameworks are often used to simplify the development of the software system. For Java projects, EJB and dependency injection frameworks are two examples of such technologies. As we explained in Section 2.5, both of the technologies are standardized and widely used. Within this section, we introduce consistency preservation rules between the architectural model PCM and source code using EJBs respectively a dependency injection framework. For both sets of the consistency preservation rules, we are able to partly reuse the package mapping consistency preservation rules.

4.6.1.1. Mapping between PCM as Architectural Model and EJB-based Source Code

For the EJB consistency preservation rules, we can partly reuse the package mapping consistency preservation rules, especially for the mapping from architecture to source code. For the mapping from source code to architecture, we can reuse them as well, but due to the use of EJB, we introduce an extension for the consistency preservation rules as follows. As EJB already defines components on code level, we can distinguish easily, which class should be used as a component-realising class, i.e. it is possible to have more EJB component-realising classes within one package. In the standard package-consistency preservation rules, however, it is only possible to have one component-realising class per package. Furthermore, we focus on the *Repository*, because we can derive the PCM *System*. To do so, we assume that each component within a *Repository* is instantiated exactly once.

Becker [Bec08] already presented a mapping between the PCM and EJB-based Java code. As we discussed for the package mapping consistency preservation rules (see Section 4.3.2) the mappings proposed by Becker make the *RequireRoles* explicit. Hence, it is possible to map all valid PCM models to Java source code. Furthermore, the mapping proposed by Becker introduces a component framework into Java source code. The understandability of the code, however, may be lowered as the mapping introduces additional classes into the source code. The additional generated classes are not an issue if the code is only generated in order to perform performance predictions or to generate code stubs. However, it becomes an issue if developers should be allowed to change existing architectural elements respectively create new architecture elements through the code. This is the reason, why we implemented a different mapping between PCM and EJB-based Java code. The mappings, however, are similar because both mappings using EJB-based Java code. For instance, a component is mapped to a class annotated with an EJB annotation.

Bidirectional Consistency Preservation Rules for Static Architecture and Source Code An overview of the bidirectional consistency preservation rules between the PCM *Repository* and EJB based source code is given in Table 4.3. From the package mapping consistency preservation rules, we reuse the mappings for *Repository*, *OperationSignatures & Parameters*, *ProvidedRoles*, *SEFFs*, and the *DataTypes*.

Hence, from an architectural perspective the interesting bidirectional consistency preservation rules are the rules for *BasicComponents*, *OperationInterfaces*, and *RequiredRoles*. For *BasicComponents*, which are added to the *Repository*, we create a new package and an EJB component class within this package. The created component class is marked as a EJB component class by adding the `Stateless` annotation. For *OperationInterfaces* that are added to the Repository, we create a new code interface in the contracts package and mark it as EJB interface by adding the `Remote` annotation. Changes to the features of *BasicComponents* and *OperationInterfaces* in the architecture or source code, can be kept consistent as in the package mapping consistency preservation rules, i.e. by updating the values of the corresponding changed features (e.g. the name feature) or by executing the matching consistency preservation operation for the changed reference (e.g. adding a new *ProvideRole*). If users only use the source code editor to evolve the software system, we create the architectural components and architectural interfaces as soon as the code structure matches the described mapping.

To ease the creation of architectural elements using the source code only, however, we propose softened consistency preservation rules for the transformation from code to architecture for *BasicComponents* and *OperationInterfaces.* This means that every class with one of the EJB component annotations (`@Stateless`, `@Stateful`, or `@MessageDriven`) is considered as a *BasicComponent.* Hence, as soon as one of the annotations is added to respectively removed from a class a new *BasicComponent* will be created respectively the existing *BasicComponent* will be deleted. This has the consequence, that one package can contain more than one *BasicComponent*, because users can create a class in the source code and add one of the component annotations to mark it as an EJB component. This leads to the challenge that it is unclear, which is the main component of this package and it is unclear for new classes that are added to a package, which contains more than one component classes, to which component they belong. It can be necessary to know to which component a class belongs for a) the execution of the incremental *SEFF* creation, and b) possible new views such as the component-class-implementation view from the Vitruvius vision (see Figure 4.4). To circumvent this, we propose the following possible solution: we decide that the main EJB component class of the package is the class that corresponds to the package itself, i.e. to the *BasicComponent* that fulfills the non-softened consistency preservation rules. If no *BasicComponent* corresponds to the package directly, we as ask the users to clarify which *BasicComponent* is the main EJB class of this package. A similar approach can be used for the new classes: they belong to the same BasicComponent as the main EJB class of the package. If no main EJB class exists, we can ask users to clarify to which *BasicComponent* the new class should belong. The fact that architectural relevant interfaces and architectural relevant components can be created at any time respectively that any class or interface can become architectural relevant has the disadvantage that all locations in the code, where the newly architectural relevant element is referenced, needs to be investigated. The reason is that after such a change other elements can be architectural relevant as well. For instance, if an interface is marked with the `@Remote` annotation it becomes architectural relevant immediately. All classes implementing this interface and corresponding to a *BasicComponent* need to make the implementation relation explicit in the architecture, i.e. a new *OperationProvideRole* needs to be created. In our prototypical implementation, however, we did not implement this behaviour, i.e. we assume that all architectural relevant elements are made explicit upon their creation respectively before they are used elsewhere.

A further softening is done for interfaces. As soon as either the `@Local` or `@Remote` annotation is added to a code interface, we consider it as an architectural relevant interface and create a corresponding *OperationInterface*. This is done even if the interface is not contained within the contracts package.

A possibility to realise the proposed mappings without softening of the mapping is the following: Instead of creating a *BasicComponent* for each class as soon as one component annotations has been added respectively creating an interface as soon as either the Remote or Local annotation is added the mapping could be forced. To do so, the EJB classes could be moved automatically to a new package and the EJB interfaces could be moved automatically to the contracts package.

For *RequiredRoles* in the architecture model, we create a private field in the class which corresponds to the requiring *BasicComponent*. The field has the type of the interface that corresponds to required *OperationInterface* and the name of the *RequiredRole*. For the mapping form code to architecture the mapping is straight forward: as soon as the `@EJB` or `@Inject` annotation has been added to a field that has a type which corresponds to an interface, we create a *RequiredRole*. A softening of this mapping is to consider a field that has a type corresponding to an *OperationInterface* as *RequiredRole* and make it explicit in the architecture. This approach allows developers to use of other EJB mechanisms to fulfill the required interfaces of a class. In EJB-based source code it is, for instance, possible to use the `lookup` method

PCM element	EJB language element
Repository	three *packages*: main, contracts, data types
Basic Component	Package in main *package* and public class that is an EJB component class annotated with `@Stateless`
Interface	*Interface* with the EJB Annotation `@Remote` in the contracts package
Signature&Parameters	*Methods&parameters*
CompositeDatatype	*Class* with getter and setter for inner types
CollectionDatatypes	*Class* that inherits from a Java collection type (e.g. `ArrayList`)
ProvidedRole	the EJB component class of the providing component implements the EJB interface
RequiredRole	a private field within the EJB component class with a) the type of the corresponding code interface, and b) the annotation `@EJB`
SEFF	*Method* in the EJB component class that implements the corresponding interface

Table 4.3.: Mapping between PCM *Repository* metamodel elements and EJB language elements. We are able to reuse the mapping for the *Repository, CompositeDatatypes, CollectionDatatypes, ProvidedRoles, SEFFs.* and *Signatures&Parameters* from the package mapping consistency preservation rules.

from the `context` class of the EJB container to decide which EJB class is used as implementation class for a field. This can be done during the runtime of a system, i.e. in this case, it is not possible to determine statically, which actual component-class is used for the field.

Figure 4.14 shows the realisation of a *BasicComponent* and its provided and required *OperationInterfaces* in source code (see Figure 4.8). The mapping is similar as the mapping shown for the package mapping consistency preservation rules. For EJB, however, we add the EJB relevant annotations.

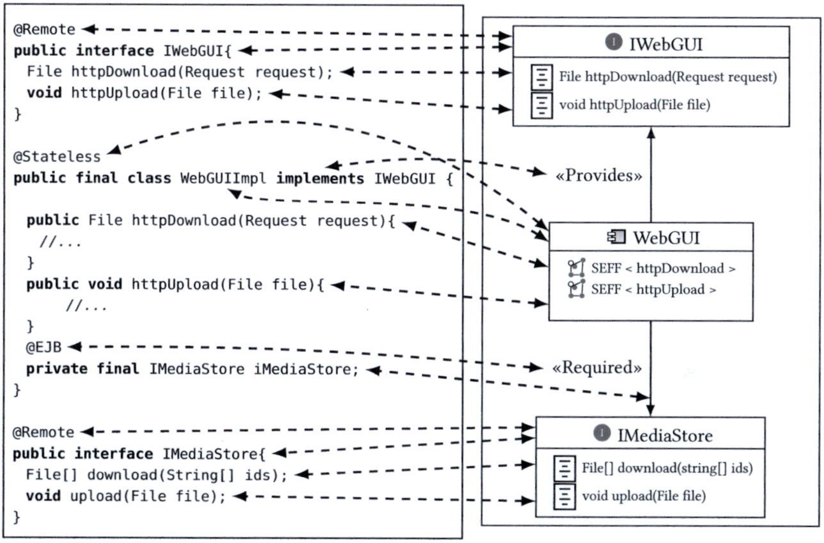

Figure 4.14.: The mapping between a *BasicComponent* and its provided and required *OperationInterfaces* to the corresponding source code elements using the EJB mapping consistency preservation rules.

Behavioural Coevolution As we explained in Section 4.5, we need to define a mapping-specific call classification and a mapping-specific required role finder to enable the incremental creation of the behaviour models in terms of the PCM *SEFF*. Since component-external method calls in EJB components can only be performed via the fields that are annotated with `@EJB` respectively `@Inject` and the destination needs to be a source code interface, we propose the following approach to define an EJB specific external call finder: All method calls that are executed using a field that is annotated with either `@EJB` or `@Inject` or a field, with the type of an EJB remote interface, are component-external method calls. Hence, it is easy to find component-external method calls if the field is used directly to execute the method call. Using this approach, the definition of a mapping-specific required role finder is also rather easy, because we have a corresponding *RequiredRole* for the used field.

If no field is used directly for the component-external method call, our Coevolution approach needs to decide whether this component-external method call is an architectural violation or not. The component-external call is no architectural violation if the component-external method call is executed directly or indirectly using a field of the EJB component-class. This is the case, for instance, if the field is passed as a parameter to another method and the parameter is than used to execute the component-external method call. Due to the halting problem it is not possible to decide, whether the call is executed using a field indirectly, using static code analysis only. Hence, using our incremental *SEFF* reconstruction approach, we could implement an over-approximation approach that considers only those calls as non-architectural violation for which the approach can decide for sure that these calls are executed using an EJB relevant field directly or indirectly.

Another approach is to detect constructor calls to EJB component-classes and consider these as architectural violation, i.e. constructor calls to classes contained in different EJB component would be forbidden using this approach. Hence, calls to other components cannot be performed using an instance that has been created using a constructor call. For the component-external method call detection this means, that we can be sure that the external-method calls, which are not executed using an EJB relevant field directly using an instance that is not created using a constructor call of another component. Hence, these calls than can be considered as regular component-external method calls. A limitation of this approach is that it does not guarantee that the detected calls are executed using the field indirectly because other approaches, such as reflection, could have been used to create an instance of an EJB class.

One limitation of the proposed approaches, is that if an EJB class requires the same EJB interface more than once, i.e. the class has more than one field with the same interface type, we cannot decide in all cases, which field has been used to execute the call (if the field is not used directly for the call). For the incremental *SEFF* reconstruction this means, that we cannot decide which *RequiredRole* should be used for the *ExternalCallAction* in the *SEFF*. In this case, we need to ask the users of our Coevolution approach to clarify, which *RequiredRole* shall be used.

For our prototypical implementation of the EJB incremental *SEFF* reconstruction, we implemented the second approach, because it introduces little overhead during the incremental *SEFF* reconstruction. During the analyses of a method, we only need to check whether a call is a constructor call to another EJB component. If a call to a constructor of a class within a different component is detected, we inform users about the introduced architectural violation.

To keep changes on behavioural architectural elements consistent with the source code, we reuse the approach from the package mapping consistency preservation rules. Hence, for changes performed to PCM *SEFFs*, we create tasks for the developers, who are responsible for implementing the behavioural models.

Assumptions and Limitations The proposed bidirectional consistency preservation rules to EJB code come with a number of assumptions and limitations.

Using the non-softened consistency preservation rules, the first assumption is that only the annotations `@EJB` and `@Inject` are used to inject dependencies into EJB components. Hence, using the non-softened consistency preservation rules, we are able not able to find the use of external interfaces that use *lookups* in the `context` class of the EJB container.

We also assume that only source code is used to describe the EJB dependencies. This means we are not considering XML descriptors yet.

A limitation for the EJB code is that we only support the definition of EJB business interfaces and EJB components. Annotations, such as `@Entity`, `@Table`, or `@PersistenceContext`, which are foreseen by EJB and provide support for the communication with a database, are not supported by the presented consistency preservation rules.

A further limitation is that the consistency preservation rules currently not support event-based communication. Event-based communication, however, is supported by EJB. PCM offers an extension that supports event-based communication as well (see [Rat13]). Hence, in future work, the consistency preservation rules can be extended using the PCM event and the EJB event mechanism in order to support event-based communication within the consistency preservation rules.

A limitation on the architectural level is that we do not support *CompositeComponents*, which are components that contain other components. In future work this limitation could be overcome by, for instance, combining EJB classes respectively components that are in the same package to a *CompositeComponent*. Another limitation on architectural level is, that we not support the PCM *System* explicit. Instead, we assume that each component in the *Repository* is instantiated once. Hence, we can can generate the *System* implicitly. This adds the following limitation to the *Repository*: each *OperationInterface* is only allowed to be provided once in the *Repository* to be able to decide which component-class shall be used for the dependency injection for the fields annotated with `@EJB`

An assumption for the incremental *SEFF* reconstruction and its architecture violation capability is that it works only correct if users do not use other features of the language, to create an instance of a class that is contained within another component. If, for instance, users use reflection in order to create an instance of a class, our current approach would not detect this kind of architectural violation. It would also create a wrong *SEFF*, if reflection is used to invoke component-external method call.

4.6.1.2. Mapping between Architectural Models and Source Code using a Dependency Injection Framework

In this section, we present source code technology-specific consistency preservation rules between the PCM and source code that is built using a dependency injection framework. This section is based on the bachelor's thesis of Monev [Mon15], where the proposed consistency preservation rules were implemented.

As dependency injection framework, we use Google Guice. The main reason for that decision is, that Google Guice allows us to assemble the dependency injection classes within the Java code itself instead of composing them within other artefacts, such as XML files. Hence, the presented consistency preservation rules are partly specific for Google Guice. Since dependency injection frameworks, however, are standardized in JSR330, parts of the proposed consistency preservation rules can be reused for all dependency injection frameworks that conform to the standard. The parts that are reusable as well as the difference between Google Juice and the JSR330 standard are explained below.

Bidirectional Consistency Preservation Rules between Static Architecture and Static Code For most elements, we are able to reuse the consistency preservation rules, we defined for the package mapping consistency preservation rules (see Section 4.3.2). To map a PCM *Repository* to code, we only need to change the consistency preservation operation for *BasicComponents*. For the source code to PCM mapping, we need to extend the consistency preservation rules for classes and for constructors. For the mapping of a *BasicComponent*, we extend the existing consistency preservation operation and create an `@Inject` annotation to the constructor of the component-realising class. Hence, we use `constructor` injection to inject the dependencies of a component-realising class. The reason for `constructor` injection instead of, for instance, injecting the dependencies via `setters`, is that we decided to compose the component-realising classes at the initialisation of the system. For the mapping from source code to architecture, we adapt the class mapping in a way that it automatically creates a constructor with the `@Inject` annotation as soon as the users decide that the class should be a component-realising class. We furthermore adapted the consistency preservation operation for constructor, in order to ensure that only one constructor with an `@Inject` annotation exists. This is a requirement from the dependency injection framework we use. Hence, the bidirectional consistency preservation rules between the PCM *Repository* and its corresponding source code only need slight changes to support a dependency injection framework.

To compose the component-realising classes respectively to assemble the classes, we can partly reuse the mapping between a PCM *System* and the composition class. Hence, as in the package mapping consistency preservation rules, a PCM *System* maps to one package and one *System*-realising class. The *System*-realising class for the mapping to the Google Guice dependency injection framework, can be implemented in two ways: It either needs to extend the class `AbstractModule` or it needs to implement the interface `Module`. The class `AbstractModule`, as well as the interface `Module`, are provided by the Google Guice framework and allow the binding respectively assembling of classes that are used within a software system and have constructors or setters marked with `@Inject`. Hence, they allow us to assemble the component-realising classes. If the *System*-realising class extends the class `AbstractModule`, it needs to override the method `configure`. If the *System*-realising class implements the interface `Module`, it needs to implement the method `configure`. In the latter case the `configure` method gets an instance of the `Binder` class as parameter, while in the first case the instance of the `Binder` class is part of the superclass `AbstractModule`. In both cases, the `configure` method is automatically called by the Google Guice framework and needs to do the actual binding of classes. For our mapping between the PCM *System* and source code this means that within this method both artefacts are mapped: the *AssemblyContexts* and the *Connectors*.

The *AssemblyContexts* are mapped to the binding of an interface to a class, i.e. an interface is bound to a component-realising class. The consistency preservation operation, creates an *AssemblyContext* for the component that corresponds to the component-realising class. The *Connectors* between *ProvidedRoles* and *RequiredRoles* in the *System* are mapped implicitly by connecting the provided interfaces of the *AssemblyContexts* to the matching required interfaces within the *System*. Hence, each interface can only be provided once and required once within one *System*. Implementing the presented consistency preservation rules between a PCM *System* and the code statements is not straight forward, as we are currently not able to use source code statements within a method body as corresponding elements. Hence, Monev [Mon15] implemented the consistency preservation as follows: The actual corresponding elements between the architectural elements *AssemblyContexts* and *Connectors*, is the `configure` method itself. If the `configure` method has been changed, we compare the old method with the new method in order to figure out which change has been performed. If elements in the PCM *System* are changed, we analyse the `configure` method in order to figure out how it needs to be updated in order to preserve the consistency.

OperationInterfaces that are provided by the *System* are mapped as follows: the *System*-realising class implements the Java interfaces that corresponds to the *OperationInterface*. Furthermore, the *System*-realising class gets a field with the type of the interface and a constructor with the `@Inject` annotation. Hence, the actual used implementation is injected. The connection of the provided roles of a *System*-realising class with the component-realising class is also done in the configure method of the *System*-realising class. To use the *System*, from e.g. a `main` method, the *System* class can be instantiated using the standard Guice mechanism.

```
public class MediaStoreSystemImpl implements IWebGUI, Module {

   private IWebGUI iWebGUI;

   public MediaStoreSystemImpl() {}

   @Inject
   public MediaStoreSystemImpl(final IWebGUI iWebGUI) {
      this.iWebGUI = iWebGUI;
   }

   @Override
   public void configure(final Binder binder) {
      binder.bind(IWebGUI.class).to(WebGUIImpl.class);
      binder.bind(IMediaStore.class).to(MediaStoreImpl.class);
   }

   @Override
   public File httpDownload(final Request request) {
      return this.iWebGUI.httpDownload(request);
   }

   @Override
   public void httpUplopad(final File file) {
      this.iWebGUI.httpUplopad(file);
   }
}
```

Listing 18: System-realisation class of the MediaStore example

Listing 18 shows the *System*-realisation class for the MediaStore example, we use throughout this thesis. In the listing, we implement the class `Module` directly instead of extending the class `AbstractModule`.

Coevolution of Behavioural Models with Source Code For the coevolution of the behavioural model, we can use a similar approach as for the EJB rules. Since we know which fields are injected using the dependency injection, we can identify external calls, which are executed via this fields, rather easily. If these fields are not directly used, we can use the same approach as for EJB consistency preservation rules. Hence, we forbid constructor calls to classes that have a corresponding *BasicComponent* and consider component-external calls as architecture relevant component-external calls. We further assume, that this calls are executed using a injected field directly or indirectly. This allows us create an *ExternalCallAction*, using the *RequiredRole* corresponding to the field, in the incrementally created *SEFF*.

To keep changes on behavioural architectural elements consistent, we use the same approach as for the EJB and package mapping consistency preservation rules: tasks for the developers, who are responsible for implementing the behavioural models are created as soon as a behavioural model element has been changed.

Compatibility with the JSR 330 standard As we explained in Section 2.5.3 the JSR 330 standard is a standard for dependency injection frameworks.

Since the above-mentioned consistency preservation rules focus on Google Guice, they are as compatible to the JSR 330 standard as Google Guice is. According to the Google Guice online documentation [4] the Guice implementation is one of the references implementations of the JSR 330 standard and most annotations are interchangeable. Important for the above-mentioned consistency preservation rules is that the `@Inject` annotation is interchangeable. Hence, the consistency preservation rules for the Repository part are compatible to the JSR 330 standard.

The consistency preservation rules for the PCM System, however, are specific for Google Guice. Hence, to support other dependency injection frameworks that are compatible with the JSR 330 standard, the consistency preservation rules for the PCM System need to be redefined specific for the used dependency injection framework.

Assumptions and Limitations For the above explained mapping between architectural models and code that is realised using Google Juice as dependency injection framework, we introduce the following assumptions respectively limitations for the PCM *System*:

1. each *BasicComponent* can only be instantiated once per *System*, i.e. it can only be represented in one *AssemblyContext*, and

[4] `https://github.com/google/guice/wiki/Guice40`

2. each interface can only be provided once per *System*.

The reason for these limitations are that the Google Guice features, we use for the mapping, allows us to bind only one code interface to one code class. Hence, it is not possible to get more than one instantiation of the same component per system.

Furthermore, we are not supporting *RequiredDelegaionRoles*. Hence, the *System* that is created is not allowed to require functions from an additional 3rd party library via required interfaces.

4.6.2. Mappings between Architectural Models, Source Code, and Additional Artefacts

The consistency preservation rules we presented above, are consistency preservation rules between source code models and architectural models only. During the development of a software system, however, additional artefacts are often used to realise and describe the architecture of a software system. Within the VITRUVIUS vision (see Figure 4.4), we propose the use of the PCM metamodel, a source code metamodel, the UML metamodel, and the PCM Sensor framework metamodel to describe the software system. These metamodels are contained in the VSUM. Using more than two metamodels within the VSUM, has the advantage that software systems using model instances of more than two metamodels can be used during the software development and software evolution. Even though supporting more than two metamodels is not the main focus of this thesis and comes with conceptual challenges and technical challenges, we give an example how to keep more than two models consistent within this section.

4.6.3. Mapping between Architectural Models, Source Code, and Eclipse Plugin Development Artefacts

Within this section, we propose a mapping between architectural models, source code, and Eclipse plugin development artefacts. We focus especially on the mapping between architectural model and the Eclipse plugin artefacts. As we explained in Section 2.5.2 Eclipse plugins are organized as Eclipse projects. For this section, it is relevant to know that in addition to plain Java projects Eclipse Plugin projects have i) a Manifest file, which contains the required bundles respectively required projects, and ii) a plugin.xml file, which contains the provided and implemented extension points of the plugin. Furthermore, so called *feature plugins* allow to combine plugin projects and other feature projects within one feature project. To do so, users need to specify the Plugins and Features that should be combined within the Eclipse Feature XML file.

We outlined the foundations of this section as proposal for a case study for multi-view modelling approaches in [KL14]. We proposed a mapping between UML composite diagrams, Eclipse plugin development artefacts, and source code. Within this section, however, we use the PCM instead of UML as architectural model. Heiss [Hei15] provides a prototypical implementation of the proposed consistency preservation rules between the PCM and the Eclipse plugin development artefacts in terms of the Manifest file and the Plugin XML file. The metamodels used for the manifest files and for the XML files, are explained in the foundations (see Section 2.5.2.2). We are able to use the Manifest metamodel and its parser and printer from the EMFtext syntax zoo[5] for the manifest files. For the XML files, we are able to use the generic XML metamodel and its parser and printer from the EMFtext syntax zoo. To ease the use of the generic XML metamodel, however, we created a set of helper methods, which are specific for the used XML files in an Eclipse plugin.

4.6.3.1. The VSUM for architectural models, source code, and Eclipse plugin development artefacts

As we use additional artefacts within these consistency preservation rules, we need to extend the VSUM, which we have presented in Figure 4.1. Additionally to Java models and the PCM as architectural models, the VSUM contains the artefacts, which are necessary for the development of Eclipse plugins. This artefacts are models of the Manifest file, models of the Eclipse plugin XML file, and models of the Eclipse Feature XML file. Even though they are defining an Eclipse plugin together, we treat these models as separate models, because there is no existing mechanism to treat Eclipse plugin

[5] http://www.emftext.org/index.php/EMFText_Concrete_Syntax_Zoo

projects and their artefacts as one model. Hence, we use the Manifest file, the Plugin XML file, and the feature XML file separately in the VSUM. The used VSUM as well as the views, we proposed in [KL14], are shown in Figure 4.15. As in the above defined consistency preservation rules the overlap can be described using the MIR languages or Xtend. The used models, monitors, and consistency preservation rules are explained in the following sections.

4.6.3.2. Used models and editors for the VSUM

As we mentioned above, we use different models for the Manifest file, the Plugin XML, and the feature XML as there is no existing single model for Eclipse Plugin projects. For the Manifest file, we can use the EMFtext grammar for Manifest files [6]. For the Plugin XML and for the feature XML file, we can use the EMFtext grammar for XML files[7]. Both grammars are available in the EMFtext syntax zoo and provide a parser and a printer as well as an editor for the file types. While the grammar and the metamodel for Manifest files is tailored specific for Manifest files and can be used easily, the grammar and the metamodel for XML files is general for XML files and not specific for the XML files used within Eclipse plugins. During the development of the consistency preservation rules, we need to ensure that we only create XML files that are compatible with the Eclipse plugin XML standard respectively the Eclipse feature XML standard.

To this end, we use the standard monitor for EMF files as monitor for the Manifest file as well as for the XML file. This means that we are only able to monitor changes performed using the editors for the EMF files. While this has no effect regarding to the consistency preservation rules, it has the disadvantage that the Eclipse GUI for Manifest files, Plugin XMLs, and Feature XMLs can currently not be used. In future work, however, a monitor can be implemented that monitors changes in the Eclipse GUI.

[6] http://www.emftext.org/index.php/EMFText_Concrete_Syntax_Zoo_Manifest

[7] http://www.emftext.org/index.php/EMFText_Concrete_Syntax_Zoo_XML

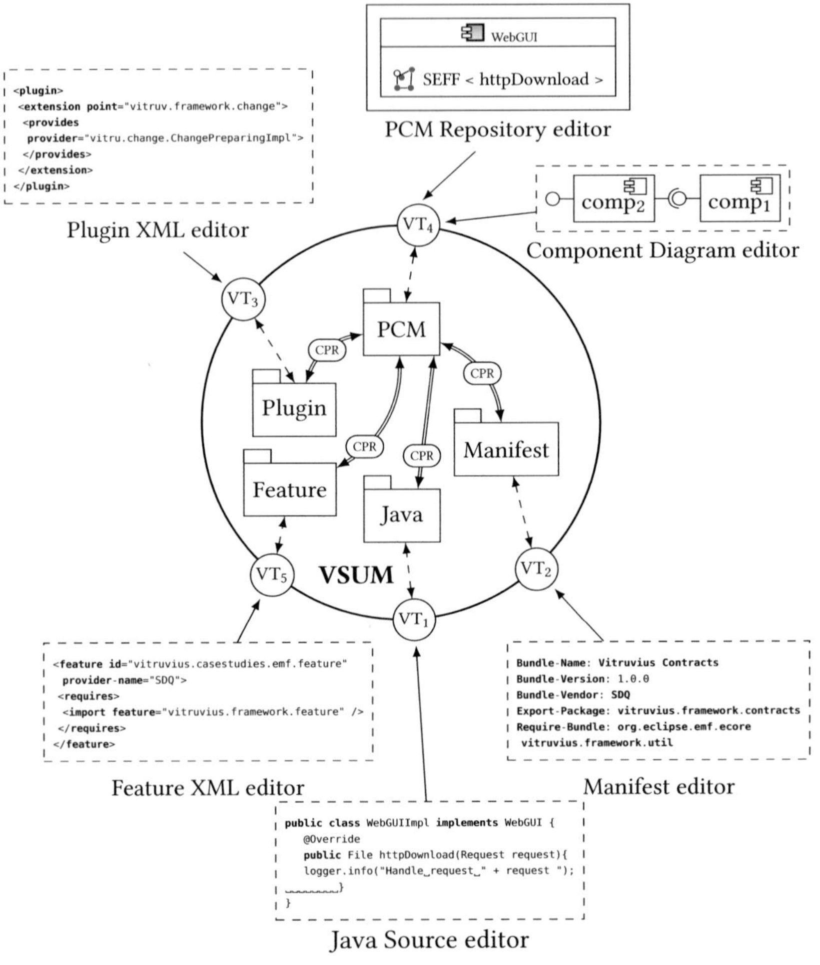

Figure 4.15.: The VSUM for the mapping between source code, architectural models, and Eclipse plugin artefacts. We use the five artefacts JaMoPP, PCM, Eclipse Plugin XML, the Eclipse Plugin Manifest file, and the Eclipse Feature XML file. As views, we [KL14] proposed the use of the standard views to each of the models as well as component-realisation view and an overall navigation view. The additional views for code and PCM, we proposed in the Vitruvius vision are intended to be used as well. To improve the clarity of this figure, we left the additional views out.

4.6.3.3. Consistency Preservation Rules between PCM, Java Source Code, Manifest Files, and Eclipse Plugin XML Files

In this section, we explain the concrete consistency preservation rules. As base for our the explanation we use the PCM. The consistency preservation rules, however, are bidirectional for all involved models unless stated otherwise.

Mapping *Repository* to Eclipse plugins For the mapping between a PCM *Repository* and Java source code, we can partly reuse the mappings we introduced for package mapping respectively the mapping to the dependency injection framework.

To be able to use our Coevolution approach for the development of Eclipse plugins, the first step is to either create a new Eclipse plugin project or create a PCM *Repository* in an existing non-Eclipse plugin project.

If a *Repository* is created in an non-Eclipse plugin project, we create a corresponding Eclipse plugin project for the *Repository*. This corresponding *Repository* is considered as the main project. As corresponding elements for the *Repository*, we use the `BundleSymbolicName` element in the Manifest file and the root Object of the Plugin XML. Within this Eclipse two corresponding packages are created: one interface and one datatype package. Both packages have the same function as the `contracts` and `datatypes` packages in the above-mentioned consistency preservation rules: they contain the corresponding Java interfaces for the *OperationInterfaces* respectively the corresponding classes for the PCM *DataTypes*. Hence, the mapping is similar to the main package in the package mappings. If users create an Eclipse plugin project first instead of a *Repository*, we create a PCM repository as well as the interface and datatype packages, and assume that the first plugin is the main Eclipse plugin project.

In the following, we describe the mapping between *OperationInterfaces* and Eclipse plugin artefacts. For each *OperationInterfaces*, an extension point with the same name as the *OperationInterface* in the Plugin XML of the main Eclipse project is created. For the mapping between architecture and code, we can use the same mapping as for the other consistency preservation rules, i.e. a new code interface is created in the contracts package of the main Eclipse plugin by our Coevolution approach.

PCM *DataTypes* are mapped as in the other consistency preservation rules. They are mapped to a class in the `datatypes` package within the main plugin project for the repository.

Each *BasicComponent* maps to a plugin project. Hence, if a *BasicComponent* is created in the Repository, we create a new Eclipse plugin project with the name of the *BasicComponent*. Similar to the *Repository* mapping the corresponding elements are the root object of the Plugin XML and the `BundleSymbolicName` in the Manifest file. If the name of the *BasicComponent* is changed, we also change the name of the corresponding project as well as the name of the corresponding `BundleSymbolicName` in the Manifest file. We furthermore, create a dependency to the main plugin for the newly created plugin project. Hence, the data types and interfaces are available in all plugins. Within the component-realising plugin poject a new component-realising class, which has the same function as the component-realisation class in the package mapping consistency preservation rules, is created. Hence, the mapping of the class is also similar as it is in the package mapping consistency preservation rules. If users create a new Eclipse plugin project, our Coevolution approach automatically creates a corresponding *BasicComponent* as well as the component-realisation class.

A *ProvidedRole* maps to a new extension in the Eclipse plugin that corresponds to the providing *BasicComponent*. This extension indicates that the Eclipse plugin provides the extension point of the Java interface. It, furthermore, specifies the class that implements the interface. In our case this class is the component-realisation class. To map a *ProvidedRole* to the code, we again use the same mapping as in the other consistency preservation rules: the component-realisation class implements the Java interface that corresponds to the provided *OperationInterface*.

For mapping of *RequiredRoles* to Eclipse plugin artefacts and Java code, we propose different strategies. Users of our Coevolution approach need to clarify which of these strategies should be used before they starting the implementation.

The first strategy is the following: For each *RequiredRole*, a new dependency from the corresponding requiring Eclipse plugin to an Eclipse plugin, which provides the required interface, is added. If more than one component provides the interface, the user needs to decide which Eclipse plugin should be used. To map a *RequiredRoles* to code, we can reuse either the mapping from the package mapping consistency preservation rules: In the component-realising class a new field with the type of the required interface is created. In the constructor this field is assigned with a new instances of the providing component-realising class. Using this strategy new instances of the required class can be created anywhere in the requiring plugin. This strategy has the disadvantage that the requiring component directly knows the providing components. Hence, the mappings mixes the PCM *Repository* mappings and the PCM *System* mappings, because the connection between the components is already distinguished during the creation of the *Repository*.

The second strategy is the following: To overcome the issue that the components know each other directly, we do not map a *RequiredRole* to a dependency between the components. Instead, we only create a mapping to the code as follows: We also create a field of the required interface in the component-implementing class. The assignment with an instance is also done in the constructor. To create this instance, we use the Eclipse mechanism to determine at runtime which plugin provides the extension point. Hence, the actual used required interfaces implementation is created during the runtime of the Eclipse plugin.

Mapping PCM *CPRE* to Eclipse plugins The mapping of the PCM *CPREs*, e.g. a PCM *System*, is done using feature plugins, i.e. one feature plugin is created for each *CPRE*. A feature plugins allows the composition of standard Eclipse plugins and other feature plugins. Within a feature plugin a user can combine standard Eclipse plugins to a feature. For each *AssemblyContext* in the *CPRE*, we create a new plugin dependency in the feature plugin of the corresponding Feature Plugin project.

Using the first strategy of mapping *RequiredRoles* to code, we can derive the connectors automatically from the dependencies in the Manifest files. Using the second strategy of mapping required roles to code, the connectors in a *CPRE* can also be created automatically, because we can connect the required roles with their matching provided roles. The reason for that is that in the constructor of a component-realisation class the interfaces are assigned via the extension point ID and that each extension point is unique using the current consistency preservation rules. Hence, the second strategy of mapping *RequiredRoles* has the limitation that (without additional effort), each interface can only be provided by one component in the *CPRE*.

4.6.3.4. Coevolution of Behavioural Models With Source Code

For the coevolution of behavioural models and source code, we need to define a mapping-specific component-external method call finder The component-external method call finder can be defined rather easily as follows: We consider all calls to interface methods, which have a corresponding *OperationSignature* as component-external method calls. As in the other mappings as well, we also consider all calls to a method within another component as a component-external method call. Hence, all calls to a method within another Eclipse plugin project that has a corresponding *BasicComponent*, is considered as component-external method call.

The finding of the used *RequiredRole* for the external call can be done similar to the package mapping consistency preservation rules, i.e. if an *OperationInterface* is required only once by one component, we use the matching *RequiredRole*. If an interface is required at least twice, we can ask the users which *RequiredRole* shall be used.

4.6.3.5. Prototypical implementation

As mentioned above, we implemented the mapping between the PCM and the Eclipse plugin development artefacts in terms of the Manifest file and the Plugin XML file (see [Hei15]). We are able to show that the PCM *Repository* can be kept consistent with the models of Eclipse plugin development artefacts. Furthermore, we can show that the Vitruvius framework, is in principle able to deal with more than two metamodels within the VSUM.

The implementation currently does neither support the feature XML in feature plugins nor the source code itself. Hence, within the prototypical implementation the Java model and the *System* are not kept consistent using our Coevolution approach. Furthermore, we have not implemented special monitors for the Manifest file and for the Eclipse Plugin XML files, yet. Our standard Vitruvius monitor for EMF files, however, can be used to monitor changes that are performed to the model elements with the standard EMF editors. This has the disadvantage that we currently are not able to monitor changes that were performed using other editors respectively the special Eclipse GUI for plugin projects.

4.6.3.6. Assumptions and Limitations

Similar to the other presented consistency preservation rules, the name of *BasicComponents* as well as the name of *OperationInterfaces* need to be unique within all used PCM *Repositories.* This is the reason, because we create Eclipse Plugins respectively Java code interfaces with the same name as the architectural elements. Even though this limitation could be avoided by creating special names for duplicated names, we decided to not allow the use of duplicate names in the PCM. As we see in the evaluation of the consistency preservation rules in Section 6.4 it turned out that this limitation is not relevant for existing PCM projects as they are not using duplicated names for *BasicComponents* or *OperationInterfaces.*

The following limitations are introduced due to the presented mapping between PCM and Eclipse Plugin artefacts:

- each *BasicComponent* can occur only once per *System,*
- using the second proposed strategy to map *RequiredRoles* from the PCM to Eclipse plugin artefacts, each *OperationInterface* is only allowed to provided by one *AssemblyContext* in the PCM *System.*

4.7. User Roles in our Coevolution Approach

In this section, we present different roles users can have if they use our Coevolution approach, i.e. the section addresses the fourth scientific challenge of this chapter (see Section 4.1).

For our Coevolution approach, we defined the following three roles: The first role is the role of architectural consistency methodologists, who are responsible for defining the architecture code consistency preservation rules and the used techniques. This role is based on the methodologist role, which has been introduced for the OSM [ASB10] approach, and which we reuse in the VITRUVIUS [Bur14; KBL13] approach. The second role is the role of software architects, who are responsible for the architecture of the software system. The third role are the software developers, who are responsible for implementing the defined software system. The role of software architects as well as software developers is based on the same role in the PCM [BKR09]. The role of the architectural consistency methodologists is the only role, we define, that is active during the design time of our Coevolution approach. The other roles we define, using the defined VSUM to create the actual software systems. Software architects and software developers are using our Coevolution approach during the implementation time of the software system. While the role of the architectural consistency methodologists is independent of the used component model, the roles of the software architects and the software developers are tailored specific for using our Coevolution approach with the PCM. However, the roles of software developers and software architects are similar for other ADLs as well. We explain these three roles in the following sections.

4.7.1. Architectural Consistency Methodologists

The first role we present, is the role of the architectural consistency methodologists. The architectural consistency methodologists have similar tasks as the methodologist in the OSM approach and the VITRUVIUS approach, where they are domain experts and decide which metamodels, view types, and views are used. Within our Coevolution approach, architectural consistency methodologists are domain experts for the architecture and code domain as well as for the used techniques, e.g. EJB. In particular, architectural consistency methodologists are responsible for the following tasks:

- deciding which architectural metamodels and source code metamodel should be used,
- defining the consistency preservation rules between architecture and source code, and
- implementing the consistency preservation rules using either our internal DSL (see Section 3.6.1) or the MIR [Kra17] languages.

Hence, the architectural consistency methodologists are responsible for creating the VSUM. Differently from the OSM approach and the Vitruvius approach, they do not need to decide which view types and views are used, because we currently use only existing view types and editors. However, if we include ModelJoin [Bur+14] in the future the architectural consistency methodologists are also responsible for creating the views.

4.7.2. Software Architects

One task of software architects within our Coevolution approach is to create the architecture of the software system. Using a component-based software architecture, as we proposed in this thesis, this means that they are responsible for creating new components in the repository or reusing existing components from other repositories and assemble them in the system. Using the PCM, they, furthermore, can specify the abstract behaviour of the services of a software component. Hence, the architect role within our Coevolution approach is a generalization of the roles of the component developers and software architects in the PCM [BKR09]. In the PCM approach, component developers specify the components and their behaviour, while software architects specify how the components are assembled. Even though we generalize both roles to the role of software architects within our Coevolution approach, they can still be separated if the PCM is used as ADL within our Coevolution approach.

The reason for the generalization is that within our Coevolution approach software architects have additional tasks. If architects change the architecture they can be requested to disambiguate the change as proposed in Section 4.4, if the change is not unique mappable to source code. Hence, interacting with our Coevolution approach and reacting to the user change disambiguation notifications is an important task of software architects within our Coevolution approach. Architects, however, also need to disambiguate changes performed in source code if they affect architectural elements and not mappable in an unique way. This is the case, for instance, if developers perform a change that need to be disambiguated to be keep it consistent with the architecture, but developers are not able to deal with the notification themselves. In this case, the architects need to figure out the intent of developers and either change the architecture accordingly or revert the change of developers in order to keep the models consistent. To interact in the right way with our Coevolution approach and to figure out how to react to the user change disambiguation notification the architects need to be aware of the consistency preservation rules.

4.7.3. Software Developers

The software developers in our Coevolution approach are responsible for implementing the software system. Using our Coevolution approach each architectural relevant change software developers perform, is kept consistent with the architectural models. Hence, if developers change the source code, the change can affect both: statical architectural elements and behavioural elements. The change of statical architectural elements, such as interfaces and components is probably not indented by developers if they only want to implement the component-internal behaviour. To support that we distinguish between component developers, who are allowed to change code that leads to a changes in the static architectural models and component-internal developers, who are only allowed to changed code that is not relevant for the static architecture. Both developer roles, we define, are allowed to perform changes that affect the behavioural elements of the architecture.

4.7.3.1. Component-internal Developers

As first role for software developers, we propose the role of *component-internal developers*. Component-internal developers are responsible for implementing the services of one or more components. To avoid changes of static architectural models during the implementation of components, component-developers are not allowed to change code elements that have corresponding static architectural elements. Component-internal developers are, furthermore, not allowed to add or delete packages, classes or interfaces that affect the architecture. They are, however, allowed to add new classes and technical interfaces within existing components. The advantage of the role is that developers cannot change the static architecture of the software system by accident, e.g. renaming an API method that is intended to be called from users. Another advantage is that component-internal developers not need to disambiguate their changes, because changes they perform cannot affect static architectural elements. Hence, they can focus on implementing the internal behaviour of a component. If component-internal developers want to introduce, for instance, new components, they need to assume the role of component developers, which is explained in the next section. Another possibility for component-internal developers to change the static architectural elements, is to create change requests for software architects or component-developers, for instance, by using a ticketing system. Software architects and component developers review the change requests and can implement them.

To figure out which changes can lead to changes of the static architecture, we can use the VITRUVIUS correspondence model. We consider changes to source code elements that have a corresponding static architectural element, e.g. a *BasicComponent*, as change of the static architecture. Having this information, however, does not help to prevent that component-internal developers change those code elements. One simple solution to prevent changes on those code elements is to role back the changes of component-internal developers if they change these elements. This approach, however, has two main disadvantages. The first one is that rolling back changes, can be confusing for component-internal developers, if they are not aware why the changes have been rolled back. The second one is that we do not know whether the current software developer is a component-internal developer or not. To overcome this disadvantages at least for code within class files or interface files and to support component-internals developers by identifying code that is relevant for the statical architecture before they actually change it, we propose a adapted code editor for component-internal developers. Within this editor, we grey out and disable the editability for the code elements that should not changed by developers. This editor can be generated dynamically based on the current VITRUVIUS correspondence model, when a component-internal developer opens a Java file using the editor for component-internal developers. Hence, we consider developers that use this editor as component-internal developers. Developers who use the standard editor are considered as component-developers.

Telpl [Tel13] showed that it is possible to grey out and prevent changes on code by implementing a plugin for the standard Eclipse Java code editor [Tel13]. Other than greying out and prevent changes for specific code elements the editor shows the same behaviour as the standard Eclipse Java code editor. In future work, we plan to integrate this approach in our Coevolution approach so that the VITRUVIUS correspondence model is used to figure out which code areas respectively code elements should be greyed out and not be editable. We currently have no tool support to prevent developers to add or delete packages, class files, or interface files that are relevant for the static architecture. It could be implemented, however, by using the first approach: we role back the changes and inform the component-internal developers that they are not allowed to perform this change. In this case, we furthermore need a method to decide whether a user is a component-internal developer or not. To do so a special Eclipse perspective, which is tailored for component-internal developers can be used.

As an example, consider the package mapping consistency preservation rules, we defined in Section 4.3.2. Using these consistency preservation rules component-internal developers are, for instance, not allowed to change interfaces in the `contracts` package, because the code interfaces have corresponding *OperationInterfaces*, while the code method have corresponding *OperationSignatures*. They are neither allowed to change a component-realisation class nor to create packages in the package that corresponds to the *Repository*. Furthermore, they are not allowed to change the method declaration of methods that correspond to a *SEFF*.

4.7.3.2. Component Developers

As second role for software developers, we propose the role of component developers. Component developers have similar tasks as component-internal developers. Hence, they are implementing the architecture, which has been outlined by the software architects. In contrast to component-internal developers, component-developers can change code that affects statical architectural elements as well. For instance, they are allowed to add packages, class files, and interface files that are relevant for the static architecture. Hence, changes a component-developer performs cannot only affect statical architectural elements, but also lead to interactions with user change disambiguation framework, if additional information is needed to keep the change consistent with the architecture. Component developers can disambiguate they changes either directly, or after consulting the architects, or by leaving a task for the architects in the task list. We assume that developers, who use the standard code editor are component developers.

5. Include Existing Artefacts

Within the previous chapter, we explained how our Coevolution approach can be used to keep architectural models and source code consistent during the software development and software evolution. The approach as it is presented in the chapters before can only be used if it is used from the beginning of the development process. Existing artefacts cannot be used or integrated within our Coevolution approach as it is presented up until now. This limitation is also true for the VITRUVIUS approach as it is presented in previous work [Bur14; KBL13; Kra+15a]. To answer the question *How can existing models be used within VITRUVIUS and within our Coevolution approach?*, we propose two different strategies to include existing artefacts. We presented the strategies and parts of their application to our Coevolution approach in [Leo+15].

This section is divided into two main parts. In the first part, we present the two strategies to integrate existing artefacts in VITRUVIUS. To realise the integration, we present the concept of a reconstructive strategy and a linking strategy. We, furthermore, introduce the role of the integrators who are responsible for implementing a reconstructive strategy or a linking strategy in order to integrate existing artefacts.

In the second part of this section, we explain the application of the strategies to the case of architectural models and source code. Within this part, we firstly explain how we can include an existing architecture model using a reconstructive strategy, and secondly how we can include existing source code using a linking strategy. For the application to our Coevolution approach, the first part of the linking strategy is to reconstruct an architecture model from source code. Therefore, existing reverse engineering approaches, such as the Source Code Model eXtractor (SoMoX) (see Section 2.4), can be used. As we developed the reverse engineering approaches *EJBmoX* and Extract [Lan+16] within the scope of this thesis, we explain them in Section 5.4.1.

We presented the integration of source code that is complaint to the used bidirectional consistency preservation rules in [Leo+15]. Petersen [Pet16] extended this approach in his master's thesis to allow the integration of arbitrary source code.

5.1. Scientific Challenges

The following scientific challenges on how to include existing models into VITRUVIUS and our Coevolution approach are addressed in this chapter:

- *Which integration strategies are necessary to enable the use of existing models within VITRUVIUS?*

  As mentioned above, VITRUVIUS is not able to deal with existing artefacts. Dealing with existing models, however, is important in order to apply VITRUVIUS to existing and historically grown projects.

- *How can the proposed integration strategies instantiated for the integration of existing architectural models and existing source code into our Coevolution approach?*

  As the VITRUVIUS approach our Coevolution approach needs to be able to work with existing projects in order to enable the use of our Coevolution approach with existing software projects. For our Coevolution approach this means that the integration of existing source code and existing architecture models is necessary. To do so, we need to instantiate the VITRUVIUS integration strategies for our Coevolution approach.

- *Which extensions are necessary to include arbitrary component-based code into our Coevolution approach?*

  A further question arises, when we deal with existing source code bases that are not compliant to the current used consistency preservation rules. The challenge is to include such non-compliant source code into our Coevolution approach so that our Coevolution approach can be used for the evolution of the software system.

5.2. Include Existing Artefacts in VITRUVIUS

The benefit of enabling the use of existing artefacts within VITRUVIUS is that it can be used within already existing projects. As a motivation why dealing with existing artifacts is necessary, consider our Coevolution approach for architectural models and source code. If we do not provide a mechanism to enable the use of already existing source code, it would be necessary to redevelop the whole project from scratch using our Coevolution approach. Especially for large projects it is unrealistic to assume that the effort will be done by development teams. To avoid the effort, we introduce a mechanism that automatically respectively semi-automatically enables the integration of existing artefacts into our Coevolution approach. Within other case studies of VITRUVIUS, for instance, the automotive software engineering domain, it is also necessary to deal with existing artefacts for the same reason.

To include existing artefacts in VITRUVIUS we propose two different strategies. The first one is the so called Reconstructive Integration Strategy (RIS), which simulates the recreation of an existing model. The second one is a Linking Integration Strategy (LIS), which connects existing models using the output of model generating tools or model creating tools, e.g. model to model transformations to link the models. We furthermore, introduce the role of the integrators, who are responsible for performing the integration of existing models or source code.

The RIS and the LIS are both based on the idea that one model instance of the models in the Virtual Single Underlying Model (VSUM) has been created already, while the other models are not created yet. For the remainder of this section, we consider the existing model as source model and the models that should be created as target models. The description of the integration strategies, which are provided in the following, address the first scientific challenge, we defined for this chapter (see Section 5.1).

Consider the small example depicted in Figure 5.1, which we use to explain the strategies in the following. In the top half of the figure, we have a metamodel A that has the classes *RootA*, *NestedA* and *Required.* The *RootA* class represents the root object for metamodel A. The *RootA* class has two containment lists. One to the *Required* class and another one to the *NestedA* class. The class *NestedA* has the *String* attribute *name.* The class *Required* has the *String* attribute *description.* Furthermore, each instance of a *NestedA* class

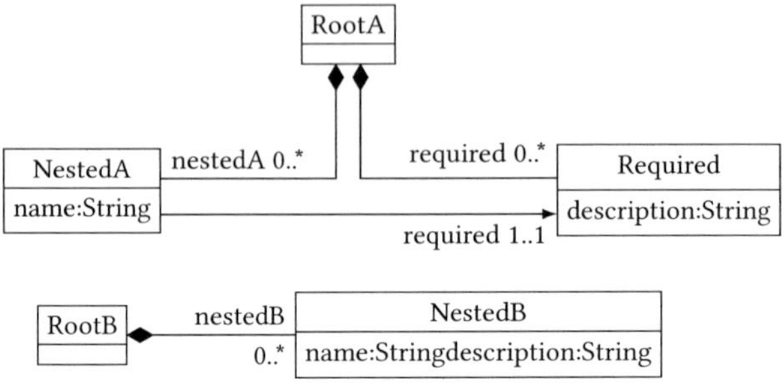

Figure 5.1.: Class diagram for metamodel A (top) and metamodel B (bottom)

needs exactly one instance of the *Required* class. In the bottom half, have metamodel B that has the root class *RootB*. This class has a containment list to the class *NestedB*, which has the attributes *name* and *description*. In addition, metamodel B has the invariant that the *name* Attribute in class *NestedB* must be unique and is not allowed to contain spaces. We also assume that we already have defined the following bidirectional consistency preservation rules using VITRUVIUS:

- *RootA* maps to *RootB*, and
- *NestedA* and *Required* map to *NestedB*. Also the *name* attributes of *NestedA* and *NestedB* are mapping to each other. Furthermore, the *description* attribute of the class *Required* maps to the *description* attribute from *NestedB*.

5.2.1. Reconstructive Integration Strategy

The idea behind the RIS is to create the other models automatically by simulating the initial creation of the already existing model. During the simulated creation, we create the changes that are the necessary input for the consistency preservation process, which we explained in Chapter 3. These changes serve as input for the VITRUVIUS framework and are processed like standard changes that are performed by users. Hence, the consistency preservation rules are executed and the corresponding model elements in all other models are created.

Before creating the changes, however, we first resolve (potential) conflicts between the source model and the target models. During this phase, we apply the invariants of the affected objects from the target models to the source model. The goal of this phase is to create models from which we are able to create valid changes and therefore valid target models. We distinguish between two different types of conflicts. The first type of conflict deals with so called syntactic conflicts, which would cause an invalid target model if we apply the transformations from the source model to get the target model. As an example for a syntactic conflict consider our small example depicted in Figure 5.1: If we want to integrate an instance of metamodel A, we need to consider the consistency preservation rules between metamodel A and metamodel B as well as the invariants of metamodel B. The invariants of metamodel B need to be applied to the attributes of metamodel A that could possibly violate the invariants during the execution of the consistency preservation rules. In our example, we need to consider the invariants for the *name* attribute of the class *NestedB* from metamodel B and apply them to the *name* attribute of class *NestedA* from metamodel A. This means that we have to check all instances of the class *NestedA* and need to make sure that their names do not contain any spaces. For instance, the *name* attribute with the value `My Name` violates the constraint that no spaces are allowed in the *name* attribute of the class *NestedB*. An obvious solution is to remove the spaces in the name. Furthermore, we need to make sure that the *name* attribute in the class *NestedA* is unique over all instances of the class *NestedA*. A simple solution here is to iterate over all instances and identify the duplicate names and append a unique number at the end of the *name* string. For instance, if we have two *name* attributes with the name *MyName* we would rename the first to *MyName1* and the second one to *MyName2*. The second type of possible conflicts are semantic conflicts. This conflicts occur if the source model instance cannot be mapped to the target model instance using the consistency preservation rules. Hence, these conflicts depend on the used consistency preservation rules. To give an example, we change the transformation from the *name* Attribute from the class *NestedA* to the *name* attribute of class *NestedB* in a way that only the first three letters from *name* are considered. This could lead to a violation of the invariant within metamodel B that the values of the attribute *name* must be unique.

To resolve the conflict, one needs to ensure that the first three letters are unique in the attribute *name* for all instances of the class *NestedA*.

Even though the invariant resolving can be done during the transformation itself we decided to do it before the integration transformation. The reason for this decision is twofold. Firstly, we can resolve conflicts before the consistency preservation rules are executed. This allows us, for instance, to resolve conflicts that cannot be resolved easily within the consistency preservation rules itself. Secondly, it is possible to solve conflicts that need the users to disambiguate the change before the actual execution of the consistency preservation rules.

After the invariant resolving phase, we perform the traversal phase to simulate the creation of the source model. This means that we need to visit every element in the model and create the creation-change for the model element as well as for its attributes. The algorithm we use relies on the fact that every model element needs to be contained in exactly one other element. This is at least true for all models in any Eclipse Modeling Framework (EMF) based model To traverse a model we first visit all elements that do not have any incoming references. Hence, the first element we visit is the root object of the model, which we consider as level 0 element. After that we visit all direct children of the root object that are contained in the root object and that do neither require other model elements to exist nor have required references to other model elements that are not created yet. We call these elements level 1 elements. We repeat the above-mentioned step for all level 1 elements and create the level 2 elements. We repeat this step until we visited all elements within model A. During each visit we create the create-changes for the visited model elements. After the application of the algorithm we have all changes that lead to the creation of the initial model.

To give an example consider metamodel A we mentioned above (see Figure 5.1). To traverse the metamodel we first would visit the *Root* class, which is the level 0 element. Both subclasses are contained within the *Root* class. The *Nested* class, however, needs to have an instance of the *Required* class to exists. Hence, the *Required* class is the level 1 element, which instances can be visited after visiting the level 0 element(s). After the creation of all *Required* classes, we can create all instances of the *Nested* class, because all elements that are needed for any *Nested* class element are already created. In our small example, the *Nested* class is a level 2 element.

This approach does not guarantee that we create the source model in the same order as users would have created it. However, the output of the simulated model creation is the same as the input source model. The above introduced approach comes with assumptions for the source model as well as for the consistency preservation rules that are executed during the creation of the elements within the source model. The assumption for the source model is that the creation order of the model elements does not haven an effect on the model itself. The assumption for the consistency preservation rules is that the creation order of the model elements must not have any effect to the consistency preservation rules. Another assumption for the transformations is that they need to be able to transform all features from a class during the creation of the class already. The reason for that assumption is that it is possible that not all changes made on a model are reported. Consider our example metamodel A from Figure 5.1: The consistency preservation transformation needs to be able to transform the *name* attribute of the class *Nested* as well as the *description* attribute from the class *Required* during the creation of each class. This is necessary, because the change for the attributes are not reported by the integration strategy. It is, however, possible to change the RIS, in order to support the creation of the changes for attributes as well.

5.2.2. Linking Integration Strategy

A LIS creates the correspondences between a source model and target models. Hence, in contrast to the RIS it does not simulate the creation of the source model. A LIS requires that the target models can be created or generated from the source model using an external tool, e.g. a Model-to-Model (M2M) transformation. It also requires that during this transformation a trace model has been created that provides the information how an element from the source model maps to the elements from the target model. Using the information from the source model, the created target models, and the trace model, a LIS creates the VITRUVIUS correspondence model. The VITRUVIUS framework can use the created VITRUVIUS correspondence model as *normal* correspondence model during the execution of the consistency preservation rules between the source model and the target models. This approach, however, has the assumption that the used model generation tools create the same target model as it would be created using the consistency preservation rules. If this is not the case, we need to create special correspondences that mark correspondence which have been created by a LIS. The elements within the correspondences marked as created by a LIS, cannot be kept consistent using the standard consistency preservation rules. Instead we need a special treatment for those elements if they are changed. A simple solution is to warn users that this change cannot be kept consistent automatically and require users to ensure the consistency manually. More advanced solutions, such as keeping at least parts of the elements consistent automatically, e.g. the name, can be implemented as well. Also, special consistency preservation rules can be created for the elements that are integrated in the approach with a LIS.

Again, consider our example for this section (see Figure 5.1). Let us assume that we already have an instance of metamodel B. Furthermore, we have defined an uni-directional model to model transformation from metamodel B to metamodel A, that creates the following elements from metamodel A:

- one *RootA* instance for every *RootB* instance;
- One *NestedA* instance and one *Required* instance for every *NestedB* instance. The *Required* instance, however, is only created if no other *Required* instance with the same *description* attribute exists already.

The M2M transformation also creates a trace model, which contains the information which model element in the instance of metamodel A was created from which element in the instance of metamodel B. The three models (the input model, the output model and the trace model) are the basis for our LIS. The LIS uses these models as input for a M2M transformation, which output is a correspondence model between the model instance A and the model instance B. The transformation creates a Vitruvius correspondence model element between the elements from metamodel B and its created model elements from metamodel A. To figure out which element from model A was created from which element in model B the transformation uses the provided trace information. This approach only works if the bidirectional consistency preservation rules match the uni-directional transformation or generation mapping, i.e. the bidirectional consistency preservation rules would have created the same output element as the uni-directional transformation if Vitruvius would have been used from the beginning of the development process. In this case the bidirectional transformations can be used directly and Vitruvius as it is can be used for the development and evolution of the models. If this is not the case a special type of Vitruvius correspondence model instances need to be created and considered during the execution of the bidirectional transformations. The latter case is explained in a more complex example for a LIS, which we present in the next section, where we apply a LIS to source code and architectural models.

To conclude, a LIS heavily depends on the source model, the creation or generation tools for the target models as well as the trace information this tools are creating. This means that a LIS often requires technology-specific or even model-specific solutions.

5.2.3. The Role of the Integrators

For the integration of existing artefacts, we define the role of integrators, who are responsible to perform the integration. If a specific model shall be integrated into a specific VSUM, the first step they have to do is to decide whether a RIS or a LIS should be used for integrating a specific model into a specific VSUM.

For a RIS they have the following two responsibilities: The first responsibility is to solve the invariants of the models if they cannot be solved automatically. Secondly, they are responsible for creating the traversal strategy for the metamodels of the models that should be integrated.

Since a LIS does not follow such a straight forward process like the RIS they have more responsibilities depending on the used LIS. Hence, responsibilities within a LIS are depending on the models that should be integrated and need to be defined specific for the used approach. In general, however, they have the following responsibilities: If no model transformation or model generation from the source model to the target model exists yet, integrators are responsible for creating such a transformation or generation. They also need to ensure that a trace model between the source model and the target model exists. They can use this trace model together with the source model and the target model to create a M2M transformation from these three input models to the Vitruvius correspondence model.

5.3. Include existing Architecture Models using Reconstructive Integration Strategy

This section introduces how we use a RIS to include an existing architecture model into our Coevolution approach, i.e. it addresses the first part of the second scientific challenge for this chapter.

Using Java Model Parser and Printer (JaMoPP) respectively Java as target model and the consistency preservation rules introduced in Chapter 4, conflicts between Palladio Component Model (PCM) and Java can occur. Table 5.1 shows the possible conflicts that can occur between PCM and Java and whether these conflicts are syntactic or semantic conflicts and how we resolve them before we traverse the model. For the semantic conflicts, which are mapping-specific, we assume that the package mapping consistency preservation rules, which we introduced in Section 4.3.2, are used. The semantic conflicts, we identified are, for instance, caused by the fact that one *OperationSignature* is provided multiple times by the same *BasicComponent*. To overcome this conflict, we could adapt the consistency preservation rules in a way that the *ProvidedRoles* are made explicit in the source code. Such an approach of mapping a PCM architectural model to source code has been introduced by Becker [Bec08] and is implemented, e.g. for ProtoCom. As we see in Section 6.4 these semantic conflicts, however, do not occur in any of the PCM instances we used as case studies.

As next step, we have to traverse the PCM elements. Therefore, two traversal algorithms are described in the following. The first one, (see Algorithm 3) shows one possible algorithm how one PCM *Repository* can be traversed, while the second one (see Algorithm 4) shows one possibility to traverse a PCM *System* respectively a *ComposedProvidingRequiringEntity*. The goal of the traversal strategy is to visit each element within the given PCM elements and create the according changes for each element in order to simulate a newly creation of the model. Hence, the first element we visit is the *Repository* element itself. Afterwards, we visit all *DataTypes* within the repository. The order in which we visit the data types is as follows: Since the *PrimitiveDataTypes* do not have any dependencies to other model elements, we visit them first. Using the consistency preservation rules we presented in this thesis, however, the creation of *PrimitiveDataTypes* does affect the source code, because we use counterparts in the Java language to represent the

Invariant name	Description	Kind	Possible Resolution strategy
Keywords	Names for elements in PCM, e.g. components, are not allowed to have the name of a keyword in Java, e.g. *class.*	syntactic	Prepend a valid letter to the begin of the identifier name.
First letter	The first letter of an identifier in Java (e.g. for a class) needs to be a letter.	syntactic	Prepend a valid letter to the begin of the identifier name.
Forbidden characters	Identifiers in Java are not allowed to contain special characters such as "-", "_", "&" etc.	syntactic	Replace the characters with "_"
Names equals	Components or Interface from the PCM with the same name, would be mapped to the same source code elements.	semantic	Append an incrementing number *i* to the conflicting name.
Signature equals	Two *OperationSignatures* in either one interfaces or two interfaces that are implemented by the same component are equal. This means they have the same name, the same Parameter types and the same return type.	semantic	Append an incrementing number *i* to the name of the conflicting *OperationSignatures.*
Double provided Interface	A component provides the same interface twice in order to provide two different implementations for the same service, e.g. one fast and one energy saving implementation.	semantic	Either restructure transformations so that they use the Broker pattern[Bec08] or restructure the PCM model instance.

Table 5.1.: Invariants between PCM and Java that need to be resolved before the integration step. We identified the invariants already for [Leo+15].

PrimitiveDataTypes from the PCM. After visiting the *PrimitiveDataTypes*, we visit all *CompositeDataTypes* and *CollectionDataTypes* to create the skeleton for the complex data types. As of now we have visited all data types and they can be used within *OperationSignatures* and as inner types in other data types. Since each *CollectionDataTypes*, however, needs to have an inner type to be a valid *CollectionDataType* the model is not valid by now. Hence, one assumption we make here is that the transformations are able to deal with the fact that the model is not in a valid state at every point in time. To complete the creation of the *DataType* we visit all *CompositeDataTypes* and *CollectionDataTypes* again and create the changes for the *InnerDataTypes* within the *CompositeDataTypes* respectively the *InnerElements* within the *CollectionDataTypes*. After the last step we have a valid model that contains all data types as well as their inner elements.

Afterwards, we can visit the remaining first level entities in the *Repository*. These are all *OperationInterfaces*, *CompositeComponents*, and *BasicComponents* in the repository and create the create-change for them. For each *OperationInterface* we also visit all *OperationSignatures*. During the visit of each *OperationSignature* we implicit visit the reference to the return type. Furthermore, we explicitly visit all *Parameters* of each *OperationSignature*. After that step, we have created a *Repository* that consists of the *DataTypes* and the *OperationInterfaces*. As next elements we visit the *BasicComponents* and the *CompositeComponents*. For the latter, we create the skeletons, but not the inner components. During the visit of the components we visit the *OperationProvidedRoles* and *OperationRequiredRoles* to establish the connection between components and interfaces. If the current component is a *BasicComponent*, we also visit the *SEFFs* of the *BasicComponents*.

As last step, for the repository we visit all *CompositeComponents* again to build their inner structure. After performing this step, we are finished with the creation of the *Repository* and can traverse the *System*. Since the *CompositeComponents* and the *System* are both from type *ComposedProvidingRequiringEntity* we traverse the inner structure of both in the same way. First, we visit the *AssemblyContext* and its encapsulated component. Since, we already visited all components, we can be sure that the encapsulated components for all *AssemblyContexts* exist. As next step, we visit the *OperationProvidedRoles* and *OperationRequiredRoles* of the *ComposedProvidingRequiringEntity*. After that we visit all *ProvidedDelegationConnector* and *RequiredDelegationConnector*, which are the delegation connectors to connect the provided respectively required interfaces with the *AssemblyContexts*. As last step we visit the *AssemblyConnectors* of a *ComposedProvidingRequiringEntity*.

The proposed Algorithm has the limitation that only one *Repository* can be traversed. If more than one *Repository* is used the limitation can be overcome by creating a virtual *Repository* that contains all elements from both *Repositories*. This virtual *Repository* can than be traversed as mentioned in the Algorithm above.

The proposed algorithm is only one possible example how an existing PCM *Repository* and an existing PCM *System* can be traversed. The important fact for any other possible traversal algorithm, is that during the creation of an element, all elements necessary to create the element have to be created already. The reason for that is that we create the create-change for the currently visited element during the visit of each element.

5.4. Include existing Source Code using a Linking Integration Strategy

To include an existing source code base into our Coevolution approach, we use a LIS. For this LIS, we present four different integration levels. These levels define the requirements on the source code that shall be integrated. The levels reach from the requirement that the source code already needs to be compliant to the consistency preservation rules that are used (Integration Level 1) over the integration of arbitrary source code (Integration Level 2 and Integration Level 3) to the generation of element-specific bidirectional consistency preservation rules (Integration Level 4). Furthermore, the four levels define to which degree the integrated source code can be kept consistent automatically with the architecture after the integration. In this dimension the degree reaches from no automatic consistency, over some defined changes can be kept consistent to all changes can be kept consistent automatically using the defined consistency preservation rules. Within this thesis, we focus on the first three levels, while the fourth level is left to future work. The definition of Integration Level 1 addresses the second part of the second scientific challenge of this chapter. The definition of Integration Level

Algorithm 3 Traversal strategy for a PCM *Repository*

```
Require: PCM ← (Set<Repository>, System)
function traversePCM(Repository,System)
    createRepository(repository)
    for all primitiveDatatype ∈ repository do
        createPrimitiveDatatype(primitiveDatatype)
    for all compositeDatatype ∈ repository do
        createCompositeDatatype(compositeDatatype)
    for all collectionDatatype ∈ repository do
        createCollectionDatatype(collectionDatatype)
    for all compositeDatatype ∈ repository do
        for all innerType ∈ compositeDatatype do
            addInnerType(compositeDatatype, innerType )
    for all collectionDatatype ∈ repository do
        setInnerType(collectionDatatype, collectionDatatype.innerType)
    for all operationInterface ∈ repository do
        createInterface(operationInterface)
        for all operationSignature ∈ operationInterface do
            createSignatureAndReturnType(operationSignature)
            for all parameter ∈ operationSignature do
                addParameter(parameter)
    for all compositeComponent ∈ repository do
        createCompositeComponent(basicComponent)
        for all opProvidedRole ∈ compositeComponent do
            createOperationProvidedRole(opProvidedRole)
        for all opRequiredRole ∈ compositeComponent do
            createOperationRequiredRole(opProvidedRole)
    for all basicComponent ∈ repository do
        for all opProvidedRole ∈ compositeComponent do
            createOperationProvidedRole(opProvidedRole)
        for all opRequiredRole ∈ compositeComponent do
            createOperationRequiredRole(opProvidedRole)
        createBasicComponent(basicComponent)
        for all seff ∈ basicComponent do
            createSeff(basicComponent, seff)
    for all compositeComponent ∈ repository do
        traverseComposedEntity(compositeComponent)
traverseComposedEntity(system)          ▷ Finally, traverse the PCM system
```

Algorithm 4 Traversal strategy for a PCM *ComposedProvidingRequiringEntity*, e.g. a PCM *System*

```
function TRAVERSECOMPOSEDENTITY(composedEntity:ComposedEntity)   ▷ a composedEntity is either a System or a CompositeComponent or a Subsystem
    for all assemblyContext ∈ composedEntity do
        CREATEASSEMBLYCONTEXT(assemblyContext)
    for all opProvidedRole ∈ composedEntity do
        CREATEOPERATIONPROVIDEDROLE(opProvidedRole)
    for all opRequiredRole ∈ composedEntity do
        CREATEOPERATIONREQUIREDROLE(opProvidedRole)
    for all providedDelegationConnector ∈ composedEntity do
        CREATEPROVIDEDDELEGATIONCONNECTOR(providedDelegationConnector)
    for all requiredDelegationConnector ∈ composedEntity do
        CREATEREQUIREDDELEGATIONCONNECTOR(requiredDelegationConnector)
    for all assemblyConnector ∈ composedEntity do
        CREATEASSEMBLYCONNECTOR(assemblyConnector)
```

2, Integration Level 3, and Integration Level 4 addresses the third scientific challenge of this chapter (see Section 5.1).

Since we use a LIS to integrate existing source code, we need to have model transformation or generation from the source in to the target models. Therefore, we use reverse engineering approaches that are able to generate an architectural model from source code. This step needs to be done for all defined integration levels. Within the work presented in this, we used the reverse engineering approaches i) SoMoX, ii) *Extract*, and iii) *EJBmoX*. We briefly explained SoMoX [Kro12] in the foundations chapter already (see Section 2.4). Since the reverse engineering approaches *Extract* and *EJBmoX* are contributions of this thesis, they are explained in the following subsections. While *Extract* is able to reverse-engineer a PCM model from arbitrary Java source code using different extraction algorithms, *EJBmoX* is able to reverse-engineer a PCM model from Java source code that is created with Enterprise Java Bean. We use the result of this extraction mechanisms to create a M2M transformation from the result of the extraction, which is a PCM as well as a link model, to the correspondence model. For the integration of existing source code we distinguish between the use cases i) integrate code that matches the consistency preservation rules, and ii) integrate code that does not match the used consistency preservation rules. Even though the integration process for the two cases is similar, the evolution of the software system using our Coevolution approach is different for the cases. For the first case, the defined consistency preservation rules can be used out of the box and the our Coevolution approach does not to distinguish, whether a correspondence has been created by the integration M2M transformation or by the consistency preservation rules itself. The reason for that is that the correspondences are the same regardless which transformation created them. The consistency preservation rules, however, cannot be applied for if code should be integrated that does not match the consistency preservation rules. Hence, an extension for the proposed consistency preservation mechanism, which we have introduced in the Chapter 3 and Chapter 4 is necessary.

In the remainder of this section, we first explain the used reverse engineering approaches. Afterwards, we four different integration levels, which can be used to integrate source code. After that, we explain how we realised the first three integration levels within our Coevolution approach. Finally, we explain the additional tasks of integrators within the different code integration levels.

Besides the fact that we can (partly) reuse existing reverse engineering approaches to integrate existing code a RIS would be impractical for the integration of source code into our Coevolution approach due to the following reasons:

1. Source code that shall be integrated, does often not match the current use consistency preservation rules. If we would simulate a creation of the model using a RIS for source code, we would force an architectural model that would have been created by the consistency preservation rules. Enforcing the architecture of the consistency preservation rules to a source code base that does not conform the consistency preservation rules would work, but would may result in a misleading architectural representation.
2. To simulate the creation of a JaMoPP model, the traversal algorithm needs to visit every element of the source code model including the

statements. Implementing a traversal strategy for that is possible but impractical.

3. The consistency preservation rules (at least the once we implemented for this thesis) from source code to architecture require users more often to disambiguate the change than the transformations from the architectural model to the source code model. Hence, users would be asked very often how to deal with the new elements that are created. Answering these questions can be challenging, especially if the users are not familiar with the consistency preservation rules or the implemented architecture.

5.4.1. Extracting Architecture Models from exiting Source Code

Extracting an architecture model from existing source code is the first step towards the integration of existing source code into our Coevolution approach. Since we use the PCM as architecture model, we need to extract a rich architecture model from source code in terms of *Components*, *OperationInterfaces*, *OperationSignatures*, *ProvidedRoles*, and *RequiredRoles*. Since we also want to integrate the behaviour of the source code we also need to extract the behaviour in terms of *SEFFs*. To integrate the source code into our Coevolution approach in the next step we also need to have the information which class belongs to which architectural artifact.

We identified three approaches that allow us to reverse-engineer source code to a PCM instance that fulfills these requirements: The first one is to use SoMoX [Kro12], which extracts an architecture based on metrics. The second one is *Extract* (see Langhammer et al. [Lan+16]), which extracts an architecture using an extraction mechanism and transforms the results to PCM. The third one is *EJBmoX*, which reverse-engineers source code that is created using Enterprise Java Bean (EJB)s.

We already explained SoMoX in Section 2.4. Since *Extract* and *EJBmoX* are contributions of this thesis, we explain them in the following two sections.

5.4.1.1. *Extract*

This section is based on Langhammer et al. [Lan+16], where we introduced *Extract*. *Extract* is able to create a PCM architecture model from source code, which is based on Plain Old Java Objects (POJOs), i.e. which does not use any specific source code technology, such as EJBs. It is, furthermore, able to create PCM *UsageModels* from test code. The latter is, however, not part of this thesis and therefore not explained here, i.e. we focus on the creation of a PCM *Repository*.

To create a PCM *Repository* using *Extract*, the work flow depicted in Figure 5.2 is executed. In the following, we first explain the reused tools. Next, we explain the four steps executed by *Extract* in order to retrieve a PCM *Repository* and a *System*.

Tools reused within the *Extract* tool chain As we can see in Figure 5.2, *Extract* uses Architecture Recovery, Change, and Decay Evaluator (ARCADE) [GIM13] to reverse-engineer the architecture of source code. ARCADE is an architecture reverse engineering tool that currently comprises ten different extraction algorithms. It can apply these different algorithms to create different views to the implemented architecture of a software system. Within this thesis, we used the Algorithm for Comprehension-Driven Clustering (ACDC), and Architecture Recovery using Concerns (ARC) as reverse engineering algorithms. As we mentioned in [Lan+16], ACDC uses the module dependencies within a system to recover its primarily structure. ARC uses information retrieval methods to recovers an semantic architectural view of the software system. Garcia et al. [GIM13] showed that the two algorithms outperformed the other available algorithms for ARCADE in terms of accuracy and scalability. As output from ARCADE, we get the output clustering of the source code, and the dependencies between classes. Consider the following example: After applying ARCADE to the running MediaStore example of this thesis, we get the two clusters shown in Figure 5.3. The clusters not only contain the actual architectural relevant classes but also used classes from third party libraries and from the Java language API. These classes, however, are ignored by *Extract* in the subsequent steps.

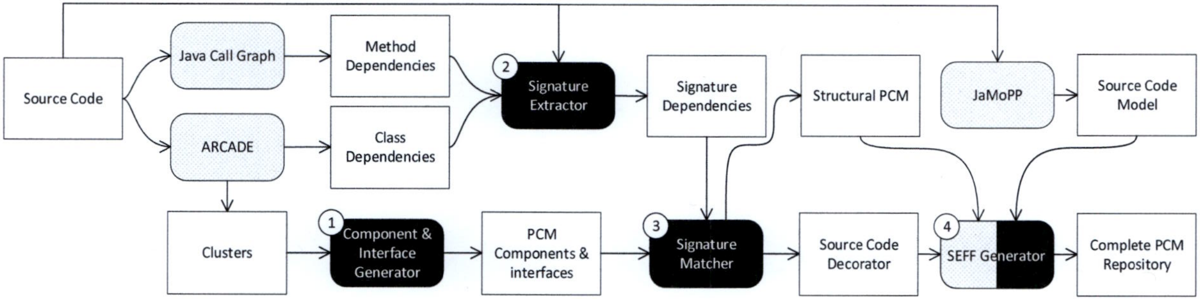

Figure 5.2.: Overview of architecture reconstruction approach *Extract*. We need to execute steps 1 through 4 to get a PCM instance from source code. The grey boxes, are approaches, we could reuse, while the black boxes are contributions of *Extract* (step 1 through 3). We were able to reuse SoMoX's *SEFF* generator for *Extract*, but we need to adapt it in order to work in the environment of *Extract*.

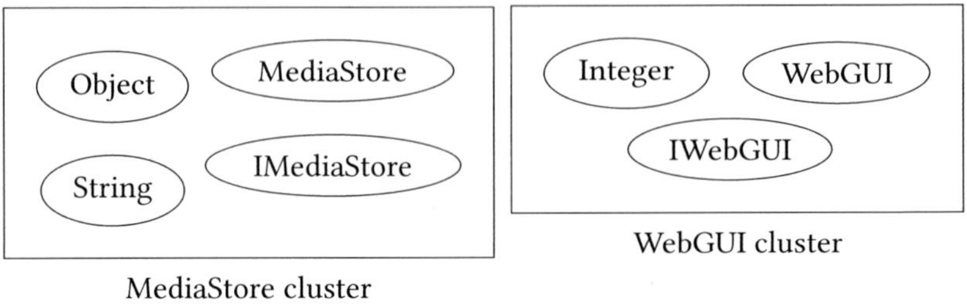

Figure 5.3.: Clusters of the MediaStore example extracted with ARCADE. We assume that two clusters are reverse-engineered by ARCADE. One cluster contains the `MediaStore` classes, while the other cluster contains the `WebGUI` classes.

From Java Call Graph[1], we get the method dependencies, i.e. we get the information which method calls with other methods. From JaMoPP [Hei+10], we get an EMF model representation of the source code.

Creating the PCM *Repository* and the PCM *System* In the following, we explain the four steps, which are used by *Extract*, to create a *Repository*:

1. create a PCM *Repository* that contains interfaces and components with their *ProvidedRoles*, and *RequiredRoles*,
2. extract the methods signatures of architectural relevant methods from source code,
3. assign signatures and data types to provided interfaces, and
4. create *SEFFs* for the provided methods of each component.

For the creation of a PCM *Repository*, we first transform each cluster in the ARCADE cluster output file into one *BasicComponent*. As ARCADE does not reverse-engineer interfaces, we create one *OperationInterface* for each cluster. This interface is provided by the *BasicComponent* through a *ProvidedRole*. As next step, we need to create the *RequiredRoles*. Therefore, we can use ARCADE's dependency output file. Using this file gives us the information which cluster depends on which other clusters, i.e, we

[1] `https://github.com/gousiosg/java-callgraph`

can find out the required *BasicComponents* for a given *BasicComponent*. As components are not allowed to depend on each other in the PCM, we create a *RequiredRole* between the *BasicComponent* and the provided interface of its required *BasicComponents*.

In step two and three, we need to create the *OperationSignatures* in the provided interfaces of each component. Within the *OperationSignatures*, we also need to create the parameters and the return types. Even though we are able to retrieve the class dependencies from ARCADE, we are not able to retrieve the method dependencies from ARCADE. To get the method dependencies between classes, we use the output of Java call-graph as input for signature matcher. The signature matcher is using the method dependencies from the Java call-graph and the class dependencies from ARCADE as input and creates signature dependencies. Therefore, the signature matcher traverses the call-graph and analyzes, for each method whether the method calls a method from a different *BasicComponent* respectively a different cluster. If this is the case, we create an *OperationSignature* for the called method in the provided *OperationInterface* of the called *BasicComponent*, because the method is called from outside its own *BasicComponent* and is therefore considered architectural relevant. After creating an *OperationSignature*, we need to create the parameters and return types. Therefore, we can reuse the data type reconstruction approach from SoMoX. Within this approach primitive data types in source code, e.g. `int` or `long`, are mapped to their corresponding PCM *PrimitiveDataTypes*. More complex data types in the source code, for instance classes, which are used as return type, are mapped to either *CompositeDataTypes* or *CollectionDataTypes*. The latter is used if a data type either implements the `Collection` interface of the Java language or if the type is an array type.

As a fourth and last step, we create a *SEFF* for each provided method of each component. Therefore, we can reuse the SoMoX *SEFF* generator. In order to be able to use SoMoX *SEFF*, we need to create a Source Code Decorator Model (SCDM) in the steps before. The SCDM contains the information how source code elements are mapped to architectural elements. Hence, we initially create an empty SCDM and update it during the creation of the components, interfaces, signatures, and data types. After this step, we are able to execute the SoMoX *SEFF* generation with this SCDM. As we mentioned in Section 2.4, the SoMoX *SEFF* generation conducts a control flow analyses on the source code. Therefore, it first classifies method calls performed within the method into either component-external method calls or component-internal method calls or library calls. Based on classified method calls it conducts the actual control flow analyses. During the control flow analyses the control flow elements, such as `loops`, `if-else`, and `switch` statements are made explicit in the *SEFF* if they contain a component-external method call.

After executing these steps, we have a complete PCM *Repository*, which consists of *BasicComponents*, *OperationInterfaces* with *OperationSignatures* and their *ReturnTypes* as well as *Parameters*. We, furthermore, retrieve the *RequiredRoles* and *ProvidedRoles* of each component. In the last step, we create *SEFFs*, which represent the behaviour of the source code. These *SEFFs* can, however, not be used for predicting the performance directly, because they do not contain performance information, such as resource demand of internal actions, for the elements within the *SEFF*. This information can be added by using approaches like Beagle Krogmann et al. [KKR10]. After applying *Extract* to our running example and the clusters, we detected according to Figure 5.3, we get a similar *Repository* as depicted in Figure 4.5. One difference is the naming of the components and clusters, as they name depends on the used reconstruction algorithm. Another difference is that the *OperationSignatures* within an *OperationInterface* are only created if the methods corresponding to the *OperationSignatures* are called from a class that is contained within another component respectively cluster.

As in SoMoX, we create an implicit PCM *System* by instantiating each of the components once in the PCM *System* and by connecting the *RequiredRoles* of the components with the matching *ProvidedRoles*.

Hence, after executing *Extract*, we have an up-to-date architectural representation of a given source code base and a SCDM, which contains the information which source code elements are mapped to which architectural elements. As we mentioned above, these artefacts are used by the following integration approach to integrate existing source code into our Coevolution approach.

5.4.1.2. EJB model eXtractor

EJBmoX, which stands for *EJB model eXtractor*, allows us to extract an architectural model from code created with EJB. As foundations for EJBs, we use the EJB version 3.1, which is defined in the JSR 318 [Sak09]. We explained the necessary foundations for EJB in Section 2.5.4. To realise the reverse engineering of EJB-based software systems, we reused the code base of SoMoX. We, however, replaced the SoMoX component and interface detection mechanism with an EJB component and interface finding mechanism. Within *EJBmoX*, we were able to reuse the following steps from SoMoX:

1. the creation mechanism for *Systems*, *ResourceEnviroment*, and *Allocation*,
2. the extraction of data types from the source code, and
3. the extraction of behaviour in terms of a *SEFF* from the source code.

The first step can be reused to create a PCM *System*, a *ResourceEnviroment*, and an *Allocation* model from a given PCM *Repository*. To create a *System* it creates an *AssemblyContext* for each component in the *Repository* and connects the provided and required roles. Composing the components is, however, only possible as long as each interface is only provided by one component. If more components provide the same interface the system architects need to specify the composition of the system. This limitation can be overcome in future work by also taking the deployment information of an EJB system into account during the reverse engineering. The first step also creates a default *ResourceEnviroment*, by creating one server. The *Allocation* model is created by deploying all created components on the one server in the *ResourceEnviroment*.

Creating a *Repository* from EJB-based source code To create a PCM *Repository* from EJB source code *EJBmoX* performs the following steps.

1. reverse engineering of *BasicComponents*, *OperationInterfaces*, and *ProvidedRoles*,
2. reverse engineering of *OperationSignatures* and *DataTypes*,
3. creation of *RequiredRoles*,

4. creation of *SEFFs* for the provided services of each *BasicComponent*.

Within the first step the EJB source code is analysed and a PCM *Repository* including *BasicComponents*, *OperationInterfaces*, and *ProvidedRoles* is created. The algorithm used by *EJBmoX* to do so, is depicted in Algorithm 5 and explained in the following. The first sub-step within the first step is the reconstruction of components. Therefore, we investigate all classes subsequently and check for each class whether it is an EJB component-class. If this is the case, we create a *BasicComponent* for the currently investigated class. Classes annotated with either `@Stateless`, `@Stateful` or `@MessageDriven` are EJB component-classes.

In the second sub-step, we create *OperationInterfaces* for all EJB business interfaces implemented by the currently investigated EJB class. The identification of EJB business interfaces is done as specified in the EJB specification [Sak09]: If an EJB component-class implements only one interface, the interface is an EJB relevant interface. If an EJB component-class implements more than one interface, only those interfaces are relevant that are annotated with either `@Remote` or `@Local`. These identification rules, however, do not apply to all interfaces. For instance, the interfaces `java.lang.Serializable`, `java.io.Externalizable`, and all interfaces in the package `javax.ejb`, are never considered as EJB business interfaces. Hence, if a class implements one of the irrelevant interfaces, *EJBmoX* also needs to ignore the interfaces during the reconstruction phase. For all other interfaces, *EJBmoX* needs to follow the above-mentioned specification, in order to create *OperationInterfaces* for all EJB business interfaces. If interfaces extend each other in the source code, for instance if class `ClassA` implements `InterfaceA`, which extends interface InterfaceB and `InterfaceA` is annotated with `@Remote`, we also consider `InterfaceB` as an architectural relevant interface. Hence, we create an *OperationInterface* for `InterfaceB` and use `InterfaceA` as parent interface. An *OperationInterface* for a Java interface, however, is only created if no *OperationInterface* has been created already for the Java interface.

After we created the *OperationInterfaces* for a component, we need to create the *ProvidedRoles* between the components and interfaces in the PCM. We create a *ProvidedRole* between a reconstructed *BasicComponent* and a reconstructed *OperationInterface*, if the EJB component-class, which corresponds to the *BasicComponent*, implements the EJB business interface, which corresponds to the *OperationInterface*.

Algorithm 5 Algorithm used by *EJBmoX* to create *BasicComponents*, *OperationInterfaces*, and *ProvidedRoles*

```
Require: sourceCodeModel←JaMoPP MODEL,
repository ← createEmptyRepository
classes ← sourceCodeModel.classes
ejbClasses ← newEmptySet
for all class ∈ classes do
    annotations ← class.annotations
    if ("Stateful" ∨ "Stateless" ∨ "MessageDrive") ∈ annotations then
                                                ▷ EJB component class found
        ejbClasses.add(class)
        basicComponent ← createBasicComponentWithName(class.name)
        repository.components.add(basicComponent)
        implementedInterfaces = class.interfaces
        implementedInterfaces.remove("Serializable")
        implementedInterfaces.remove("Externalizable")
        implementedInterfaces.remove("javax.ejb.*")
        ejbInterfaces = newEmptySet
        if implementedInterfaces.size = 1 then
            ejbInterfaces.add(implementedInterfaces.first)
        else if implementedInterfaces.size > 1 then
            for all interface ∈ implementedInterfaces do
                if ("Remote" ∨ "Local" ∈ interface.annotations then
                    ejbInterfaces.add(interface)
        for all ejbInterface ∈ ejbInterfaces do
            opInterface ←
repository.interfaces.getInterfaceWithName(ejbInterface.name)
            if opInterface = ∅ then             ▷ create interface if not existing
                opInterface      ←      createOperationInterfaceWith-
Name(ejbInterface.name)
                repository.interfaces.add(opInterface)
            providedRole ← createProvidedRole         ▷ create providedRole
            providedRole.component ← basicComponent
            providedRole.interface ← opInterface
```

As second step, we need to create PCM *OperationSignatures* with parameters and return types as well as PCM *DataTypes* for the types of parameters and return types. For each method in the EJB business interface we create one *OperationSignature* in the corresponding PCM *OperationInterface.* For the creation of PCM data types, we are able to reuse the data type reconstruction approach from SoMoX. This approach creates PCM data types for each Java object used as parameter or return type and adds it to the *OperationSignature.*

After the creation of the *OperationSignature,* we need to create the *RequiredRoles* between components and interfaces. A required relation between a *BasicComponent* and an *OperationInterface* in the PCM means that the component needs the functionality of the interface to fulfill its own contracts. In EJB dependencies from an EJB component class to an Java interface can be injected into the component class fields by annotating the fields with either `@EJB` or `@Inject`. The runtime environment of EJB respectively the used EJB container, ensures that the correct EJB component class that implements the interface is injected. This mechanism is similar to the PCM definition of a required role. Hence, to create the *RequiredRoles,* we need to investigate every field of every EJB component-class and check, whether the field is annotated with `@EJB` or `@Inject` and if the type of the field is an Java interface for which we created an *OperationInterface.* If this is the case, we can create a *RequiredRole* between the *BasicComponent,* which corresponds to the EJB component-class, and the *OperationInterface,* which corresponds to the type of field.

As the last step to complete the PCM repository, we need to create *SEFF*s for the components. This is done by creating one *SEFF* for each provided *OperationSignature* of a *BasicComponent.* Therefore, we can also partly reuse the SoMoX implementation. To run the SoMoX *SEFF* reconstruction, we need to have an up-to-date SCDM, which contains the information how architectural elements are mapped to the source code. In the case of *EJBmoX*, we create the SCDM with the following information:

- a component-to-class relation between each EJB component-class and its corresponding *BasicComponent,*
- an interface-to-interface relation between for each EJB business interface and its corresponding *OperationInterface,*

- a signature-to-method relation between each interface method in EJB business interface and its corresponding *OperationSignature*, and
- a data-type-to-class relation between each EJB data type class, which are usually represented by POJOs, and the PCM data types.

These information are added to the SCDM during the above-mentioned reconstruction steps, i.e. during the creation of *BasicComponents*, for instance, we also create the component- to-class entries in the SCDM.

Having the SCDM allows us to run the *SEFF* reconstruction approach from SoMoX, which executes a control flow analysis. The starting points for the control flow analyses are all class methods that implements an architectural relevant interface method, i.e. each method that implements an interface method from an EJB interface we found in the first step. As we mentioned in Section 2.4, the first step of the control flow analysis is to recursively visit all method calls within a method and classify them as either *internal* calls, *external* calls or *library* calls. We adapted the classifying mechanism of SoMoX in order to support *EJBmoX*. The classifying mechanism used in SoMoX classifies all calls to another component as component *external* calls, all calls to a used third party library or another used API, such as *java.lang.*, as *library* call, and all calls to component-internal methods as *internal* call. We can reuse the SoMoX classification for library calls and internal calls. The classification of *external* calls, however, needs to be implemented for EJB components as follows: *EJBmoX* needs to check whether a method call is a call to a method of a required interface. If this is true we found an external call. As in the SoMoX implementation, *EJBmoX* identifies all calls to a used API or third party library as *library* call. Furthermore, calls to data types are considered as *library* calls. This means that *EJBmoX* assumes that within data types no external calls are performed. As in the SoMoX implementation, *internal* calls are calling a method within the same component. After the classification is done we execute the *SEFF* generating mechanism from SoMoX, which uses the classified method calls to reverse-engineer the *SEFF* of a given method. To use the reverse-engineered *SEFF* for the coevolution within our Coevolution approach, *EJBmoX* is able to generate *ResourceDemandingInternalBehaviour* and *InternalCallAction* for component-internal method calls instead of inlining them directly into the *SEFF*.

Extensions for *EJBmoX* We developed two extensions for *EJBmoX*, which allows *EJBmoX* to also reverse-engineer software systems that do not completely follow the above-mentioned mapping. The first extension, reverse-engineers fields within an EJB component-class that have the type of an EJB interface to *RequiredRoles* in the architecture. Hence, *RequiredRoles* are created even if the fields are not annotated with `@EJB` or `@Inject`. Using this extension those fields are treated the same way as fields annotated with `@EJB` or `@Inject`. Hence, they are reverse-engineered to *RequiredRoles* within the *BasicComponent*, which corresponds to the class containing the field. This extension allows us to reverse-engineer software system, where developers composed EJB components manually, e.g. through the `lookup` method of the `Context` class used by the EJB container. Using the first extension, however, has the disadvantage that *EJBmoX* is not able to reverse-engineer the correct PCM *System* in a fully-automated fashion.

The second extension creates an *OperationInterface* in the reconstructed PCM *Repository* for classes, which are annotated with an EJB component-annotation, but not providing an EJB interface. To do so, we create one *OperationSignature* for each public method in the class.

Example reconstruction using *EJBmoX* Listing 19 shows an EJB implementation of the running MediaStore example. The simplified version of the MediaStore consists of two EJB component-classes and two `remote` EJB business interfaces. The EJB class `WebGUIImpl` implements the interface `IWebGUI` and requires an instance of the interface `IMediaStore` (Listing 19).

For this simple example, *EJBmoX* creates two *BasicComponents*: one for the class `WebGUIImpl` and one for the class `MediaStoreImpl`, because both are annotated with `@Stateless`. *EJBmoX*, furthermore, creates two *OperationInterface* for the two Java interfaces `IWebGUI` and `IMediaStore`, because both interfaces are annotated with `@Remote`. In the second step, *EJBmoX* creates one *OperationProvidedRole* between the *BasicComponent WebGUIImpl* and the *OperationInterface* `WebGUI` and one between the *BasicComponent MediaStoreImpl* and the *OperationInterface MediaStore*. The *ProvidedRoles* are created, because the classes corresponding to the *BasicComponents* implementing the EJB interfaces correspond to the *OperationInterfaces*.

```
@Remote
public interface IWebGUI{
  File httpDownload(Request request);
  void httpUpload(File file);
}
@Remote
public interface IMediaStore{
  File[] download(String[] ids);
  void upload(File file);
}
@Stateless
public final class WebGUIImpl implements IWebGUI {
  @EJB
  private final IMediaStore iMediaStore

  @Override
  public File httpDownload(Request request){
        Integer id = request.getFirstId();
        String idStr = id.toString();
        String[] ids = new String[]{idStr};
        File[] file = this.iMediaStore.download(ids);
        logger.info("File␣" + file + "␣retrieved.");
        return file[0];
  }

  @Override
  public void httpUpload(File file){
    //...
  }
}
@Stateless
public final class MediaStoreImpl implements IMediaStore{
  @Override
  public File[] download(String[] ids){
      //...
  }

  @Override
  public void upload(File file){
      //...
  }
}
```

Listing 19: Simple example for EJB code

During the interface reconstruction, we also create the signatures in terms of *OperationSignatures* for the methods within the Java interface. Hence, *EJBmoX* creates the *OperationSignatures download* and *upload* in *IMediaStore* and *httpDownload* as well as *httpUpload* in *IWebGUI*. During the creation of the *OperationSignatures*, *EJBmoX* also creates the PCM *CompositeDatatypes Request* and *File* for the types used as parameters in the *OperationSignatures*. Furthermore, *EJBmoX* creates a *CollectionDatatype* named *FileList* for the array of files `File[]`.

In the next step, *EJBmoX* creates an *OperationRequiredRole* between the *BasicComponent* `WebGUIImpl` and the *OperationInterface* `IMediaStore`, because the `IMediaStore` field in the class `IWebGUI` has the `@EJB` Annotation. During the above-mentioned steps, *EJBmoX* creates a SCDM, which contains the links between the architectural elements and their matching source code elements. As last step to complete the PCM repository we reconstruct the *SEFFs* for the class methods. As example, we consider the method `httpDownload` in the `WebGUIImpl`. As mentioned above, we can reuse the *SEFF* creation mechanism from SoMoX. Therefore, the following steps are executed: First, all method calls within the method `httpDownload` are visited and classified as either *component-external* call, *component-internal* call or *library* call. The result of this visiting is that only the call `download` is a component-external call. All other calls are library calls. Now we can execute the control flow analysis for the method. The first element in the resulting *SEFF* is an *InternalAction* for all calls before the component-external call. For the `download` call, the *SEFF* reconstruction creates an *ExternalCallAction*. For the last library call in the method, the *SEFF* reconstruction creates another *InternalAction*.

As we are now finished creating the PCM *Repository*, we can create the PCM *System* for the simple example. Therefore, we create one *AssemblyContext* for each *BasicComponents* in the *Repository*, i.e. we create one for the *BasicComponent* `MediaStoreImpl` and one for the *BasicComponent* `WebGUIImpl`. The *AssemblyContexts* are connected using an *AssemblyConnector* between the provided interfaces and required interface. The simple example, is an EJB implementation of the running example for this thesis. Hence, *EJBmoX* reverse-engineers the PCM repository depicted in Figure 4.5 from the EJB example source code. *EJBmoX*, furthermore, extracts the PCM System depicted in Figure 4.6.

Assumptions and Limitations We make similar assumptions for the structure of the EJB code as we make for the bidirectional consistency preservation rules between PCM and EJB code (see Section 4.6.1.1). One assumption, we currently have, is that only source code artefacts are used to describe the EJB components, EJB interfaces, and EJB dependencies. This means other approaches, for instance XML descriptors, to describe EJB component-classes, EJB interfaces, and dependencies between EJBs are not considered yet. In future work, however *EJBmoX* can be extended in order to take such XML descriptors into count during the reverse engineering of a software system. Furthermore, we assume that EJB relevant business interfaces are contained in the source code. This means, we are currently not dealing with business interfaces contained in external libraries or JAR files. We also assume that data types do not have any component relevant behaviour. Hence, we require that data types do not contain external calls. If the mentioned assumptions do not hold for source code, which should be analysed, *EJBmoX* creates a wrong architecture and/or wrong *SEFF*s.

A limitation on the architectural level is that we do not support *CompositeComponents*, which are components that contains other components. In future work this limitation could be overcome by, for instance, combining EJB component-classes contained in the same package or in the same project to a *CompositeComponent*.

5.4.2. The Four Code Integration Levels

In the following, we explain the concepts for the four code integration levels, we defined for the integration of existing source code. In the next section the integration of source code for our Coevolution approach is explained based on this levels.

5.4.2.1. Integration Level 1

The first level of integration can be used if the following requirements are fulfilled:

- The source code base that shall be integrated needs to be compliant to the consistency preservation rules that are used for the consistency preservation.
- The reverse-engineered architecture, which has been created by the used reverse engineering tool, needs to be equal to the architecture that would have been created if our Coevolution approach has been used from the beginning of the development, i.e. it the reverse-engineered architecture needs to be compliant to the used consistency preservation rules as well.

The level has two advantages: The first one is that the integrated code can be treated like the code that would have been created if our Coevolution approach has been used from the beginning of the development process. Hence, changes performed to any architectural element or source code element can be kept consistent using the current used bidirectional consistency preservation rules. The second advantage of Integration Level 1 is that the process of the integration and the development process after the integration are simple, because no special treatment for the integrated parts of the source is needed. Hence, neither software architects nor software developers need to deal with the fact that some of the elements have been integrated. However, Integration Level 1 has the disadvantage that existing source code usually not fulfills the bidirectional consistency preservation rules, because source code can be build up in an arbitrary way. Even if the code follows a certain consistency preservation rule, it is not guaranteed that no architecture violation occurs within the code or that certain parts of the code do not follow the intended consistency preservation rules. If the latter is the case, an approach such as Archimetrix [DPB13] can be used to align the code base to an intended architecture. Integrating Archimetrix, however, is left to future work. Hence, Integration Level 1 is suited for existing source code that already fulfill the used consistency preservation rules.

In contrary to Integration Level 1 the other integration levels can be used for an arbitrary code base. Hence, there are no special requirements to the source code and the reverse-engineered architecture model.

5.4.2.2. Integration Level 2

The second integration level is the first level that supports source code that is not compliant to the used bidirectional consistency preservation rules. To realise this a special treatment is necessary for the integrated source code elements and their corresponding reverse-engineered architectural elements. During the integration these elements are marked as integrated elements. The special treatment and the marking is only necessary if the elements are not compliant to the used bidirectional consistency preservation rules. Hence, during the integration a matcher is executed that checks which source code elements and their corresponding architectural elements do not fulfill the used consistency preservation rules. If during the evolution of a software system one of these elements has been changed by users, the elements cannot be kept consistent automatically. Instead users get a notification though the user change disambiguation framework of our Coevolution approach that contains the information that the performed change cannot be kept consistent automatically. Furthermore, it contains the information, which element corresponds to the changed element and should be changed manually to preserve consistency.

Hence, the advantage of this approach is that arbitrary code can be integrated, while the disadvantage is that the integrated elements cannot be kept consistent automatically. Instead the users are notified that the integrated elements need to be kept consistent manually.

New elements that are added to the architecture, are kept consistent using the defined consistency preservation rules. For new elements that are added to the source code, we need to decide whether they are part of an integrated component or not. If they are part of an integrated component, they are treated as integrated elements. Otherwise they are treated as new elements and can be kept consistent using the defined bidirectional consistency preservation rules. This level has the advantage that an arbitrary code base can be integrated. It has, however, the disadvantage that included code that does not fulfill the consistency preservation rules cannot be kept consistent automatically. Integration Level 2 is suited if a) the existing source code of a project does not fulfill the used consistency preservation rules, and b) the existing source code is not changed frequently. Hence, it is suited for projects that like to include their code base into our Coevolution approach and use our Coevolution approach and the provided bidirectional consistency preservation rules for the implementation of new components and features.

5.4.2.3. Integration Level 3

The third level is similar to the second level, but it overcomes the disadvantage that no elements can be kept consistent automatically. Therefore, it allows to keep defined changes consistent automatically during the software evolution. As in Integration Level 2, the integrated architectural elements and source code elements are marked as integrated during the integration. Furthermore, the integrators needs to identify changes that can be kept consistent. For these changes the integrators needs to define integration-specific consistency preservation rules that are executed if an element, which is marked as integrated, has been changed. The more integration-specific consistency preservation operations can be defined by the integrators the more effort is omitted for keeping the models consistent manually.

To figure out, whether a change that occurs during the evolution of the software system can be kept consistent automatically, we check after each change a) if an integrated element has been changed, and if yes, b) whether an action has been defined by the integrators for the integrated element. If both conditions are true, the consistency between the elements can be preserved automatically. If only the first condition (a) is true, we fall back to the approach that is used in Integration Level 2, i.e. the users get the notification that the change needs to be kept consistent manually. If neither of conditions are true, either a new element has been introduced or the changes does not affect integrated elements. In this case, we can use the standard consistency preservation rules to preserve consistency. The advantage of Integration Level 3 is that integrated elements, which do not follow the standard consistency preservation rules, can be kept consistent automatically with their corresponding elements during the software evolution. The disadvantage is that the integration process needs more effort, because the integrators needs to define which changes to integrated elements can be kept consistent automatically and need to implement the consistency preservation rules for these changes. Integration Level 3 is suited for projects, where the integrated elements are changed during the evolution of the software system, and defined changes should be kept consistent automatically.

5.4.2.4. Integration Level 4

For the forth integration level, we propose the creation of element-specific consistency preservation rules during the integration process. This element-specific consistency preservation rules can be used for consistency preservation during the evolution of the software system. In this thesis, we focus on the first three integration levels. Hence, we consider the fourth level is as future work. However, we can give some initial ideas about the realisation of Integration Level 4. As a first step, the integration needs to be extended in a way that element-specific mappings are created for each architectural element, which has been created during the reverse engineering procees, and its corresponding source code element. Since currently, mapping-specific rules are neither supported by our Coevolution approach nor supported by the VITRUVIUS framework, the next step is to enable the support of element-specific consistency preservation rules. Therefore, the reaction language developed by Klare [Kla16] and Kramer [Kra17] or our internal DSL to create consistency preservation rules, can be extended. During the software evolution, a similar process as in Integration Level 3 can be used to check whether a change affects an element for which an element-specific consistency preservation operation exist. If an element-specific consistency preservation operation exists for the changed element, this consistency preservation operation needs to be executed in order to preserve the consistency. If this is not the case, the standard consistency preservation rules can be used. The advantage of Integration Level 4 compared to Integration Level 3 is that all elements can be kept consistent automatically based on the element-specific consistency preservation rules. The approach is suited if the source code that should be integrated is changed frequently and if the source code does not fulfill any consistency preservation rules.

5.4.3. Integration Level 1: Include Architecture-Code-Mapping Compliant Source Code

This section explains, how the integration of existing source code using Integration Level 1 for source code is realised within our Coevolution approach. Integration Level 1 means, that the code we integrate needs to be compliant with the current used bidirectional consistency preservation rules between architecture and code. This can be, for example, code that uses EJB and matches our EJB consistency preservation rules or it could be code that either is compliant or was refined to be compliant to the package mapping consistency preservation rules we explained in Section 4.3.

5.4.3.1. Overview of the integration process

Figure 5.4 gives an overview how the integration process works. For all code integration levels the first step is to reverse-engineer the source code base that shall be integrated. Therefore, we can use one of the above-mentioned reverse engineering approaches to get an architecture model of a given source code. The result of the reverse engineering process are two artefacts: i) an architectural model, which represents an architectural view onto the source code base, and ii) the linking information between the source code and the architectural model. If we use one of the above-mentioned reverse engineering approaches, we get a SCDM that contains the linking information. These two artefacts and the source code can be used as input models for the LIS. The reason why we need these three models as input models for the LIS is explained below. The main part of the presented LIS, is to create an instance of the Vitruvius correspondence model that contains the correspondences between the architectural element and its corresponding source code element(s). This Vitruvius correspondence model can be used for the evolution of the software system using our Coevolution approach.

5.4.3.2. Using a LIS to Create a Vitruvius Correspondence Model

A first idea is to create the Vitruvius correspondence model instance from the available information in the SCDM. It turned out, however, that the information in the SCDM is not sufficient to create a VITRUVIUS correspondence model. To give an example, where the information in the SCDM is not sufficient, consider the parameters of a method in the source code model. For our Coevolution approach, we need to have the correspondence from each method parameter from the source code model to a corresponding parameter of an *OperationSignature* in the architecture model. This information is not represented directly in the SCDM. To get the missing information, one approach is to extend the SCDM with the necessary information as well as the reverse engineering approaches in a way that they are able to create the necessary information. Another approach is to use the information from the SCDM together and combine them with information from the source code model and the architectural model to get the necessary information. In order to avoid the effort of extending the reverse engineering approaches, we decided for the latter approach, which is also depicted in Figure 5.4. To give an example how this approach works consider, again, the parameters of a method. Even though the correspondence between the parameters of a method and its corresponding *Parameters* of an *OperationSignature* are not made explicit in the SCDM, we can create the correspondence by using the information from the correspondence between the methods and *OperationSignatures* to create the correspondence between the parameters of a method and the *Parameters* of an *OperationSignature*. Hence, for Integration Level 1, the linking integration strategy performs a simple M2M transformation from the SCDM, the architecture model and the source code model to the VITRUVIUS correspondence model. This M2M transformation creates one entry in the VITRUVIUS correspondence model for each linking information in the SCDM. If the information from the SCDM is not sufficient, the transformation uses additional information from the Java model and the architectural model.

It might be necessary to adapt this M2M transformation according to the used bidirectional consistency preservation rules. For the package mapping consistency preservation rules, for instance, we need to perform the following two modifications for the consistency preservation rules: Firstly, it is necessary to ensure that only for one class per package an entry in the VITRUVIUS correspondence model is created, and secondly it is necessary to create a correspondence for each package of its corresponding component.

Using this approach to integrate the source code creates the same correspondence model that would have been created if our Coevolution approach

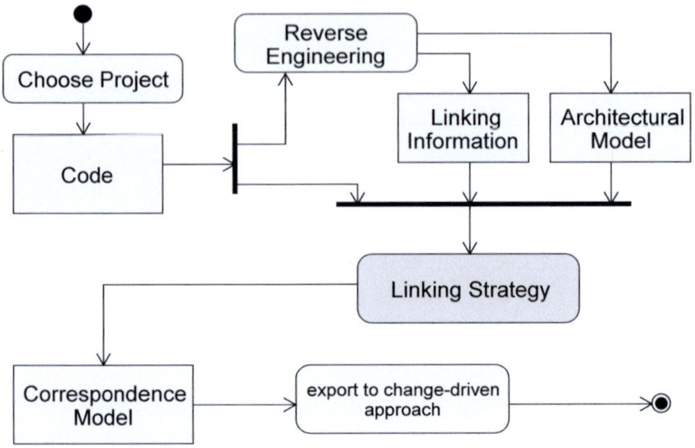

Figure 5.4.: Diagram that shows the steps executed by the proposed LIS to include source code that is compliant with the used architecture to code consistency preservation rules. We published the diagram already in [Leo+15].

has been used from the beginning of the development process. Hence, the integrated source code can be kept consistent using the already existing bidirectional consistency preservation rules. This means, furthermore, that after the integration our Coevolution approach can be used as if it has been used from the beginning of the development process. Within the next section, we explain how it is possible to include arbitrary component-based source code.

5.4.4. Integration Level 2: Include Non-Compliant Source Code

Including source code that is non-compliant with the used bidirectional transformations is possible in Integration Level 2. In this section, we describe how we realise Integration Level 2 for our Coevolution approach, by changing respectively extending the above-mentioned integration of source code. The Integration Level 2 has the requirements that i) integrated elements are marked as integrated elements, and ii) after each change during the software evolution a check is performed whether an integrated element has been changed. To realise these requirements, we performed the following three extensions compared to the integration of mapping compliant code:

1. extending the VITRUVIUS correspondence metamodel,
2. extending the integration transformation, and
3. extending the coevolution process in order to check whether a change has been performed on an integrated model element or not.

For the first necessary extension, we introduce the new class `IntegrationCorrespondence` to the correspondence metamodel, which has the standard `Correspondence` as base class. Hence, it can be treated as a standard correspondence model element, but it marks its instances as integrated elements. The second change, we made to the above-mentioned integration process occurs during the integration itself. Instead of creating a standard VITRUVIUS correspondence model containing instances of `Correspondences`, we create `IntegrationCorrespondences`, for elements that are integrated by default. Instead of creating `IntegrationCorrespondences` only, it is, however, also possible to create standard `Correspondences` for elements that fulfill the used consistency preservation rules. To do so, we integrated a check, which is executed before the creation of an `IntegrationCorrespondence`. This check needs to be implemented mapping-specific and needs to decide whether a given architecture model element and a given source code element fulfill the bidirectional consistency preservation rules. To do so, this check can access the VITRUVIUS correspondence model, the SCDM as well as all architectural model elements and source code elements. If the result of the check is that the given elements fulfill the consistency preservation rules a standard `Correspondences` can be created for that elements. Hence, the elements can be kept consistent during the evolution of a software system using the standard consistency preservation rules.

As last step, we need to extend our coevolution process. Therefore, we developed a mechanism that checks for each change that is performed on either an architectural element or a source code element, whether the changed element affects an integrated element respectively an integrated area or not. An existing element that has been changed, is considered as integrated element respectively as element contained in an integrated area if either of the following two statements is true: i) the VITRUVIUS correspondence model

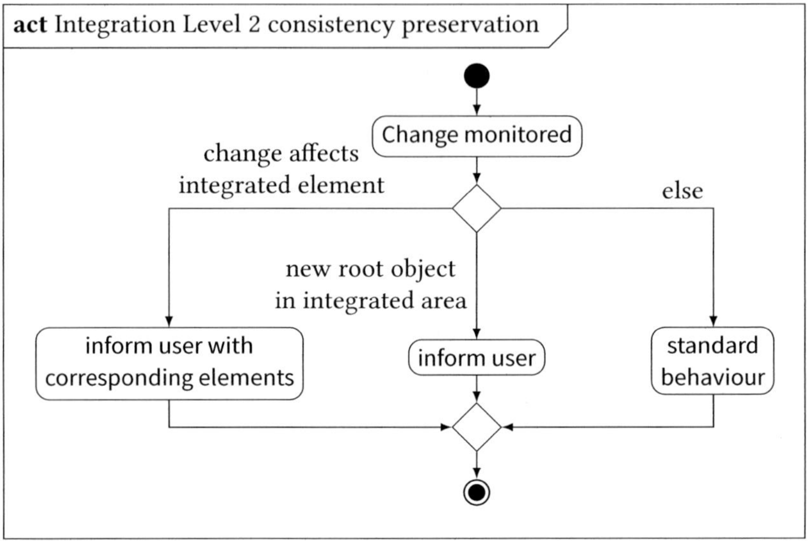

Figure 5.5.: Change processing in Integration Level 2. After we monitored a change, we check whether the change has been performed to an element within an integrated or not. In the first case, we need to inform users about the change (either with the corresponding element or without the corresponding element). In the latter case, we can use the standard consistency preservation rules can be used (standard behaviour)[Pet16].

contains an `IntegrationCorrespondence` for that element, or ii) one parent element of the changed element is an integrated element. If the element is considered as integrated element, the standard consistency preservation rules are not executed. Instead the users get a notification via the user change disambiguation that specifies which element needs to be updated manually to achieve consistence between the models. Figure 5.5 shows, how a change is processed within our Coevolution approach using the extended development process.

Newly added elements cannot kept consistent using the standard consistency preservation rules if they are contained within an integrated element or an integrated area. Hence, we need to figure out whether a newly added element has been added into an integrated area and should be treated as integrated element, or whether it should be treated as standard element. We decided that newly added elements within a compilation unit should be treated by default the same way as their compilation unit respectively the class or interface within this compilation unit. Hence, it is simple to figure out whether a new element that has been added within a compilation unit should be treated as integrated element or not by checking the parents of the newly added elements until a class or interface is reached. A challenge arises, however, for compilation units respectively classes, interfaces, and packages that are newly added. For these elements, it is unclear whether they have been added into an integrated area or not. However, it can be decided depending on the consistency preservation rules, whether these elements are contained in an integrated area or not. For the package mapping consistency preservation rules, for instance, newly added packages, classes or interfaces are considered as being part of an integrated area if they are added within a package or sub-package that a) contains at least one integrated class or interface already, or b) is contained in an integrated area itself.

5.4.5. Integration Level 3: The Definition and Execution of Special Bidirectional Consistency Preservation Rules for Non-Compliant Source Code

To realise Integration Level 3 for our Coevolution approach, we extend the realisation for Integration Level 2 in the following way: A new task is added for the integration phase: During this phase the integrators need to specify specific consistency preservation rules for changes that affect integrated elements. These specific consistency preservation rules have the same structure as the standard consistency preservation rules and can be either written in the Mapping Invariant Response (MIR) languages [Kra17] or in our internal DSL (see Section 3.6.1). The difference to the standard consistency preservation rules and the specific consistency preservation rules is the execution time within the consistency preservation process. During the software evolution phase, the specific consistency preservation rules are executed if the following two conditions are true: i) the change occurred in an integrated area, and ii) an integration specific consistency preservation operation that is defined in the specific consistency preservation rules matches the occurred change (e.g. rename of an interface method). A typical change, which can be kept consistent automatically for integrated elements, is if they are renamed by users, e.g. the rename of an interface method can be kept consistent with the name of the corresponding *OperationInterface*. Figure 5.6 shows, how a change is processed within our Coevolution approach if Integration Level 3 is used. The processing is similar as the one, we presented for Integration Level 2 (see Section 5.4.4). It only adds the possibility to keep the change consistent using the integration specific consistency preservation rules.

5.4.6. Tasks for the Integrators during the Code Integration

In this section, we explain the task of the integrators that are specific for the code integration. The general tasks of the integrators are explained in Section 5.2.3. For the code integration in Integration Level 1 the integrators have the additional task of refining the specified M2M transformation from the SCDM to the Vitruvius correspondence model if needed. This refinement might be necessary in order to allow the automatic coevolution of the reverse-engineered architectural model and the source code. To be able to execute the refinement, integrators need to be aware of the used standard consistency preservation rules.

For Integration Level 2 the integrators have the additional task of implementing the mapping-specific integration-area-finder for newly added classes, interfaces, and packages. The finder is used to figure out, whether newly added elements are contained in an integration area or not. To realise this task, integrators need to be aware of the standard consistency preservation rules.

As mentioned above, within Integration Level 3, the integrators need to define the integration specific consistency preservation rules and implement them. For the implementation of the consistency preservation rules integrators can, e.g. use the Reaction language [Kla16] or our internal DSL. As in Integration Level 2, they also need to define a mapping-specific integration-area-finder. To do so, they also need to be aware of the used standard consistency preservation rules. Hence, the integrators need to be aware of the used standard consistency preservation rules in all realised integration levels.

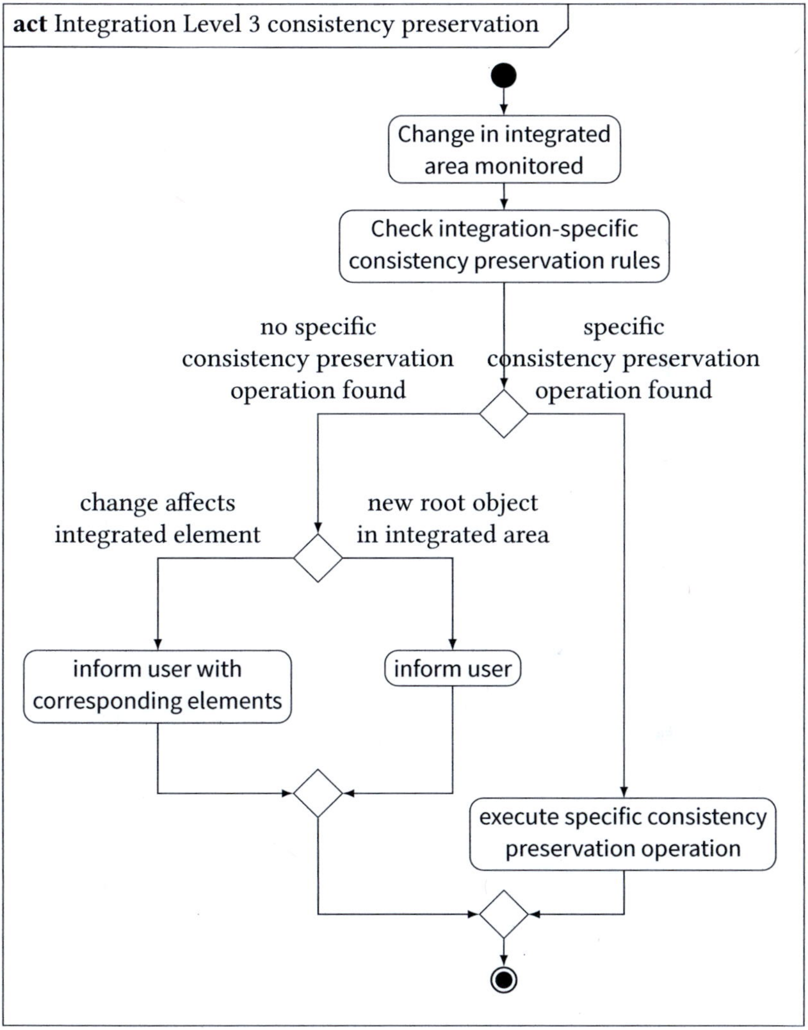

Figure 5.6.: Change processing in Integration Level 3. The figure shows the necessary steos if a change in an integrated area has been monitored. To simplify the figure, we did not include the standard Vitruvius case[Pet16].

6. Evaluation

In this section, we present the evaluation of our Coevolution approach. The main goal of our Coevolution approach is to keep architectural models and source code consistent during software evolution. Hence, the evaluation is aligned to the goals and research questions, which we introduced in the Section 1.2. We evaluated our Coevolution approach, the developed reverse engineering tools, and the integration of existing projects on existing Palladio Component Model (PCM) instances and open source case studies. We showed that our Coevolution approach can be used to keep changes performed to real world projects consistent by extracting changes from a Version Control System (VCS) and replaying them. Furthermore, we evaluated that the coevolved models can be used for model-based analyses by predicting the performance of a software system using coevolved models.

The remainder of this section is structured as follows. In Section 6.1, we give an overview of the performed evaluation and classify them according to the validation levels presented by Böhme and Reussner [BR05]. Next, we present the Goal Question Metric (GQM) plan for the evaluation (see Section 6.2). Based on the GQM plan, we describe the performed evaluation. We first evaluate the contributions of including existing artefacts (see Chapter 5) before we evaluate the contributions of the architectural code consistency (see Chapter 4). The reason that we first evaluate the contributions of Chapter 5 is that we need to have an up-to date architecture model for an existing source code base before we can evaluate the contributions of Chapter 4, i.e. before we can evaluate that our Coevolution approach is able to keep architectural models and source code consistent during the software evolution.

6.1. Evaluation Overview

In this section, we present an overview of the performed evaluation and classify them into the different validation levels presented by Böhme and Reussner [BR05]. We also give a brief overview of the evaluation results.

6.1.1. Overview of the Performed Evaluation

First, we evaluate the developed reverse engineering approaches *Extract* and *EJBmoX* by analysing existing open source projects using the reverse engineering approaches to show how architecture models can be reverse-engineered from source code. To evaluate the contributions of the thesis, we perform different evaluation case studies. Next, we evaluate the consistency preservation rules between component-based architecture models and source code, which we presented in Chapter 4, as follows: We use a Reconstructive Integration Strategy (RIS) as explained in Section 5.3 to simulate the creation of existing PCM *Repositories*. During this reconstruction, the defined consistency preservation rules are executed to create the corresponding source code respectively Eclipse Plugin artefacts. Next, we evaluate the levels of code integration to show how existing source code can be integrated into our Coevolution approach. Therefore, we use the reverse-engineered software systems from the first evaluation. Based on the integrated projects, we use the ChangeReplayTool (see Section 2.5.5) to replay changes, which were performed on the open source systems, we integrated before. During the replay of the changes, our Coevolution approach keeps changes to architectural relevant source code consistent respectively informs users that changes are performed on an integrated element. Hence, we are able to evaluate that our Coevolution approach is able to keep architectural models consistent with source code changes. We, furthermore, used the replay of changes to evaluate the

- functionality of the incremental*SEFF* reconstruction,
- the scalability of our Coevolution approach, and
- the performance of our Coevolution approach.

As last evaluation, we show that it is possible to perform model-based analyses using PCM's performance predicting capabilities. As case study system, we use the open source system "modular Rice University Bidding System" (mRUBiS) and predict the performance of

- a model reversed engineered with *EJBmoX*, and
- a coevolved architectural model.

6.1.2. Validation Levels of the performed Evaluations

Table 6.1 classifies the performed evaluations into the validation levels introduced by Böhme and Reussner [BR05]. As we presented in Section 2.6.2 we interpret the levels as follows for our Coevolution approach: The first level (*Level I*) is the metric validation respectively result validation, which can be used to compare the result of an approach with the reality. The second level (*Level II*) represents the applicability validation, which shows the applicability of an approach to real world project. The third level (*Level III*) is the benefit validation, which shows the benefit of one approach compared to other approaches. As mentioned in 2.6.2 Böhme and Reussner [BR05] do not define an explicit *Level 0*, which would be considered as implementation validity level.

We are not performing a *Level III* validation, as it would require too much effort. Instead, we focus on *Level I* and *Level II* validations. All performed evaluations are also *Level 0* validations, because all evaluations require a working prototypical implementation of our Coevolution approach.

6.1.3. Evaluation Results

In this section, we give a brief overview of the evaluation results.

We were able to integrate most existing PCM instances using the consistency preservation rules presented in this thesis. We successfully evaluated the developed reverse engineering tools *Extract* and *EJBmoX* on 14 respectively 2 open source projects. We integrated the mRUBiS case study system, and evaluated Integration Level 1 successfully. We also integrated and replayed changes to four open source projects and were able to identify changes

performed evaluation	**Level I**	**Level II**
RIS for existing PCM models using different consistency preservation rules	✗	
Evaluation of reverse engineering approach using case study system and open source systems		✗
Evaluation of Linking Integration Strategy (LIS) based on a reversed engineered case study system	✗	
Evaluation of LIS based on reverse-engineered open source systems		✗
Evaluation of Integration Level 1 using a case study system	✗	
Evaluation of Integration Level 2 and Integration Level 3 by replaying changes on reverse engineered and integrated open source systems		✗
Incremental *SEFF* reconstruction on open source systems during change replay		✗
Performance evaluation of Java monitor	✗	
Performance measurement and scalability analysis during change replay	✗	
Model-based performance prediction with coevolved architectural model		✗

Table 6.1.: A classification of the performed evaluation into the validation levels of Böhme and Reussner [BR05]. An "✗" means that the performed evaluation is an evaluation of the validation level.

on integrated elements and keep them consistent with the architecture respectively inform the users about the changes. During this evaluation, we were also able to keep the *SEFF* consistent incrementally. Hence, we were able to evaluate Integration Level 2 and Integration Level 3 using open source systems. Even though the performance of our Coevolution approach can be improved, the performance measurement showed that our Coevolution approach can be used for typical sized classes. As performance bottleneck, we identified the parsing of source code into a Java Model Parser and Printer (JaMoPP) representation.

Finally, we were able to predict the performance of a software system using a coevolved architectural model. For this case study, we used mRUBiS as software system.

6.2. GQM Plan for the Evaluation

The evaluation is aligned to the GQM approach presented by Basili et al. [BCR94]. We shortly gave a brief overview of the GQM approach in Section 2.6.1. To use the GQM concept for the evaluation, we first need to define the goals for the evaluation. Next, we need to define questions, which allow us to check whether the goals are reached. Finally, we need to define metrics, which can be used to answer the questions.

The goals, which we present for the evaluation, are closely aligned to the goals and questions, which we proposed in Section 1.2. Note: to follow the structure of the evaluation section, the goals are first defined for the evaluation of Chapter 5 and secondly defined for Chapter 4.

6.2.1. Include existing Artefacts

G1 To enable the use of existing source code artefacts, we first need to reverse-engineer the architecture of an existing source code base. Hence, one goal of this thesis is to revere engineer the architecture of a software system from an existing source code.

- **Q1.1** Are the presented reverse engineering approaches applicable for real open source software systems of reasonable size and produce valid architecture models, which abstract from the source code?
  - **M1.1.1** Source Lines of Code (SLoC) of the reverse-engineered software systems.
  - **M1.1.2** Number of violated OCL constraints in the reverse-engineered architectural models.

M1.1.3 Ratio between number of compilation units (classes and interfaces) in source code vs. number of components and interfaces in the architectural model.

Q1.2 How accurate are the architectural models, which are reverse-engineered using *EJBmoX* w.r.t. the extraction strategies?

M1.2.1 Number of extracted *BasicComponents* compared to the number of annotated Enterprise Java Bean (EJB) component classes.

M1.2.2 Number of extracted *OperationInterfaces* compared to the number of annotated EJB Java interfaces.

M1.2.3 Number of the *RequiredRoles* in each *BasicComponent* compared to the number of fields in the corresponding *EJB* component class.

M1.2.4 Number of *ProvidedRoles* in each *BasicComponent* compared to the number of implements relations in the corresponding *EJB* component class.

Q1.3 What are the differences between a reverse-engineered architectural model, which was created using *EJBmoX*, compared to a manual created architectural model of the same software system?

M1.3.1 Differences, in terms of number of elements and level of abstraction, between a manually created architectural model and a reverse-engineered model for the same software system.

G2 To enable the use of existing artefacts, one goal of our Coevolution approach is to enable the integration of existing architectural models and existing source code bases.

Q2.1 How many PCM elements in existing case study systems can be mapped to code using the different consistency preservation rules we presented in Chapter 4?

M2.1.1 Percentage of existing PCM elements that can be mapped to code using the RIS, which we presented in Section 5.3.

Q2.2 How often are users informed about changes on integrated elements when using Integration Level 2?

M2.2.1 Ratio of changes that led to user notification vs. changes that can be kept consistent using the standard consistency preservation rules.

Q2.3 How many changes on integrated elements can be kept consistent using Integration Level 3?

M2.3.1 Ratio between elements that can be kept consistent automatically vs. elements that only inform users about a change.

6.2.2. Coevolution of Architectural Models and Source Code

G3 The main goal of our Coevolution approach is to enable the coevolution of architectural models and source code during the evolution of a software system.

Q3.1 Which changes to architectural relevant source code can be kept consistent w.r.t. to the current consistency preservation rules during the software evolution?

M3.1.1 Number of changes performed on source code that can be kept consistent during the performed case studies vs. number of changes that could not be kept consistent during the performed case studies.

Q3.2 To which extend can our Coevolution approach deal with open source systems of reasonable size, i.e. can our Coevolution approach be applied for real world projects?

M3.2.1 The overhead our Coevolution approach creates for open source projects of reasonable size compared to the overhead our Coevolution approach creates for relatively small projects.

- **Q3.3** How much time is consumed by our Coevolution approach to keep architectural models and source code consistent after a change has been performed?
  - **M3.3.1** Average time our Coevolution approach needs to update an architectural model after an architectural relevant change in the source code occurred.
  - **M3.3.2** The time our Coevolution approach needs to update a behavioural model after a method body has been changed in the source code.

6.2.3. Model-based Analyses using coevolved Architecture Models

- **G4** One goal of our Coevolution approach is that the coevolved models can be used for model-based analyses.
  - **Q4.1** Which steps are necessary to use a coevolved model for performance prediction?
    - **M4.1.1** The number of steps that can be omitted if our Coevolution approach and the coevolved model are used for performance prediction compared to steps that are necessary to prepare the model for performance prediction manually.
  - **Q4.2** How accurate are the performance predictions that are performed with a coevolved model?
    - **M4.2.1** Prediction error of the response time between the predicted performance and the measured performance of the case study system.

6.3. Evaluation of reverse engineering approaches

Within this section, we explain the evaluation of the developed reverse engineering approaches *Extract* and *EJBmoX*. The evaluation of *Extract* is done by analyzing 14 different open source systems. To evaluate *EJBmoX*, we analysed two open source software systems.

6.3.1. Evaluation of Extract

The evaluation presented in this section is based on the evaluation we showed in Langhammer et al. [Lan+16]. *Extract* itself is not only able to reconstruct the architecture of a software system, but it is also able to reconstruct *UsageModels* from test cases. In this thesis, however, the reconstruction of *UsageModels* is not in the focus. Hence, we present the evaluation results of *Extract* only with respect to the architectural model in terms of a PCM *Repository*. Details about the reconstruction of *UsageModels* and their evaluation can be found in [Lan+16].

The evaluation of *Extract* is performed as a case study, where we investigated different open source projects. Executing *Extract* for a software system gives us the architectural model as described in Section 5.4.1.1, i.e. we get a PCM model in terms of *BasicComponents*, *OperationInterfaces* with *OperationSignatures*, and *RequiredRoles* as well as *ProvidedRoles*. For provided services of a component, we also retrieve the *SEFFs*. As additional artifact, we get a Source Code Decorator Model (SCDM), which contains the information how the source code elements are mapped to architectural elements. These models can be used as input for the LIS, that is used to integrate existing source code into our Coevolution approach.

The investigated open source projects, their versions and the created *BasicComponents* for the used architecture recovery algorithms can be seen in Table 6.2. As recovery algorithms we used Architecture Recovery using Concerns (ARC) and Algorithm for Comprehension-Driven Clustering (ACDC). We choose these two algorithms as they outperformed the other available algorithms for *Extract* in terms of accuracy and scalability[GIM13]. The investigated projects are all Apache projects written in Java. The projects were used by Le et al. [Le+15] to validate reverse engineering algorithms including ARC and ACDC. Even though the projects are all Apache projects, the software systems have different sizes and different domains (cf. [Le+15]). Hence, by using these projects, we can show that *Extract* can be applied to various Java projects. We investigated 14 open source projects with sizes from 46 KSLoC to 644 KSLoC and an overall size of more than 2.4 million

SLoC. The resulting models as well as the corresponding versions of the software systems, and a description how to set up *Extract* are available online [1]. In this analysis, we showed the principle applicability of *Extract* to open source software systems and showed its scalability. The extraction itself needs approximately 5 minutes for the smaller systems, such as *Log4j*. For the larger systems, however, the extraction needs up to five hours on standard hardware (Mac OSX with 2.2 GHz Intel core i7, and 8GB RAM). In future work the extraction performance can be improved by either optimising the JaMoPP parser or replacing JaMoPP with a faster Java parser, such as the Model Discovery (MoDisco) [Bru+10] parser or the Eclipse Java Development Tools (JDT) Abstract Syntax Tree (AST) parser.

From this evaluation, we can answer the question 1.1 as follows: As we can see from the evaluation we performed for *Extract*, the developed reverse engineering approach is applicable to real world projects. As we expected, none of the reverse-engineered architectural models violated an OCL constraint of the PCM metamodel. This result is expected, because we tailored *Extract* in order to create valid PCM instances. For instance, during the implementation of *Extract*, we figured out that the generic reverse-engineered *CollectionDataTypes* violates a PCM constrains, because it does not contain an inner element. To overcome this issue, we created and used the generic *CompositeDataType* `Object` as default value for an inner element in a *CollectionDataType*. The ratio between the compilation units and the created interfaces and components can be found in Table 6.3. The abstraction ratio for all investigated compilation units to all created components and interface is 0.31 for ARC and 0.08 for ACDC. Hence, we create far less components and interfaces than compilation units exist in the source code, i.e. the models abstract from the source code by composing classes to components. Furthermore, *Extract* abstracts from statements and component-internal calls during the *SEFF* reconstruction.

6.3.2. Evaluation of *EJBmoX*

As mentioned above, we investigated two different EJB software systems to evaluate *EJBmoX*. These systems are the MediaStore[Koz+08; SK16], and

[1] `https://sdqweb.ipd.kit.edu/wiki/Extract`

System	Domain	Version	KSLoC	ARC	ACDC
ActiveMQ	Message Broker	3.0	95	116	88
Cassandra	Distributed DBMS	2.0.0	184	285	52
Chukwa	Data Monitor	0.6.0	39	74	43
Hadoop	Data Process	0.19.0	224	388	101
Ivy	Dependency Manager	2.3.0	68	128	40
JackRabbit	Content Repository	2.0.0	246	294	72
Jena	Semantic Web	2.12.0	384	766	36
JSPWiki	Wiki Engine	2.10	56	77	31
Log4j	Logging	2.02	62	187	61
Lucene Solr	Search Engines	4.6.1	644	115	41
Mina	Network Framework	2.0.0	46	93	44
PDFBox	PDF Library	1.8.6	113	127	41
Struts2	Web Apps Framework	2.3.16	153	75	26
Xerces	XML Library	2.10.0	112	143	28
Total			**2426**	**2876**	**696**

Table 6.2.: Overview of the analysed open source systems using *Extract*, we performed for [Lan+16]. ARC, and ACDC columns display the number of recovered components for each system. Note: The lines of code do not include test code.

mRUBiS[2]. Both systems are designed as evaluation systems and span approximately 5.000 SLoC. Both projects are EJB based.

[2] https://www.hpi.uni-potsdam.de/giese/public/mdelab/mdelab-projects/case-studies/mrubis/

Project	#Comp.Units	#Components + Interfaces		Ratio	
		ARC	ACDC	ARC	ACDC
ActiveMQ	1036	232	176	0.22	0.17
Cassandra	886	570	104	0.64	0.12
Chukwa	338	148	86	0.44	0.25
Hadoop	1647	776	202	0.47	0.12
Ivy	474	256	80	0.54	0.17
JackRabbit	1948	588	144	0.30	0.07
Jena	3822	1532	72	0.40	0.02
JSPWiki	351	154	62	0.44	0.18
Log4j	585	174	122	0.30	0.21
Lucene Solr	2996	230	82	0.08	0.03
Mina	1852	186	88	0.10	0.05
PDFBox	852	254	82	0.30	0.10
Struts2	479	150	52	0.31	0.11
Xerces	762	286	56	0.38	0.07
Total	18028	5536	1408	0.31	0.08

Table 6.3.: Ratio between compilation units and components and interfaces in the reverse-engineered models. Note: We counted the compilation units in production code only, i.e. only the compilation units represented in the reverse-engineered architecture are taken into account. Test code and example code are not counted.

The MediaStore system was introduced by Koziolek et al. [Koz+08] to evaluate the PCM approach. A more recent version of the MediaStore and an up-to-date implementation as well as a PCM model are provided by Strittmatter and Kechaou [SK16]. The MediaStore allows users to download audio files, upload audio files, and purchase audio files. Our running example, which we introduced in Section 4.3.2.4, is a simplified version of this MediaStore.

The mRUBiS system is provided by the System Analysis and Modelling Group of the Hasso Platner Institut. It is a case study system created to simulate an auction site prototype similar to eBay. To realise this functionality, users can authenticate themselves, add items, bid for items, and finally purchase items if they win the auction.

The mRUBiS system can be analysed using the *EJBmoX* standard configuration, i.e. mRUBiS only uses the `@EJB` annotation to indicate the required interfaces within the component-classes. Furthermore, all component-classes implement at least one EJB `Remote` interface or one EJB `Local` interface. Each Java interface is only implemented by one component, i.e. *EJBmoX* is able to derive the PCM *System* implicitly during the reconstruction of mRUBiS.

For the MediaStore system, however, we need to use the extension configuration of *EJBmoX*. Hence, fields of an EJB component-class with the type of an EJB Java interface, which are not annotated with `@EJB` or `@Inject`, are considered as *RequiredRoles* in the architecture as well. We, furthermore, create an implicit *OperationInterface* in the reconstructed PCM *Repository* for classes, which are annotated with an EJB component-annotation, but not providing an EJB interface. The results of the analysed projects can be seen in Table 6.4. The resulting models are available online[3].

The table also allows us to answer the question 1.2 from the GQM plan as follows: *EJBmoX* is able to reverse-engineer all EJB component-classes to *BasicComponents* and all architectural relevant Java interfaces to *OperationInterfaces*. It can also reverse-engineer *ProvidedRoles*, which are represented by an `implements` realisation between an EJB component class and an architectural relevant Java interface *EJBmoX* is also able to reverse-engineer *RequiredRoles*, which are represented by a private field, with the type of an architectural relevant Java interface, in an EJB component class. It is also able to create implicit interfaces for classes not providing an EJB interface, but considered as EJB component-classes. Even though we only applied *Extract* to larger projects, we can indicate that *EJBmoX* can be applied to larger projects as well, because both approaches share the same infrastructure. The architecture models created with *EJBmoX* do not violate any OCL constraint from the PCM metamodel. The reason is the same as for *Extract*: We tailored *EJBmoX* specifically in order to not violate any OCL constraints in the PCM metamodel. To calculate the ratio between compilation units

[3] `https://sdqweb.ipd.kit.edu/wiki/EJBmox`

System	MediaStore	mRubis
KSLoC	2.9	4.8
BasicComponent	12	14
EJB component-classes	12	14
OperationInterface	16	14
EJB interfaces	16	14
RequiredRole	16	14
EJB fields in component-classes with type of EJB interface	16	14
ProvidedRole	12	27
implements-relations between a EJB component-class and an architectural relevant EJB interface	12	27

Table 6.4.: Result for the analysing software systems using *EJBmoX*. As we can see the reverse-engineered number of *BasicComponents*, *OperationInterfaces*, *RequiredRoles*, and *ProvidedRoles* matches the number of actual implemented counterparts in the source code.

and created components and interfaces, we can use the information about the reverse-engineered components and reverse-engineered interfaces from Table 6.4. We, furthermore, need the information that mRUBiS consists of 69 compilation units, while the MediaStore consists of 59 compilation units. Hence, we have a ratio of 0.41 for mRUBiS, while we have a ratio of 0.47 for the MediaStore. Even though the ratio is higher as for *Extract*, we can state that *EJBmoX* gives an high-level overview of the analysed software systems and abstracts from the source code.

6.3.3. Comparison of a Revere Engineered Model with a Manually created Model

As Strittmatter and Kechaou [SK16] created an up-to date PCM model from the implementation of the MediaStore manually, we can use the MediaStore system to compare the reversed engineered *Repository* with a manually crafted one. By performing this comparison, we answer the research question 1.3 from our GQM plan. The manually created *Repository* is depicted

Figure 6.1.: The manually created PCM *Repository* model of the MediaStore

in Figure 6.1, while the reverse-engineered *Repository* is depicted in Figure 6.2.

As we can see from the figures, the numbers of the components and interfaces are similar. The names of the components are slightly different in the automatically created *Repository*. The names differ, because *EJBmoX* creates the name of a component using the name of its corresponding EJB component-class. The names for EJB component-classes are usually ending with `Impl` in the implementation of the MediaStore. Hence, the names of the *BasicComponents* also ending with `Impl`. To overcome this issue, it would be possible to remove `Impl` from the end of a components name automatically during the reverse engineering process. The following main differences between the automatic reverse-engineered model and the manual created one can be observed:

Figure 6.2.: The reverse-engineered PCM *Repository* model of the MediaStore

- No matching component can for the three components `FileStorage`, `DownloadLoadBalancer`, and `ParallelWatermarking` are present in the reverse-engineered model. For the components `DownloadLoadBalancer` and `ParallelWatermarking` this is the case, because no implementation is currently available for these components. Similar to the other two components, *EJBmoX* is not able to reverse-engineer a component for the `FileStorage` component in the manual model, because the `FileStorage` component is not present in the code directly. It is used in the manual model to represent communication with the HDD or external storage.
- Two *BasicComponents* and two *OperationInterfaces* called `DBManager` are present in the reverse-engineered model. They are responsible for the interaction with the database. In the manually created model, however, only one *BasicComponent*, called `DB`, is present, which handles the database interaction. The difference occurs, because two EJB component-classes called `DBManager` exist in the code. The `DBManager` classes in the code both interact with the database. One class is responsible for the database access in order to retrieve and store audio files, while the other class is responsible for the database access for user information. The manually created architecture abstracts from these two classes and combines them in one component.
- The used data types are different, because *EJBmoX* creates one architectural data type for each Java data type used in the implementation. For instance, *EJBmoX* creates a PCM *CollectionDatatype*, with the name `BYTEList`, which uses the *PrimitiveDataType* `BYTE` as inner type, for the code data type `byte[]` (a byte array). The manually created model can abstract from these details and uses only `FileContent` and `AudioCollectionRequest` as custom PCM *DataTypes*. The reverse-engineered model, however, also contains data types for `AudioFile` and `AudioFileInfo` as well as *CollectionDataTypes* for both of the types.
- The code interfaces, which are marker interfaces for the `IDownload` interface, have an explicit representation in the reverse-engineered architecture, while the manually created architecture can abstract from the marker interfaces. These interfaces are necessary in the

code to mark classes that implement `IDownload` more specific. They, however, do not add functionality.

- Some *OperationSignatures*, e.g. the *OperationSignatures* within `IDownload`, are different in terms of parameters. The reason is, again, that the manually created architecture abstracts from parameters, which are unnecessary for the performance prediction. The manually created architecture model, furthermore, combines the requests in an own PCM data type, which is not directly represented in the code. Hence, this data type is not reverse-engineered by *EJBmoX*.

The main reason for the observed differences is that manual created architectural models can abstract from more implementation details, while the reverse-engineered models cannot easily abstract from all this details. Hence, the automatically created architecture model elements are more detailed as the manually created one, because the automatic create architecture models are closely aligned with the underlying source code. They also provide a consistent abstraction level for the extracted source code. The advantage of the manually created model is that users can get a higher-level overview that omits unnecessary details. *EJBmoX*, however, is not able to abstract from those details. Hence, we can observe the same result for reverse-engineered architectural models as Krogmann [Kro12]: the automatically reverse-engineered architectural models are precise and have a consistent abstraction level. They, however, also contain non-performance relevant information, from which manually created architecture models can abstract away.

6.4. Evaluation of the Consistency Preservation Rules and the PCM RIS

In this section, we present the evaluation of the RIS for the PCM (see Section 5.3) as well as the evaluation of the consistency preservation rules we proposed in Chapter 4. To do so, we use existing PCM models and include them using the RIS for the PCM. During the integration, we simulate the atomic creation of the existing PCM model. During the integration, our Coevolution approach to reacts to these changes with the current active consistency preservation rules and creates the corresponding source code elements for the existing PCM models.

To create the evaluation data, we use the prototypical implementation of our Coevolution approach with the prototypical implementation for the consistency preservation rules. For the evaluation of the consistency preservation rules between PCM and artefacts of Eclipse plugins, we reuse the data Heiss [Hei15] carried out in his bachelor's thesis.

6.4.1. Existing PCM Models

This section gives an overview of the existing PCM models, we used for the evaluation of the PCM RIS and the consistency preservation rules. We use seven existing PCM case studies, which have been used in different case studies over the last years to evaluate the PCM itself and its extensions. Hence, these models can be seen as representative PCM models. Table 6.5 lists the number of elements each of the case studies contains. We later compare how many of these elements can be integrated using the proposed consistency preservation rules.

MediaStore

The MediaStore case study was created by Koziolek et al. [KBH07] to show the applicability of the Palladio approach. Since the initial presentation of the MediaStore, the system has been used to show the applicability of extensions developed for the PCM. An up-to-date model and EJB based implementation has been introduced by Strittmatter and Kechaou [SK16]. As our running example of this thesis, the system itself allows users to upload and download media files from a server.

CoCoME

The Common Component Modelling Example (CoCoME) by Herold et al. [Her+08] is a case study system that has been developed to compare different modelling approaches for component-based software systems. It is an example software system that describes processes and workflows in supermarkets and retail stores. It supports use cases, such as buying products and paying them as well as, and administrative processes, such as ordering new products and inventory management. Krogmann and Reussner [KR08] introduce the first PCM version of the CoCoME system, which has been refined and extended by Heinrich et al. [HRR16].

Open Reference Case

The Open Reference Case system is service-oriented variant of the CoCoME system developed in the SLA@SOI project. As stated in [HRR16] an additional web service layer has been introduced to the original CoCoME architectural model.

Desktop Search

As the name indicates the PCM model of the Desktop Search models a program that allows the search on a desktop system.

DPS

The Dynamic Positioning System (DPS) system, is a model of a Dynamic Positioning System, which can be used to navigate and finding the position of a deepwater oil platform (see Duarte et al. [Dua+10], Gouvêa et al. [Gou+11], and Gouvêa et al. [Gou+12]). Within [Gou+11] and [Gou+12] a PCM instance of a DPS has been introduced.

Industrial Control System

The Industrial Control System (ICS) is an industrial case study for the PCM and has been introduced by Koziolek et al. [KSB10] and refined by Brosch et al. [Bro+12]. The system is an industrial size process control system from ABB.

BRS

The Business Reporting System (BRS) has been introduced by Koziolek [Koz11] to show the applicability of PerOpteryx and is, according to [Koz11], loosely based on a real system introduced by Wu and Woodside [WW04]. According to Koziolek [Koz11], the BRS system allows users to retrieve data, such as reports and statistical data, about business processes from a database.

6.4.2. Execution of the Case Study

To automatically execute the above-described case study and allow the repetition and ease the reproducibility of our results, we implemented a small evaluation tool, which is available as part of the Vitruvius framework and as part of the implementation of our Coevolution approach. This tool executes a set of consistency preservation rules for a given set of PCM models. At first it counts the elements in each of the PCM models. During the execution of each consistency preservation rule for each PCM model it furthermore logs the number of changes, which can be kept consistent using the active consistency preservation rules. The process of the evaluation tool is described in the activity diagram in Figure 6.3. As last step, we manually aggregated the numbers and calculated the percentage of changes that can be kept consistent for each consistency preservation rules in relation to the overall model elements. We, furthermore, checked the output models manually to ensure that the generated output is correct w.r.t. the consistency preservation rules.

6.4.3. Results of the Integration Case Study

In this section, we describe the results and findings of the case study using the RIS for PCM and existing models and answer evaluation question 2.1. An overview of the elements that can be integrated is given in Table 6.6. Within this table the results of all implemented consistency preservation rules are shown. In Section A.2, the integrated elements for each used case study project is shown.

Project	*Repository*									*System*					
	BasicComponents	*CompositeComponents*	*OperationInterfaces*	*CompositeDataTypes*	*CollectionDataTypes*	*OperationSignatures*	*OperationProvideRoles*	*OperationRequiredRoles*	*SEFFs*	*AssemblyContexts*	*AssemblyConnectors*	*SystemRequiredRoles*	*RequiredDelegationConnectors*	*SystemProvideRoles*	*ProvidedDelegationConnectors*
MediaStore	14	0	9	2	0	20	15	16	26	10	11	0	0	1	1
CoCoME	8	0	8	19	9	29	7	13	31	20	24	2	2	1	1
Open Reference Case	15	0	15	20	8	54	14	23	52	13	19	1	2	4	4
Desktop Search	3	0	3	0	1	3	3	2	3	3	2	0	0	1	1
DPS	5	0	3	0	0	4	5	4	6	5	4	0	0	5	5
Industrial Control System	14	0	10	0	0	10	14	28	14	11	18	0	0	6	6
BRS	14	2	10	2	1	28	15	14	44	9	11	0	0	2	2
Total	73	2	58	43	19	148	73	100	176	71	89	3	4	20	20
Total w.o. Industrial Control System & Desktop Search & DPS	51	2	42	43	18	131	51	66	153	52	65	3	4	8	8

Table 6.5.: Overview of the elements in existing PCM case study systems

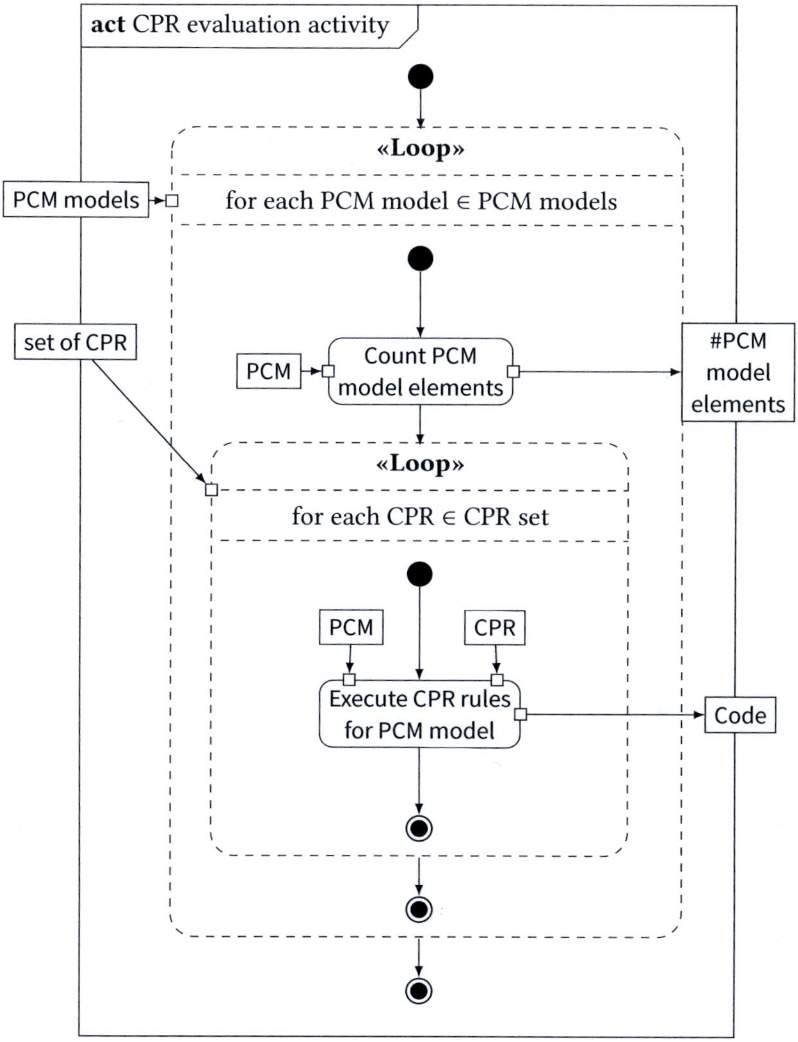

Figure 6.3.: Activity diagram of the evaluation helper tool. The tool applies a given set of consistency preservation rules to a given set of PCM models.

PCM element	Pack. map.			EJB			Dep. Inject.			Eclipse plugin		
	#el.	#cf.	pct.	#el.	#cf.	pct.	#el.	#cf.	pct.	#el	#cf.	pct.
BasicComponents	73	0	100	73	0	100	73	0	100	51	0	100
CompositeComponents	2	0	100	–	0	0	2	0	100	–	0	0
OperationInterfaces	58	0	100	58	0	100	43	0	100	42	0	100
CompositeDataTypes	43	0	100	43	0	100	43	0	100	–	0	0
CollectionDataTypes	19	0	100	19	0	100	19	0	100	–	0	0
OperationSignatures	148	0	100	148	0	100	148	0	100	–	0	0
OperationProvideRoles	73	0	100	73	17	77	73	0	100	51	0	100
OperationRequiredRoles	100	0	100	100	0	100	100	0	100	66	0	100
SEFFs	176	0	100	176	0	100	176	0	100	–	0	0
AssemblyContexts	71	0	100	–	0	0	71	21	70	–	0	0
AssemblyConnectors	89	0	100	–	0	0	89	0	100	–	0	0
SystemRequiredRoles	3	0	100	–	0	0	3	0	0	–	0	0
RequiredDelegationConnectors	4	0	100	–	0	0	4	0	0	–	0	0
SystemProvideRoles	20	0	100	–	0	0	20	0	100	–	0	0
ProvidedDelegationConnectors	20	0	100	–	0	0	20	0	100	–	0	0

Table 6.6.: Integrated and conflicting overall elements per consistency preservation rule

The #el. column of Table 6.6 shows the number of elements created by the RIS for the PCM instances.The #cf. column of Table 6.6 shows the number of conflicting elements, i.e. elements that can be integrated into our Co-evolution approach, but lead to a validation error. The pct. column shows the percentage included elements using the active consistency preservation rules. Columns containing "–" indicate that the consistency preservation rule is not able to transform these models.

Note: the overall number of elements for Eclipse plugins is lower, because we did not perform the case study for all of the above-mentioned projects, because we reused the results from the bachelor's thesis of Heiss [Hei15]. Hence, for the integration of existing PCM elements to Eclipse plugins, we only present results for the MediaStore, CoCoME, the Open References Case, and the BRS system.

As the #el. column in Table 6.6 equals the number of elements contained in all projects, which were used for the evaluation of the consistency preservation rule, we can state that the RIS for PCM is able to simulate the creation of a PCM instance. However, due to additional limitations, which are introduced by the consistency preservation rules, some elements cannot be integrated. As we mentioned above, the conflicting elements are such elements that con not be mapped to source code respectively to Eclipse plugin artefacts. For the package mapping consistency preservation rules and Eclipse plugins, all elements of the case study projects could be integrated.

Using the EJB consistency preservation rules, we introduce the constraint that each interface only is allowed to be provided once in the *Repository*, because we implicitly derive the PCM *System* from the repository. Hence, the provided interfaces need to be unique over all *OperationProvidedRoles*. This constraint does not hold for 17 out of 73 *OperationProvidedRoles*. For the dependency injection consistency preservation rules between architectural models and code, we introduce the following two constraints: a) it is not allowed to provide one interface more than once per *System*, and b) the components in all *AssemblyContexts* need to be unique, i.e. one component is only allowed to be present once per *System*. For both constraints the conflicting elements are *AssemblyContexts*. Both constraints occur a in a total of 21 times, which means that only 50 out of 71 *AssemblyContexts* can be integrated using the Dependency Injection consistency preservation rules.

Mapping	#int. elem.	#total elem.	$\frac{\#int.\ elem.}{\#total\ elem.}$	#sup. elem.	$\frac{\#int.\ elem.}{\#sup.\ elem}$
Pack. map.	899	899	1	899	1
EJB	673	899	0.75	690	0.98
Dep. Inject	871	899	0.97	892	0.98
Eclipse plugin	210	697	0.30	210	1
Total	2653	3394	0.78	2691	0.99

Table 6.7.: Ratio between integrated elements and total elements respectively supported elements per consistency preservation rule. The ratio represents metric 2.1.1 and allows us to answer the research question 2.1.
Legend: #int. elem. represents the number of integrated elements using the consistency preservation rule over all case study projects, #total elem. is the sum of all elements in all case study projects, #sup. elem. is the number of supported elements in all case study projects for the consistency preservation rule

Conflicts, which can be resolved automatically, are not listed in this table. Automatically resolvable conflicts are, for instance, white spaces in names of PCM elements or duplicate names for PCM elements. The latter did not occur within the investigated case study projects. The reason for that might be that the understandability of models decreases and the effort for the evolution of those models of increases. For instance, if two or more *OperationInterfaces* have the same name and an architect wants to use the interface within a *ProvidedRole* or an external-call the actual used interface needs to be identified by its unique identifier, which is a random string, if the name is equal. If users assign a unique name, it is easier to find the desired interface.

Table 6.7 shows the sum of all elements our Coevolution approach was able to integrate for the different consistency preservation rules. In the table, we distinguish between the ratio of integrated element to total elements and the ratio between integrated elements to supported elements. Supported elements are elements, which can conceptually be integrated using the mentioned consistency preservation rules. Not supported element are elements, which cannot be integrated using the mentioned consistency preservation rules, for instance, elements contained in a *System* are not supported by the EJB consistency preservation rules.

After performing the RIS for PCM, we can answer the research question 2.1 with the metric 2.1.1 as follows:. Using the RIS for PCM, we are able to integrate 99% of the elements, which are supported by the consistency preservation rules, and 78% elements in total. Hence, we are able to map most existing PCM models to source code respectively to Eclipse plugin artefacts using the presented consistency preservation rules.

6.5. Integrating Existing Source Code and Replaying Changes

In this section, we explain the evaluation of integrating existing open source code projects into our Coevolution approach. We show that changes performed to the integrated source code can be kept consistent with the architectural model. Therefore, we replay changes from a VCS. Hence, within this section we answer the remaining research questions for research goal 2 (in particular 2.2, and 2.2), and research questions 3.1 for research goal 3.

6.5.1. Used Open Source Projects

In this section, we explain how we decided which open source projects are used for the evaluation. Therefore, we first give an overview of the requirements, we have for open source projects. As next step, we explain the process how we actually chose the open source projects and give a short description about the chosen projects. The requirements and the process itself are similar to the requirements and the process Petersen [Pet16] described in his master's thesis.

6.5.1.1. Requirements to Open Source Projects

For the evaluation, we have the following two mandatory requirements for open source projects:

1. As we evaluate our Coevolution approach using the package mapping consistency preservation rules, the projects we use for the evaluation need to use plain java objects to realise the architecture.
2. As we replay changes from a VCS the projects also need to have a complete history within a VCS repository. Since the change replay tool we use, currently only supports GIT, projects need to have either a GIT repository or a repository, which we can transform to a GIT repository. SVN projects, for instance, are also possible, as tools exist that allow the transformation of an SVN repository to a GIT repository.

Optional requirements the projects should fulfill are:

- Projects should be standalone projects and have a low number of external dependencies, because we do not consider external dependencies in the architectural model.
- Projects should include package-info.java files for each package, because we use the package mapping consistency preservation rules for our evaluation. Within these rules, we use the package-info.java file respectively the `Package` element in the files as corresponding element between source code and architectural model, yet. This requirement is a technical requirement, because JaMoPP is not able to deal with the hierarchical folder structure within a Java project, but is able to deal with package-info.java files. The requirement, however, is not a strong requirement, because we can overcome the technical issue by creating package-info.java files in each package of a given project.

One goal of our evaluation is to check, whether the consistency preservation process of our Coevolution approach kept the right model elements consistent. As we perform this evaluation manually, the projects need to be reasonable small in terms of SLoC[4]. Another goal is, however, to show that our Coevolution approach is also able to deal with projects of reasonable size. Therefore, we also need projects of bigger size. As there is no exact distinction when a project is to be considered as small or big project, we can only give a vague estimation of when we consider a project as a small project or big project. During the selection process, which is explained in

[4] SLoC representing the lines of code without empty lines and without comment lines.

the following, it turned out that for the projects we used, it is possible to manually check the results for projects with less than 20 KSLoC (excluding test code). Hence, such projects are considered small projects in the evaluation. Projects with more SLoC are considered as bigger projects and used for the scalability analyses. This estimation is only valid for the performed evaluation and for the considered projects.

6.5.1.2. Selection Process and chosen Evaluation Projects

To choose potential evaluation projects, we focus on Apache projects, because of the following reasons:

- Apache projects usually have a complete VCS history,
- all versions of Apache projects can be accessed easily, and
- Apache projects can be considered as state of the art open source software systems, because they are wildly used and accepted.

To find potential Apache projects, we used the same approach as Petersen [Pet16]. Petersen [Pet16] implemented a script [5] to count the lines of Java source code for all Apache projects, which are available at the Apache homepage [6]. To count the lines of code in a project, we used the tool cloc, which is available on Github [7]. Please note: The SLoC we get for each project are not the actual SLoC that we used in the actual evaluation, because the evaluation has been performed for a specific version of the project and without test code. Even though the script counts SLoC for the current version and including the test code, we can use it to filter all projects and find those of adequate size for the actual evaluation.

As result from the script run, we have a data set that contains the name, the SLoC, and the number of Java files for 173 Apache projects. The SLoC in the projects, we analysed, range from 174 SLoC in the Apache Lucy project to 2.6 million SLoC in the Apache Harmony project.

To find possible evaluation projects, we automatically filtered out projects with less than 10.000 SLoC and less than 100 Java files. To find projects,

[5] `https://github.com/FrederikP/projectfinder`

[6] `https://projects.apache.org/`

[7] `https://github.com/AlDanial/cloc`

for which we are able to perform a manual check whether our Coevolution approach changed the correct model elements, we also filtered out projects with more than 30 KSLoC and more than 500 Java files. Again, please note that the filtering has been performed for the projects including the KSLoC for the test code, while the actual evaluation has been performed for a specific version of each project and without the test code, i.e. production code only. This is the reason why we applied the filter using 30 KSLoC instead of 20 KSLoC, which we considered as small projects in the section above. After we applied the automatic filter, we have 31 projects left. To apply both filters, we used the KSLoC including test code. For the actual evaluation, we use non-test code only. As Petersen [Pet16] pointed out, from the remaining 31 projects only nine projects are standalone projects and Java only projects. From these nine projects Petersen identified Apache Any23[8] as best fit for our requirements, because it has a native GIT repository and maintained package-info.java files for each Java package. Apache Any23 is separated in different projects, which can be investigated as standalone sub-projects of Apache Any23. We decided to use the Apache Any23 core project for our evaluation. Petersen also pointed out, that Apache Gora[9] is a good fit as it is not to big in size and has a GIT mirror on Github. Similar to Any23, Apache Gora is separated in different Eclipse projects. As for Any23, we decided to use the core project of Apache Gora for our evaluation. Hence, as small projects, we used Any23[10] and the core project of Apache Gora in our evaluation. We also use these two projects to evaluate the incremental *SEFF* reconstruction during the change replay.

For the evaluation of projects with more than 20 KSLoC, we choose Apache Velocity, and Apache Xerces. Apache Velocity[11] has been chosen because it is standalone Java project (see Petersen [Pet16]) and because it is only slightly above the 20 KSLoC limit. We choose Apache Xerces[12], because we already were able to successfully extract the architecture using *Extract*.

Table 6.8 gives an overview of the four used evaluation projects.

[8] `https://any23.apache.org/`
[9] `https://gora.apache.org`
[10] `https://any23.apache.org`
[11] `http://velocity.apache.org`
[12] `http://xerces.apache.org/xerces2-j/`

Project	Short description
Gora (gora-core)	Apache Gora is an open source framework providing an in memory data persistence for big data. Users can, amongst others, persist data to a column store. Furthermore, it allows users to analyze the stored data.
Any23	Apache Any23 (Anything to triples) is a library that allows the extraction of structured data in RDF format. It supports multiple formats, such as Resource Description Framework (RDF)a and Comma-Separated Values (CSV). It can be used, for instance, as a library in own program code, from command line, or as web service.
Velocity	Apache Velocity is a template engine for Java. It allows users to reference objects defined in Java via a simple template language.
Xerces2	Apache Xerces is a XML library. Hence, it allows users to parse XML files and create XML files.

Table 6.8.: overview of the used open source systems for the evaluation of the LIS for source code and PCM and the change replay study.

6.5.2. Reverse Engineering of the Case Study Systems

We used *Extract* to reverse-engineer the architectural model from the source code. Within *Extract*, we used ACDC as clustering algorithm for classes.

For Xerces, we can reuse the results from the evaluation of *Extract* itself, while we need to run *Extract* for Gora, Any23, and Velocity specific for this evaluation. Table 6.9 gives an overview of the integrated versions of the evaluation projects and the result of the reverse engineering process. As mentioned above, the KSLoC for the actually integrated versions are different from the KSLoC we counted for the project using the script from Petersen [Pet16]. This difference results from the fact that we counted the KSLoC for the actually integrated versions and without test, i.e. we counted the actual production code only.

Project	Integrated version	KSLoC	Java files	BC	OpIf
Gora (gora-core)	0.6	5.7	76	16	16
Any23 (core)	0.90	12.6	190	16	16
Velocity	1.60	26	229	18	18
Xerces	02.10	112	705	20	20

Table 6.9.: overview of the integrated versions of the evaluation projects and the result of the reverse engineering process. The KSLoC represents the KSLoC for the version number, we used for our evaluation. As we only investigated production code, we counted the KSLoC without test code. The BC column shows the number of extracted *BasicComponents* for each system. The OpIf column shows the number of extracted *OperationInterface* for each system.

6.5.3. Integrating the Case Study Systems

As next step, within the integration process, the actual integration needs to be performed.

As a prior step to the actual integration, we need to ensure that each package folder of all projects contains a `package-info.java` file. As we explained above, this step is necessary, because we use the package mapping consistency preservation rules for the evaluation. These rules need to have `package-info.java` files in each package to determine the package of a compilation unit respectively Java file correctly. From the four integration projects only Any23 has already included `package-info.java` files in all but one package. We added the `package-info.java` file manually for this package. For the remaining three projects, we added `package-info.java` files to all packages.

As next step, we perform the actual integration for the four projects by executing the integration transformation, we described in Section 5.4.3.2. During the integration, the transformation uses the source code, the SCDM, and the existing architectural model to create an instance of the Vitruvius correspondence model. This model can be used by our Coevolution approach to preserve the consistency between architecture and code during the software

Project	IC	IC with*SEFF*	Target version	Changes
Gora (gora-core)	336	525	0.6.1	419
Any23 (core)	555	733	1.0	164
Velocity	1130	–	1.64	737
Xerces	3598	–	2.11	684

Abbreviations: IC = created *IntegratedCorrespondences*, IC with *SEFF* = created *IntegratedCorrespondences* if *SEFF* elements are integrated as well

Table 6.10.: Detailed information created integration artefacts and the changes between the versions

evolution. During the execution, the transformation checks for each element that shall be integrated, whether it fulfills the consistency preservation rules already. As we expected, none of the reverse-engineered components, interfaces, and data type elements can be kept consistent with its corresponding source code elements using the package mapping consistency preservation rules. As the elements corresponding to a class or an interface, already did not adhere to the package mapping consistency preservation rules, none of their child elements are able to adhere to the consistency preservation rules. Hence, none of the integrated elements can be kept consistent using the package mapping consistency preservation rules. Hence, during the execution of the transformation we created `IntegrationCorrespondences` only. This allows us to evaluate Integration Level 2 and Integration Level 3 for the evaluation projects. To evaluate Integration Level 3, however, we have to define specific consistency preservation rules for changes on integrated elements. The defined actions are described in the next section.

The first two columns of Table 6.10 show the number of created `IntegrationCorrespondences` for each project. As we can see from these two columns, the number of created `IntegrationCorrespondences` increases with the size of the projects and the size of the projects and also increases if the `IntegrationCorrespondences` are created between methods in code and *SEFFs* in the architectural model.

6.5.4. Replaying Changes Extracted from a VCS

After the integration of an existing project, we can replay changes from a VCS. To replay the changes, we use the change replay tool (see Section 2.5.5), which was introduced by Petersen [Pet16]. To use the change replay tool, we need to specify a reachable target version based on the source version, i.e. within the history of the VCS a path valid path between the two versions must exist. The third column of Table 6.10 shows the target versions, we choose, for the replaying of changes. One requirement for the target versions is the need of a direct path within the VCS from the source to the target version. For the target versions, we choose the next minor or major version depending on how much changes occurred between the versions. The fourth column of the table shows the number of changes respectively edit operations the change replay tool extracted between the integrated version and the target version. We performed different replaying scenarios during the evaluation. In the first run, we evaluated Integration Level 1 for each of the projects. After this run, we included the specific consistency preservation rules for integrated elements we defined in the reactions language [Kla16; Kra17]. For each of the evaluation projects, we counted whether the change could be kept consistent using either the standard package mapping consistency preservation rules, the specific consistency preservation rules, or whether the users need to preserve the consistency manually. To evaluate the coevolution and the UML editor, we performed a third run where we performed architectural relevant changes via the UML class diagram editor respectively the PCM architectural editor. The results of theses case studies are shown in the next sections.

6.5.4.1. Technical Remarks

Due to technical reasons the number of occurrence of the different changes can vary between different executions of the change replay tool. This is the reason why we have different numbers for changes replayed for Integration Level 2 and Integration Level 3. This behaviour is caused by the interaction between the change replay tool and the Java monitor. For each change, the change replay tool resets the content of the whole compilation unit. Even though the whole content is set, the Java monitor only reacts to the actually changed elements as it reacts to Eclipse AST notifications. If the change replay is executed more than once for the same project, the change kind can vary for the same change as the notifications from the Eclipse AST can report different changes. For instance, if a method has been renamed, it is possible that the Eclipse AST first reports the deletion of a method with the old name and secondly reports the insertion of a new method with the new name. However, even if the number of changes differs, the result after the change replay remains the same.

We furthermore observed that the Java monitor reports more changes than the consistency preservation reacts to. On the one hand this is caused, because the Java monitor is able to detect more change types than it actually reports to the consistency preservation process. This is the case for changes that introduce a super class to or remove one from an existing class. On the other hand this is caused by another issue in the interaction between the Java monitor and the change replay tool. If a Java file is moved by the change replay tool, the Java monitor is currently not able to detect this kind of change reliably Hence, our Coevolution approach does not react to this change and updates the correspondence information. If further changes are performed to this Java file, the Java monitor reports these changes, but they are neither considered as changes to an integrated element nor as changes to a non-integrated element. Hence, we consider changes performed to this files as non-architectural relevant changes, which they are probably not. We observed this case mainly in the case study for Xerces.

From this technical limitations, we can draw the following two conclusions for future work:

- if consistency preservation rules need to react to additive changes respectively removing changes for super classes, we need to extend the Java monitor and enable reporting of these changes, and
- the interoperability between the change replay tool and Java monitor can be improved respectively the Java monitor can be improved to ensure monitoring of all changes.

Even though we currently have these technical issues, our Coevolution approach is still able to react to most changes that were recorded by the Java monitor.

6.5.4.2. Results for Integration Level 2

During the evaluation of Integration Level 2, users get notified if they changed an element that is contained in an integrated area. They need to preserve the consistency between the changed element and its corresponding elements manually.

The diagram in Figure 6.4 shows the aggregated changes replayed for all evaluation projects. In Section A.3, we provide the information specific for each project. The results, however, are the same for all projects and can be discussed together. The diagram in Figure 6.4 also shows, whether the changes handled by the integration extension or by the standard consistency preservation rules.

As the results show, most changes affect integrated elements or integrated areas. Only a fraction of the changes is performed within non-integrated areas and therefore handled by the standard consistency preservation rules. Even though our Coevolution approach points to the elements that need to be kept consistent, users are required to keep most of the changes consistent manually. Keeping changes consistent manually can be time consuming and error prone. In the next section, we explain to which extend Integration Level 3 is able to overcome this limitation.

After performing the change replay evaluation for Integration Level 2, we can answer research question 2.2 as follows: Out of the 335 changes our Coevolution approach reacted to, only 2 (0.6%) can be handled by the standard consistency preservation rules. For the remaining 333 (99.4%) changes the users get the notification that they need to keep the architectural model consistent manually.

We can also answer research question 3.1 as follows: For the case study performed for Integration Level 2, our Coevolution approach is able to react to 73.5 % of the overall recorded changes. Even though the Java monitor records the add super class changes and remove super class changes, we are not reacting to these changes. If we take out these changes from the calculation, our Coevolution approach is able to react to 91.3% of the overall changes. For the case study performed for Integration Level 3 the numbers are almost identical and are not explained separately.

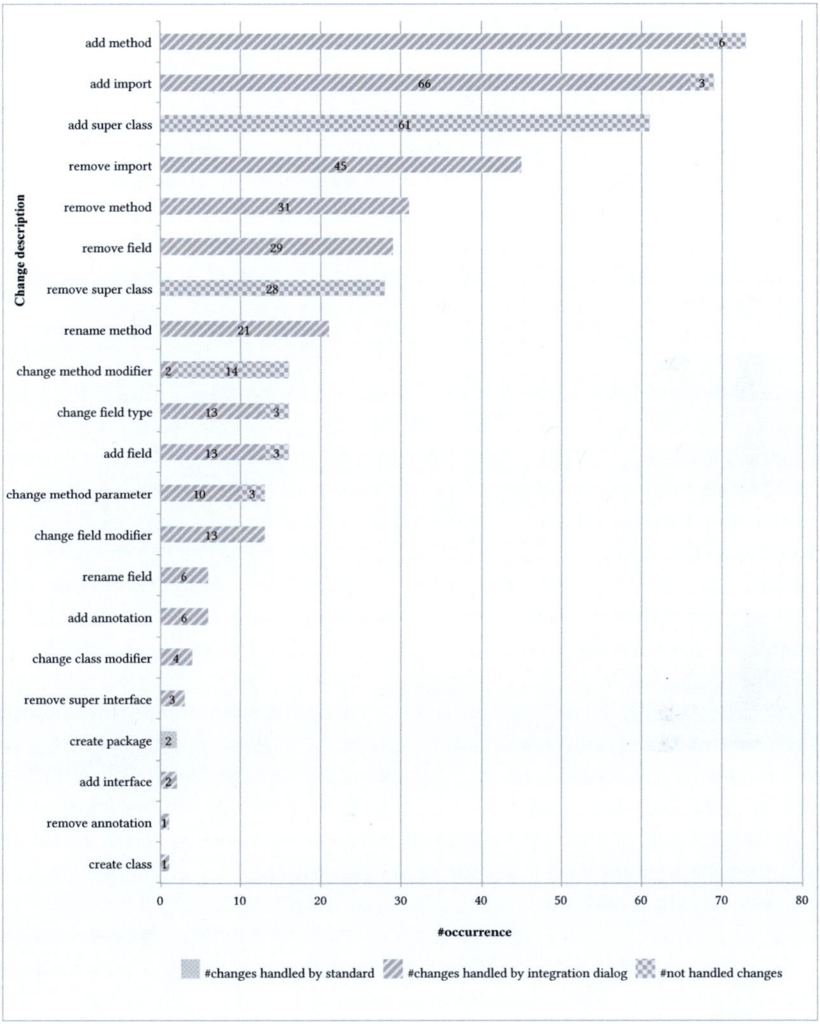

Figure 6.4.: Result of the change replay case study for Integration Level 2

6.5.4.3. Results for Integration Level 3

As we can see from the evaluation of Integration Level 2 most of the changes affect integrated elements, while only a fraction of the changes is performed within not-integrated areas. The goal of this Integration Level 3 is to allow a similar level of automatic consistency preservation for integrated code areas, which our Coevolution approach reaches for standard code using the active consistency preservation rules. To reach this goal, special consistency preservation rules need to be defined for code contained in integrated areas (see Section 5.4).

Defined Reactions for Automatic Consistency Preservation of integrated Code Areas For the evaluation of Integration Level 3, we added the following reaction definitions: As neither the package mapping consistency preservation rules nor the consistency preservation rules for the integrated code uses import statements to preserve consistency, we can implement empty reactions for adding and removing import statements. For the renaming of architectural relevant methods, we assume that the architectural elements should automatically be renamed accordingly. Hence, we can implement a specific consistency preservation rule for the renaming of methods. A similar approach is used for removing architectural relevant methods. If an architectural relevant method is removed, we remove the corresponding architectural elements (*OperationSignatures* or *SEFFs*) and notify the users. If a new public method is added, we cannot automatically decide, whether this is an architectural relevant method or not. However, we implemented a specific consistency preservation rule, which asks users in order to clarify whether the new method is architecture relevant or not. If a change affects a `Parameter` that is contained in an architectural relevant method, we automatically keep the *Parameter* consistent using the same consistency preservation rules as for the package mapping consistency preservation rules. During the reverse engineering, fields of classes are extracted to *InnerDeclarations* if the class of the field is reverse-engineered to a *CompositeDataType*. To keep changes to fields consistent with their corresponding *InnerDeclarations*, we defined a specific consistency preservation rule, which checks whether a corresponding *InnerDeclaration* exists. If this is the case the consistency preservation rule keeps the *InnerDeclaration* consistent with the changed field. Therefore, the name of the *InnerDeclaration* is changed if the field has been renamed and the type of the *InnerDeclaration* is changed if the type of the field has been changed.

All defined consistency preservation can also be defined from the architectural model to source code. Hence, if users change architectural elements that have corresponding source code elements in the integrated code area, the consistency preservation can be achieved using these rules.

Results for Static Architectural Elements and Static Code Elements We performed the replay case study again, and used the above-mentioned consistency preservation rules for integrated code elements. The diagram in Figure 6.5 shows the result for consistency preservation between static code elements and static architectural elements, i.e. without using incremental *SEFF* reconstruction during the change replay. As one can see, most changes that needed manual interactions in Integration Level 2 can be kept consistent using the defined consistency preservation rules for integrated code elements. For instance, no messages or question is displayed if an `import` has been changed.

After performing the change replay evaluation for Integration Level 3, we can answer research question 2.3 as follows: As for the evaluation of Integration Level 2 only 2 (0.6%) changes can be handled by the standard consistency preservation rules. The above defined integration reactions are able to handle 303 (92.1%) changes. For the remaining 24 (7.3%) changes the users need to keep the architectural model consistent manually. This number can be reduced further in future work, by defining more specific consistency preservation rules. We did not count the user notifications or how often users are requested to disambiguate the change within the integration reactions, because this kind of user change disambiguation can be avoided by implementing the specific consistency preservation as a fully automatic rule.

During the change replay and the consistency preservation, we observed a speciality in the Velocity project: It contains one component with parser functionality for parsing a Velocity template. The classes implementing the parser functionality are generated using the Java Compiler Compiler (JavaCC)[13] and its preprocessor JJTree. Both tools are part of the JavaCC and can be used as a

[13] `http://javacc.org`

parser generator, which can be used by Java applications. The parser classes in Velocity, e.g. `Parser`, `ParserConstants`, and `Token`, are generated into the `parser` package. Within our Coevolution approach, the parser classes are architectural relevant and some of them contain public methods with a corresponding *OperationSignature*. Between version 1.60 and 1.64 the parser has been changed and the parser classes have been regenerated, which led to new methods in the `Parser` class. As the `Parser` class is architectural relevant users evolving the software system get asked by our Coevolution approach, whether they want to create corresponding *OperationSignatures* within the interface provided by the `Parser.ss` component as soon as a method in the class `Parser` has been added. To avoid these questions, we can decide upfront that each method should be reflected within the architecture. To do so, we defined specific consistency preservation rules, which are used if one of the parser classes has been changed. Hence, we use element-specific consistency preservation rules for the parser classes.

The diagram in Figure 6.5 the changes handled using the specific rules are not made explicit but represented within the last column. In the appendix (see Section A.3), these changes are made explicit for the Velocity project. Two other approaches to deal with the parser classes, which we not realised, are:

- Exclude the parser classes from by either excluding them from the coevolution or even exclude them from the reverse engineering, because they are not meant to be changed by users anyway.
- Include the parser classes as infrastructure in the architecture, as these classes can be seen as existing infrastructure, which can be used by other components in the architecture.

Results with incremental *SEFF* reconstruction We evaluated the incremental *SEFF* reconstruction using Any23 and Gora. For Any23 50 changes were classified as changes on method bodies by the Java monitor, while 285 changes for Gora were classified as changes on method bodies. For the architectural relevant method changes, our Coevolution approach was able to reconstruct the corresponding *SEFF* respectively the corresponding *ResourceDemandingInternalBehaviour*. As we only investigated the core projects of Any23 and Gora, not all methods, however, were considered as

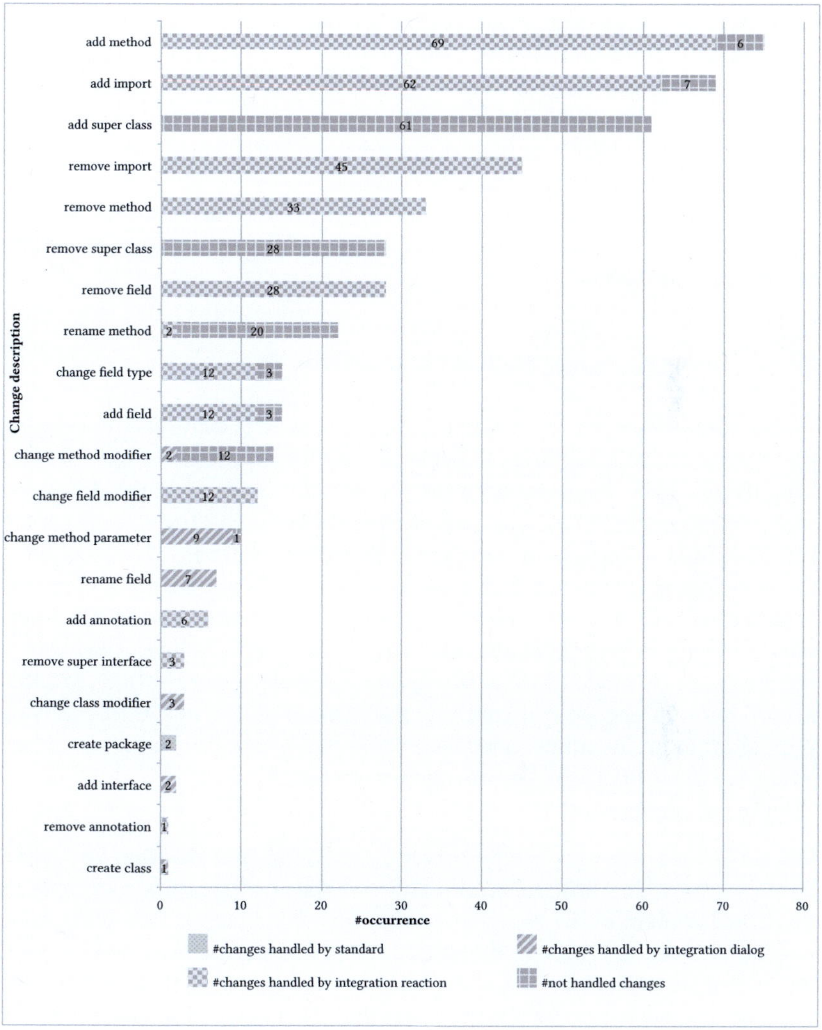

Figure 6.5.: Result of the change replay case study for Integration Level 3

architectural relevant methods as they are called from outside of the core projects only. If we would have included all projects of Any23 respectively Gora, more methods in the core projects would have been considered as architectural relevant by the reverse engineering approach, because the methods are called from outside of the core project. Hence, these methods would have been considered as architectural relevant methods also by our Coevolution approach. From the performed evaluation, however, we can state that our Coevolution approach is able to incrementally reconstruct the behaviour of a method.

6.5.4.4. Using an Architectural Editor to perform Changes

Within this section, we show how we can use the architectural editor during the change replay evaluation, to perform architectural relevant changes and keep the changes consistent with the source code. To prepare this study, we first need to perform the standard change replay using the change replay tool. During the replay, we monitor architectural relevant changes. After this initial step, we know which changes affect which architectural elements. Now we are able to replay the changes again and perform the architectural relevant changes in the architectural model. After performing the changes to the architectural model, we check whether the source code has been updated accordingly. If yes, we can continue the change replay in the source code until another architectural relevant change will occur. To conduct this case study, we need to extend the change replay tool for code in order to allow skipping of changes.

We performed the case study only for renaming and deletion of *OperationSignatures.* This has technical reasons, as the change replay tool replaces the whole content of the compilation unit for each change. The source code monitor, however, is able to determine the actual performed change based on the Eclipse AST. If we would, for instance, add a new method through the architecture, we would be able to determine the correct class but we would not be able to determine the correct position for the method. This would lead to errors in later steps of the change replay, as the change replay tool would remove this method with the next replay it performs.

We performed this evaluation for Any23 and Gora. In the first run we figured out which changes are architectural relevant. For Any23, one change renamed an architectural relevant method between version 0.9 and 1.0. None of the delete method changes were relevant for the architecture. For Gora, one change renamed an architectural relevant method and one change deleted an architectural relevant method.

In the second run, we performed these changes on the architectural model, while skipping the specific changes in the replay tool. As soon as we changed the architectural elements our Coevolution approach renamed respectively removed the code methods, i.e. we showed that it is possible to perform architectural relevant changes on architectural models during the coevolution.

6.6. Performance Evaluation of our Coevolution Approach

In this section, we present a performance evaluation of our Coevolution approach. As the execution of the consistency preservation rules are occurs in background jobs of the IDE they are not blocking users of our Coevolution approach directly. Hence, achieving a high performance is not the main focus of the work, we present in thesis. It is, however, necessary to achieve a feasible performance for our Coevolution approach, because:

- users are involved in the process for consistency preservation, and
- to allow a usable coevolution approach between architecture and code the consistency preservation rules should be executed within an acceptable timeframe.

Hence, the goals of the performed performance evaluation are:

- getting an estimate how our Coevolution approach performs on common hardware,
- showing that the performance for a single change the does not depend on the overall size of the project,
- getting an evidence about the magnitude how long our Coevolution approach needs for the consistency preservation, and

- pointing to possible performance issues during the coevolution.

The performance evaluation is divided in two parts. First, we evaluate the performance of the Java code monitor. It is evaluated separately, because JaMoPP, which is also used within the Java code monitor, turned out to be the bottleneck for revere engineering. Secondly, we evaluate the performance of our Coevolution approach during the change replay evaluation.

6.6.1. Performance Evaluation for the Java Monitor

As first part of the evaluation, we evaluate the performance of the Java code monitor to find out, whether our Coevolution approach is in principle able to deal with Java classes of reasonable size. This part of the evaluation has been performed by Messinger for his master's thesis [Mes14]. It is also part of our paper [Kra+15a] and its associated technical report [Kra+15b]. The time the Java monitor consumes is composed of two main parts. The first part starts as soon as the Java monitor is notified about a change in a Java source file by the Eclipse framework. The task of the first part is to classify the changes. The second part is composed of following three sub parts: parsing the JaMoPP instance of the changed compilation unit, creating a Vitruvius change based on the monitored AST change and the JaMoPP compilation unit, and. and submitting the created change to the consistency preservation components within the Vitruvius framework. The two main parts are measured separately and added up to get the overall time the Java monitor needed.

6.6.1.1. Evaluation setup

For the evaluation we and Messinger used the Apache Hadoop[14] HDFS (Hadoop Distributed File System) as system under study. Hadoop HDFS is a distributed file system developed to enable high-throughput access to large data sets stored on clusters[15]. Hadoop HDFS consists of more than 200 KSLoC and is embedded in the Hadoop framework. It includes manual

[14] `http://hadoop.apache.org/`

[15] `http://wiki.apache.org/hadoop/HDFS`

Compilation unit	LLoC	modified method
`ByteArray`	28	`getBytes`
`INode`	350	`getParent`
`FSEditLog`	1045	`initJournals`
`DFSClient`	2050	`connectToDN`
`DataTransferProtos`	15812	`registerAllEvents`

Table 6.11.: Overview of compilation units used for the Java code monitor performance evaluation. Note: As we reuse the data from Messinger [Mes14], the LoC are presented in LLoC, which represents the total number of statements within a compilation unit. The difference between the two LoC measurements is not crucial for the presented evaluation.

written compilation units various sizes as well as large generated compilation units. Hence, it is a good fit for our performance evaluation.

To perform the evaluation, we executed three different changes:

- Renaming of a method. Therefore, we toggled the name of a specific method by appending "0" or "1" to the method name. The toggling has been done depending on whether "0" or "1" is already present, which depends on the current iteration.
- Changing the modifier of a method. Therefore, we replace `public` with `private` respectively `private` with `public` within each iteration.
- Adding and removing a filed. We added the field `String lorem="lorem ipsum dolor sit amet";` if it is not present and removed it if it is present already. Hence, we consecutively added or added or removed the field in the iterations.

To measure the performance for compilation units (Java files) of different size, we choose to measure the performance for five compilation units, which are presented in Table 6.11. For the first four compilation units in the table, we repeated each of the above-mentioned changed 100 times. Because of the size and the required amount of time, we repeated each change 25 times for `DataTransferProtos`. Hence, for the first four compilation units, we repeated the renaming 100 times. The toggling from public to private and from private to public as well as the adding and removing of a filed has been repeated 50 times each.

As hardware we used a 4 core Intel Xeon CPU with 3.40 Ghz with 8 GB of RAM and a 64-bit Windows 7 Professional installation as operating system. As environment for the Java monitor, we used a 64-bit Eclipse 3.5 (Kepler) instance with a workspace containing the Hadoop HDFS project. As Java runtime environment, we used the Java Runtime Environment (JRE) 1.7 64-bit.

6.6.1.2. Results

The aggregated results of the performance measurement for the different changes for each compilation units as well as the standard deviation is shown in Table 6.12. The Diagram 6.6 visualizes the results from the table. The results from the table and the diagram indicate two findings: i) the time needed to process a change increases with the size of the changed compilation unit, and ii) the performed change itself has no performance influence. Hence, regardless whether we added/remove a filed, renamed a method, or changed the modifier of a filed the time the Java monitor needs compute a change remains the same given the same compilation unit. The first change, however, consumed more time as the remainder of the changes as JaMoPP needs to initialize itself. Hence, we consider the first change as an outlier and remove it from the result.

Table 6.13 shows the relation between the time needed by the Java monitor for the first part (classifying the AST changes) and the second main part (creating VITRUVIUS changes using JaMoPP). As we can see from this table, the second part consumes at least 90% of the overall time. For the larger compilation units the JaMoPP parsing consumes 99% of the overall time. Within the second part itself the bottleneck is the parsing of a compilation unit using JaMoPP. We discuss the findings and draw conclusions for this width=observations in Section 6.6.3.

Compilation Unit	LLOC	Rename Method		Replace Method Modifier		Add or Remove Field	
		$\bar{t}[ms]$	s	$\bar{t}[ms]$	s	$\bar{t}[ms]$	s
ByteArray	28	57	0.94	50	0.34	57	0.33
INode	350	292	0.22	278	0.32	324	0.33
FSEditLog	1045	832	0.09	856	0.16	865	0.10
DFSClient	2050	1776	0.17	1676	0.16	1954	0.16
DataTransferProtos	15 812	14 683	0.09	14 334	0.09	14 880	0.10

Table 6.12.: Results of the performance evaluation for the Java code monitor. The table shows the measured total monitoring time for the Java code monitor for the above-mentioned edit operations. For each operation, *average* total time consumption in milliseconds $\bar{t}[ms]$ and the *standard deviation/average* s is given. The table has been published already in [Mes14] and [Kra+15a; Kra+15b].

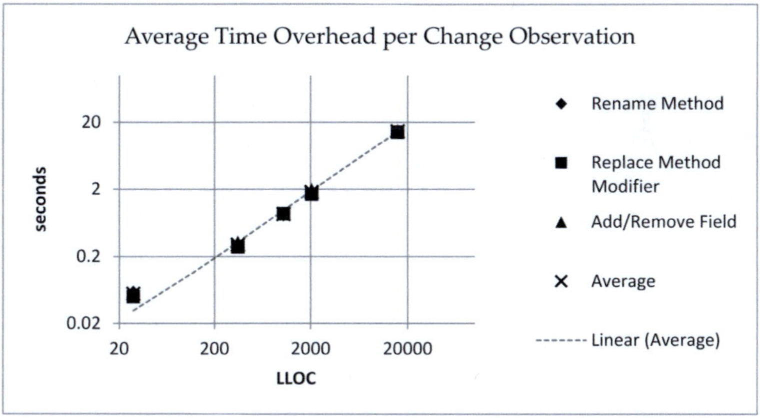

Figure 6.6.: Average time consumed by the Java monitor in ms. The axes are logarithmic to base 10.

Compilation Unit	**LLOC**	**Rename Method**		**Replace Method Modifier**		**Add or Remove Field**	
		AST	JaMoPP	AST	JaMoPP	AST	JaMoPP
ByteArray	28	0.06	0.94	0.06	0.94	0.04	0.96
INode	350	0.02	0.98	0.02	0.98	0.01	0.99
FSEditLog	1045	0.01	0.99	0.01	0.99	0.01	0.99
DFSClient	2050	0.01	0.99	0.01	0.99	0.01	0.99
DataTransferProtos	15812	0.01	0.99	0.01	0.99	0.01	0.99

Table 6.13.: Relation between the time needed for AST change classifying and JaMoPP-based creation of a Vitruvius change to the total time consumed by the Java monitor. The table contain *average* AST or JaMoPP time consumption divided by the *total average* time consumption. From the results, we can conclude that the Vitruvius change generation based on JaMoPP consumes more than 90% of the overall time. The table has been created by Messinger [Mes14] and is published in his master's thesis already.

6.6.2. Performance during Change Replay

In this section, we evaluate the performance of our Coevolution approach during the change replay. Hence, we evaluate the time our Coevolution approach consumes to keep changes in code consistent with the architecture. Therefore, we combine the measurement implemented for the Java monitor with a newly introduced time measurements for the consistency preservation. As result, we get the time consumed by the Java monitor and the time consumed by the consistency preservation mechanism. Adding up the results gives us the information how long our Coevolution approach needs to process one change.

As we showed in the section above, parsing the change compilation unit using JaMoPP consumes more than 90% of the overall time. Hence, the hypotheses for this performance evaluation is that the JaMoPP performance still consumes the biggest amount of time.

6.6.2.1. Experiment Setup

We measured the performance of our Coevolution approach during the change replay of the projects Any23 and Xerces. For both projects, we measured the performance without the incremental *SEFF* reconstruction. For Any 23 we also performed a measurement with the incremental *SEFF* reconstruction. In all cases, we measured the performance with activated consistency preservation rules for integrated elements. For both projects, we investigated the first 51 atomic changes, to which our Coevolution approach reacted, during the change replay. The performance of the first change is considered as an outlier, because JaMoPP needs to initialize itself during the parsing of the first change. We also ignore composite changes, because composite changes combine more than one change and would falsify the performance measurements, because we would compare composite changes with atomic changes. In order to avoid user notifications and user clarification during the performance measurement, we use a modified user change disambiguation mechanism, which randomly answers questions immediately. In order to rule out possible false measurements due to other tasks, such as garbage collection, we repeated the experiment three times for each project. Even though the number of repetitions is not very high it is sufficient for the evaluation for the following reasons, because we only want to show the magnitude of the consistency preservation duration.

As hardware, we used a standard laptop with a 2.2 GHz Intel i7 processor and 8 GB RAM with Mac OSX 10.11 as operation system. As IDE, we used 64-bit Eclipse 4.5 (Mars) and the JRE 1.8 64 bit as Java environment.

6.6.2.2. Results

The results without the incremental *SEFF* reconstruction show two similarities with the results for the standalone Java monitor performance measurement:

- the parsing of compilation units using JaMoPP consumes most of the time, and
- the time consumed to process a change does not depend on change itself.

Knowing these two facts allows us, to present the results aggregated for the changed compilation units independently from the actual performed change. The diagram 6.7 shows the result for the change replay performance for Any23, while the diagram in Figure 6.8 shows the result for the change replay performance for Xerces. As we can see from those diagrams, the consistency preservation usually consumes less than 20% of the time. We have, however, observed one exception for Xerces, where the consistency preservation step consumes almost 50% of the time. Another finding is that we cannot confirm the finding from the Java monitor performance evaluation, that larger files always require more time to be parsed by JaMoPP. Even though larger files tend to need more time to be parsed by JaMoPP some smaller files also need quite a long time to get parsed.

For Any23, we also measured the time need by our Coevolution approach to reconstruct the *SEFF* incrementally during the change replay evaluation, i.e. we measured the time to keep a change performed to a method body consistent with the architectural model. We again, present the results aggregated for the changed compilation units. The results are visualized in diagram 6.9. The results indicate that our Coevolution approach needs more time to process for method body changes as for non-method body changes.

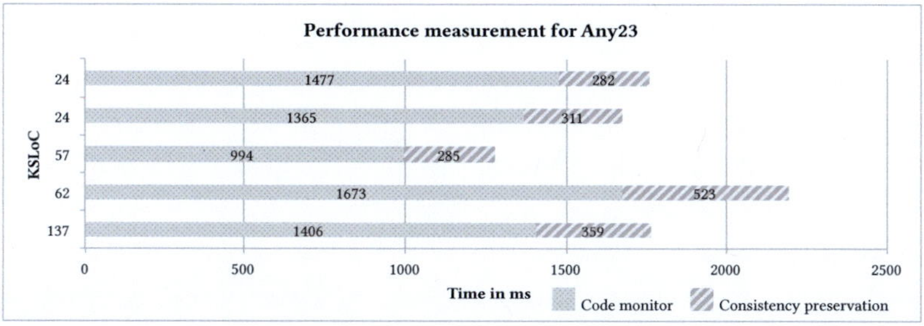

Figure 6.7.: Performance evaluation for the first 50 changes for Any23 during the change replay evaluation. The changes only affected five compilation units with sizes from 24 SLoC up to 137 SLoC. Note: This diagram excludes changes affecting method body changes, i.e. it excludes the performance measurement for the incremental *SEFF* reconstruction.

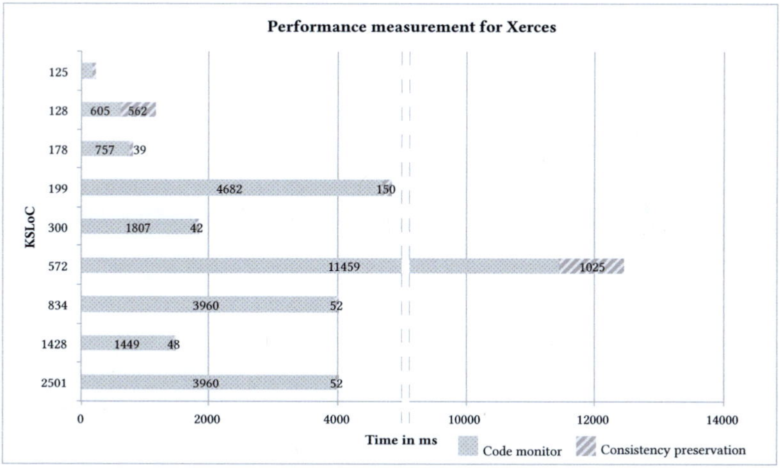

Figure 6.8.: Performance evaluation for the first 50 changes for Xerces during the change replay evaluation. As we can see the changes affected compilation units from size from 125 SLoC up to 2501 SLoC.

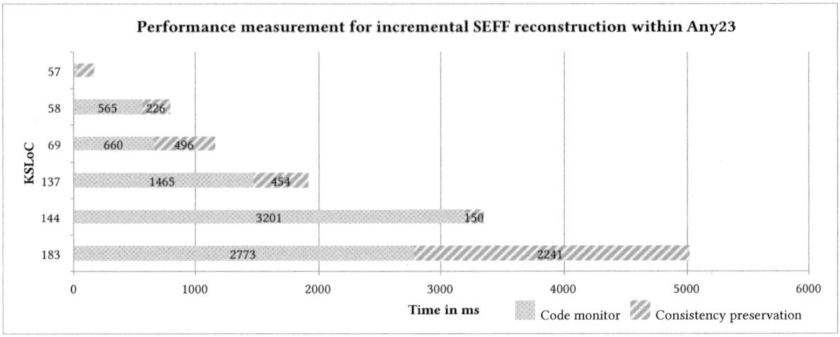

Figure 6.9.: Performance evaluation for the first 25 method body changes for Any23 during the change replay evaluation. This diagram only shows changes affecting method body changes, i.e. it only shows the performance measurement for the incremental *SEFF* reconstruction. We can see the actual consistency preservation step requires more time for changes affecting method bodies as for changes affecting static code only. Hence, the incremental *SEFF* reconstruction requires more time than executing the "normal" consistency preservation rules.

However, the parsing of compilation units into a JaMoPP still consumes the most time. The consistency preservation required between 4% and 82% of the overall time. The time required varies as the necessary actions to create a *SEFF* incrementally vary depending on the size and the method calls within the method, which has been changed.

6.6.3. Discussion

In this section, we discuss the results of the performed performance evaluations. Both evaluations show that the most time is consumed by the parsing of compilation units into JaMoPP representation. The time needed to process a change increases almost linearly with increasing compilation unit size.

We can argue, that the performance of our Coevolution approach is sufficient for compilation units with reasonably small size. For the experiments, we performed, our Coevolution approach is able to keep preserve consistency between code and architecture for file sizes with less than 300 SLoC within a couple of seconds. As Messinger [Mes14] pointed out, Hatton [Hat97] analysed software projects of different programming languages. Hatton

[Hat97] concludes that classes realising components should be in the range between 200 and 400 LoC to minimize fault-density. As we seen in the evaluation, however, many classes consist of more than the denoted size. As we also seen in the evaluations for Xerces and especially Any23 the JaMoPP parser requires more time for some files even for files with smaller size. Hence, in future work one task is to increase the performance of the parsing component of the Java monitor. Improving the performance would also provide a benefit for the incremental *SEFF* reconstruction, because the incremental *SEFF* reconstruction needs to operate on the extracted JaMoPP model and needs to resolve Java elements within other compilation units as the changed one.

After performing the performance evaluation, we can answer research question 3.3. The time, our Coevolution approach requires to process a performed change on the source code, depends on the size of the changed compilation unit. The time to process a change varies between under one second to more than 10 seconds. If dynamic code is changed, i.e. a method body has been changed, our Coevolution approach requires more time, because the incremental *SEFF* creation needs to be performed. Detailed information about the time consumed is shown in the diagrams 6.7 6.8, and 6.9.

Hence, we can the research question 3.2 as follows using 3.2.1: our Coevolution approach requires approximately the same amount of time for open source software of reasonably size (in our case 112 KSLoC for Xerces) as for smaller open source systems case studies. Hence, the overhead it adds is reasonable small and we can argue that our Coevolution approach is able to deal with open source projects of reasonable size.

To increase performance in future work, one of the following solution can be considered:

- optimizing the JaMoPP parser,
- parsing only the changed fractions of compilation units, or
- replacing the JaMoPP parser by a faster parser.

In 8.2, we show a first idea how the standard Eclipse JDT AST parser can be used to replace JaMoPP. Therefore, we propose to convert the classes within the Eclipse JDT AST into Eclipse Modeling Framework (EMF)-based classes.

Although our Coevolution approach respectively the Java code monitor requires more time to process larger code files, it is possible to process this large compilation units.

6.7. Model-based Performance Prediction using Coevolved Architecture Models

In this section, we explain how a model extracted with *EJBmoX* and a model coevolved based on the extracted model can be used to predict the performance of a software system. As case study system, we use the mRUBiS system, which we already explained in Section 6.3.2.

Even though developing approaches to enrich existing models with performance information and developing simulators for the Palladio approach is out of the scope of this thesis, we performed this evaluation to show an end-to-end validation of our Coevolution approach. In particular, we show how a) performance prediction for an extracted model can be realised, and b) how we can use a coevolved model for performance prediction after a new requirement has been implemented into an existing software system. After showing a) and b), we can show that the accuracy of the performance prediction using the coevolved model is as good as the performance prediction for the reverse-engineered model

In the remainder of this section, we first explain the used evolution scenario for mRUBiS and the necessary steps to implement the evolution scenario. As second step, we explain how we performed the coevolution of the architectural model and the source code during the implementation. After these two steps, we have the models, which we can use for the performance prediction. As next step, we explain how we enrich an existing architectural model, which is based on EJB component-code, with performance information. Therefore, we explain the experiment setup to get the performance data from the software system we used. As last step, we show the results of the performance prediction using the enriched models and compare the predicted performance with the measured performance.

6.7.1. Evolution Scenario for mRUBiS

This section introduces the performed evolution for the mRUBiS system. We introduce the following two requirements for the evolution:

1. allow users to upload one initial image of an item during the registration of the item.
2. creating a thumbnail of the uploaded image, in order to present the thumbnail in a later step, e.g. within an overview site of the item or an overview site of similar items.

To implement these requirements, we need to extend the `registerItem` signature in the `ItemRegistrationService` interface in order to allow users to upload an image. The component `ItemRegistrationServiceBean` needs to be extended in order to realise the functionality. To create the thumbnail, we introduce a new `ImageMgmtServiceBean`, which provides the new interface `ImageMgmtService`. Hence, the new component provides the mechanism to scale an image. The `ItemRegistrationServiceBean` requires the new interface `ImageMgmtService` and uses it to create the thumbnail within `registerItem`. In order to store the image as well as the thumbnail in the database, we need to extend the database interface `BusinessObjectsPersistenceService` and the realising component `BusinessObjectsPersistenceServiceBean` as well. Furthermore, we need to extend the classes `Item` and `EItem` in order to support the image as well as the thumbnail. The `Item` class represents the business object of an item, while the class `EItem` represents the persistent entity of the Java Persistence API (JPA), which is stored in the database. As a last step, we need to extend the database itself. Except for the extension of the database itself, all steps can be performed using the editors supported by our Coevolution approach.

6.7.2. Coevolution during the Implementation of the Evolution Scenario

As next step of the performance evaluation process, we implemented the described changes into the existing mRUBiS implementation and evolved the existing PCM model using our Coevolution approach. Figure 6.10 shows the activity diagram of `registerItem` before the evolution and after we conducted the evolution scenario. As PCM model for the existing implementation, we can use the PCM model for mRUBiS, which we created during the evaluation of *EJBmoX* (see Section 6.3.2). Before we can perform the coevolution, however, we need to integrate the model into our Coevolution approach. Therefore, we can use the integration mechanism described in Section 5.4.6. As our goal is to use the coevolved model for a performance prediction, we integrate the *SEFFs* and their corresponding methods as well into our Coevolution approach. Hence, we keep the *SEFFs* consistent with method body changes during the evolution of mRUBiS. The mRUBiS system maps the EJB components and interfaces conform with the consistency preservation rules, we defined for EJB (see Section 4.6.1.1). As a consequence, we can use these consistency preservation rules, to keep changes consistent between source code and the architectural model, i.e. for the integration and coevolution of the mRUBiS system, we can use Integration Level 1. This is a difference to the integrated systems in Section 6.5, where none of the integrated elements already fulfilled the used consistency preservation rules. Hence, by performing this evaluation, we also evaluate Integration Level 1, which has not been evaluated yet.

After this integration step, we can coevolve the architectural model and the source code. Therefore, we perform the changes described above and used our Coevolution approach for the mRUBiS project. Hence, after performing the changes, we have both the evolved source and the evolved architectural model. Users using our Coevolution approach in this scenario have the following advantages compared to users not using our Coevolution approach:

- they do not need to update the architectural model manually,
- during the evolution architectural relevant changes can be performed using the architectural model,
- they can reuse the existing *System* and *Allocation* diagram, as the elements within the *Repository* remain the same, and
- changes performed to parts of the architectural model not affected from the evolution scenario because the model is not fully regenerated but updated incrementally based on the source code changes.

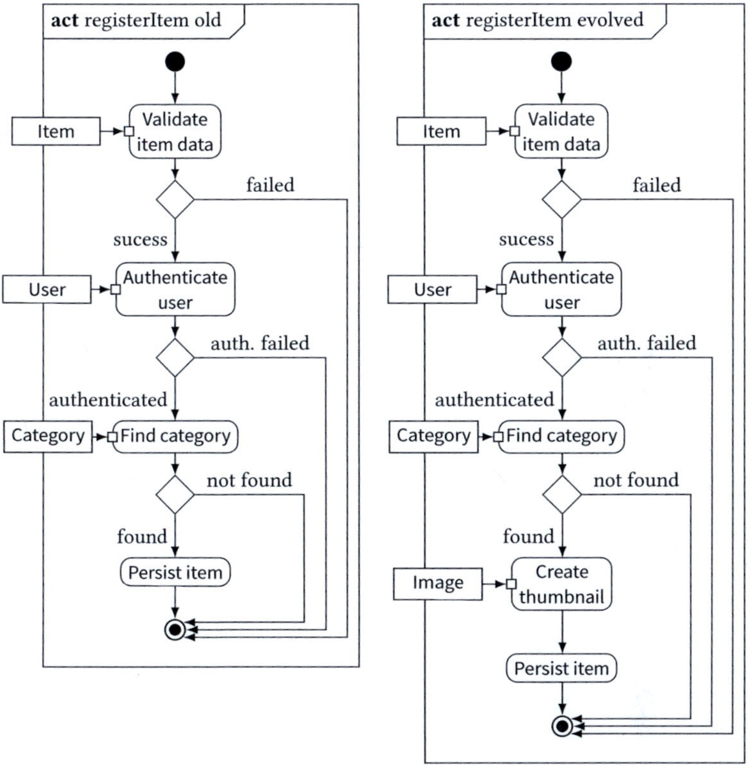

Figure 6.10.: Activity diagram of the `registerItem` service before the evolution scenario (left) and after we performed the evolution scenario (right). We added the creation of the thumbnail, which needs to be done during the registration of a new item.

To allow the repetition and ease the reproducibility of this case study, we performed the changes in source code and committed them into a GIT repository. Hence, we can use the change replay tool to coevolve the architectural model with the source code changes.

6.7.3. Enriching the Architectural Model with Resource Demands

Before we can use the Palladio approach for the actual performance prediction, we need to enrich respectively parametrise the architectural model with resource demands. This needs to be done for the model extracted with *EJBmoX* as well as for the coevolved model.

For the model enriching, we reuse the approach of Merkle [Mer17], which we explain in short in the following. We extended this approach in order to allow the enriching of a coevolved model. In the following, we first introduce the parametrisation process itself, which is used for the parametrisation of the models solely. We secondly explain the measurement process, which uses realistic workload in order to get realistic measurement data. The realistic measurement results are later compared with simulated results for the same realistic workload.

6.7.3.1. Model Parametrisation Process

To be able to parametrise an architectural model with performance information, the first step is to execute the software system and measure the execution time to get performance data from the software system. Therefore, it is necessary to set up the software system on a server and enabling monitoring of the application. For the monitoring, we use InspectIT[16], which is able to instrument a running Java application and measure the performance of each method. InspectIT, therefore, installs an agent in the software system under test and sends the results to an InspectIT server running either on the same server or on a different server.

After the initial setup and instrumentation steps, the software system needs to be executed using a load driver. The load driver executes one scenario at a time, i.e. it calls one provided interface method of the software system repeatedly. During the execution a warm-up phase is executed to avoid side effects, such as just in time compiling, during the actual measuring, which would falsify the measurement. At the end of this run, the collected invocation traces are stored in the Central Management Repository (CMR)

[16] `http://www.inspectit.rocks`

of the InspectIT database. Each invocation trace contains all calls to an EJB business interfaces in the context of the current system call. From the invocation trace, we get the order of EJB calls as well as they execution duration.

In our scenario, we register an item in the mRUBiS system by calling the service `registerItem`. Therefore, we execute 2000 warm-up requests and 1000 requests to get the actual parameterisation information for the non-evolved system. For the evolved system we execute 500 warm-up requests and 1000 requests to get the actual parameterisation information. In the evolved system less warm-up runs are required, because the generation of the thumbnail and storing the information in the database dominate the overall response time. We, furthermore, did not observe any side effects caused which indicate that the system is still in the warm-up phase, during the actual parameterisation phase. After the execution, we have stored 3000 respectively 1500 trances in the InspectIT database. As workload, we use a closed workload with one user, i.e, we have 3000 respectively 1500 sequential traces without contention of different users accessing the software system simultaneously. As think time for the one user, we choose 10 ms for both case studies, i.e. after completing the measurement, we wait 10 ms until a new request is created.

As next step, a the parameterisation extension, developed by Merkle [Mer17] for *EJBmoX*, is executed. The parameterisation extension needs a running InspectIT server, that contains the traces in its CMR database. The first step of the parameterisation extension is to skip the the warm-up runs, i.e, for the actual parameterisation only the remaining runs are used. As second step, the parameterisation extension needs to match the reconstructed methods and external calls within these methods with the methods monitored by InspectIT. Therefore, the parameterisation extension scans an invocation sequence sequentially and creates events for observed EJB component-external method calls and component-internal method calls. A matcher component traverses the *SEFF* actions and listens to these events and matches the events from the scanner with the *SEFF* elements, e.g. an *ExternalCallAction* or the beginning respectively the ending of an *InternalAction*. If the matcher retrieves the expected event a match has been found and the *SEFF* can be annotated with the necessary information, e.g. the resource demand of an *InternalAction*. After the scanning and matching phase, we have the necessary performance information for the *SEFF* elements. This information is added as a Stochastic

Expression (StoEx) in the *SEFF* actions, i.e. we use a probability distribution to determine the execution time of a specific *SEFF* action. More details about this approach can be found in Merkle [Mer17].

As an optional third step, SQL statements can be retrieved and annotated as well. This is helpful for the Palladio extension introduced by Merkle and Knoche [MK15], Merkle [Mer17]. For our evaluation, however, we did not use this optional extension.

After this step, we have the automatically enriched performance model. The performance model contain the resource demands in milliseconds, i.e. a processor with a processing rate of 1 can be used to simulated the same CPU speed used for the measurement. If a faster CPU should be simulated the simulated processing rate of the CPU can be increased accordingly.

An optional step, after the automatic enrichment is a manual refinement of the resulting PCM model. In the example of `registerItem`, we needed to adjust the model on one position: Within the service `persistItem` of the component `BusinessObjectsPersistenceServiceBean` the data of the thumbnail is stored on the hard drive. For this scenario the time the hard drive needs dominates the time the CPU needs to process this scenario. The automatic extraction, however, currently cannot differentiate between I/O and CPU demands and attributes observed execution times completely to the CPU. For the evolved mRUBiS system this scenario consumes most of the overall time needed to process the whole `registerItem` request. Without manual adaption, however, the simulation would assign the demand to the CPU. This results in an increased contention for the CPU, i.e. the CPU is not able to compute other requests during this time. We found out that this leads to a prediction error. Hence, we changed the demand from the CPU to the HDD for the operation `persistItem`, in order to reflect reflect the reality better in the used PCM model.

6.7.3.2. Performance Measurement Process

The actual performance measurement of the software system is done in a separate phase as the measurement for the parameterisation phase for the following reasons:

- the performance measurement should be performed with a realistic workload, and
- the instrumentation introduces overhead during the execution of the parameterisation run, which should not be considered during the measurement phase.

Note: Even though the instrumentation introduces overhead this overhead is not measured by InspectIT itself but in the load driver, because the load driver measures the response time of the called service. Hence, the response time measured by the load driver during the parameterisation phase are reflecting the response time including the overhead. As we disable InspectIT during the actual measurement run the response time measured by the load driver during the measurement run reflects the response time without the overhead.

As for the measurement run, we also call the service `registerItem` using a load driver. Again, we execute 2000 runs of warm-up and 1000 to measure the performance for the non-evolved workload, while we execute 500 runs of warm-up and 1000 performance measurements for the coevolved model. For both cases, we use an open workload with exponentially distributed mean interarrival times, i.e. new users arrive constantly at the system, executing a request, and leaving the system. For the non-evolved model, we use a mean interarrival time of 150 ms, while we use a mean interarrival time of 1000 ms for the coevolved model. The reason for the difference in the mean interarrival is the duration the system needs to process the request. In the evolved model, this time is significantly higher, because the system needs to calculate the thumbnail and store the new image in the database. As the mean interarrival time is significantly higher as the time needed to process a request, the contention within our scenario is relatively low. Lowering the interarrival time would increase the contention, but it would probably also overload the system, which would lead to measurement and prediction errors. We argue that this is acceptable for the evaluation performed in this thesis, because we only want to show that it is possible to use our coevolved models for performance prediction. Optimizing the performance prediction in cases where the contention is high is not part of this thesis.

As result of this runs, we have the information about the actual measured performance of the software system. In a later step, we compare this measured performance with the predicted performance. Technically this data is stored in an R[17] database.

6.7.3.3. Used Setup for Enriching Architectural Models and for Measuring the Performance

We need to measure the software system to enrich the architecture models and to measure the actual performance for a realistic work load. To do so, we need to deploy the software system and the necessary additional components. The deployment, we use, is depicted in Figure 6.11. As environment, we used two different virtual machines (VM1 and VM2). Both are running on the same physical hardware environment, which is a SunFire x4440 equipeed with 4 Six-Core AMD Opteron Processors à 2400 MHz, 128 GB RAM and 8*300GB HDD.

On the first virtual machine (VM1), we deployed the mRUBiS system, the load driver, and the R server. The R server on VM1 is used by the load driver to store the measured data. The stored measured data can be used for the comparison between the performance prediction and the actual measured data. As database for the mRUBiS system, we use a MySQL[18] data set. The database for the mRUBiS system is initialized with 2000 users, 100 items, and 20 categories for the items before each run. For each call of `registerItem`, a new item is created within one of the existing categories and a new randomly generated image from a size between 300x700 pixels and 400x800 pixels is uploaded. The first virtual machine is equipped with 4GB RAM and one AMD Opteron CPU core with 2.4 GHz. As operation system we used 64bit Windows 2012 Server. We only assigned one CPU core to this server to avoid incorrect measurements due to the use of multiple cores. In the case of more than one CPU core, we currently cannot determine how the execution time is distributed over the different CPUs. We argue that the evaluation using one CPU core only, is sufficient for the evaluation performed in this thesis, because our goal is not to optimize the performance prediction for multicore processors. Instead we want to show that the coevolved models can be used to predict the performance of a software system.

[17] `https://www.r-project.org`

[18] `https://www.mysql.com`

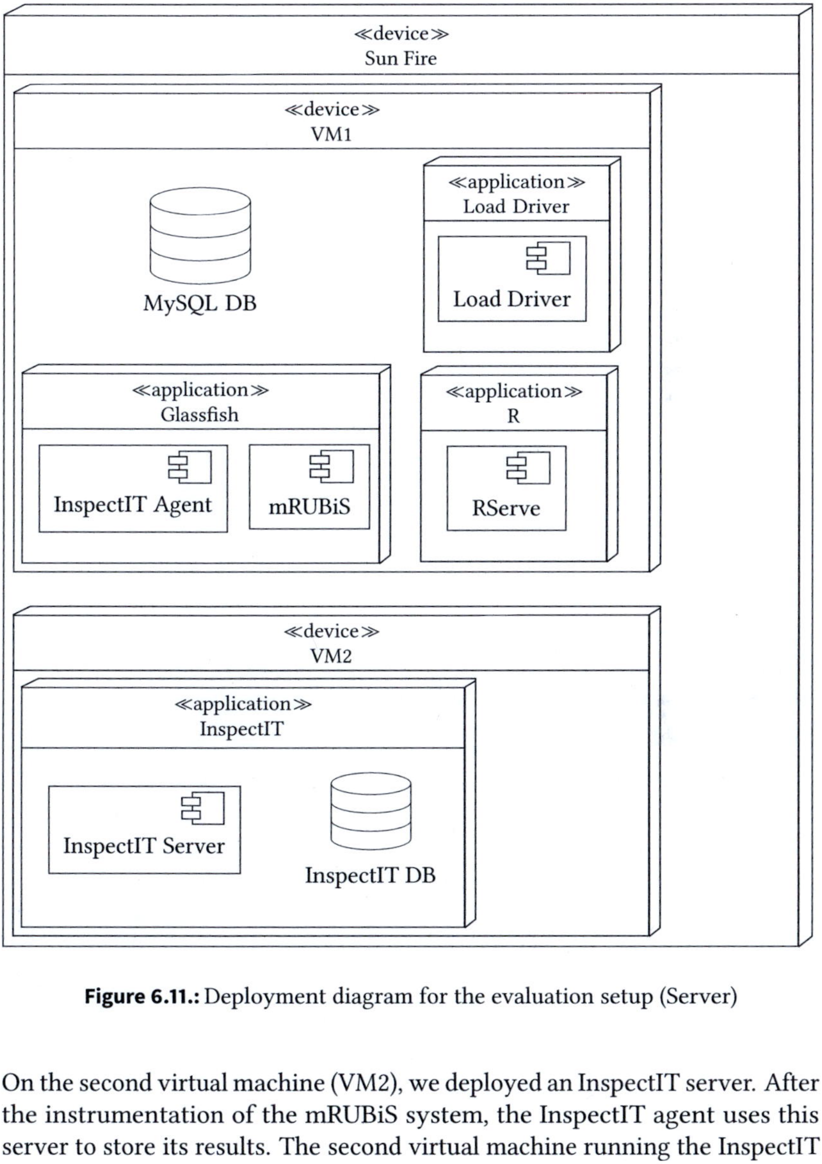

Figure 6.11.: Deployment diagram for the evaluation setup (Server)

On the second virtual machine (VM2), we deployed an InspectIT server. After the instrumentation of the mRUBiS system, the InspectIT agent uses this server to store its results. The second virtual machine running the InspectIT server is not critical for the performance, because it runs the InspectIT server

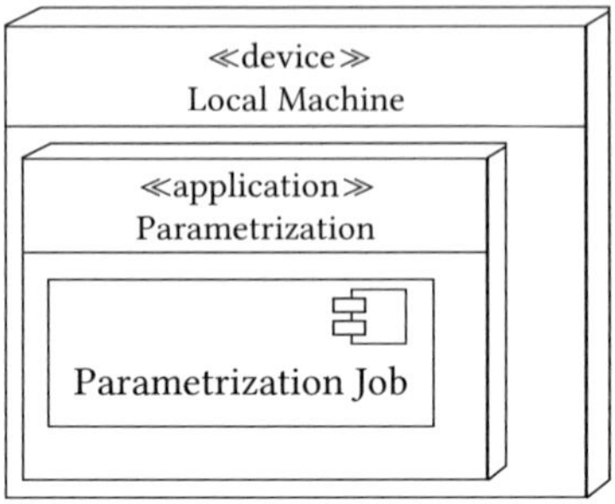

Figure 6.12.: Deployment diagram for the evaluation setup (Local Machine)

only and stores the information in a database. It turned out, however, that this functionality needs to be on a second virtual machine as the performance drain on the main machine would be to high otherwise. This virtual machine is also equipped with an AMD Opteron CPU with 2.6 GHz and 4 GB RAM. As operating system it uses a 64 bit Centos Linux.

The local machine in Figure 6.12 is a PC running the Parametrization Job after the parameterisation run has been completed. It communicates with the InspectIT application in order to retrieve the data, which is necessary for the parameterisation, from the InspectIT DB.

6.7.3.4. Enriching a Coevolved Architectural Model with Performance Information

The process described above requires source code, a consistent architecture model, and a SCDM. The architecture model needs to contain interfaces, components, and *SEFFs*. Within the *SEFFs* the behaviour needs to be specified, i.e. *Branches*, *Loops*, and *InternalActions* need to be present. It is, however, not necessary for the *SEFFs* to contain performance information already. These three artefacts are the output of the architecture reconstruction performed with *EJBmoX*. The parameterisation extension of *EJBmoX* is embedded in to the *EJBmoX* run and is able to enrich the extracted PCM.

Within the work presented in this thesis, our goal is to enrich a coevolved model with performance information. Therefore, we implemented a small tool, which realizes the enriching of an architectural model without the need of running the architecture extraction step of *EJBmoX* upfront. The tool creates the SCDM from the VITRUVIUS correspondence model using a model to model transformation. Using the SCDM, the source code, and the coevolved architecture model, we can execute the *EJBmoX* extension, which enriches the architecture model with performance information. Hence, we can retrieve an architectural model enriched with performance information from a coevolved architecture model. The implemented tool is available as Eclipse plugin and available within the VITRUVIUS framework. After enriching the model, we are able to answer research question 4.1 from the GQM plan as follows: Using our Coevolution approach omits the effort to update the statical architectural elements and the behavioural architectural elements manually. The measuring of the software system and enriching the model with performance information remains the same. Using the proposed setup, however, most steps for the enriching process can be done automatically.

6.7.4. Experiment Results

After we enriched the models, we can execute the performance prediction using one of the available simulators for the Palladio approach. For the simulation, we use EventSim, which has been introduced by Merkle [Mer11] and Merkle and Henss [MH11]. As allocation and resource environment for the simulation, we use the environment generated by *EJBmoX*, i.e. we used one server with one CPU and all assemblies are deployed on this server. As the CPU has a processing rate of 1, we simulate the same CPU as the CPU used for the measurements. For the results, we compare the measured values with the predicted values of the simulation. To illustrate the model's generalization capability, we used different workloads for the measurement and the prediction as we used in the parameterisation run in the enriching phase. We compare the mean response time, the empirical cumulative density of the response time, and the mean CPU utilization between the simulated results and the measured results.

The diagram in Figure 6.13 shows the empirical cumulative density of the response time for the model extracted with *EJBmoX*, i.e. the non-evolved model. The diagram in Figure 6.14 shows the empirical cumulative density

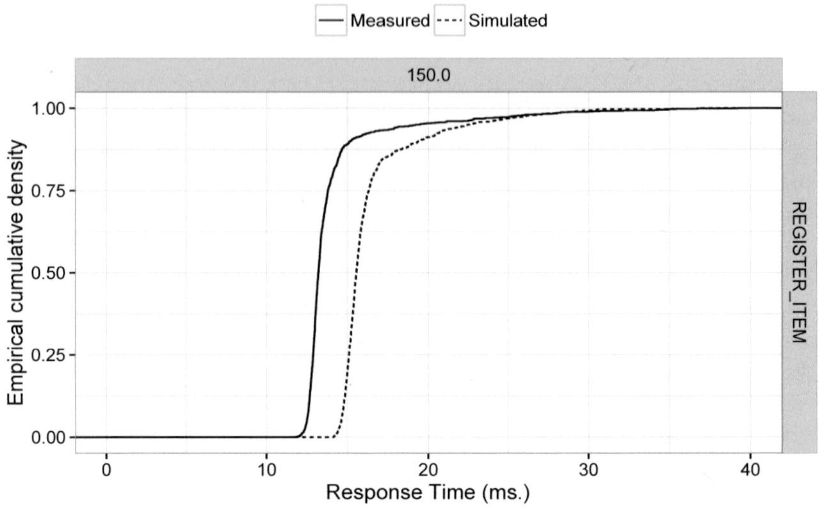

Figure 6.13.: Cumulative response time distribution of measurements compared to simulation results for the extracted model. The x-axis shows the response time in milliseconds. In the simulated run as well as in the measured run nearly all requests are processed within the first 25 ms. The mean interarrival time of new users is 150 ms.

for the coevolved model. As we can see the simulated curve and the measured curve have the same shape in both diagrams. As expected, the time needed to process the request for `registerItem`, increases dramatically for the coevolved model, because the thumbnail needs to be created and the image needs to be stored in the database. In both diagrams the simulated performance is slightly slower as the actual measured performance. The reason for this behaviour of the simulation seems to be twofold: first, might be the lack HDD monitoring during the parameterisation phase. Instead of split the load to HDD and CPU as the load occurs the load is only assigned to the CPU. This leads to the fact that contention scenarios are predicted slightly wrong in the simulation, because some requests need to wait longer in the simulation until they are processed than in the real time. We observed this behaviour especially for the `persistItem` service using the evolved system. As mentioned above, this service is used to store the data in the database and

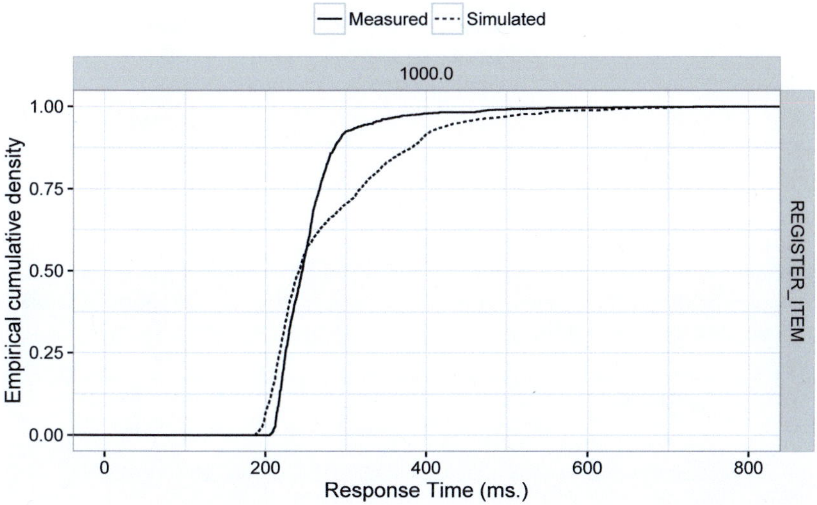

Figure 6.14.: Cumulative response time distribution of measurements compared to simulation results for the coevolved model. The x-axis shows the response time in milliseconds. The evolved system requires more time to process requests, i.e. most requests are processed within a range of 200 and 500 ms. The mean interarrival time of new users is 1000 ms.

is HDD intensive, i.e. we changed the demand from the CPU to the HDD. As part of future work, the monitoring could be improved in order to consider HDD demand of the system under test as well.

Table 6.14 the mean response time per user is shown for both experiments. As we can see, the accuracy of the performance prediction using the coevolved model is not degenerate for the coevolved model.

Table 6.15 shows the mean measured utilization of the CPU compared with the mean simulated utilization of the CPU. The error is for both experiments greater than 50 %. This difference is partly caused by the additional load introduced by the load driver and R server. Both processes have an impact on the measured CPU utilization, but not on the simulated utilization. The additional load, however, does not explain the large gap between the simulated and measured mean CPU utilization. System processes executed by

Experiment	Meas. time (ms)	Sim. time (ms)	Error abs. (ms)	Error rel. (%)
extracted model	14.92	16.45	1.53	10.25
evolved-model	256.67	277.25	20.58	8.01

Table 6.14.: Comparison of the mean response time in the measured run and the simulated run for both experiments. As we can see, the relative error for both cases is approximately 10%, i.e, the prediction of the response time can be used to make reliable statements about the behaviour of the software system.

Experiment	Utili. measured	Utili. simulated	Error abs.	Error rel.
extracted model	0.14	0.05	−0.08	61.89
evolved model	0.27	0.12	−0.14	53.62

Table 6.15.: Comparison of the mean CPU utilization in the measured run and the simulated run. All numbers are in percentage. As we can see, the error is greater than 50 percent for both experiments, i.e. the prediction of the utilization cannot be used to make reliable statements about the behaviour of the software system.

the used SQL database to store the uploaded images on the HDD might be another explanation for the observed behaviour. To improve the prediction of the CPU utilization, the measurement can be improved in order to only consider the actual CPU utilization of the process under test. Furthermore, the load driver and the R server can be moved to a separate VM.

After performing the experiments, we can answer research question 4.2 as follows: The relative prediction error for the mean response time using the evolved model is 8.01%. Brosig et al. [Bro+15] pointed out that, according to Menascé et al. [MAD94] [MA00], in capacity planning, prediction errors of the response time are acceptable up to a relative error of 30% percent. Hence, the results we get for the response time can be used for the capacity planning. The prediction error for the mean CPU utilization, however, is greater than 50%, i.e. the results are currently not usable for a prediction of the CPU utilization.

6.8. Threats to validity

In this section, we present the threats to validity for the performed evaluation.

For the evaluation of *Extract* and *EJBmoX*, we identified the following threats to validity: To evaluate *Extract*, we only used Apache projects. The projects, however, are of different size, from different domains, and widely used. Hence, we argue that the projects represent typical open source software systems. We also did not compare an architectural model reverse-engineered with *Extract* with a manual created one, yet. Hence, we are not able to make statements about their accuracy. For the evaluation of *EJBmoX*, we used only two relatively small open source software systems, which were designed as case study systems. Hence, we cannot make a statement whether realistic open source EJB systems or industrial sized EJB systems can be investigated using *EJBmoX* as it is or whether further extensions for *EJBmoX* are needed to cope with those projects.

For the evaluation of the consistency preservation rules using the PCM RIS, we identified the following threat to validity: We used only a limited amount of existing PCM models. Some of them, such as CoCoME, however, are widely used to evaluate the PCM itself. Hence, we can argue that the used models are representative PCM model instances.

For the replay of changes from a VCS and the coevolution evaluation, we identified the following threats to validity: The changes are not performed by developers in our scenario but by the change replay tool. Even though the changes we replay, are performed to the actual source code, it is unclear, whether developers would have performed the changes in the same order. Hence, we cannot make a statement, whether developers and architects would use our Coevolution approach as we did in this scenario. Another threat to validity is that the change replay tool in combination with the source code monitor showed slightly different behaviour during repetitions of the change replay for the same project. However, we can argue that this behaviour only occurred in a minor cases of changes and that the result after the change replay remains the same. A threat to validity for the coevolution is that we only used four open source projects and replayed possible changes. As for *Extract*, all of them are Apache projects. However, as in *Extract*, we used projects of different sizes and different domains.

For the performance evaluation of our Coevolution approach, we identified the following threats to validity: The performance evaluation of the Java monitor has been conducted with only a few test methods and only a subset from the possible changes. We can argue, however, that the JaMoPP parser required the biggest amount of time in each test, i.e. changing the actual change would not lead to a much different result. For the performance evaluation of the coevolution approach, we also used only limited amount of changes performed to a limited set of classes. We furthermore, only executed three repetitions. We can, however, similar as above and state that the JaMoPP parser required the biggest amount of time, i.e. the time is dominated by the JaMoPP parser, which we cannot influence. Furthermore, the goal was to give the order of magnitude of the time required to coevolve a model.

For the performance prediction using a coevolved model, we identified the following threats to validity:

- the evaluation has been performed using one case study project only,
- within the project, we considered only one scenario,
- we only used one server for the prediction and for the measurement, and
- the contention during the performance prediction was low.

We can argue, however, that we only wanted to show that the coevolved models can be used in principle for the performance prediction.

7. Related Work

In this chapter, we present related work to the approach presented in this thesis. We have presented an approach capable of coevolving architectural models and source code (see Section 4.2) within this thesis. As architectural model, we use the Palladio Component Model (PCM). As source code, we use the Java language, which is an object-oriented programming language. Our Coevolution approach is also able to coevolve UML class diagrams using the defined UML class diagram editor, which we presented in Section 4.2.4. It is also capable of coevolving source code and its behavioural models. Our Coevolution approach is, furthermore, able to integrate existing architectural models and existing source code. The approach we use, is based on the Vitruvius, framework, which is a view-based engineering framework using Model-Driven Software Development (MDSD) techniques.

The related work is structured according to the contributions of our Coevolution approach. Therefore, we first present approaches, which are able to coevolve architectural models and source code. Next, we explain architecture reverse engineering approaches that have the goal to reverse-engineer an architectural model from source code, which is afterwards used for the coevolution with the source code. Finally, we focus on view-based approaches that use MDSD techniques in order to keep models consistent.

7.1. Approaches that keep Architectural Models and Source Code Consistent

The first major area of related work are approaches that keep architectural models and source code consistent during software development and software evolution. We first explain approaches capable of coevolving source code and high-level architectural models. Next, we explain approaches that are able to keep behavioural models consistent with source code. Next, we present approaches that keep UML class diagrams and source code consistent during software evolution. Finally, we present approaches that integrate high-level architectural information into source code.

7.1.1. Coevolution Approaches for Source Code and High-Level Architectural Models

One goal of approaches coevolving source code and high-level architectural models, is to avoid architecture drift and architecture erosion. Silva and Balasubramaniam [SB12] have presented a survey on approaches that can be used to control software architecture erosion. The classification of approaches is depicted in Figure 7.1. Our Coevolution approach can be seen as an approach that *prevents* software architecture erosion using *architecture to implementation linkage*. Most approaches that fall into this category, such as ArchJava [ACN02], embed architectural information into the source code. We explain the relation between those approaches and our Coevolution approach in Section 7.1.4. Our Coevolution approach, however, does not embed the architectural models directly but uses a correspondence model to trace between architectural models and its corresponding source code elements. ArchWare [Oqu+04], which also falls into this category, presents an explicit Architecture Description Language (ADL) and a textual syntax to create the architecture and its implementation. Hence, the created models are detailed enough to generate the complete source code of a system. To create these detailed models, users first need to model high-level architectural models and refine them in next steps. As the high-level architectural models are part of the executable software system, they are kept consistent with their refined models automatically. Within our Coevolution approach, however, we use a stricter separation between the source code and the architectural model. We do not consider the architectural model as part of the running application.

KobrA [Atk+01] (Komponentenbasierte Anwendungsentwicklung) is a component-based application development environment that allows to create the architecture of a software system. Therefore, it supports different UML diagrams, for instance, the UML composite diagram, UML class diagrams, and UML behaviour models such as the activity diagram. The different

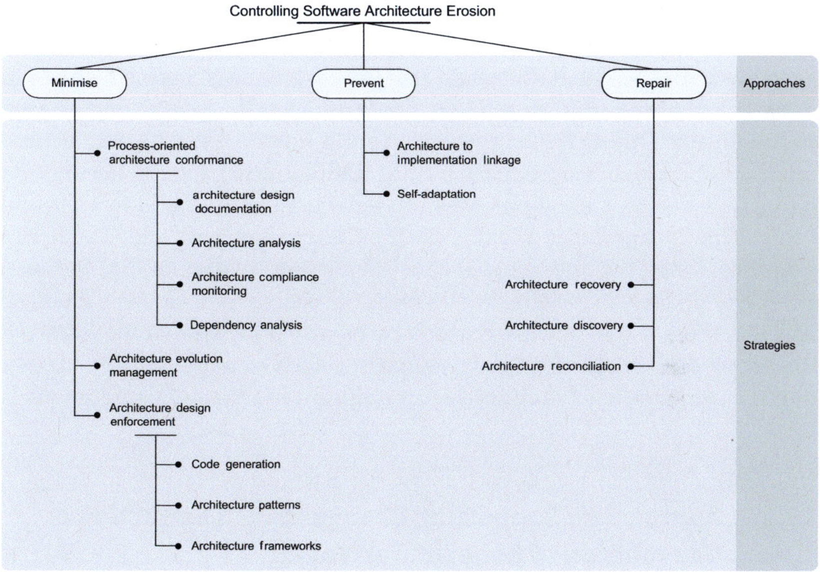

Figure 7.1.: The classification of software architecture erosion presented by Silva and Balasubramaniam [SB12].

diagrams are different views on a Single Underlying Model (SUM). Hence, KobrA is an implementation of the view-based engineering approach Orthographic Software Modelling (OSM) [ASB10]. In recent work KobrA has been applied to the open source project Common Component Modelling Example (CoCoME) [Dac16]. Dacic [Dac16] provides an up-to-date KobrA model for CoCoME as well as a prototypical implementation. Using KobrA has the advantages that the used models are kept consistent as they use the same SUM. Dacic [Dac16], however, did not propose a coevolution for the implemented source code and the KobrA models as we do in our Coevolution approach.

IBM Rational Rhapsody[1] supports model-driven software developments in multiple ways. It allows the creation of UML models such as package

[1] `http://www-03.ibm.com/software/products/en/ratirhapfami`

diagrams, class diagrams and different behaviour models such as activity diagrams and sequence diagrams. From these models, source code can be generated. IBM Rational Rhapsody also has reverse engineering features in order to include existing code. Users need to trigger the reverse engineering step manually. During the reverse engineering, however, not all architectural models are created automatically. IBM Rational Rhapsody also supports bidirectional consistency preservation between architectural models and code. This is supported for the UML package diagrams and UML class diagrams. Using the bidirectional consistency preservation of IBM Rational Rhapsody updates the diagrams as soon as the source code has been changed and vice versa. A difference to our Coevolution approach is that IBM Rational Rhapsody does support language elements, such as packages and classes, only, i.e. no high-level architecture description in terms of components is used.

7.1.2. Approaches Supporting Change-driven Extraction or Coevolution of Behavioural Models

The extraction respectively coevolution of behavioural models is usually either done to achieve one or more of the following goals: i) allow users to get a high-level overview of the behaviour of the source code in order to ease the understanding of the code and to enable the detection of architecture violation, ii) allow users to edit up-to-date behavioural models in order to update the source code. From the tools and approaches explained in the following, Architexa, ArchLint, and JITTAC achieve the first goal, while mbeddr and Fujaba achieve the second goal.

ArchLint[2] [Maf+13] can be used to detect architectural violations. Therefore, ArchLint uses static code analysis and the history of the source code. As input it needs the source code history data as well as a high-level architecture representation. Based on the input data ArchLint uses heuristics in order to detect possible architecture violations. ArchLint is able to detect the so called absence violation[Maf+13], which is defined as a dependency that exists in the architecture but is not present in the source code. It is, furthermore, able to detect divergence violation, which is a dependency that exists in the source code, but that is not allowed according to the architectural model. A

[2] `http://aserg.labsoft.dcc.ufmg.br/archlint`

difference to our Coevolution approach is that the architecture violation is not detected during the actual development time but in a separate analysis step.

The Just-in-Time Tool for Architectural Consistency (JITTAC)[3] presented by Buckley et al. [Buc+13], can be used to detect architectural violation respectively architecture erosion during the development time of a software system. To do so, architects first need to create a software architecture in terms of componetns from existing code. Therefore, they need to map source code elements in terms of packages, interfaces, and classes to components. During this process dependencies between the components are created dynamically. Furthermore, architects are allowed to define new dependencies between components. If developers add dependencies in the code that are not present in the architecture yet, the architectural model gets updated accordingly and a warning is shown to architects. Architects then need to decide whether the new dependency is considered as architecture violation or whether they accept the new dependency in the architectural model. A notable feature of JITTAC is that it warns developers if they are about to violate respectively already violated the architecture. This feature is included within the Eclipse IDE. Different as our Coevolution approach, however, JITTAC does not allow coevolution of source code and architecture and it uses a different component definition as we do.

Architexa[4] allows the creation of UML sequence diagrams dynamically from source code. The diagrams are dynamically created and read only views. Architexa focuses on the creation of UML sequence diagrams for classes. In our Coevolution approach, we focus, however, on the incremental creation of activity like diagrams (the *SEFFs*) for components. The components in our Coevolution approach, can comprise a set of classes.

Voelter et al. [Voe+13] introduce mbeddr, which is a language based on C, that allows the creation of source code using either an editor that integrates a source code editor with editors for UML behaviour models, such as activity diagrams. It is based on the JetBrains MPS (Meta Programming System) [PSV13], which is a integrated environment for language engineering. Users of mbeddr can view and edit parts of the source code directly as models or as source code. As the code as well as the model are projective views that show

[3] `http://actool.sourceforge.net`

[4] `http://www.architexa.com`

the same single underlying model the consistency is preserved automatically. In Section 7.1.4, we explain how mbeddr can be used to coevolve architectural elements, such as components, with the source code, by embedding them into the source code and defining specific keywords for the architectural elements.

From UML to Java and back again (Fujaba) allows round-trip engineering between behavioural models and source code. Nickel et al. [NNZ00] describe how Fujaba can be used for the coevolution between source code and UML activity diagrams as well as source code and UML statecharts. The coevolution of both is based on method bodies within classes. Hence, users can change, for instance, activity diagrams to update the code and vise versa. Fujaba focuses on the coevolution of method bodies within classes. Within our Coevolution approach, we focus on the reconstruction of component-behaviour, i.e. the reconstruction approach we propose is not based on a single method body but can span multiple method bodies.

7.1.3. Approaches supporting Round-trip Engineering between UML Class Diagrams and Source Code

Many famous related coevolution and round-trip engineering approaches focus on the coevolution of source code and UML class diagrams. The approaches often refer to their consistency preservation process as synchronization mechanism between models. These approaches are related to our Coevolution approach, yet they are different because the mapping between UML class diagrams and object-oriented source code is quite clear. Hence, usually the approaches do not need to allow for different consistent preservation rules between architectural models and source code. The approaches, however, closely related to our UML class diagram editor *Projective UML class diagram editor for Java (ProjUMLed4J)*, which we have presented in Section 4.2.4. In [KLK16], we already identified approaches able to keep UML class diagrams and source code consistent. We divided these tools in three different classes depending on how they enable coevolution respectively round-trip engineering between source code and UML class diagrams. Approaches within the first category use an explicit model, which contains the UML information. Approaches that fall into second category, use a central model to store all information about all used artefacts. Approaches in the third category do not use any additional artefacts, i.e. they use the source code only.

Tools within the first category are, for instance, IBM Rational Software Architect [Cla10], MagicDraw [No 12], UML Lab[5], and Fujaba [NNZ00]. MagicDraw allows users to integrate changes in one artefact into the other artefact. Therefore, it uses an explicit synchronization mechanism for the source code and the UML class diagram model. The synchronization is explicit because it needs to be triggered by users. As UML Lab arose from Fujaba they share the same consistency preservation process and can be explained together. The used consistency process combines implicit and explicit consistency preservation. Implicit means that changes to either the source code or the architectural model are kept consistent directly without an explicit triggering of the consistency preservation process. UML Lab and Fujaba using such implicit changes if both the architectural editor and the source code editors are open. If one of them is closed the consistency preservation process needs to be triggered manually, i.e. explicitly. Information, which are only contained in the UML class diagram, such as multiplicities, are stored within structured comments in the source code. Hence, to share this information it is sufficient to share the source code itself. The diagrams do not need to be shared. A similar approach is used by Rational Software Architect for UML class diagrams and source code. It provides an implicit synchronization mechanism, which transfers information, i.e. changes in the UML class diagram are kept consistent with the source code and vice versa.

Enterprise Architect [Spa14], which is a popular tool for allowing coevolution between UML class diagrams and code, falls into the second category. If users modify the UML class diagram, Enterprise Architect persists the changes in a central model. The synchronization of the source code has to be called explicitly. Hence, concurrent modifications in the UML class diagram and the source code are not possible, as one change would overwrite the other change.

Tools falling in the third category are, for instance, UML Aid Explorer[6], Architexa, a GMF-based editor [Hei+09b] based on JaMoPP, and Together [Bor05] from Borland. UML Aid and Architexa use the source code of

[5] `http://www.uml-lab.com/`

[6] http://www.objectaid.com

a project to show an UML class diagram for a specific set of classes and interfaces. The created UML diagram, however, are read-only class diagrams, i.e. it is not possible to change UML class diagrams. Even though UML Aid and Architexa not support round-trip engineering, we mention them here as they both use the source code as underlying model and create a projectional view onto the source code. The GMF-based editor presented by Heidenreich et al. [Hei+09b] uses JaMoPP as model for the source code and provides an editable UML class diagram editor. It is, however, not UML compliant and is also not compatible with the latest Eclipse versions. The most popular tool falling into the third category is Together from Borland. The tool supports a so called LiveSource mechanism, which allows for editing the source code using UML class diagrams. The used UML class diagrams are generated dynamically from the underlying source code as projective view. Information that is represented by the UML class diagram only, e.g. multiplicities of associations, are stored in structured code comments.

The above mentioned list of tools and approaches, which we already presented in [KLK16], does not claim to be complete, as they are many tools allowing for the coevolution between source code and UML class diagrams. The important fact is that these approaches are optimized for UML class diagrams. Defining the consistency preservation rules between UML class diagrams and object-oriented source code is rather easy, as most UML class diagram elements have a direct representation in source code. As mentioned above, the approaches are, however, related to ProjUMLed4J. The differences between ProjUMLed4J and approaches from the first category is that ProjUMLed4J does not have an explicit model for storing the UML class diagram. Instead, it generates the UML class diagram as projective view from the underlying source code. The main differences to the tools from the second category is that we do not use an additational central model. The tools from the third category that allow editing of UML class diagrams, i.e. Borland Together and the GMF editor for JaMoPP, are similar to ProjUMLed4J. However, they do not support annotations in order to store information that do not have a direct representation in source code, e.g. multiplicities between classes. Also ProjUMLed4J is tailored in order to work with the techniques used in our Coevolution approach and it is thous used as UML class diagram editor in our Coevolution approach.

7.1.4. Approaches Embedding Architectural Information in to Source Code

Another approach of keeping architectural information and source code consistent is to embed architectural information into the source code. To do so, four approaches are common:

1. defining architecture in the source code using features of the used programming language,
2. defining architecture in additional features of the used programming language, e.g. annotations within Java,
3. extending the programming language with architectural artefacts, or
4. using built-in mechanisms of the programming language to define an architecture.

The first approach, is to implement the architecture in the source code directly. An example for this idea is the Programming-in-the-small-and-many (PRISM) approach presented by Mikic-Rakic and Medvidovic [MM03]. PRISM allows developers to specify a component-based architecture in source code using features of the used source code language, e.g. Java. PRISM is considered by the authors as middleware platform, which is able to develop software architectures. Therefore, it enables users to define architectural level elements, for instance, components, connectors, events, and configurations, within the source code. Hence, software developers can implement architectural decisions directly in the source code. Therefore, software developers need to specify the architecture and define how the components are connected and how events are send among the components. The advantage of such an approach is that no explicit consistency preservation mechanism is necessary, because the architecture is implemented directly into the source code. No explicit architectural model, however, exists to represent architectural elements. Also no behavioural model exists, as the behaviour is described by the realising source code itself. Hence, the approach cannot contain information which is not contained in the source code directly. In future work, we can define consistency preservation rules between architectural models and source code, which is based on PRISM. Hence, PRISM architectural models can be combined with our Coevolution approach.

An example for the second approach is provided by Konersmann et al. [Kon+13]. They present the idea of using Java annotations to embed architectural information in source code. An architectural view is dynamically created, from the underlying source code, on demand. Even though the technique used by Konersmann et al. [Kon+13] is different as the technique we use in our Coevolution approach, from a users perspective the approaches are similar because Konersmann et al. [Kon+13] also use the PCM as architectural model. Konersmann and Holschbach [KH16] recently extended the approach in order to keep the PCM *Allocation* consistent with a software system running with Java Enterprise Edition. A difference between our Coevolution approach and the the approach presented by Konersmann et al. [Kon+13] is that Konersmann et al. [Kon+13] do not store the architectural model explicitly, but store it within the source code. They also currently do not provide a concept of coevolving behavioural models in terms of the *SEFF*. Furthermore, they are also not providing an approach for integrating existing source code using reverse engineering approaches and different integration levels.

A famous approach that extends the source code with architectural artefacts is ArchJava [ACN02]. ArchJava introduces new languages elements as keywords for Java. The newly introduced language elements are, for instance, *components*, *ports*, *requires*, *provides* and *connect*. They extending the Java language and can be used to define components and their connection amongst each other in the source code. Classes, for instance, can be specified as `component classes`. To compile ArchJava code, however, a special Java compiler is necessary that is able to compile the source code with the additional keywords. Similar to PRISM, we can combine our Coevolution approach with ArchJava by defining consistency preservation rules between architectural models and ArchJava based source code.

A similar approach as ArchJava is used by mbeddr [Voe+13], which we already mentioned above. It supports the integration of components, interfaces, ports, and connectors into the C programming language respectively a programming language that is almost C. As the PRISM approach, ArchJava and mbeddr omit the need of a consistency preservation mechanism, because the architectural elements are embedded in the source code. Both, however, do not have an explicit architectural model available.

The last method for embedding is to use built-in mechanisms of the used programming language. With the upcoming Java version 9 [7], Java introduces so called *modules*. The module concept allows to define modules and their relations in the source code. A module combines a set of classes and packages. It also specifies the exported classes and interfaces and the required modules. Java 9 modules have the advantage that they are a built-in feature of the upcoming Java language. Java super packages, which are similar to Java 9 modules, have been proposed in 2006 [Sun06]. They can be used to collect other Java packages and Java classes in a super package to ease the handling of large projects. They are, however, not integrated in the Java language specification. Instead Java modules are favored. The differentiation between our Coevolution approach and the proposed Java built-in mechanisms, however, is the same and explained in the following for Java 9 modules. Similar to the other approaches falling into the category of embedding architectural information in source code Java modules do not provide an explicit architecture model. Similar to PRISM and ArchJava, we can define consistency preservation rules between architectural models and Java 9 modules. In the future work section of this thesis (see Section 8.2), we outline how this can be done.

7.2. Architecture Reverse Engineering Approaches

In this section, we focus on architecture reverse engineering approaches that have the goal to use the reverse-engineered model for coevolution with the source code. Those approaches are related to the source code integration strategies, we presented in Section 5.4.

Ducasse and Pollet [DP09] present a taxonomy of software architecture reconstruction approaches. Within this taxonomy they classified different approaches according to their *goals*, *processes*, *input*, *techniques* and *outputs* on the top level. The detailed classification is depicted in Figure 7.2.

As the integration of existing source code into our Coevolution approach is done by using either Source Code Model eXtractor (SoMoX), *Extract*, or *EJBmoX* as reverse engineering approaches, our Coevolution approach

[7] `http://openjdk.java.net/projects/jigsaw/spec/sotms/`

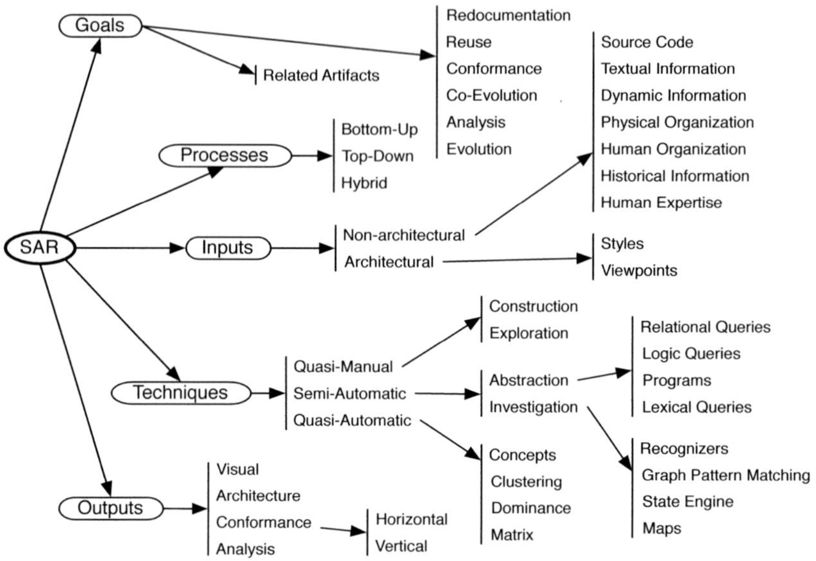

Figure 7.2.: Process-oriented taxonomy for reverse Engineering approaches (taken from Ducasse and Pollet [DP09])

falls into the following categories of the taxonomy: The main *goal* of our Coevolution approach is *coevolution*. As *process*, we use a *bottom-up* process, because we use the source code as information for the reverse engineering. As *inputs*, we use *non-architectural* information. In particular, we use *source code* only as input model. The used *techniques* during the reconstruction is *quasi-automatic*. The *output* of the reverse engineering approaches are i) an *architecture* of the software system, and ii) a *visualisation* of the software architecture. Using the reverse-engineered architecture also allows the *analysis* of Non-Functional Properties (NFP) if the performance models are parametrised in a subsequent step.

In the following, we present approaches related to our Coevolution approach, which use a reversed engineered architecture in order to coevolve architectural model and source code. The approaches were identified by Ducasse and Pollet [DP09] and have the *goal* of *coevolution*.

First, we present the approach presented by Tran and Holt [TH99]. They introduce an approach to repair the architecture of a software system. As input models they use existing architecture models and evolved source code. They differentiate between the following two different repair approaches: i) forward architecture repair, which means that the source code (concrete architecture) is repaired in order to match the architecture (conceptual architecture), and ii) reverse architecture repair, which means that the architecture (conceptual architecture) is repaired in order to match the source code (concrete architecture). The difference to our Coevolution approach is that they do not coevolve the architecture with source code during the development but restore the consistency at one time.

Another approach that reconstructing architecture with the goal of coevolution is presented by Huang et al. [HMY06]. They propose an online recovery and manipulation approach for software architecture. Therefore, they use the runtime information and recover the architecture of a software system based on the reflection mechanism of the used component-framework. The recovered architecture can be transformed into an ADL. The ADL contains information about the architecture, its runtime behaviour, and deployment information of the software system. Changes performed to the ADL model are kept consistent, for instance, with the deployment environment, i.e. the deployement can be changed during the runtime via the architectural view. Hence, they focus on coevolution between the runtime architecture and the runtime environment. The focus of our Coevolution approach, however, is to keep architectural models and source code consistent during the development time.

The last approach, we present, that allows coevolving an reconstructed system is the tool suite IntensiVE (Intensional View Environment) introduced by Mens et al. [Men+06]. We mentioned them again in the section for related view-based approaches, because IntensiVE is a tool, which can be seen as view-based. Wuyts [Wuy01] present an approach for reverse engineering IntensiVE views from source code and use them for coevolution. The proposed high-level views are, however, not a component-based architectural model, which we use in our Coevolution approach. We, furthermore, introduce the different integration levels in order to decide whether the reconstructed and integrated elements can be used for coevolution with the standard consistency preservation rules, or whether integration specific consistency preservation rules need to be defined.

7.3. View-based Software Development Approaches

In this section, we focus on related approaches from the view-based software development domain.

Atkinson et al. [ATM15] present different strategies for the realisation of multi-view environments. Our Coevolution approach can be seen as a multi-view approach that uses a source code view, a UML class diagram view, and a component-based architectural view. In the following, we classify our Coevolution approach in the five *dichotomies* presented by Atkinson et al. [ATM15].

The first dichotomy presented is *rigorous versus relaxed.* Approaches that use multiple views, which explain how the views need to be kept consistent, and define what should be contained within the views, are considered rigorous. Approaches that use multiple views but do neither explain how they need to be kept consistent nor what the precise form in these views takes, are considered relaxed. Our Coevolution approach is rigorous, because we define how the used views respectively models need to be kept consistent.

The second dichotomy is *synthetic versus projective views.* As we also mentioned in the foundations (see Section 2.2.2), view-based software development differentiates synthetic views form projective views. Projective views are views generated from an underlying model, which also ensures the consistency. Synthetic views need to be kept consistent amongst each other. Our consistency preservation process between source code and the architectural model as described in this thesis is synthetic. The UML class diagram editor we presented, is a projective view onto the source code. The Vitruvius approach in general, which is the base for our Coevolution approach, however, can be seen as projective as well, because it allows for the generation of views from a Virtual Single Underlying Model (VSUM).

The third dichotomy is *Explicit versus Implicit Correspondences.* It describes whether the correspondences between elements in the views are made explicitly by using so called inter-view correspondences or whether the correspondences are represented implicitly using intra-view pointers. Our Coevolution approach uses explicit correspondences, as we build the correspondences between the model elements using a correspondence model.

Dichotomy	Our Coevolution approach
Rigorous versus Relaxed	rigorous
Synthetic versus Projective Views	mixed
Explicit versus Implicit Correspondences	explicit
Extensional versus Intentional Correspondence Definition	intensional
Essential SUM versus Pragmatic SUM	pragmatic

Table 7.1.: A Classificaiton of our Coevolution approach into the realisation strategies for multi-view approaches presented by Atkinson et al. [ATM15] for multi-view approaches

The fourth dichotomy is *Extensional versus Intensional Correspondence Definition.* It distinguishes approaches, whether they define the correspondences extensionally or intensionally. Extensional approaches describe the correspondence information at the instance level, i.e. directly between views. Intensional approaches, however, define the correspondence rules also at type level. As we describe the correspondence rules on the type level respectively on the metamodel level, our Coevolution approach can be considered as an intensional approach.

The fifth and last dichotomy is *Essential SUM versus Pragmatic SUM.* An essential SUM is minimalistic, i.e. it is free of internal redundancy. A pragmatic SUM is allowed to be constructed using sum-models, which are not free from redundancy. The VSUM within our Coevolution approach is a pragmatic SUM, because it contains the source code and the architectural models, which are not redundancy free.

Even though we mentioned the OSM ([ASB10]) approach in the foundations already (see Section 2.2.1), it is a related view-based development approach as well. The idea in OSM is to store all information used in the development process in a SUM and creating projective views onto this SUM. We reused the idea of having a SUM for Vitruvius and our Coevolution approach. However, we use a VSUM, which allows the reuse of existing metamodels. In our Coevolution approach, we use the Java metamodel and the PCM metamodel within the VSUM. We already mentioned KobrA, which can be seen as implementation of OSM, in Section 7.1.1 and identified it as related work to our Coevolution approach.

Meier and Winter [MW16] present a view-based approach using reference metamodels (RMMs) to keep instances of different metamodel consistent. Therefore, they propose to create reference metamodels of all involved metamodels respectively viewpoints. For object-oriented languages, for instance, such a reference metamodel would contain all elements that are common for object-oriented langues (e.g. classes, methods, and fields). From this reference metamodels one reference single underlying metamodel (RSUMM) is derived. This RSUMM defines the common concepts of the references metamodels. The consistency preservation is achieved using the following process: First, changes in a viewpoint are propagated to the reference models. Secondly the changes are propagated to the RSUMM. From the RSUMM they are propagated to the other involved references models. From there the changes are propagated to the other involved viewpoints to achieve consistency. Even though Meier and Winter [MW16] do not provide an implementation of their approach yet, they plan to apply their approach to architectural models and source code as well. Furthermore, they plan to integrate requirements and test cases.

Intensional View Environment, introduced by Mens et al. [Men+06], is an approach that keeps high-level architectural views consistent with the source code. As high-level views they use, for instance, structural views and component-like views. This views can be generated dynamically from the underlying source code. The main difference to our Coevolution approach is that they do not use component-based architectural models as we use. Furthermore, the consistency preservation only works from code to the architectural views.

8. Conclusions and Future Work

Within this chapter, we first summarize the approach, the contributions and the evaluation of this thesis. Afterwards, we present open questions and provide an overview of possible future work based on the open questions.

8.1. Summary

In this thesis, we have presented a novel approach for coevolving source code and architectural models during the development and evolution of a software system. The approach supports software architects and software developers by avoiding the well-known problems architecture drift and architecture erosion. These problems can occur, for instance, if architectural models are used for the evolution of a software system but not kept up-to-date with source code changes. The presented approach is a change-driven approach that uses consistency preservation rules to achieve the consistency between the models. The approach enables the coevolution of source code and behavioural models. It also allows for integrating existing architectural models and existing source code. The evaluation showed that i) the consistency preservation rules can be applied to existing architectural models, ii) it is possible to integrate existing source code, and iii) our Coevolution approach is able to keep changes performed to the source code consistent with the architectural model and vice versa. We implemented our Coevolution approach to support the Palladio Component Model (PCM) as architectural model and Java as source code language.

To realise the approach, we first presented the used consistency preservation process, which is able to keep arbitrary models consistent during the development and evolution of a software system. This process can be used in our Coevolution approach as well as in the view-based engineering approach

Vitruvius. As the proposed consistency preservation process is change-driven, we need changes as input for the process. To retrieve the changes, we decided to monitor the used editors. As one goal is to enable the reuse of existing editors to allow users to use familiar editors, we implemented monitors for the PCM architectural models and the Eclipse Java source code editor.

Next, we presented how our Coevolution approach can be used to keep architectural models and source code consistent. From the Vitruvius approach, we reuse the idea of using a Virtual Single Underlying Model (VSUM), which contains all necessary models for the development of a system. Hence, in our case the VSUM contains architectural models and source code. We showed how consistency preservation rules can be used for the coevolution. Therefore, we defined three dimensions for consistency preservation rules: i) a technology-specific dimension, ii) a project-specific dimension, and iii) an element-specific dimension. Within this thesis, we introduced the following four concrete consistency preservation rules from the architectural models to source code: We first introduced the package mapping consistency preservation rules, which can be used to keep PCM architectural models consistent with Java source code using Plain Old Java Objects (POJOs). Secondly, we introduced two technology-specific consistency preservation rules. The first one can be used to keep instances of the architectural model PCM consistent with Java source code built with Enterprise Java Beans (EJBs). The second technology-specific consistency preservation rules can be used to keep instances of PCM architectural models consistent with Java source code build with a dependency injection framework. Finally, we introduced consistency preservation rules between architectural models and artefacts of Eclipse plugin development. To do so, we focused on the development of consistency preservation rules between instances of PCM and the Eclipse Manifest files and plugin XML files.

We, furthermore, introduced the concept of user change disambiguation, which is used if the consistency preservation rules are not able to automatically decide how a model shall be kept consistent with a change performed to another model. In this case the users of our Coevolution approach need to clarify they intention and decide how the consistency between the models can be preserved.

We also presented an approach to keep behavioural models consistent with source code during the software evolution. Therefore, we introduced an approach, which is able to incrementally reverse-engineer the *Service Effect Specifications (SEFF)* from a method body as soon as the method body has been changed. During the incremental *SEFF* creation our Coevolution approach is able to detect architecture violations.

We introduced different roles users can assume if they use our Coevolution approach for the software development. During the design time phase, architectural consistency methodologists defines the consistency preservation rules. During the actual development of a software system, software architects and software developers use our Coevolution approach and the defined consistency preservation rules to implement the software system.

As one goal of this thesis is to allow the reuse of already existing models, we present two integration strategies that are able to integrate existing models. The first integration strategy, which we called Reconstructive Integration Strategy (RIS), simulates the creation of a model. It is used within our Coevolution approach to integrate existing architectural models. During the simulated creation of the architectural models, we use the monitors to record the changes. These changes can be used by our Coevolution approach to create the corresponding source code elements. The second proposed integration strategy, is called Linking Integration Strategy (LIS). The LIS uses existing Model-to-Model (M2M) transformation or Model-to-Text (M2T) generation steps in order to create an instance of the model that shall be integrated. Based on this generation respectively transformation step, it creates the Vitruvius correspondence model. We implemented a LIS in order to integrate existing source code. Therefore, we first need to reverse-engineer an architectural model from existing source code. Therefore, we used the reverse engineering approaches *Extract*, Source Code Model eXtractor (SoMoX), and *EJBmoX*. We contribute the two reverse engineering approaches *Extract* and *EJBmoX*. *Extract* can be used to reverse-engineer an architectural model from Java source code, while *EJBmoX* is tailored in order to reverse-engineer Java source code build with EJBs. We use the extracted architectural model, the source code, and the information how the source code elements are mapped to the architectural elements to create a Vitruvius correspondence model. This correspondence model can be used within our Coevolution approach, in order to allow coevolution of the source code and reverse-engineered architectural model. The elements integrated with the LIS for source code are grouped into four different groups depending on the integration level used for they integration. Integration Level 1 is used for integrated elements, which can be kept consistent using the consistency preservation rules, while elements of the remaining integration levels cannot be kept consistent using the standard consistency preservation rules. Hence, they either need to be kept consistent manually (Integration Level 2) or by using consistency preservation rules specific for a set of integrated elements (Integration Level 3), or even by element consistency preservation rules (Integration Level 4).

We have evaluated our Coevolution approach in different case studies. We showed that the developed reverse engineering approaches *Extract* and *EJBmoX* are able to reverse-engineer an architectural model from source code. Therefore, we reverse-engineered 14 open source projects with *Extract* and two open source case study with *EJBmoX*. Next, we showed that the four consistency preservation rules can be applied to existing PCM architectural models. Therefore, we used the developed RIS to simulate the creation of seven existing PCM models for each of the developed consistency preservation rules. Within this evaluation, we were able to integrate between 98% and 100% of the supported elements per consistency preservation rule set. Next, we evaluated the integration of existing source code. Therefore, we integrated four open source projects from sizes up to 112.000 Source Lines of Code (SLoC) into our Coevolution approach. To show that our Coevolution approach is able to keep changes performed to source code consistent with the architectural model, we integrated an old version from the Version Control System (VCS) and replayed changes to a newer version using a change replay tool. During the change replay, our Coevolution approach was able to keep the architectural model consistent with architectural relevant source code changes. During this evaluation, we also showed that our Coevolution approach is able to i) keep method body changes consistent with the behavioural model, and ii) that changes performed to the architectural model can be kept consistent with the source code.

We conducted a performance evaluation of our Coevolution approach to measure the overhead our Coevolution approach introduces during the software evolution. Within this evaluation, we showed that our Coevolution approach is in most cases able to keep the architectural model consistent after changes performed to the source code within one to five seconds. Hence, the overhead introduced by our Coevolution approach is acceptable for the coevolution.

We showed, furthermore, that the overhead does not increase with the size of the project. The overhead introduced by our Coevolution approach, however, depends on the time needed to parse the changed compilation unit into the Eclipse Modeling Framework (EMF) model representation. Even though we observed some exceptions, the duration of parsing a compilation unit into an EMF model usually increases with the size of the compilation unit. Hence, the performance can be improved by either optimizing the used Java parser or replacing it with a faster parser.

Finally, we evaluated that the coevolved architectural models can be used for performance prediction. To conduct a performance prediction, we first need to parametrise the models with resource demands. To do so, we need to set up the software system and measure the execution time of the provided services and its internal methods for a given workload. Using this information allows us to parametrise the architectural model. After the parameterisation step, we execute the performance prediction using the performance prediction capabilities of the PCM. To analyse the accuracy of the performance prediction, we compare the predicted value with actual measured values. The prediction error for the response time is approximately 10%. Hence, the performance prediction based on the coevolved models can be used to estimate the performance of the real software system.

8.2. Limitations and Outlook on Future Work

In the approach presented in the thesis, we focus on the coevolution and consistency preservation between architectural models and source code during software development. The approach itself, however, currently has some limitations, which can be part of future research. In the following, we provide an overview of possible future work:

Changing the used technology of a project Within the presented thesis, we presented different consistency preservation rules, e.g. the package mapping consistency preservation rules. Currently, users need to specify the consistency preservation rules, which should be used, at the beginning of the development process. Changing them during the software evolution is currently not supported. Changing the consistency preservation rules, however, would allow software architects and developers to adapt the software system to new requirements or technologies. For instance, our Coevolution approach could support changing the used technology from POJOs to EJBs by changing the used consistency preservation rules from the package mapping consistency preservation rules to the EJB consistency preservation rules. In this case our Coevolution approach could be used to generate the necessary EJB annotations for classes and for the refactoring of affected parts in the source code, such as the fields in classes.

Replacing Java Model Parser and Printer (JaMoPP) with the Eclipse Java Development Tools (JDT) Abstract Syntax Tree (AST) parser Within this thesis, we used the JaMoPP parser to parse Java into an EMF model representation. EMF models are necessary within the implemented consistency preservation process and within the used change metamodel. The results of the performance evaluation, however, show that parsing Java source code into EMF models consumes the most time during the consistency preservation process between architectural models and source code. Furthermore, JaMoPP currently supports Java only up to version 5. Hence a part of future work could be to replace JaMoPP by using a faster parser and printer that also supports newer versions of Java. Therefore, we can use, for instance, the parser and printer is provided by the Eclipse JDT AST. Even though the Eclipse parser is a fast parser and creates a model representation of the source code, it does not create an EMF model. Instead, it creates a model, which is based on plain Java classes. To enable the use of the Eclipse JDT AST parser and keep the advantages of having EMF model, we plan to transform the classes of the Eclipse JDT AST parser into EMF model classes. To avoid the manual transformation effort, we plan to develop and implement a novel approach, which is able to transform a set of Java classes into EMF-based model classes.

Integrating our Coevolution approach within the continuous integration of a project Modern software development projects often use continuous integration in order to build the software system and run tests after each commit automatically. As we showed in the evaluation of our Coevolution approach, we are able to reverse-engineer an architectural model of a software system and replayed changes, which we extracted from a VCS. The change replay step and a headless version of our Coevolution approach can be integrated within the continuous integration of a software system to keep the architectural model up-to date as follows: Therefore, the initial step is to reverse-engineer the architectural model from the current version and integrate it into the headless version of our Coevolution approach. After each new commit the continuous integration can execute the change replay tool in order to extract the changes performed in the current commit. These changes can be passed to the headless version of our Coevolution approach, which can use the changes to keep the architectural model consistent with these changes. Using this approach would allow us to maintain an up-to-date architectural model and warn users if the change introduces, for instance, architectural violations. Combining this with an automatic approach for parameterisation the coevolved model can be used to simulate the performance after each commit and point out, for instance, possible scalability performance problems, which were introduced with this commit.

Integrating software systems with existing source code and existing corresponding architectural models In this thesis, we propose an approach for the integration of an existing architectural model and existing source code. We are, however, currently not able to integrate a software system with an already existing architectural model that corresponds to existing source code. This limitation can be overcome in future work. Therefore, for instance, a special RIS for PCM can be created. Instead of using the simulated changes to create the source code elements as in the standard RIS for PCM, it is possible to define specific RIS consistency preservation rules. This specific consistency preservation rules can be used to check whether a corresponding source code element already exists for the architectural element contained in the simulated change. If this is the case the existing element can be used as corresponding model. If this is not the case the standard consistency preservation rules can be used to create the corresponding source code elements. Mazkatli [Maz16] already proposed a similar approach for integrating existing artefacts. Mazkatli [Maz16], however, applied this approach for the automotive standards AMALTHEA and ASCET.

Creating consistency preservation rules between PCM and Java 9 modules In this thesis, we presented consistency preservation rules between PCM as architectural model and Java source code adhering to current Java versions, i.e. we use packages, classes, and interfaces for the mapping of architectural elements. With the upcoming Java version 9[1], however, Java introduces a new module concept. Using the module concept allows developers to define modules and their relations in the source code. Java 9 modules combine a set of classes and packages. They also allow the specification of exported classes and interfaces as well as the definition of required modules, classes, and interfaces. In future work, a concept can be developed that specifies how to map architectural models from the PCM to Java 9 modules. Combining this concept with the support of the Eclipse JDT AST would allow us to implement consistency preservation rules between PCM and Java 9 modules. The consistency preservation rules could map, for instance, PCM components to modules and PCM *OperationInterfaces* to the methods within exported interfaces of a module. *RequiredRoles* and *ProvidedRoles* could be mapped to required relations and export relations of Java 9 modules.

Extending the consistency preservation process to support more than two metamodels The work in this thesis focuses on the consistency preservation of source code and architectural models. Hence, we use two metamodels in the VSUM and during the consistency preservation process. Extending the consistency preservation process to allow more than two metamodels in the VSUM, would allow us to keep other artefacts used in the software development, such as UML class diagrams and UML component diagrams, consistent with the PCM and Java source code. For the consistency preservation rules between PCM and Eclipse plugin artefacts, we showed that it is in principle possible to keep instances of three metamodels consistent. However, the consistency preservation process currently provides only limited support for keeping more than two metamodels consistent. Moreover, the task of keeping instances of more metamodels consistent is becoming more complex the more metamodels are used within the VSUM. Hence, a part of future work can be to define strategies how the consistency preservation process can support the consistency preservation or multiple metamodels within the VSUM.

1 `http://openjdk.java.net/projects/jigsaw/spec/sotms/`

Performing an experiment with users To show the benefit of our Coevolution approach during the software evolution, an experiment that involves different users performing the same evolution task, can be conducted. For this experiment, the users can be separated into two groups. The task within the experiment can be, to evolve a given software system and its architectural model in order to fulfill a new requirement. For the execution of the evolution task, one user group performs the evolution with our Coevolution approach, while the control group performs the evolution without our Coevolution approach. After the experiment, we can compare the time needed by the participants within the different groups and evaluate whether the architectural models are still up-to date with the source code. The experiment can be extended with a third user group. The third group is allowed to use another approach for coevolving architectural models and source code, such as IBM Rational Rhapsody, to perform the evolution scenario. This would allow us to compare our Coevolution approach with other approaches.

Extending the consistency preservation process in order to support multiple users The approach we presented in this thesis, is focused on the consistency preservation in one IDE involving one user at a given time. In real software development processes, however, multiple users are usually involved simultaneously. To support multiple users developing a software system simultaneously, the introduced consistency preservation process can be extended in order to support versioning and simultaneously editing of artefacts used for the software development and software evolution.

A. Appendix

A.1. Change Catalog for the Source Code Monitor

In this section, we present the complete change catalogue for the source code monitor. The catalogue has been developed by Messinger [Mes14] for his master's thesis. It was necessary to define a own catalogue as existing catalogues did not fulfill our needs. The tables are taken from Messinger [Mes14].

Primitive Changes		
Create/Delete	*Structural*	*Modification*
Create Class	Add Supertype	Rename Class
Delete Class	Remove Supertype	Add Class Modifier
Create Interface	Add Import	Remove Class Modifier
Delete Interface	Remove Import	Rename Interface
Create Enum	Add Method	Add Interface Modifier
Delete Enum	Remove Method	Remove Interface Modifier
Create Package	Add Field	Rename Enum
Delete Package	Remove Field	Add Enum Modifier
	Add Parameter	Remove Enum Modifier
	Remove Parameter	Rename Package
	Add Variable	Rename Method
	Remove Variable	Add Method Modifier
	Add Statement	Remove Method Modifier
	Remove Statement	Change Return Type
	Add Comment	Rename Field
	Remove Comment	Add Field Modifier
	Add Enum Literal	Remove Field Modifier
	Remove Enum Literal	Change Field Type
		Rename Parameter
		Add Parameter Modifier
		Remove Parameter Modifier
		Change Parameter Type
		Rename Variable
		Add Variable Modifier
		Remove Variable Modifier
		Change Variable Type
		Change Comment

Table A.1.: Primitive changes in the change catalogue. They are grouped into the three subcategories *create/delete, structural* and *modification* [Mes14].

Composite Changes	
1st Order	*2nd Order*
Move Class	Extract Variable
Move Interface	Inline Variable
Move Enum	Extract Field
Move Method	Inline Field
Move Field	Extract Method
Move Enum Literal	Inline Method
Convert Variable to Field	Extract Class
Convert Field to Variable	Inline Class
Toggle Comment	Split Interface
	Merge Interface
	Split Enum
	Merge Enum
	Split Package
	Merge Package

Table A.2.: Composite changes in the change catalogue, which are subdivded into two groups: first order, which consists of composed primitive changes, and second order, which consists of composed composite changes [Mes14].

Type Hierarchy Specific		
Change Type	*Move*	*Composite Move*
Specialize Return Type	Pull Up Method	Extract Superclass
Generalize Return Type	Push Down Method	Inline Superclass
Specialize Parameter Type	Pull Up Field	Extract Subclass
Generalize Parameter Type	Push Down Field	Inline Subclass
Specialize Variable Type		Extract Superinterface
Generalize Variable Type		Inline Superinterface
		Extract Subinterface
		Inline Subinterface

Table A.3.: Type hierarchy specific changes in the change catalogue, which consider the type hierarchy of object-oriented languages[Mes14].

A.2. Results of the Integration Case Study per Project

In this section, we present the results of the integration case study for Reconstructive Integration Strategy (RIS) per project. In Section 6.4.3, we presented the results combined for all projects. The results for the MediaStore are shown in Table A.4. The results for CoCoME are shown in Table A.5. The results for the Open Reference Case are shown in Table A.6. The results for DSP can are shown in Table A.7. The results for DPS can are shown in Table A.8. The results for ICS system are shown in Table A.9. The results for the BRS project are shown in Table A.10.

PCM element	**#elem**	**POJO**		**EJB**		**Dep. Inject.**		**Eclipse plugin**	
		#cf.	pct.	#cf.	pct.	#cf.	pct.	#cf.	pct.
BasicComponents	14	0	100	0	100	0	100	0	100
CompositeComponents	0	0	100	0	100	0	100	–	0
OperationInterfaces	9	0	100	0	100	0	100	0	100
CompositeDataTypes	2	0	100	0	100	0	100	–	0
CollectionDataTypes	0	0	100	0	100	0	100	–	0
OperationSignatures	20	0	100	0	100	0	100	–	0
OperationProvideRoles	15	0	100	6	60	0	100	0	100
OperationRequiredRoles	16	0	100	0	100	0	100	0	100
SEFFs	26	0	100	0	100	0	100	–	0
AssemblyContexts	10	0	100	–	0	2	80	–	0
AssemblyConnectors	11	0	100	–	0	0	100	–	0
SystemRequiredRoles	0	0	100	–	0	–	0	–	0
RequiredDelegationConnectors	0	0	100	–	0	–	0	–	0
SystemProvideRoles	1	0	100	–	0	0	100	–	0
ProvidedDelegationConnectors	1	0	100	–	0	0	100	–	0

Table A.4.: Integrated and conflicting elements for the MediaStore project

	#elem	POJO		EJB		Dep. Inject.		Eclipse plugin	
PCM element		#cf.	pct.	#cf.	pct.	#cf.	pct.	#cf.	pct.
BasicComponents	8	0	100	0	100	0	100	0	100
CompositeComponents	0	0	100	-	0	0	100	–	0
OperationInterfaces	8	0	100	0	100	0	100	0	100
CompositeDataTypes	19	0	100	0	100	0	100	–	0
CollectionDataTypes	9	0	100	0	100	0	100	–	0
OperationSignatures	29	0	100	0	100	0	100	–	0
OperationProvideRoles	7	0	100	0	100	0	100	0	100
OperationRequiredRoles	13	0	100	0	100	0	100	0	100
SEFFs	31	0	100	0	100	0	100	–	0
AssemblyContexts	20	0	100	–	0	12	40	–	0
AssemblyConnectors	24	0	100	–	0	0	100	–	0
SystemRequiredRoles	2	0	100	–	0	–	0	–	0
RequiredDelegationConnectors	2	0	100	–	0	–	0	–	0
SystemProvideRoles	1	0	100	–	0	0	100	–	0
ProvidedDelegationConnectors	1	0	100	–	0	0	100	–	0

Table A.5.: Integrated and conflicting elements for the CoCoME project

	#elem	POJO		EJB		Dep. Inject.		Eclipse plugin	
PCM element		#cf.	pct.	#cf.	pct.	#cf.	pct.	#cf.	pct.
BasicComponents	15	0	100	0	100	0	100	0	100
CompositeComponents	0	0	100	-	0	0	100	–	0
OperationInterfaces	15	0	100	0	100	0	100	0	100
CompositeDataTypes	20	0	100	0	100	0	100	–	0
CollectionDataTypes	8	0	100	0	100	0	100	–	0
OperationSignatures	54	0	100	0	100	0	100	–	0
OperationProvideRoles	14	0	100	0	100	0	100	0	100
OperationRequiredRoles	23	0	100	0	100	0	100	0	100
SEFFs	52	0	100	0	100	0	100	–	0
AssemblyContexts	13	0	100	–	0	0	100	–	0
AssemblyConnectors	19	0	100	–	0	0	100	–	0
SystemRequiredRoles	1	0	100	–	0	–	0	–	0
RequiredDelegationConnectors	2	0	100	–	0	–	0	–	0
SystemProvideRoles	4	0	100	–	0	0	100	–	0
ProvidedDelegationConnectors	4	0	100	–	0	0	100	–	0

Table A.6.: Integrated and conflicting elements for the Open Reference Case project

	#elem	POJO		EJB		Dep. Inject.		Eclipse plugin	
PCM element		#cf.	pct.	#cf.	pct.	#cf.	pct.	#cf.	pct.
BasicComponents	3	0	100	0	100	0	100	NA	NA
CompositeComponents	0	0	100	-	0	0	100	NA	NA
OperationInterfaces	3	0	100	0	100	0	100	NA	NA
CompositeDataTypes	0	0	100	0	100	0	100	NA	NA
CollectionDataTypes	1	0	100	0	100	0	100	NA	NA
OperationSignatures	3	0	100	0	100	0	100	NA	NA
OperationProvideRoles	3	0	100	0	100	0	100	NA	NA
OperationRequiredRoles	2	0	100	0	100	0	100	NA	NA
SEFFs	3	0	100	0	100	0	100	NA	NA
AssemblyContexts	3	0	100	–	0	0	100	NA	NA
AssemblyConnectors	2	0	100	–	0	0	100	NA	NA
SystemRequiredRoles	0	0	100	–	0	–	0	NA	NA
RequiredDelegationConnectors	0	0	100	–	0	–	0	NA	NA
SystemProvideRoles	1	0	100	–	0	0	100	NA	NA
ProvidedDelegationConnectors	1	0	100	–	0	0	100	NA	NA

Table A.7.: Integrated and conflicting elements for the Desktop Search project

PCM element	#elem	POJO		EJB		Dep. Inject.		Eclipse plugin	
		#cf.	pct.	#cf.	pct.	#cf.	pct.	#cf.	pct.
BasicComponents	5	0	100	0	100	0	100	NA	NA
CompositeComponents	0	0	100	-	0	0	100	NA	NA
OperationInterfaces	3	0	100	0	100	0	100	NA	NA
CompositeDataTypes	0	0	100	0	100	0	100	NA	NA
CollectionDataTypes	0	0	100	0	100	0	100	NA	NA
OperationSignatures	4	0	100	0	100	0	100	NA	NA
OperationProvideRoles	5	0	100	2	60	0	100	NA	NA
OperationRequiredRoles	4	0	100	0	100	0	100	NA	NA
SEFFs	6	0	100	0	100	0	100	NA	NA
AssemblyContexts	5	0	100	–	0	2	60	NA	NA
AssemblyConnectors	4	0	100	–	0	0	0	NA	NA
SystemRequiredRoles	0	0	100	–	0	–	0	NA	NA
RequiredDelegationConnectors	0	0	100	–	0	–	0	NA	NA
SystemProvideRoles	5	0	100	–	0	0	100	NA	NA
ProvidedDelegationConnectors	5	0	100	–	0	0	100	NA	NA

Table A.8.: Integrated and conflicting elements for the DPS project

	#elem	POJO		EJB		Dep. Inject.		Eclipse plugin	
PCM element		#cf.	pct.	#cf.	pct.	#cf.	pct.	#cf.	pct.
BasicComponents	14	0	100	0	100	0	100	NA	NA
CompositeComponents	0	0	100	-	0	0	100	NA	NA
OperationInterfaces	10	0	100	0	100	0	100	NA	NA
CompositeDataTypes	0	0	100	0	100	0	100	NA	NA
CollectionDataTypes	0	0	100	0	100	0	100	NA	NA
OperationSignatures	10	0	100	0	100	0	100	NA	NA
OperationProvideRoles	14	0	100	4		0	100	NA	NA
OperationRequiredRoles	28	0	100	0	100	0	100	NA	NA
SEFFs	14	0	100	0	100	0	100	NA	NA
AssemblyContexts	11	0	100	–	0	4	63	NA	NA
AssemblyConnectors	18	0	100	–	0	0	100	NA	NA
SystemRequiredRoles	0	0	100	–	0	–	0	NA	NA
RequiredDelegationConnectors	0	0	100	–	0	–	0	NA	NA
SystemProvideRoles	6	0	100	–	0	0	100	NA	NA
ProvidedDelegationConnectors	6	0	100	–	0	0	100	NA	NA

Table A.9.: Integrated and conflicting elements for the Industrial Control System project

PCM element	#elem	POJO		EJB		Dep. Inject.		Eclipse plugin	
		#cf.	pct.	#cf.	pct.	#cf.	pct.	#cf.	pct.
BasicComponents	14	0	100	0	100	0	100	0	100
CompositeComponents	2	0	100	-	0	0	100	–	0
OperationInterfaces	10	0	100	0	100	0	100	0	100
CompositeDataTypes	2	0	100	0	100	0	100	–	0
CollectionDataTypes	1	0	100	0	100	0	100	–	0
OperationSignatures	28	0	100	0	100	0	100	–	0
OperationProvideRoles	15	0	100	5	66	0	100	0	0
OperationRequiredRoles	14	0	100	0	100	0	100	0	100
SEFFs	44	0	100	0	100	0	100	–	100
AssemblyContexts	9	0	100	–	0	1	88	–	0
AssemblyConnectors	11	0	100	–	0	0	100	–	0
SystemRequiredRoles	0	0	100	–	0	–	0	–	0
RequiredDelegationConnectors	0	0	100	–	0	–	0	–	0
SystemProvideRoles	2	0	100	–	0	0	100	–	0
ProvidedDelegationConnectors	2	0	100	–	0	0	100	–	0

Table A.10.: Integrated and conflicting elements for the BRS project

A.3. Results of the Change Replay Case Study per Project

Within this section, we present the results of the change replay case study from Section 6.5.4 for each project.

A.3.1. Results for the core project of Apache Any23

Table A.11 shows the results for the change replay evaluation for the core project of Apache Any23. We replayed changes from version 0.9 to version 1.0 for Any23. Please note: Renaming changes for parameters and type changes of parameters are combined in the row "changes method parameter".

		handled by standard		handled by dialog		handled by integration reaction
Change	**#occ.**	IL2	IL3	IL2	IL 3	IL 3
remove import	18	0	0	18	0	18
remove method	14	0	0	14	0	14
add import	7	0	0	7	0	7
remove field	7	0	0	7	0	7
add method	4	0	0	4	0	4
ch. method parameter	4	0	0	4	4	0
add super class	3	0	0	0	0	0
rem. super interface	3	0	0	3	0	3
ch. method modifier	2	0	0	2	2	0
add annotation	1	0	0	1	0	1
remove super class	1	0	0	0	0	0
create package	1	1	1	0	0	0

Table A.11.: Change replay evaluation results for the core project of Apache Any23

A.3.2. Results for the core project of Apache Gora

The results for the change replay for the core project of Apache Gora is shown in Table A.12. We replayed changes from version 0.6 to version 0.6.1 for Gora. During the evaluation of Gora, we can observe different number of occurenc for rename method, remove method and add method. As we mentioned above, this can occur due to the indirect interaction between the change replay tool and the Java monitor. The resulting code after the change replay remains the same for both cases. The difference is that the change replay for Integration Level 2 was either faster as the change replay for Integration Level 3 or the Java monitor was not notified in a different way by the Eclipse Java Development Tools (JDT) Abstract Syntax Tree (AST) notificaiton mechanism. From this behaviour, we get the difference between renaming of a method respectively "removing" the method and "adding" it again.

		handled by standard		handled by dialog		handled by integration reaction
Change	**#occ.**	IL2	IL3	IL2	IL 3	IL 3
add super class	29	0	0	0	0	0
add import	17	0	0	17	0	17
remove import	16	0	0	16	0	16
change field modifier	6	0	0	6	0	6
change field type	6	0	0	6	0	6
add annotation	5	0	0	5	0	5
add field	4	0	0	4	0	4
rename method	2(IL2)/ 1(IL3)	0	0	2	0	1
create package	1	1	1	0	0	0
remove annotation	1	0	0	1	0	1
remove method	0(IL2)/ 2(IL3)	0	0	0	0	2
add method	1	0	0	0	0	1

Table A.12.: Change replay evaluation results for the core project of Apache Gora

A.3.3. Results for Apache Velocity

All changes performed to Apache Velocity are performed to integrated areas, i.e. no changes are handled by the standard consistency preservation rules. We replayed changes from version 1.6 to version 1.6.4 for Velocity. Hence, all changes (except for remove super class and add super class), are handled by integration dialogs when Integration Level 2 is used. If Integration Level 3 together with element-specific reactions for the Parser classes is used all changes are handled by integration reactions respectively by the element-specific reactions. Table A.13 shows the detailed results of the evaluation for Apache Velocity.

Change	#occ.	IL2: handled by dialog	IL3: handled by integra-tion reaction	IL3: handled by element-specific reaction
add method	25	25	7	18
rename method	19	19	19	0
remove method	17	17	17	0
add import	16	16	16	0
add field	6	6	6	0
remove import	5	5	5	0
change field modifier	4	4	1	3
remove field	3	3	3	0
remove super class	2	0	0	0
add super class	2	0	0	0
change field type	1	1	1	0

Table A.13.: Change replay evaluation results for Apache Velocity

A.3.4. Results for Apache Xerces

Table A.14 shows the result for the change replay evaluation for Xerces. For Xerces, we replayed the changes from version 2.10.0 to 2.11.0. Due to technical reasons, we observed different occurrences for some changes during the different evaluation runs. Please note: As in the table for Any23, renaming changes for parameters and type changes of parameters are combined in the row “changes method parameter”.

	#occ.		**handled by standard**		**handled by dialog**		**handled by integration reaction**
Change	IL2	IL3	IL2	IL3	IL2	IL 3	IL 3
add method	43	45	0	0	38	0	40
add import	29	29	0	0	26	0	22
remove super class	25	25	0	0	0	0	0
add super class	25	25	0	0	0	0	0
remove field	19	18	0	0	19	0	18
ch. method modifier	14	12	0	0	0	0	0
ch. field type	9	8	0	0	6	0	5
ch. method param.	9	6	0	0	6	5	0
rename field	6	7	0	0	6	7	0
add field	6	5	0	0	3	0	2
remove import	6	6	0	0	6	0	6
ch. class modifier	4	3	0	0	4	3	0
ch. field modifier	3	2	0	0	3	0	2
add interface	2	2	0	0	2	2	0
create class	1	1	0	0	1	1	0

Table A.14.: Change replay evaluation results for core Apache Xerces

Bibliography

[ACN02] Jonathan Aldrich, Craig Chambers, and David Notkin. "ArchJava: Connecting Software Architecture to Implementation". In: *Proceedings of the 24th International Conference on Software Engineering*. ICSE '02. Orlando, Florida: ACM, 2002, pp. 187–197. ISBN: 1-58113-472-X. DOI: 10.1145/581339.581365. URL: http://doi.acm.org/10.1145/581339.581365.

[ASB10] Colin Atkinson, Dietmar Stoll, and Philipp Bostan. "Orthographic Software Modeling: A Practical Approach to View-Based Development". In: *Evaluation of Novel Approaches to Software Engineering*. Ed. by LeszekA. Maciaszek, César González-Pérez, and Stefan Jablonski. Vol. 69. Communications in Computer and Information Science. Berlin/Heidelberg: Springer, 2010, pp. 206–219. ISBN: 978-3-642-14819-4.

[Atk+01] C. Atkinson, B. Paech, J. Reinhold, and T. Sander. "Developing and applying component-based model-driven architectures in KobrA". In: *Proceedings Fifth IEEE International Enterprise Distributed Object Computing Conference.* 2001, pp. 212–223. DOI: 10.1109/EDOC.2001.950441.

[ATM15] Colin Atkinson, Christian Tunjic, and Torben Möller. "Fundamental Realization Strategies for Multi-view Specification Environments". In: *Enterprise Distributed Object Computing Conference (EDOC), 2015 IEEE 19th International.* IEEE. 2015, pp. 40–49.

[Bal91] R. Balzer. "Tolerating inconsistency [software development]". In: *[1991 Proceedings] 13th International Conference on Software Engineering*. May 1991, pp. 158–165. DOI: 10.1109/ICSE.1991.130638.

[BCR94] Victor R. Basili, Gianluigi Caldiera, and H. Dieter Rombach. "The Goal Question Metric Approach". In: *Encyclopedia of Software Engineering - 2 Volume Set*. Ed. by John J. Marciniak. John Wiley & Sons, 1994, pp. 528–532.

[Bec+07] Bernhard Beckert et al. "The KeY system 1.0 (deduction component)". In: *Proceedings, International Conference on Automated Deduction*. Lecture Notes in Computer Science. Bremen, Germany: Springer Berlin Heidelberg, 2007, pp. 379–384. URL: http://link.springer.com/chapter/10.1007/978-3-540-73595-3%5C_26.

[Bec08] Steffen Becker. *Coupled Model Transformations for QoS Enabled Component-Based Software Design*. Vol. 1. The Karlsruhe Series on Software Design and Quality. Universitätsverlag Karlsruhe, 2008.

[Ber+12] Gábor Bergmann, István Ráth, Gergely Varró, and Dániel Varró. "Change-driven model transformations". English. In: *Software & Systems Modeling* 11.3 (2012), pp. 431–461. ISSN: 1619-1366. DOI: 10.1007/s10270-011-0197-9. URL: http://dx.doi.org/10.1007/s10270-011-0197-9.

[BKR09] Steffen Becker, Heiko Koziolek, and Ralf Reussner. "The Palladio component model for model-driven performance prediction". In: *Journal of Systems and Software* 82 (2009), pp. 3–22. DOI: 10.1016/j.jss.2008.03.066. URL: http://dx.doi.org/10.1016/j.jss.2008.03.066.

[Bor05] Borland Software Corporation. *Borland Together UML 2.1 Guide Version 2008 R3*. 2005. URL: http://techpubs.borland.com/together/2008R3/EN/TogetherUML21.pdf (visited on 10/15/2015).

[BP08] Cédric Brun and Alfonso Pierantonio. "Model Differences in the Eclipse Modelling Framework". In: *UPGRADE The European Journal for the Informatics Professional* IX.2 (2008), pp. 29–34. URL: http://www.cepis.org/upgrade/files/2008-II-pierantonio.pdf.

[BR05] Rainer Böhme and Ralf Reussner. "Validation of Predictions with Measurements". In: *Dependability Metrics*. Ed. by Irene Eusgeld, Felix C. Freiling, and Ralf Reussner. Vol. 4909. Lecture Notes in Computer Science. Springer, 2005, pp. 14–18. ISBN:

978-3-540-68946-1. URL: http://dx.doi.org/10.1007/978-3-540-68947-8%5C_3.

[Bro+12] Franz Brosch, Heiko Koziolek, Barbora Buhnova, and Ralf Reussner. “Architecture-based Reliability Prediction with the Palladio Component Model”. In: *IEEE Transactions on Software Engineering* 38.6 (Nov. 2012), pp. 1319–1339. ISSN: 0098-5589. DOI: 10.1109/TSE.2011.94.

[Bro+15] Fabian Brosig et al. “Quantitative Evaluation of Model-Driven Performance Analysis and Simulation of Component-based Architectures”. In: *Software Engineering, IEEE Transactions on* 41.2 (Feb. 2015), pp. 157–175. ISSN: 0098-5589. DOI: 10.1109/TSE.2014.2362755.

[Bru+10] Hugo Bruneliere, Jordi Cabot, Frédéric Jouault, and Frédéric Madiot. “MoDisco: a generic and extensible framework for model driven reverse engineering”. In: *Proceedings of the IEEE/ACM international conference on Automated software engineering*. ASE ’10. Antwerp, Belgium: ACM, 2010, pp. 173–174. ISBN: 978-1-4503-0116-9. DOI: 10.1145/1858996.1859032. URL: http://doi.acm.org/10.1145/1858996.1859032.

[BS16] Erik Burger and Oliver Schneider. “Translatability and Translation of Updated Views in ModelJoin”. In: *Theory and Practice of Model Transformations: 9th International Conference, ICMT 2016, Held as Part of STAF 2016.* (Vienna, Austria). Ed. by Pieter van Gorp and Gregor Engels. Vol. 9765. Lecture Notes in Computer Science. Cham: Springer International Publishing, July 2016, pp. 55–69. ISBN: 978-3-319-42064-6. DOI: 10.1007/978-3-319-42064-6_4.

[BT14] Erik Burger and Aleksandar Toshovski. “Difference-based Conformance Checking for Ecore Metamodels”. In: *Proceedings of Modellierung 2014.* Vol. 225. GI-LNI. Vienna, Austria, Mar. 2014, pp. 97–104. URL: http://sdqweb.ipd.kit.edu/publications/pdfs/burger2014a.pdf.

[Buc+13] Jim Buckley, Sean Mooney, Jacek Rosik, and Nour Ali. “JITTAC: A Just-in-time Tool for Architectural Consistency”. In: *Proceedings of the 2013 International Conference on Software Engineering.* ICSE ’13. San Francisco, CA, USA: IEEE Press, 2013, pp. 1291–1294. ISBN: 978-1-4673-3076-3. URL: http://dl.acm.org/citation.cfm?id=2486788.2486987.

[Bur+14] Erik Burger, Jörg Henß, Martin Küster, Steffen Kruse, and Lucia Happe. "View-Based Model-Driven Software Development with ModelJoin". In: *Software & Systems Modeling* 15.2 (2014). Ed. by Robert France and Bernhard Rumpe, pp. 472–496. ISSN: 1619-1374. DOI: 10.1007/s10270-014-0413-5.

[Bur13] Erik Burger. "Flexible Views for Rapid Model-Driven Development". In: *Proceedings of the 1st Workshop on View-Based, Aspect-Oriented and Orthographic Software Modelling*. VAO '13. Montpellier, France: ACM, 2013, 1:1–1:5. ISBN: 978-1-4503-2070-2. DOI: 10.1145/2489861.2489863. URL: http://doi.acm.org/10.1145/2489861.2489863.

[Bur14] Erik Burger. "Flexible Views for View-based Model-driven Development". PhD thesis. Karlsruhe, Germany: Karlsruhe Institute of Technology, July 2014. ISBN: 978-3-7315-0276-0. DOI: 10.5445/KSP/1000043437. URL: http://digbib.ubka.uni-karlsruhe.de/volltexte/1000043437.

[CA78] Liming Chen and Algirdas Avizienis. "N-version programming: A fault-tolerance approach to reliability of software operation". In: *Digest of Papers FTCS-8: Eighth Annual International Conference on Fault Tolerant Computing*. 1978, pp. 3–9.

[Cla10] Claire Liu. *Round Trip Engineering Scenario using Rational Software Architect and ClearCase Remote Client*. 2010. URL: http://www.ibm.com/developerworks/rational/library/10/roundtripengineeringscenariosusingrsaandccrcv7-5-5/roundtripengineeringscenariosusingrsaandccrcv7-5-5-pdf.pdf (visited on 10/15/2015).

[CS13] Daniel Calegari and Nora Szasz. "Verification of model transformations: A survey of the state-of-the-art". In: *Electronic notes in theoretical computer science* 292 (2013), pp. 5–25.

[Dac16] Muamer Dacic. "A KobrA Model and Implementation of the CoCoME". MA thesis. Universität Mannheim, 2016.

[DJ06] Danny Dig and Ralph Johnson. "How do APIs evolve? A story of refactoring". In: *Journal of software maintenance and evolution: Research and Practice* 18.2 (2006), pp. 83–107.

[DP09] Stéphane Ducasse and Damien Pollet. “Software architecture reconstruction: A process-oriented taxonomy”. In: *Software Engineering, IEEE Transactions on* 35.4 (2009), pp. 573–591.

[DPB13] Markus von Detten, Marie Christin Platenius, and Steffen Becker. “Reengineering Component-Based Software Systems with Archimetrix”. In: *Journal of Software and Systems Modeling* (2013). Theme Issue on Models for Quality of Software Architecture.

[Dua+10] Flavio Duarte et al. “Experience with a new architecture review process using a globally distributed architecture review team”. In: *2010 5th IEEE International Conference on Global Software Engineering*. IEEE. 2010, pp. 109–118.

[EV06] Sven Efftinge and Markus Völter. “oAW xText: A framework for textual DSLs”. In: *Eclipsecon Summit Europe 2006*. Nov. 2006. URL: `http://eclipsecon.org/summiteurope2006/presentations/ESE2006-EclipseModelingSymposium12_xTextFramework.pdf`.

[Fal+14] Jean-Rémy Falleri, Floréal Morandat, Xavier Blanc, Matias Martinez, and Martin Monperrus. “Fine-grained and Accurate Source Code Differencing”. In: *Proceedings of the 29th ACM/IEEE International Conference on Automated Software Engineering*. ASE ’14. Vasteras, Sweden: ACM, 2014, pp. 313–324. ISBN: 978-1-4503-3013-8. DOI: `10.1145/2642937.2642982`. URL: `http://doi.acm.org/10.1145/2642937.2642982`.

[FKL16] Sebastian Fiss, Max E. Kramer, and Michael Langhammer. “Automatically Binding Variables of Invariants to Violating Elements in an OCL-Aligned XBase-Language”. In: *Proceedings of Modellierung 2016*. Ed. by Andreas Oberweis and Ralf Reussner. Vol. P-254. Lecture Notes in Informatics (LNI). Bonn, Germany: Gesellschaft für Informatik e.V. (GI), 2016, pp. 189–204. ISBN: 978-3-88579-648-0.

[Fow+99] Martin Fowler, Kent Beck, John Brant, William Opdyke, and Don Roberts. *Refactoring: Improving the Design of Existing Code*. Addison-Wesley, Reading, MA, USA, 1999.

[GBB12] Thomas Goldschmidt, Steffen Becker, and Erik Burger. "Towards a Tool-Oriented Taxonomy of View-Based Modelling". In: *Proceedings of the Modellierung 2012*. Ed. by Elmar J. Sinz and Andy Schürr. Vol. P-201. GI-Edition – Lecture Notes in Informatics (LNI). Bamberg: Gesellschaft für Informatik e.V. (GI), Mar. 2012, pp. 59–74. ISBN: 978-3-88579-295-6.

[GBU10] Thomas Goldschmidt, Steffen Becker, and Axel Uhl. "Incremental Updates for Textual Modeling of Large Scale Models". In: *Proceedings of the 15th IEEE International Conference on Engineering of Complex Computer Systems (ICECCS 2010) - Poster Paper*. IEEE, 2010.

[GIM13] Joshua Garcia, Igor Ivkovic, and Nenad Medvidovic. "A comparative analysis of software architecture recovery techniques". In: *Automated Software Engineering (ASE), 2013 IEEE/ACM 28th International Conference on*. 2013, pp. 486–496. DOI: 10.1109/ASE.2013.6693106.

[Gou+11] Daniel Dominguez Gouvêa et al. "Experience Building Non-Functional Requirement Models of a Complex Industrial Architecture". In: *Proceedings of the second joint WOSP/SIPEW international conference on Performance engineering (ICPE 2011)*. Ed. by Samuel Kounev, Vittorio Cortellessa, Raffaela Mirandola, and David J. Lilja. Karlsruhe, Germany: ACM, 2011, pp. 43–54. ISBN: 978-1-4503-0519-8. DOI: 10.1145/1958746.1958757. URL: http://icpe2011.ipd.kit.edu/call_for_papers/industrialexperience_track/.

[Gou+12] Daniel Dominguez Gouvêa et al. "Experience with Model-based Performance, Reliability and Adaptability Assessment of a Complex Industrial Architecture". In: *Journal of Software and Systems Modeling* (2012). Special Issue on Performance Modeling, pp. 1–23. ISSN: 1619-1366. DOI: 10.1007/s10270-012-0264-x.

[Hat97] Les Hatton. "Reexamining the Fault Density-Component Size Connection". In: *IEEE Softw.* 14.2 (Mar. 1997), pp. 89–97. ISSN: 0740-7459. DOI: 10.1109/52.582978. URL: http://dx.doi.org/10.1109/52.582978.

[Hei+09a] Florian Heidenreich, Jendrik Johannes, Sven Karol, Mirko Seifert, and Christian Wende. "Derivation and Refinement of Textual Syntax for Models". In: *Model Driven Architecture - Foundations and Applications: 5th European Conference, ECMDA-FA 2009, Enschede, The Netherlands, June 23-26, 2009. Proceedings.* Ed. by Richard F. Paige, Alan Hartman, and Arend Rensink. Berlin, Heidelberg: Springer Berlin Heidelberg, 2009, pp. 114–129. ISBN: 978-3-642-02674-4. DOI: 10.1007/978-3-642-02674-4_9. URL: http://dx.doi.org/10.1007/978-3-642-02674-4_9.

[Hei+09b] Florian Heidenreich, Jendrik Johannes, Mirko Seifert, and Christian Wende. *Jamopp: The java model parser and printer.* Tech. rep. 2009.

[Hei+10] Florian Heidenreich, Jendrik Johannes, Mirko Seifert, and Christian Wende. "Closing the Gap between Modelling and Java". In: *Software Language Engineering.* Ed. by Mark van den Brand, Dragan Gašević, and Jeff Gray. Vol. 5969. Lecture Notes in Computer Science. Springer Berlin Heidelberg, 2010, pp. 374–383. ISBN: 978-3-642-12106-7. DOI: 10.1007/978-3-642-12107-4_25. URL: http://dx.doi.org/10.1007/978-3-642-12107-4_25.

[Hei15] Simon Heiss. "Coevolution von komponentenbasierten Architekturmodellen und Eclipse Plugins". Bachelor's Thesis. Karlsruhe Institute of Technology (KIT), 2015.

[Her+08] Sebastian Herold et al. "CoCoME - The Common Component Modeling Example". In: *The Common Component Modeling Example.* Ed. by Andreas Rausch, Ralf Reussner, Raffaela Mirandola, and František Plášil. Vol. 5153. Lecture Notes in Computer Science. Springer Berlin Heidelberg, 2008, pp. 16–53. ISBN: 978-3-540-85288-9. DOI: 10.1007/978-3-540-85289-6_3. URL: http://dx.doi.org/10.1007/978-3-540-85289-6_3.

[HMY06] Gang Huang, Hong Mei, and Fu-Qing Yang. "Runtime recovery and manipulation of software architecture of component-based systems". In: *Automated Software Engineering* 13.2 (2006), pp. 257–281. ISSN: 1573-7535. DOI: 10.1007/s10515-006-7738-4. URL: http://dx.doi.org/10.1007/s10515-006-7738-4.

[HRR16] Robert Heinrich, Kiana Rostami, and Ralf Reussner. *The CoCoME Platform for Collaborative Empirical Research on Information System Evolution*. Tech. rep. 2016,2; Karlsruhe Reports in Informatics. Karlsruhe Institute of Technology, Feb. 2016. URL: http://digbib.ubka.uni-karlsruhe.de/volltexte/1000052688.

[HVW11] Markus Herrmannsdoerfer, Sander D Vermolen, and Guido Wachsmuth. "An extensive catalog of operators for the coupled evolution of metamodels and models". In: *Software Language Engineering*. Springer, 2011, pp. 163–182.

[ISO11] ISO/IEC/IEEE 42010:2011(E). *Systems and software engineering – Architecture description*. International Organization for Standardization, Geneva, Switzerland, Dec. 2011, pp. 1–46. DOI: 10.1109/IEEESTD.2011.6129467.

[JK06] Frédéric Jouault and Ivan Kurtev. "Transforming models with ATL". In: *Satellite Events at the MoDELS 2005 Conference*. Springer. 2006, pp. 128–138.

[KBH07] Heiko Koziolek, Steffen Becker, and Jens Happe. "Predicting the Performance of Component-based Software Architectures with different Usage Profiles". In: *Proc. 3rd International Conference on the Quality of Software Architectures (QoSA'07)*. Vol. 4880. Lecture Notes in Computer Science. Springer-Verlag Berlin Heidelberg, July 2007, pp. 145–163. URL: http://sdqweb.ipd.uka.de/publications/pdfs/koziolek2007b.pdf.

[KBL13] Max E. Kramer, Erik Burger, and Michael Langhammer. "View-centric engineering with synchronized heterogeneous models". In: *Proceedings of the 1st Workshop on View-Based, Aspect-Oriented and Orthographic Software Modelling*. VAO '13. Montpellier, France: ACM, 2013, 5:1–5:6. ISBN: 978-1-4503-2070-2. DOI: 10.1145/2489861.2489864. URL: http://doi.acm.org/10.1145/2489861.2489864.

[KH16] Marco Konersmann and Jens Holschbach. "Automatic Synchronization of Allocation Models with Running Software". In: *Softwaretechnik-Trends* 36.4 (2016). URL: http://pi.informatik.uni-siegen.de/stt/36_4/./01_Fachgruppenberichte/S

SP2016/ssp-stt/24-Automatic_Synchronization_of_Allocation_Models_with_Running_Software.pdf.

[KKR10] Klaus Krogmann, Michael Kuperberg, and Ralf Reussner. "Using Genetic Search for Reverse Engineering of Parametric Behaviour Models for Performance Prediction". In: *IEEE Transactions on Software Engineering* 36.6 (2010). Ed. by Mark Harman and Afshin Mansouri, pp. 865–877. ISSN: 0098-5589. DOI: http://doi.ieeecomputersociety.org/10.1109/TSE.2010.69. URL: http://sdqweb.ipd.kit.edu/publications/pdfs/krogmann2009c.pdf.

[KL14] Max E. Kramer and Michael Langhammer. "Proposal for a Multi-View Modelling Case Study: Component-Based Software Engineering with UML, Plug-ins, and Java". In: *Proceedings of the 2nd Workshop on View-Based, Aspect-Oriented and Orthographic Software Modelling*. VAO '14. York, United Kingdom: ACM, 2014, 7:7–7:10. ISBN: 978-1-4503-2900-2. DOI: 10.1145/2631675.2631676. URL: http://doi.acm.org/10.1145/2631675.2631676.

[KL86] J. C. Knight and N. G. Leveson. "An Experimental Evaluation of the Assumption of Independence in Multiversion Programming". In: *IEEE Trans. Softw. Eng.* 12.1 (Jan. 1986), pp. 96–109. ISSN: 0098-5589. DOI: 10.1109/TSE.1986.6312924. URL: http://dx.doi.org/10.1109/TSE.1986.6312924.

[Kla14] Benjamin Klatt. "Consolidation of Customized Product Copies into Software Product Lines". PhD thesis. Karlsruhe, Germany: Karlsruhe Institute of Technology (KIT), Oct. 2014. URL: http://digbib.ubka.uni-karlsruhe.de/volltexte/1000043687.

[Kla16] Heiko Klare. "Designing a Change-Driven Language for Model Consistency Repair Routines". Master's Thesis. Karlsruhe: Karlsruhe Institute of Technology (KIT), 2016. DOI: 10.5445/IR/1000080138. URL: http://dx.doi.org/10.5445/IR/1000080138.

[KLK16] Heiko Klare, Michael Langhammer, and Max E. Kramer. "Projecting UML Class Diagrams from Java Code Models". In: *4th Workshop on View-Based, Aspect-Oriented and Orthographic Software Modelling (VAO)*. VAO '16. Karlsruhe, Germany, Mar.

2016, pp. 11–18. URL: http://digbib.ubka.uni-karlsruhe.de/volltexte/1000053686.

[Kon+13] Marco Konersmann, Zoya Durdik, Michael Goedicke, and Ralf Reussner. "Towards Architecture-Centric Evolution of Long-Living Systems (The ADVERT Approach)". In: *Proceedings of the 9th ACM SIGSOFT International Conference on the Quality of Software Architectures (QoSA 2013).* June 2013.

[KOS06] Philippe Kruchten, Henk Obbink, and Judith Stafford. "The Past, Present, and Future for Software Architecture". In: *IEEE Software* 23.undefined (2006), pp. 22–30. ISSN: 0740-7459. DOI: doi.ieeecomputersociety.org/10.1109/MS.2006.59.

[Koz+08] Heiko Koziolek, Steffen Becker, Jens Happe, and Ralf Reussner. "Evaluating Performance of Software Architecture Models with the Palladio Component Model". In: *Model-Driven Software Development: Integrating Quality Assurance.* Ed. by Jörg Rech and Christian Bunse. IDEA Group Inc., Dec. 2008, pp. 95–118.

[Koz08] Heiko Koziolek. *Parameter Dependencies for Reusable Performance Specifications of Software Components.* Vol. 2. The Karlsruhe Series on Software Design and Quality. Universitätsverlag Karlsruhe, 2008. ISBN: 978-3-86644-272-6.

[Koz11] Anne Koziolek. "Automated Improvement of Software Architecture Models for Performance and Other Quality Attributes". PhD thesis. Karlsruhe, Germany: Institut für Programmstrukturen und Datenorganisation (IPD), Karlsruher Institut für Technologie, July 2011. URL: http://digbib.ubka.uni-karlsruhe.de/volltexte/1000024955.

[KR08] Klaus Krogmann and Ralf H. Reussner. "The Common Component Modeling Example". In: vol. 5153. Lecture Notes in Computer Science. Springer-Verlag Berlin Heidelberg, 2008. Chap. Palladio: Prediction of Performance Properties, pp. 297–326. URL: http://springerlink.com/content/63617n4j5688879h/?p=9666cb29a31b453aba8a1ae6ee7831b6&pi=11.

[Kra+15a] Max E. Kramer, Michael Langhammer, Dominik Messinger, Stephan Seifermann, and Erik Burger. "Change-Driven Consistency for Component Code, Architectural Models, and Contracts". In: *Proceedings of the 18th International ACM SIGSOFT*

Symposium on Component-Based Software Engineering. CBSE '15. Montréal, QC, Canada: ACM, 2015, pp. 21–26. ISBN: 978-1-4503-3471-6. DOI: 10.1145/2737166.2737177. URL: http://doi.acm.org/10.1145/2737166.2737177.

[Kra+15b] Max E. Kramer, Michael Langhammer, Dominik Messinger, Stephan Seifermann, and Erik Burger. *Realizing Change-Driven Consistency for Component Code, Architectural Models, and Contracts in Vitruvius*. Tech. rep. Karlsruhe: Karlsruhe Institute of Technology, Department of Informatics, 2015. URL: http://nbn-resolving.org/urn:nbn:de:swb:90-456541.

[Kra14] Max E. Kramer. "Synchronizing Heterogeneous Models in a View-Centric Engineering Approach". In: *Software Engineering 2014 – Fachtagung des GI-Fachbereichs Softwaretechnik*. Ed. by Wilhelm Hasselbring and Nils Christian Ehmke. Vol. 227. GI Lecture Notes in Informatics. Doctoral Symposium. Kiel, Germany: Gesellschaft für Informatik e.V. (GI), 2014, pp. 233–236. ISBN: 978-388579-621-3. URL: http://subs.emis.de/LNI/Proceedings/Proceedings227/P-227.pdf.

[Kra15] Max E. Kramer. "A Generative Approach to Change-Driven Consistency in Multi-View Modeling". In: *Proceedings of the 11th International ACM SIGSOFT Conference on Quality of Software Architectures*. QoSA '15. 20th International Doctoral Symposium on Components and Architecture (WCOP '15). Montréal, QC, Canada: ACM, 2015, pp. 129–134. ISBN: 978-1-4503-3470-9. DOI: 10.1145/2737182.2737194. URL: http://doi.acm.org/10.1145/2737182.2737194.

[Kra17] Max Emanuel Kramer. "Specification Languages for Preserving Consistency between Models of Different Languages". PhD thesis. Karlsruhe, Germany: Karlsruhe Institute of Technology (KIT), 2017. 278 pp. DOI: 10.5445/IR/1000069284. URL: http://nbn-resolving.org/urn:nbn:de:swb:90-692845.

[Kro12] Klaus Krogmann. *Reconstruction of Software Component Architectures and Behaviour Models using Static and Dynamic Analysis*. Vol. 4. The Karlsruhe Series on Software Design and Quality. KIT Scientific Publishing, 2012. DOI: 10.5445/KSP/1000025617.

URL: http://digbib.ubka.uni-karlsruhe.de/volltexte/1000025617.

[KSB10] Heiko Koziolek, Bastian Schlich, and Carlos Bilich. “A Large-Scale Industrial Case Study on Architecture-based Software Reliability Analysis”. In: *2010 IEEE 21st International Symposium on Software Reliability Engineering*. IEEE. 2010, pp. 279–288.

[Lan+16] Michael Langhammer, Arman Shahbazian, Nenad Medvidovic, and Ralf H. Reussner. “Automated Extraction of Rich Software Models from Limited System Information”. In: *2016 13th Working IEEE/IFIP Conference on Software Architecture (WICSA)*. Apr. 2016, pp. 99–108. DOI: 10.1109/WICSA.2016.35.

[Lan13] Michael Langhammer. “Co-Evolution of Component-based Architecture-Model and Object-Oriented Source Code”. In: *Proceedings of the 18th international doctoral symposium on Components and architecture*. ACM. 2013, pp. 37–42.

[LBR99] GT Leavens, AL Baker, and Clyde Ruby. “JML: A Notation for Detailed Design”. In: *Behavioral Specifications of Businesses and Systems*. Ed. by Haim Kilov, Bernhard Rumpe, and Ian Simmonds. Boston, USA: Springer Berlin Heidelberg, 1999, pp. 175–188. URL: http://link.springer.com/chapter/10.1007/978-1-4615-5229-1%5C_12.

[Le+15] Duc Minh Le et al. “An Empirical Study of Architectural Change in Open-Source Software Systems”. In: *12th IEEE Working Conference on Mining Software Repositories* (2015), pp. 235–245.

[Leo+15] Sven Leonhardt, Benjamin Hettwer, Johannes Hoor, and Michael Langhammer. “Integration of Existing Software Artifacts into a View- and Change-Driven Development Approach”. In: *Proceedings of the 2015 Joint MORSE/VAO Workshop on Model-Driven Robot Software Engineering and View-based Software-Engineering*. MORSE/VAO ’15. L’Aquila, Italy: ACM, 2015, pp. 17–24. ISBN: 978-1-4503-3614-7. DOI: 10.1145/2802059.2802061. URL: http://doi.acm.org/10.1145/2802059.2802061.

[LK14] Michael Langhammer and Max E. Kramer. "Determining the Intent of Code Changes to Sustain Attached Model Information During Code Evolution". In: *Fachgruppenbericht des 2. Workshops "Modellbasierte und Modellgetriebene Softwaremodernisierung".* Vol. 34 (2). Softwaretechnik-Trends. Gesellschaft für Informatik e.V. (GI), 2014. URL: http://pi.informatik.uni-siegen.de/stt/34_2.

[LK15] Michael Langhammer and Klaus Krogmann. "A Co-evolution Approach for Source Code and Component-based Architecture Models". In: *17. Workshop Software-Reengineering und-Evolution.* Vol. 4. 2015. URL: http://fg-sre.gi.de/fileadmin/gliederungen/fg-sre/wsre2015/WSRE2015-Proceeedings-preliminary.pdf#page=40.

[MA00] Daniel A. Menascé and Virgilio A. F. Almeida. *Scaling for E-Business: Technologies, Models, Performance, and Capacity Planning.* Prentice Hall, Englewood Cliffs, NJ, USA, 2000.

[MAD94] Daniel A. Menascé, Virgilio A. F. Almeida, and Larry W. Dowdy. *Capacity Planning and Performance Modeling: From Mainframes to Client-Server Systems.* New Jersey: Prentice-Hall, Mar. 1994, p. 432. ISBN: 0-13-035494-5.

[Maf+13] Cristiano Maffort, Marco Tulio Valente, Nicolas Anquetil, Andre Hora, and Mariza Bigonha. "Heuristics for discovering architectural violations". In: *Working Conference on Reverse Engineering (WCRE'13).* 2013.

[Maz16] Manar Mazkatli. "Automotive Systems Modeling with Vitruvius". MA thesis. Karlsruhe Institute of Technology (KIT), Germany, 2016.

[Men+06] Kim Mens, Andy Kellens, Frédéric Pluquet, and Roel Wuyts. "Co-evolving Code and Design with Intensional Views: A case study". In: *Comput. Lang. Syst. Struct.* 32.2-3 (July 2006), pp. 140–156. ISSN: 1477-8424. DOI: 10.1016/j.cl.2005.09.002. URL: http://dx.doi.org/10.1016/j.cl.2005.09.002.

[Mer+16] Philipp Merkle, Jörg Henss, Sebastian Lehrig, and Anne Koziolek. "Under the Hood". In: *Modeling and Simulating Software Architectures – The Palladio Approach.* Ed. by Ralf H. Reussner et al. Cambridge, MA: MIT Press, Oct. 2016. Chap. 8, pp. 167–

191. URL: http://mitpress.mit.edu/books/modeling-and-simulating-software-architectures.

[Mer11] Philipp Merkle. “Comparing Process- and Event-oriented Software Performance Simulation”. MA thesis. Karlsruhe Institute of Technology (KIT), Germany, 2011.

[Mer17] Philipp Merkle. “Guiding the Design of Transactional Information Systems by Architecture-level Modeling and Simulation”. to appear. PhD thesis. Karlsruhe, Germany: Karlsruhe Institute of Technology, 2017.

[Mes14] Dominik Messinger. “Incremental Code Architecture Consistency Support through Change Monitoring and Intent Clarification”. MA thesis. Karlsruhe Institute of Technology (KIT), 2014.

[MH11] Philipp Merkle and Jörg Henss. “EventSim – An Event-driven Palladio Software Architecture Simulator”. In: *Palladio Days 2011 Proceedings (appeared as technical report).* Ed. by Steffen Becker, Jens Happe, and Ralf Reussner. Karlsruhe Reports in Informatics ; 2011,32. Karlsruhe: KIT, Fakultät für Informatik, 2011, pp. 15–22. URL: http://digbib.ubka.uni-karlsruhe.de/volltexte/1000025188.

[MK15] Philipp Merkle and Holger Knoche. “Extending the Palladio Component Model to Analyze Data Contention for Modernizing Transactional Software Towards Service-Orientation”. In: *Proceedings of the Symposium on Software Performance (SSP) 2015.* Softwaretechnik-Trends. 2015. URL: http://sdqweb.ipd.kit.edu/publications/pdfs/merkle2015a.pdf.

[MM03] Marija Mikic-Rakic and Nenad Medvidovic. “Adaptable Architectural Middleware for Programming-in-the-small-and-many”. In: *Proceedings of the ACM/IFIP/USENIX 2003 International Conference on Middleware.* Middleware ’03. Rio de Janeiro, Brazil: Springer-Verlag New York, Inc., 2003, pp. 162–181. ISBN: 3-540-40317-5. URL: http://dl.acm.org/citation.cfm?id=1515915.1515927.

[Mon15] Alexander Monev. "Injecting Component Dependencies into Architecture and Code Co-Evolution Transformations using a Dependency Injection Framework". Bachelor's Thesis. Karlsruhe Institute of Technology (KIT), 2015.

[MW16] Johannes Meier and Andreas Winter. "Towards Metamodel Integration Using Reference Metamodels". In: *4th Workshop on View-Based, Aspect-Oriented and Orthographic Software Modelling (VAO)*. VAO '16. Karlsruhe, Germany, Mar. 2016, pp. 19–22. URL: http://digbib.ubka.uni-karlsruhe.de/volltexte/1000053686.

[Nic+00] Ulrich A Nickel, Jörg Niere, Jörg P Wadsack, and Albert Zündorf. "Roundtrip engineering with FUJABA". In: *Proceedings of the 2nd Workshop on Software-Reengineering (WSR), August*. 2000.

[NNZ00] Ulrich Nickel, Jörg Niere, and Albert Zündorf. "The FUJABA Environment". In: *Proceedings of the 22Nd International Conference on Software Engineering*. ICSE '00. Limerick, Ireland: ACM, 2000, pp. 742–745. ISBN: 1-58113-206-9. DOI: 10.1145/337180.337620. URL: http://doi.acm.org/10.1145/337180.337620.

[No 12] No Magic, Inc. *MagicDraw Technical Overview*. 2012. URL: http://www.nomagic.com/files/brochures/letter/MagicDraw_TechOverview_2012.pdf (visited on 10/15/2015).

[Obj09] Object Management Group (OMG). *Meta Object Facility (MOF) 2.0 Query/View/Transformation Specification – Version 1.1 Beta 2*. Dec. 2009. URL: http://www.omg.org/spec/QVT/1.1/Beta2/.

[Obj15] Object Management Group (OMG). *OMG Unified Modeling Language TM (OMG UML): Version 2.5*. 2015. URL: http://www.uml.org.

[Obj16] Object Management Group (OMG). *MOF 2.5.1 Core Specification (formal/2016-11-01)*. Nov. 2016. URL: http://www.omg.org/spec/MOF/2.5.1/.

[Oqu+04] Flavio Oquendo et al. "ArchWare: Architecting Evolvable Software". In: *Software Architecture: First European Workshop, EWSA 2004, St Andrews, UK, May 21-22, 2004. Proceedings*. Ed. by Flavio Oquendo, Brian C. Warboys, and Ron Morrison. Berlin, Heidelberg: Springer Berlin Heidelberg, 2004, pp. 257–271. ISBN:

978-3-540-24769-2. DOI: 10.1007/978-3-540-24769-2_23. URL: http://dx.doi.org/10.1007/978-3-540-24769-2_23.

[Pet16] Frederik Petersen. "Extending an Architecture and Code Co-Evolution Approach to Support Existing Software Projects". MA thesis. Karlsruhe Institute of Technology (KIT), 2016.

[PSV13] Vaclav Pech, Alex Shatalin, and Markus Voelter. "JetBrains MPS As a Tool for Extending Java". In: *Proceedings of the 2013 International Conference on Principles and Practices of Programming on the Java Platform: Virtual Machines, Languages, and Tools.* PPPJ '13. Stuttgart, Germany: ACM, 2013, pp. 165–168. ISBN: 978-1-4503-2111-2. DOI: 10.1145/2500828.2500846. URL: http://doi.acm.org/10.1145/2500828.2500846.

[PW92] Dewayne E. Perry and Alexander L. Wolf. "Foundations for the Study of Software Architecture". In: *ACM SIGSOFT Software Engineering Notes* 17.4 (Oct. 1992), pp. 40–52.

[Rat13] Christoph Rathfelder. *Modelling Event-Based Interactions in Component-Based Architectures for Quantitative System Evaluation.* Vol. 10. The Karlsruhe Series on Software Design and Quality. Karlsruhe, Germany: KIT Scientific Publishing, 2013. URL: http://www.ksp.kit.edu/shop/isbn2shopid.php?isbn=978-3-86644-969-5.

[Reu+11] Ralf Reussner et al. *The Palladio Component Model.* Tech. rep. Karlsruhe: KIT, Fakultät für Informatik, 2011. URL: http://digbib.ubka.uni-karlsruhe.de/volltexte/1000022503.

[Reu+16] Ralf H. Reussner et al. *Modeling and Simulating Software Architectures – The Palladio Approach.* Cambridge, MA: MIT Press, Oct. 2016. 408 pp. ISBN: 9780262034760. URL: http://mitpress.mit.edu/books/modeling-and-simulating-software-architectures.

[RVV09] István Ráth, Gergely Varró, and Dániel Varró. "Change-Driven Model Transformations". In: *Model Driven Engineering Languages and Systems.* Ed. by Andy Schürr and Bran Selic. Berlin, Heidelberg: Springer, 2009, pp. 342–356. ISBN: 978-3-642-04425-0. DOI: 10.1007/978-3-642-04425-0_26. URL: http://dx.doi.org/10.1007/978-3-642-04425-0_26.

[Sak09] Kenneth Saks. *JSR 318: Enterprise JavaBeansTM,Version 3.1 EJB Core Contracts and Requirements.* Tech. rep. JCP (Java Community Process), 2009. URL: `http://download.oracle.com/otn-pub/jcp/ejb-3.1-pfd-oth-JSpec/ejb-3_1-pfd-spec.pdf`.

[SB12] Lakshitha de Silva and Dharini Balasubramaniam. “Controlling software architecture erosion: A survey”. In: *Journal of Systems and Software* 85.1 (2012). Dynamic Analysis and Testing of Embedded Software, pp. 132–151. ISSN: 0164-1212. DOI: `http://dx.doi.org/10.1016/j.jss.2011.07.036`. URL: `http://www.sciencedirect.com/science/article/pii/S0164121211002044`.

[Sei14] Stephan Seifermann. “Model-Driven Co-Evolution of Contracts, Unit-Tests and Source-Code”. MA thesis. Karlsruhe Institute of Technology (KIT), Germany, 2014.

[SGM02] Clemens Szyperski, Dominik Gruntz, and Stephan Murer. *Component Software: Beyond Object-Oriented Programming.* 2nd ed. New York, NY: ACM Press and Addison-Wesley, 2002.

[SK16] Misha Strittmatter and Amine Kechaou. *The Media Store 3 Case Study System.* Tech. rep. 2016,1. Faculty of Informatics, Karlsruhe Institute of Technology, Feb. 2016. URL: `http://digbib.ubka.uni-karlsruhe.de/volltexte/documents/3792054`.

[Spa14] Sparx Systems. *Enterprise Architect User Guide.* 2014. URL: `http://www.sparxsystems.com.au/bin/EAUserGuide.pdf` (visited on 10/15/2015).

[Sta73] Herbert Stachowiak. *Allgemeine Modelltheorie.* Wien: Springer Verlag, 1973. ISBN: 3-211-81106-0.

[Ste+08] David Steinberg, Frank Budinsky, Marcelo Paternostro, and Ed Merks. *EMF: Eclipse Modeling Framework.* second revised. Eclipse series. Addison-Wesley Longman, Amsterdam, Dec. 2008. ISBN: 978-0321331885.

[Sun06] Sun Microsystems. *JSR 294: Improved Modularity Support in the Java Programming Language.* Tech. rep. 2006.

[Tel13] Christian Telpl. “Partial Lock for Eclipse Source Code Editors against User Input”. Bachelor’s Thesis. Karlsruhe Institute of Technology (KIT), 2013.

[TH99] John B. Tran and Richard C. Holt. "Forward and Reverse Repair of Software Architecture". In: *Proceedings of the 1999 Conference of the Centre for Advanced Studies on Collaborative Research*. CASCON '99. Mississauga, Ontario, Canada: IBM Press, 1999, pp. 12–. URL: http://dl.acm.org/citation.cfm?id=781995.782007.

[Van08] Robbie Vanbrabant. *Google Guice : Agile Lightweight Dependency Injection Framework*. firstPress. Berkeley, CA: Apress, 2008. ISBN: 978-1-59059-997-6. URL: http://swbplus.bsz-bw.de/bsz303965231cov.htm.

[VMP14] Vladimir Viyovic, Milan Maksimovic, and Branko Perisic. "Sirius: A rapid development of DSM graphical editor". In: *Intelligent Engineering Systems (INES), 2014 18th International Conference on*. IEEE. 2014, pp. 233–238.

[Voe+13] Markus Voelter, Daniel Ratiu, Bernd Kolb, and Bernhard Schaetz. "mbeddr: instantiating a language workbench in the embedded software domain". English. In: *Automated Software Engineering* 20.3 (2013), pp. 339–390. ISSN: 0928-8910. DOI: 10.1007/s10515-013-0120-4. URL: http://dx.doi.org/10.1007/s10515-013-0120-4.

[Vog13] Lars Vogel. *Eclipse 4 RCP : The complete guide to Eclipse application development; second edition based on eclipse 4.3*. [2. ed.] vogella series. Leipzig[Druckort]: Lars Vogel, 2013. ISBN: 9783943747072.

[VS06] Markus Völter and Thomas Stahl. *Model-Driven Software Development – Technology, Engineering, Management*. Chichester, England: John Wiley & Sons, Ltd, 2006. ISBN: 978-0-470-02570-3.

[Wer16] Dominik Werle. "A Declarative Language for Bidirectional Model Consistency". MA thesis. Karlsruhe Institute of Technology (KIT), 2016.

[Wuy01] Roel Wuyts. "A Logic Meta-Programming Approach to Support the Co-Evolution of Object-Oriented Design and Implementation". PhD thesis. Vrije Universiteit Brussel, 2001.

[WW04] Xiuping Wu and Murray Woodside. "Performance Modeling from Software Components". In: *SIGSOFT Softw. Eng. Notes* 29.1 (2004), pp. 290–301. ISSN: 0163-5948. DOI: http://doi.acm.org/10.1145/974043.974089.

The Karlsruhe Series on Software Design and Quality

Edited by Prof. Dr. Ralf Reussner // ISSN 1867-0067

Band 1 **Steffen Becker**
Coupled Model Transformations for QoS Enabled Component-Based Software Design.
ISBN 978-3-86644-271-9

Band 2 **Heiko Koziolek**
Parameter Dependencies for Reusable Performance Specifications of Software Components.
ISBN 978-3-86644-272-6

Band 3 **Jens Happe**
Predicting Software Performance in Symmetric Multi-core and Multiprocessor Environments.
ISBN 978-3-86644-381-5

Band 4 **Klaus Krogmann**
Reconstruction of Software Component Architectures and Behaviour Models using Static and Dynamic Analysis.
ISBN 978-3-86644-804-9

Band 5 **Michael Kuperberg**
Quantifying and Predicting the Influence of Execution Platform on Software Component Performance.
ISBN 978-3-86644-741-7

Band 6 **Thomas Goldschmidt**
View-Based Textual Modelling.
ISBN 978-3-86644-642-7

Band 7 **Anne Koziolek**
Automated Improvement of Software Architecture Models for Performance and Other Quality Attributes.
ISBN 978-3-86644-973-2

Die Bände sind unter www.ksp.kit.edu als PDF frei verfügbar oder als Druckausgabe bestellbar.

Band 8 **Lucia Happe**
Configurable Software Performance Completions through Higher-Order Model Transformations.
ISBN 978-3-86644-990-9

Band 9 **Franz Brosch**
Integrated Software Architecture-Based Reliability Prediction for IT Systems.
ISBN 978-3-86644-859-9

Band 10 **Christoph Rathfelder**
Modelling Event-Based Interactions in Component-Based Architectures for Quantitative System Evaluation.
ISBN 978-3-86644-969-5

Band 11 **Henning Groenda**
Certifying Software Component Performance Specifications.
ISBN 978-3-7315-0080-3

Band 12 **Dennis Westermann**
Deriving Goal-oriented Performance Models by Systematic Experimentation.
ISBN 978-3-7315-0165-7

Band 13 **Michael Hauck**
Automated Experiments for Deriving Performance-relevant Properties of Software Execution Environments.
ISBN 978-3-7315-0138-1

Band 14 **Zoya Durdik**
Architectural Design Decision Documentation through Reuse of Design Patterns.
ISBN 978-3-7315-0292-0

Band 15 **Erik Burger**
Flexible Views for View-based Model-driven Development.
ISBN 978-3-7315-0276-0

Band 16 **Benjamin Klatt**
Consolidation of Customized Product Copies into Software Product Lines.
ISBN 978-3-7315-0368-2

Band 17 **Andreas Rentschler**
Model Transformation Languages with Modular Information Hiding.
ISBN 978-3-7315-0346-0

Band 18 **Omar-Qais Noorshams**
Modeling and Prediction of I/O Performance in Virtualized Environments.
ISBN 978-3-7315-0359-0

Band 19 **Johannes Josef Stammel**
Architekturbasierte Bewertung und Planung von Änderungsanfragen.
ISBN 978-3-7315-0524-2

Band 20 **Alexander Wert**
Performance Problem Diagnostics by Systematic Experimentation.
ISBN 978-3-7315-0677-5

Band 21 **Christoph Heger**
An Approach for Guiding Developers to Performance and Scalability Solutions.
ISBN 978-3-7315-0698-0

Band 22 **Fouad ben Nasr Omri**
Weighted Statistical Testing based on Active Learning and Formal Verification Techniques for Software Reliability Assessment.
ISBN 978-3-7315-0472-6

Band 23 **Michael Langhammer**
Automated Coevolution of Source Code and Software Architecture Models.
ISBN 978-3-7315-0783-3